S0-ACK-677

ORIGINAL NARRATIVES
OF EARLY AMERICAN HISTORY

REPRODUCED UNDER THE AUSPICES OF THE
AMERICAN HISTORICAL ASSOCIATION

GENERAL EDITOR, J. FRANKLIN JAMESON, PH.D., LL.D.
DIRECTOR OF THE DEPARTMENT OF HISTORICAL RESEARCH IN THE
CARNEGIE INSTITUTION OF WASHINGTON

NARRATIVES OF EARLY MARYLAND

1633—1684

ORIGINAL NARRATIVES
OF EARLY AMERICAN HISTORY

NARRATIVES
OF EARLY MARYLAND

1633—1684

EDITED BY

CLAYTON COLMAN HALL, LL.B., A.M.

OF THE MARYLAND HISTORICAL SOCIETY

WITH A MAP AND TWO FACSIMILES

CHARLES SCRIBNER'S SONS
NEW YORK

COPYRIGHT, 1910, BY
CHARLES SCRIBNER'S SONS

Printed in the United States of America

CONTENTS

NARRATIVES OF EARLY MARYLAND

Edited by Clayton Colman Hall

MAP AND FACSIMILE REPRODUCTIONS

AN ACCOUNT OF THE COLONY OF THE LORD BARON OF BALTAMORE, 1633

INTRODUCTION

THE Account of Lord Baltimore's Colony in Maryland is a translation from the Latin original transcribed about the year 1832 by the late Father William McSherry, S. J., from the Archives of the Society of Jesus in Rome (Angl. Histor., IV. 877–880). The Latin text of Father McSherry's copy, together with an English translation, was published by the Maryland Historical Society in 1874 (*Fund Publication* no. 7). In 1898 this text was compared with the record in the Jesuit archives by Father Thomas Hughes, S. J., and several minor corrections noted.[1] In the following text these corrections have been embodied and the whole translation carefully revised.

The original document, prepared, as the text indicates, some months before the departure of the first colonists of Maryland, and in anticipation of that event, was written by Father Andrew White, S. J.,[2] and doubtless transmitted either by him directly or through the Provincial in England to the General of the Society at Rome, the Very Reverend Father Mucio Vitelleschi, for the better information of the latter as to the nature of the new field in which the writer was to be engaged.

The sources from which the facts were derived are stated in the document itself. George, the first Lord Baltimore and father of Cecilius, the first Proprietary of Maryland, was in

[1] Maryland Historical Society, *Calvert Papers* no. 3 (*Fund Pub.* no. 35), app. B.

[2] The note on page 53 of the Maryland Historical Society *Fund Publication* no. 7, which ascribes the authorship of this account to Cecilius Lord Baltimore, is obviously due to an error, either of the transcriber or of the editor. The note does not appear in the original record in the Archives of the Society of Jesus.

fact an "eye-witness," as he had explored the country upon the occasion of his visit to Virginia in 1629–1630 after recognizing the unpromising condition of his projected colony at Avalon in Newfoundland; and the account of Captain John Smith referred to is doubtless that contained in the *Description of Virginia*, etc., published in 1612.[1] The writer of this document was evidently familiar with the Conditions of Plantation offered by Cecilius Lord Baltimore as inducements to persons to embark in the adventure, from which he freely quotes.

The zealous missionary dwells much upon the prospect of extending the light of the Gospel in a new field, but at the same time he does not overlook the material advantages offered by the Proprietary to such as would join in the enterprise either in person or by contribution of money.

A translation of this document was made, from a manuscript copy formerly in the possession of the Maryland Historical Society, by the late N. C. Brooks, LL.D., and published in 1847 in Force's *Tracts*, IV., no. 12. In 1872 the Latin text was printed in the *Woodstock Letters* for private circulation among members of the Society of Jesus, with a revision of this translation.

C. C. H.

---

[1] *Narratives of Early Virginia*, in this series, p. 73.

AN ACCOUNT OF THE COLONY OF THE LORD BARON OF BALTAMORE, 1633

An Account of the Colony of the Lord Baron of Baltamore, in Maryland, near Virginia: in which the character, quality and state of the Country, and its numerous advantages and sources of wealth are set forth.

THIS province is near the English Colony in Virginia. The Most Serene King of England desired that it should be called the land of Maria or Maryland, in honor of Maria, his wife.[1] The same Most Serene King, out of his own noble disposition, recently, in the month of June, 1632, gave this Province to the Lord Baron of Baltamore and his heirs forever; and this gift he has confirmed and ratified by the public seal of his whole kingdom. Therefore the Most Illustrious Baron has already determined to lead a colony into those parts, first and especially, in order that he may carry thither and to the neighboring places, whither it has been ascertained that no knowledge of the true God has as yet penetrated, the light of the Gospel and the truth; then, also with this intent, that all the associates of his travels and toils may be invited to a share in the gain and honor, and the empire of the King be more widely extended.

For this purpose he is seeking, with all speed and diligence, for men to accompany him on this voyage, both such as intend to try their fortunes with him, and others also. Indeed, after attentively considering the whole matter, and taking the advice of men, distinguished for their experience and wisdom, he has now weighed with great care all the advantages as well as disadvantages which have hitherto advanced or hindered other colonies; and found nothing which does not

[1] The grant of the province of Maryland was made to Lord Baltimore by Charles I., king of England. It was named in honor of the queen, Henrietta Maria.

tend strongly to confirm him in his design, and promise him the most prosperous success. For both the writings which his most noble father has left behind him—an eye-witness, reliable and worthy of all credit—and the constant reports of those men who come to us every day from that country, or places not far from it; and besides, the very faithful account written and published by Captain Smith, who first discovered the country—what he says of the fertility and excellence of its soil is truly wonderful and almost incredible— add to these also the unanimous agreement and testimony of numberless men, living here in London, who formerly came from those countries, and intend to return there; and who, with one voice, verify and confirm what Smith has written.

Wherefore the Most Noble Baron intends, by the aid of God, to sail for those parts, about the middle of next September; and to those whom he shall find to accompany and assist him in so glorious an undertaking, he offers many inducements, in the most generous and liberal spirit.

Of which this is the first and most important, (to say nothing of those rewards of station and preferment, which will be liberally given in honor of worth, valor, fortitude and noble deeds), that whoever shall pay a hundred pounds,[1] to carry over five men, (which will be enough for arms, implements, clothing and other necessaries); whether they shall think best to join us themselves, or intrust the men and money to those, who shall have charge of this matter, or to any one else, to take care of them and receive their share of the lands: to all the men so sent, and to their heirs forever, shall be allotted the right to two thousand acres of good land. Besides this, if in the first expedition they prove themselves faithful followers, and do good service, they shall receive no small share in the profits of trade—of which hereafter—and in other privileges: concerning which they will be more fully informed, when they come to the aforesaid Baron. Moreover, as to what was said before concerning a hundred pounds, this shall also be understood, in proportion, of a smaller or larger sum of money, whether given by one man, or contributed and furnished by several together.

The first and most important design of the Most Illustrious

---

[1] See Conditions of Plantation, p. 91, *infra*.

Baron, which also ought to be the aim of the rest, who go in the same ship, is, not to think so much of planting fruits and trees in a land so fruitful, as of sowing the seeds of religion and piety. Surely a design worthy of Christians, worthy of *angels*, worthy of *Englishmen*.[1] The English nation, renowned for so many ancient victories, never undertook anything more noble or glorious than this. Behold the lands are white for the harvest, prepared for receiving the seed of the Gospel into a fruitful bosom. The Indians themselves are everywhere sending messengers, to seek after fit men to instruct the inhabitants in saving doctrine, and to regenerate them with the sacred water. There are also men here in the city, at this very time, who declare that they have seen ambassadors, who were sent by their kings[2] for this same purpose to Jamestown in Virginia; and infants brought to New England to be washed in the saving waters. Who then can doubt, that by one such glorious work as this, many thousands of souls will be brought to Christ? I call the work of aiding and saving souls glorious: for it was the work of Christ, the King of Glory. For the rest, since all men have not such enthusiastic souls and noble minds, as to think of nothing but divine things, and to consider nothing but heavenly things; because most men are more drawn, secretly or openly, by pleasures, honor and riches, it was ordained by the wonderful wisdom of God, that this one enterprise should offer to men every kind of inducement and reward.

It is acknowledged that the situation of the country is excellent and very advantageous, as it extends to the 38th or 40th degree of north latitude, and is in location and climate not unlike Seville, Sicily, Jerusalem, and the best parts of Arabia Felix and China. The climate is serene and mild, not oppressively hot like that of Florida and old Virginia, nor bitterly cold like that of New England; but preserves, so to speak, a middle temperature between the two, and enjoys the

---

[1] The Latin text reads *dignum angelis, dignum anglis* (Md. Hist. Soc. *Fund Pub.* no. 7, p. 47), in allusion to the words attributed to the Pope Gregory the Great, uttered more than one thousand years before at the sight of certain blond English youths, captives exposed for sale in Rome:—"*Non Angli sed Angeli.*" The play upon words is necessarily lost in translation.

[2] For explanation of this and corresponding titles of rank, see pp. 84, 125.

advantages, and escapes the evils, of each. On the east it is washed by the ocean; on the west it borders upon an almost boundless continent, which extends to the Chinese Sea. It has two very large arms of the sea, both of them bays abounding in fish. One of these, named the Chesa-peack, is twelve miles wide, and spread out between two districts, runs from south to north a hundred and sixty miles. It is navigable for large ships, and is interspersed with various large islands suitable for grazing; and at these islands can be caught, in the greatest abundance, the fish called *shad*.

The other they call the Dilaware,[1] in which cod-fish are caught all the year round; but the most convenient time to catch them is in the colder months, for the warm weather interferes with salting them. Now this great abundance of fish arises from the following cause: the wind, which uniformly blows from the Canaries, from the north-east, drives the water of the ocean, and with it the fish, into the Gulf of Mexico; from which, since there is no escape for it either to the east or the south, it is driven with great force towards the north, and carries with it large numbers of fish along the shores of Florida, Virginia, Maryland and New England. These, flying from the larger fish, take refuge in shallow places, where they are more easily caught by the fishermen.

There are various notable rivers. The chief of these they call the Attawomech,[2] a navigable river running eastward 140 miles, where there is such a lucrative trade with the Indians, that a certain merchant in the last year exported beaver skins to the value of 40,000 gold crowns, and the profit of the traffic is estimated at thirty fold.

On the plains and in the open fields there is a great abundance of grass; but the country is, for the most part, thickly wooded. There are a great many hickory trees, and oaks so straight and tall that beams, sixty feet long and two and a half feet wide, can be made of them. The cypress trees also grow to a height of 80 feet, before they have any branches, and three men with arms extended can barely reach round their trunks. There are plenty of mulberry trees to feed silkworms. The Chinese grain which the Portuguese call *Sove del' Hierva* is also found there. There are alder, ash and chest-

---

[1] Delaware.   [2] Potomac.

nut trees, as large as those which grow in Spain, Italy, and France; and cedars equalling those which Libanus boasts of.

Why should I speak of the pine, laurel, fir, sassafras and the other trees, with various kinds besides, which yield balsam and fragrant gums? trees useful in every way, for building, ship-building, for making planks, pitch, tar, turpentine, sinegma, perfumes, and plasters. The woods moreover are passable, not filled with thorns or undergrowth, but arranged by nature for pasture for animals, and for affording pleasure to man. There are fruitful vines, from which wine can be made, and a grape as large as cherries, the juice of which is thick and oily. The inhabitants call these Mesamines. There are cherries as big as damsons, and gooseberries just like ours. There are three kinds of plums. Mulberries, chestnuts and walnuts, are so plentiful that they are used in various ways for food. Strawberries and raspberries are also to be found there.

Of the fishes the following kinds are already known: sturgeons, *turciones* (?), seals (?), *aristoci*, shrimps, skates, trouts, three kinds of *melanurae*, (black-tailed perch), *erechini*, roaches, white salmon, mussels, periwinkles, and numberless others of that sort, the names and species of which are unknown.

For the rest, there are such numbers of swine and deer that they are rather an annoyance than an advantage. There are also vast herds of cows, and wild oxen, fit for beasts of burden and good to eat, besides five other kinds of large animals unknown to us, which the neighboring people use for food. Sheep, as well as asses and mules, have to be procured either from our country or from the Canaries.

The nearest woods are full of horses and wild bulls and cows. Five or six hundred thousand of the skins of these animals are carried every year to Seville, from that part of the country which lies westward towards New Mexico. Any number of wild goats can be procured from the neighboring people. Add to these muskrats, ciuri, beavers, foxes, martens and weevils [weasels], which do not destroy hens and eggs as ours do. Among the birds are found a very ravenous eagle, various kinds of birds of prey, which live, for the most part, on fishes, and partridges no larger than quails, but in almost endless numbers.

There are also great quantities of wild turkeys, which are twice as large as our tame and domestic ones. There are blackbirds too, and thrushes, and many and various kinds of small birds, some red, and some blue, etc., etc. In the winter, there are plenty of swans, geese, cranes, herons, ducks, *kirthei, glauci* (birds of a green color), parrots, and a great many others, unknown in our country. The best of citrons and quinces grow there. Peaches also are so abundant, that an honorable and reliable man positively declared, that he gave a hundred bushels to his pigs last year. Why should I speak of the excellent lupines, beans, roots, and other things of that kind? For even the peas in those parts grow ten inches long in ten days. It is such a good grain country, that, in the worst years, the seed yields two hundred fold; at other times, and generally, for one grain, five or six hundred, and in the best years, fifteen or sixteen hundred; and this too in one harvest, while the soil is so rich, as to afford three harvests a year.

It is probable that the soil will prove to be adapted to all the fruits of Italy, figs, pomegranates, oranges, olives, etc;— to pass over the rest briefly. There is no lack of those things that can be made useful to fullers and apothecaries, and no small supply of tin, iron, hemp and flax. There is also hope of finding gold, for the neighboring people wear bracelets of gold, which indeed is as yet unwrought, and long strings of pearls. It is also to be expected that the provident industry and long experience of men will discover many other advantages and sources of wealth.

INSTRUCTIONS TO THE COLONISTS BY
LORD BALTIMORE, 1633

INTRODUCTION

LORD BALTIMORE's letter of instructions to the colonists of Maryland is printed from an original manuscript now in the possession of the Maryland Historical Society, having been acquired by it among a large collection of Calvert Papers obtained by the society in 1888 from a descendant of the last Lord Baltimore. This document is specially valuable as disclosing the mind, purpose and character of Cecilius Lord Baltimore, the founder of Maryland, for it is an autograph, written entirely by his own hand, with his own interlineations and corrections. An endorsement shows it to be a copy of the letter delivered to the commissioners for the government of the province. It is without doubt the original draft of the instructions which was probably transcribed in a fair hand or engrossed for signature.

It is noteworthy that in the very first paragraph disputes concerning religion are prohibited—thus showing the determination of Lord Baltimore, himself a Roman Catholic, that upon this subject there should from the beginning be both liberty and peace within the province.[1] His loyalty to the crown is shown by his insistence upon the taking of the oath of allegiance to the King as an absolute condition for permission to settle in the colony and enjoy the benefits offered[2] to the colonists.

The sailing which had been planned for September[3] did not occur until November, the delay being chiefly caused by the efforts of members of the old Virginia Company, the charter of which had been annulled, to defeat Lord Baltimore's enterprise altogether. For this reason he too was prevented

[1]See p. 250, *infra.*   [2]See p. 91, *infra.*   [3]See p. 6, *supra.*

13

from carrying out his intention of personally accompanying the colonists, finding it necessary, as he states in the letter, to remain in England in order to defend his charter rights. This fact also explains the careful instructions given to the commissioners to ascertain what persons had sought to incite mutiny among the sailors before departure, and the cautions to avoid anchoring under the guns of the fort at Point Comfort, (where Fort Monroe now stands); to inquire into the disposition of the more influential settlers in Virginia; to do what they could with prudence to oblige members of the Council there; but otherwise to have as little to do with them as possible during the first year.

This first company of colonists was composed of two classes: the gentlemen adventurers who went out to take up lands and become, under the Conditions of Plantation,[1] lords of manors; and the indentured servants.[2] Of the former, the ruling class, the large majority was of the Roman Catholic faith; of the latter, the majority was Protestant, and these being the more numerous, the larger number of the whole ship's company was of the latter faith. That among the gentlemen adventurers there were some who were conformable to the Church of England is shown by the fact that from their number were to be chosen messengers, the one to convey letters, including one from the King, to Sir John Harvey, governor of Virginia, and the other to convey letters to Captain William Claiborne, who had established a trading-post on Kent Island and who, claiming prior possession, was during a long life Lord Baltimore's untiring antagonist. Obviously the persons to be selected for these important and delicate missions were not servants.

The remainder of the instructions, as to place of settlement, mode of building fortifications, planting of corn, training of the men in military discipline, and inquiry as to the

[1] See p. 91, infra.   [2] See pp. 99, 100, infra.

existence of material for the manufacture of gunpowder, call for no special comment. They are the prudent and practical directions of a wise proprietary governor.

It is worthy of note that the author of this letter, Cecilius Lord Baltimore, upon whom as the result of the death of his father the planting of Maryland had suddenly devolved, was, at this time, but twenty-seven years of age.

This document was printed by the Maryland Historical Society in *Calvert Papers* no. 1, *Fund Publication* no. 28.

C. C. H.

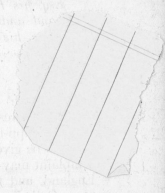

INSTRUCTIONS TO THE COLONISTS BY LORD BALTIMORE, 1633

Instructions 13 Novem: 1633 directed by the Right Hono^ble^*. Cecilius Lo: Baltimore and Lord of the Provinces of Mary Land and Avalon unto his well beloved Brother Leo: Calvert Esq*^r^*. his Lop*^s^* Deputy Governor of his province of Mary Land and unto Jerom Hawley and Thomas Cornwaleys Esqrs. his Lo*^pps^* Commissioners for the government of the said Province.*[1]

1. INPRI: His Lo^pp^ requires his said Governor and Commissioners th.^t^ in their voyage to Mary Land they be very carefull to preserve unity and peace amongst all the passengers on Shipp-board, and that they suffer no scandall nor offence to be given to any of the Protestants, whereby any just complaint may heereafter be made, by them, in Virginea or in England, and that for that end, they cause all Acts of Romane Catholique Religion to be done as privately as may be, and that they instruct all the Romane Catholiques to be silent upon all occasions of discourse concerning matters of Religion; and that the said Governor and Commissioners treate the Protestants wth as much mildness and favor as Justice will permitt. And this to be observed at Land as well as at Sea.

2. That while they are aboard, they do theyre best endeavors by such instruments as they shall find fittest for it, amongst the seamen and passengers to discover what any of them do know concerning the private plotts of his Lo^pps^

---

[1] The original document has the following endorsement:—"15 Novem. 1633. A Coppy of Instructions to Mr. Leo. Calvert, Mr. Jerom Hawley and Mr. Tho. Cornwaleys the Lo: Baltimores Governor and Commissioners of his province of Maryland. In the 5th Article some directions is given concerning Cap. Cleyborne."

adversaries in England, who endeavored to overthrow his voyage: to learne, if they cann, the names of all such, their speeches, where and when they spoke them, and to whom; The places, if they had any, of their consultations, the Instruments they used and the like; to gather what proofes they cann of them; and to sett them downe particulerly and cleerely in writing wth all the Circumstances; together wth their opinions of the truth and validity of them according to the condition of the persons from whom they had the information; And to gett if they can every such informer to sett his hand to his Informacion. And if they find it necessary and that they have any good probable ground to discover the truth better, or that they find some unwilling to reveale that w^{ch} (by some speeches at randome, that have fallen from them) they have reason to suspect they do know concerning that buisness: that at their arrivall in Mary Land they cause every such p'son to answer upon oath, to such questions as they shall thinke fitt to propose unto them: And by some trusty messenger in the next shipps that returne for England to send his Lo^{pp} in writing all such Intelligences taken either by deposition or otherwise.

3. That as soone as it shall please god they shall arrive upon the coast of Virginea, they be not perswaded by the master or any other of the shipp, in any case or for any respect whatsoever to goe to James Towne, or to come wthin the command of the fort at Poynt-Comfort: unless they should be forct unto it by some extremity of weather, (wch god forbidd) for the preservation of their lives and goodes, and that they find it altogether impossible otherwise to preserve themselves: But that they come to an Anchor somewhere about Acomacke,[1] so as it be not under the command of any fort; and to send ashoare there, to inquire if they cann find any to take wth them, that cann give them some good informatione of the Bay of Chesapeacke and Pattawomeck River, and that may give them some light of a fitt place in his Lo^{pps} Countrey to sett downe on; wherein their chiefe care must be to make choice of a place first that is probable to be healthfull and fruitfull, next that it may be easily fortified, and

---

[1] Accomac, on the eastern side of Chesapeake Bay, the fort mentioned being on the west shore.

thirdly that it may be convenient for trade both wth the English and savages.

4. That by the first oportunity after theyr arrivall in Mary Land they cause a messenger to be dispatcht away to James Town such a one as is conformable to the Church of England, and as they may according to the best of their judgments trust; and he to carry his ma^{ties} letter to Sr John Harvie the Governor[1] and to the rest of the Councell there, as likewise his Lo^{pps} letter to S^r Jo: Harvie, and to give him notice of their arrivall: And to have in charge, upon the delivery of the said letters to behave himself wth much respect unto the Governor, and to tell him th^t his Lo^{pp} had an intention to have come himself in person this yeare into those parts, as he may perceive by his ma^{ties} letter to him but finding that the setling of that buisness of his Plantation and some other occasions, required his presence in England for some time longer than he expected, he hath deferred his owne coming till the next yeare, when he will not faile by the grace of god to be there; and to lett him understand how much his Lo^{pp} desires to hold a good correspondency wth him and that Plantation of Virginea, wch he wilbe ready to shew upon all occasions and to assure him by the best words he cann, of his Lo^{pps} particular affection to his person, in respect of the many reports he hath heard of his worth, and of the ancient acquaintance and freindshipp wch he hath understood was between his Lo^{pps} father and him as likewise for those kind respects he hath shewne unto his L^{opp} by his letters since he understoode of his L^{opps} intention to be his neighbor in those parts: And to present him wth a Butt of sacke from his L^{opp} wch his L^{opp} hath given directions for, to be sent unto him.

5. That they write a letter to Cap: Clayborne[2] as soone as conveniently other more necessary occasions will give them leave after their arrivall in the Countrey, to give him notice of their arrivall and of the Authority and charge committed to them by his L^{opp} and to send the said letter together wth his L^{opps} to him by some trusty messenger that is likewise

[1] Sir John Harvey, governor of Virginia, 1629–1639.
[2] For an account of the subjects of difference between Lord Baltimore and Captain William Claiborne, see p. 50 et seq., infra.

conformable unto the Church of England, wth. a message also
from them to him if it be not inserted in their letter wch is
better, to invite him kindly to come unto them, and to signify
that they have some buisness of importance to speake w^th
him about from his L^opp wch. concernes his good very much;
And if he come unto them then that they use him courteously
and well, and tell him, that his L^opp understanding that he
hath settled a plantacion there wth in the precincts of his L^opps
Pattent, wished them to lett him know that his L^opp is willing
to give him all the encouragement he cann to proceede; And
that his L^opp hath had some propositions made unto him by
certaine m^rchants in London who pretend to be partners w^th
him in that plantation, (viz) M^r. Delabarr, M^r. Tompson
Mr Cloberry, M^r. Collins, and some others, and that they desired to have a grant from his L^opp of that Iland where he is:
But his L^opp. understanding from some others that there was
some difference in partnershipp between him and them, and
his L^opp finding them in their discourse to him, that they
made somewhat slight of Cap: Clayborne's interest, doubted
lest he might prejudice him by making them any grant his
Lo^pp being ignorant of the true state of their buisness and of
the thing they desired, as likewise being well assured that by
Cap: Clayborne his care and industry besides his charges,
that plantation was first begunn and so farr advanced, was for
these reasons unwilling to condescend unto their desires, and
therefore deferred all treaty wth them till his Lo^pp. could
truly understand from him, how matters stand between them,
and what he would desire of his L^opp in it, wch his Lo^pp
expects from him; that thereupon his L^opp may take it into
farther consideration how to do justice to every one of them
and to give them all reasonable satisfaction; And that they
assure him in fine that his L^opp intends not to do him any
wrong, but to shew him all the love and favor that he cann,
and that his L^opp gave them directions to do so to him in his
absence; in confidence that he will, like a good subject to his
ma^tie, conforme himself to his higness gratious letters pattents granted to his Lo^pps whereof he may see the Duplicate
if he desire it together wth their Commission from his L^opp.
If he do refuse to come unto them upon their invitation, that
they lett him alone for the first yeare, till upon notice given

to his L^{opp} of his answere and behaviour they receive farther directions from his L^{opp}; and that they informe themselves as well as they cann of his plantation and what his designes are, of what strength and what Correspondency he keeps wth Virginea, and to give an Account of every particular to his L^{opp}.

6. That when they have made choice of the place where they intend to settle themselves and that they have brought their men ashoare wth all their provisions, they do assemble all the people together in a fitt and decent manner and then cause his ma^{ties} letters pattents to be publikely read by his L^{opps} Secretary John Bolles, and afterwards his L^{opps} Commission to them, and that either the Governor or one of the Commissioners presently after make some short declaration to the people of his L^{opps} intentions wch he means to pursue in this his intended plantation, wch are first the honor of god by endeavoring the conversion of the savages to Christianity, secondly the augmentation of his ma^{tie's} Empire and Dominions in those parts of the world by reducing them under the subjection of his Crowne, and thirdly by the good of such of his Countreymen as are willing to adventure their fortunes and themselves in it, by endeavoring all he cann, to assist them, that they may reape the fruites of their charges and labors according to the hopefulnes of the thing, wth as much freedome comfort and incouragement as they cann desire; and wth all to assure them, that his L^{opps} affection and zeale is so greate to the advancement of this Plantacion and consequently of their good, that he will imploy all his endeavors in it, and that he would not have failed to have come himself in person along wth them this first yeare, to have beene partaker wth them in the honor of the first voyage thither, but that by reasons of some unexpected accidents, he found it more necessary for their good, to stay in England some time longer, for the better establishment of his and their right, then it was fitt that the shipp should stay for him, but that by the grace of god he intends w^{th}out faile to be wth them the next year: And that at this time they take occasion to minister an oath of Allegeance to his ma^{tie} unto all and every one upon the place, after having first publikely in the presence of the people taken it themselves; letting them

know that his Lo^pp gave particuler directions to have it one of
the first things that were done, to testify to the world that
none should enjoy the benefitt of his ma^ties gratious Grant
unto his L^opp of that place, but such as should give a publique assurance of their fidelity and allegeance to his ma^tie.

7. that they informe themselves what they cann of the
present state of the old Colony of Virginea, both for matter of
government and Plantacon as likewise what trades they drive
both at home and abroade, who are the cheife and richest
men, and have the greatest power amongst them whether
their clamors against his Lo^pps pattent continue and whether
they increase or diminish, who they are of note that shew
themselves most in it, and to find out as neere as they cann,
what is the true reason of their disgust against it, or whether
there be really any other reason but what, being well examined proceedes rather from spleene and malice then from any
other cause; And to informe his L^opp exactly what they
understand in any of these particulers.

8. That they take all occasions to gaine and oblige any of
the Councell of Virginea, that they shall understand incline to
have a good correspondency wth his L^opps plantation, either
by permission of trade to them in a reasonable proportion,
w^thin his L^opps precincts, or any other way they can, so it be
cleerely understood that it is by the way of courtesy and not
of right.

9. That where they intend to settle the Plantacon they
first make choice of a fitt place, and a competent quantity of
ground for a fort w^thin wch or neere unto it a convenient
house, and a church or a chappel adjacent may be built, for
the seate of his L^opp or his Governor or other Commissioners
for the time being in his absence, both wch his Lo^pp would
have them take care should in the first place be erected, in
some proportion at least, as much as is necessary for present
use though not so compleate in every part as in fine afterwards they may be and to send his L^opp a Platt of it and of
the scituation, by the next oportunity, if it be done by that
time, if not or but part of it nevertheless to send a Platt of
what they intend to do in it. That they likewise make choise
of a fitt place neere unto it to seate a towne.

10. That they cause all the Planters to build their houses

in as decent and uniforme a manner as their abilities and
the place will afford, and neere adjoyning one to an other,
and for that purpose to cause streetes to be marked out where
they intend to place the towne and to oblige every man to
buyld one by an other according to that rule and that they
cause divisions of Land to be made adjoyning on the back
sides of their houses and to be assigned unto them for gardens and such uses according to the proportion of every ones
building and adventure and as the conveniency of the place
will afford wch his L^{opp} referreth to their discretion, but is
desirous to have a particuler account from them what they
do in it, that his Lo^{pp} may be satisfied that every man hath
justice done unto him.

11. That as soone as conveniently they cann they cause
his L^{opps} surveyor Robert Simpson to survay out such a proportion of Land both in and about the intended towne as likewise wthin the Countrey adjoyning as wilbe necessary to be
assigned to the present adventurers, and that they assigne
every adventurer his proportion of Land both in and about
the intended towne, as alsoe wthin the Countrey adjoyning,
according to the proportion of his adventure and the conditions of plantacion propounded by his Lo^{pp} to the first adventurers, wch his L^{opp} in convenient time will confirme unto
them by Pattent. And heerein his L^{opp} wills his said Governor and Commissioners to take care that in each of the
aforesaid places, that is to say in and about the first intended
Towne and in the Countrey adjacent they cause in the first and
most convenient places a proportion of Land to be sett out for
his L^{opps} owne proper use and inheritance according to the
number of men he sends this first yeare upon his owne account; and as he alloweth unto the adventurers, before any
other be assigned his part; wth w^{ch} (although his Lopp might
very well make a difference of proportion between himself
and the adventurers) he will in this first colony, content himself, for the better encouragement and accomodation of the
first adventurers, unto whom his L^{opp} conceive himself more
bound in honor and is therefore desirous to give more satisfaction in everything then he intends to do unto any that shall
come heereafter. That they cause his Lo^{pps} survayor likewise to drawe an exact mapp of as much of the countrey as

they shall discover together wth the soundings of the rivers and Baye, and to send it to his L^{opp}.

12. That they cause all the planters to imploy their servants in planting of sufficient quantity of corne and other provision of victuall and that they do not suffer them to plant any other commodity whatsoever before that be done in a sufficient proportion wch they are to observe yearely.

13. That they cause all sorts of men in the plantation to be mustered and trained in military discispline and that there be days appoynted for that purpose either weekely or monthly according to the conveniency of other occasions; wch are duly to be observed and that they cause constant watch and ward to be kept in places necessary.

14. That they informe themselves whether there be any convenient place wthin his L^{opps} precincts for the making of Salt, whether there be proper earth for the making of saltpeeter and if there be in what quantity; whether there be probability of Iron oare or any other mines and that they be carefull to find out what other commodities may probably be made and that they give his L^{opp} notice together wth their opinions of them.

15. That In fine they bee very carefull to do justice to every man wthout partiality, and that they avoid any occasion of difference wth those of Virginea and to have as litle to do wth them as they cann this first yeare that they connive and suffer litle injuryes from them rather then to engage themselves in a publique quarrell wth them, wch may disturbe the buisness much in England in the Infancy of it. And that they give unto his L^{opp} an exact account by their letters from time to time of their proceedings both in these instructions from Article to Article and in any other accident that shall happen worthy his Lo^{pps} notice, that thereupon his L^{opp} may give them farther instructions what to doe and that by every conveyance by wch they send any letters as his Lo^{pp} would not have them to omitt any they send likewise a Duplicate of the letters wch they writt by the last conveyance before that, least they should have failed and not be come to his Lo^{pps} hands.

A BRIEFE RELATION OF THE VOYAGE UNTO MARYLAND, BY FATHER ANDREW WHITE, 1634

INTRODUCTION

THIS version of the Relation of the Voyage to Maryland is from an original manuscript in English in the possession of the Maryland Historical Society by which it was acquired in 1894, and published in 1899, in a volume entitled *Calvert Papers* no. 3, *Fund Publication* no. 35. This manuscript was sent by Leonard Calvert, brother of Lord Baltimore, and first governor of the province of Maryland, to his partner in business, Sir Richard Lechford. It was enclosed in a letter dated from Point Comfort, May 30, 1634, a little more than two months after the landing of the colonists at St. Mary's, and was despatched by the *Ark*, in which those colonists were conveyed, upon the return voyage of that vessel.

There is a Latin version of the *Relatio Itineris in Marylandiam*, known as Father Andrew White's Narrative, in the Archives of the Society of Jesus ("Angl. Histor.," IV. 413–440). A copy of this, together with an English translation, was published by the Maryland Historical Society in 1874, *Fund Publication* no. 7. This Latin text is undoubtedly the record of the report of the voyage, rendered by Father White, who accompanied the colonists, and was the first Superior of the Maryland Mission, to the General of the Society at Rome.

The two versions, the Latin and the English, differ but little, the former being more full in some particulars, while in others the latter is more amplified. The chief points of contrast are, that in the Latin, devout expressions and acknowledgments of Divine favor and protection are more frequent, as would be natural in a letter addressed by a priest to his spiritual superior; and in the English the description of the climate, the soil, and the products of the earth are more full, as would be natural in a letter intended for the information of those pecuniarily or personally interested in the colony. The narrative of events is the same in each.

Leonard Calvert, the governor, describes the English manuscript as having been written by "a most honest and discreet gentleman." It is safe to attribute its authorship to Father White. It has been conjectured, and not without reason, that he probably kept an exact journal of the voyage, from which he was able to draw for material in writing reports, expanding or condensing, according to the occasion and the purpose of the letter. Leonard Calvert's letter enclosing it contains some of the language of the narrative; but he probably had it before him as he wrote.

The English version, as an historical document, has the advantage over the Latin text, that it is an original manuscript, whereas the latter is known only at second hand, through its record in the Jesuit Archives.

The substance of this narrative was printed in pamphlet form in London in 1634 under the title *A Relation of the Successful Beginnings of the Lord Baltimore's Plantation in Maryland*, and was reprinted in 1865 from an original in the British Museum, in Shea's *Early Southern Tracts*, being no. 1 of that series.

A translation of the Latin text, made by the late N. C. Brooks, LL.D., was published with one of the "Account" of Maryland in 1847,[1] and with it reprinted in Force's *Tracts*, IV., no. 12. The Latin text was printed in 1872, in the *Woodstock Letters*, with a revision of Dr. Brooks's translation, for the use of members of the Society of Jesus. The original text is also given in Father Thomas Hughes's *History of the Society of Jesus in North America, Documents*, I., pt. I., 94.

C. C. H.

---

[1] See p. 4, *supra*.

A BRIEFE RELATION OF THE VOYAGE UNTO MARYLAND, BY FATHER ANDREW WHITE, 1634[1]

ON S.[t] Cecilias day, the 22 of November 1633 with a gentle Northerne gale we set saile from the Cowes about 10 in the morninge, toward the needles, being rockes at the south end of Ile of Wight, till by default of winde we were forced to ankour at Yarmouth, w.[ch] very kindly saluted us, how beit we were not out of feare, for the seamen secretly reported that they expected the post with letters from the Counsell at London: but God would tende the matter, and sent th.[t] night soe strong a faire winde as forced a ffrench barke from her ankor hold driveing her foule upon our pinnace forced her to set saile with losse of an ankour, and take to Sea, that being a dangerous place to floate in, whereby we were necessarily to follow, least we should part companie, and thus God frustrated the plot of our Seamen. This was the 23 of Novemb: on S.[t] Clements day who wonne his Crowne by being cast into the Sea fastned to an ankor. That morneing by 10 a clocke we came to Hurste Castle, and thence were saluted with a shot, and soe passed by the dangerous needles, being certaine sharpe rockes at the end of the Iland, much feared by Seamen for a double tyde which she carried to Shipwrecke, tone upon the rockes, t- other upon the sand.[2] I omitt our danger passed Yarmouth, where by dragging anchour in a strong winde and tide we almost runne of our shipp a ground.

All this Saturday and the night following the winde served us so well, that next day by 9 of Clocke we got beyond the westerne Cape of England, and so steered along not soe strongly as wee might because of our pinnace slow saileinge, whome

---

[1] The original manuscript is not divided into paragraphs and contains but little punctuation. The beginnings of sentences are not even marked by capital letters. The punctuation and capitalization of this text are such as the sense requires.   [2] "The one upon the rocks, the other," etc.

we feared to leave behinde, for feare shee might meet w^th
Turkes or some other pirates though we see none. By this
meanes a faire shipp of London overtooke us of 600 tunne.
Here we had a greate recreation to see that ship and ours runne
for the fame with all the cloath they could make, an howers
space with faire winde and weather, and pleasant sound of
trumpetts, but ours gave the other a topsaile and yet held
with her. This done we stroke one course of our sailes, and
staied for our pinnace, which was farre short of us, and the
Draggon, for soe shee was called, runne from us out of sight
that evening.

Soe all Sunday and Munday the 24th and 25th of Novemb:
we sailed afore the winde, till night, when the winde changed
to Northwest so violent, and tempestuous, as the *Dragon* was
forced backe to ffamouth,[1] not able to keep the sea, being yet
not to goe southwest, but right south to Angola, and our pinnace mistrusting her strength came up to us to tell that if shee
were in distresse shee would shew two lights in her shroodes.
Our master was a very sufficient seaman, and shipp as strong
as could be made of oake and iron, 400 tunne, kingbuilt: make-
inge faire weather in great stormes. Now the master had his
choise, whether he would returne England as the *Draggon* did,
or saile so close up to the winde, as if he should not hold it he
must necessarily fall upon the Irish shoare, so infamous for
rockes of greatest danger: of these two, out of a certaine har-
dinesse and desire to trie the goodnesse of his shipp, in which
he had never beene at Sea afore, he resolved to keep the sea,
with great danger, wanting Sea-roome. The winde grew still
lowder and lowder, makeing a boysterous sea, and about mid-
night we espied our pinnace with her two lights, as she had
forewarned us, in the shroodes, from wch time till six weekes,
we never see her more, thinkeing shee had assuredly beene
foundred and lost in those huge seas, but it happened otherwise, for before shee came to the Irish Channell, where we
were now tossinge, shee returned for England, and entered
into the Scilley Iles, whence afterward in the *Dragons* Company shee came to the long reach[2] and Canarie Iles, God pro-
videing a convenient guard for that small vessell.

[1] Falmouth.

[2] The long stretch of open sea from the Canaries to the West Indies.

This night thus frightfull being past, the winde came about to South west, full against us, though not very stronge, so that with many tackes about we scarce crept on our way, soe all the 26 27 and 28 dayes the winde altered little. On the 29th the windes were all day a gathering and toward night poured forth such a sea of winde as if they would have blowen our shipp under water at every blast. All next day beinge the blessed apostle St Andrewes day, the like cloude gathered in fearefull manner, terrible to the beholders, so that ere it began to blow it seemed all the sprightes and witches of Maryland were now set in battaile array against us. This evening the master saw the sunne fish to swimme against the sunnes course, a thing evidently shewing fearfull stormes to come: about 10 in the night a blacke cloud shede a pittifull shower upon us, and presently such a furious winde followed as wee were able to beare noe cloath at all, and yet before we could take in our maine Course,[1] wch we onely carried, a furious impression of winde suddainely came, and splitt it from top to toae, and cast one part of it into the sea. This amazed the stoutest hearte, even of the sailours, who confessed they had seene ships cast away with lesse violence of weather, all the Catholiques fell to praier, Confessiones, and vowes, and then the helme being bound up, and ship left without saile or government to the windes and waves, floated at hull like a dish till god were pleased to take pittie upon her. Thus we were in feare of imminent death all this night never lookeing to see day in this world, till at length it pleased God to send some ease, and by little and little still more, till we were with milder weather freed from all those horrours. This deliverie in a manner assured us of Gods mercy towards us, and those infidells Conversion of Maryland, his holy Goodness be forever praised, Amen.

From this time to our journeyes end, about 3 monethes, we had not one howre of bad weather, but soe prosperous a navigation, as our mariners never saw so sweet a passage: when I say 3 months, I meane not we were so long at sea but reckon the time spent at Barbadoes and St Christophers, for we were at sea onely 7 weekes and 2 daies, wch is held a speedy passage. From this time all alonge the Spanish Coast we had

[1] Mainsail.

nor good, nor very bad windes, in wch time we looked for Turkes but saw none, it seemes they were returned home to celebrate their Tamisom,[1] a great feast which happeneth about that time. After we had passed the Straits-mouth[2] and the Maderas, and now went full afore the winde, which is here trade, and ever constant on one point of the Compasse, still servinge for south and Southwest, as we sailed we made 3 ships bigger then ours, 3 leagus west from us, labouring as we imagined towards us. We feared the might be turkes, and therefore made readie for fight, neither wanted some who imprudently wished the master to make towards them, but he answered he could not justifie that to the owners of the ship, and indeed he might well have found a hard bargaine of it. Happily they were Canarie merchants and feared us as we them.

In the long reach we feared nought but Calmes, which sometimes held a fortnight or 3 weekes together, and starve men, but this happens not above once in an age. There are often tedious stayes for fault of winde, but when it comes it is ever the same for our way. We sailed 3000 miles in this reach in a sea of milke without any calme in the dead of winter, where we had every as hote, as the hotest day of summer in England, so that in summer tis intolerable for heat, where I see that *diligentibus Deum omnia cooperantur in bonum*,[3] for if we had not had those Crosses, rubbs, and difficulties before our comeing forth, we had got the hote weather which had doubtlesse cost most of our lives. From our setting forth till Christmas day our sickenesse onely sea-sicknesse, then indeed for the celebrity of the daye wine being given over all the ship, it was soe immoderately taken as the next day 30 sickened of fevers, whereof about a dozen died afterward amongest which one Catholique venturer, Mr Nicholas ffarefax, and one very faithfull servant of my L^rde named Mr Barefoot.

Some curiosities we see in our way, as flieinge fishes, wch use their finnes as well to flie as swimme. They are of the

---

[1] Presumably Ramazan is meant, the month of Mohammedan fasting. In the Latin text of this Relation it is called " solemne jejunium," a solemn *fast*. Md. Hist. Soc., *Calvert Papers*, no. 3, p. 11.

[2] Of Gibraltar.

[3] "All things work together for good to them that love God." Rom. viii. 28.

bignesse of sparling fish or great smelt very dainty for meat.
Some of them as they rise in hundreds pursued by the dolphins
fell into our ship, being not able to flie above two or three acres,
when their finnes being dried, they must neede dippe them
into the water to flie a fresh againe.   After we came within 21
and some odd minutes of the Aquinoctiall, where begins the
tropicke, we saw the tropicke bird, bigge as falcons, with 2 white
feathers in their traines and noe more.   Whether they alwaies
keep in the aire, or sometimes rest on the water I know not.

When we had passed the Canaries our governour begunne to
bee sollicitous for fraight homeward, fearinge we should come
to late for it to Virginia, and likewise that the Virginians wd
stand but our heavie freinde, though the could perhaps furnish us in that kinde.   After talke had with the commissioners and gentlemen, resolution was made to beare up to Bonavista directly south, and an Iland right against Angola, on the
Coast of Affrique 14 degrees from the line[1] whither the Hol-
lander since the losse of S[t] Martines useth to goe for salt,
thence carrieing it to Newfoundland to make fish.   This Iland
abounds with goats, haveing in it none inhabitantes but some
40 or 50 Portingalls banished thither for crimes committed by
them.   Both the salt for fraight and goates for fresh food
invited us thither, though if the yeare were wet, as it had
beene the yeare afore, noe salt can be made.

We had not gone full 200 miles, when the Commissioners
seeing all the commodity redounded to my L[rd], and that their
land provision was like to be spent by this circuit, caused the
governour to question the purser what provision of bread was
aboard, and findeing it short we altered againe our course to
S[t] Christophers, and soe began to thinke at what season we
were like to come to Maryland, and how we should procure
our seed corne.   As for Virginia we expected little from them
but blows, although we carried the kings letters to their
Governour, and the governour himselfe much esteemed and
loved my L[rd], yet wee feared he could or would doe us little

---

[1] Boavista, the easternmost of the Cape Verde Islands, in 16° N. lat., is doubtless meant.   These islands lie directly off the coast of Senegambia; but the
name Angola was formerly applied in a general way to a much larger portion
of the west coast of Africa than that to which it is now limited.   The Dutch
lost St. Martin, W. I., in 1633.

good being overawed by his councell.   As for the Salvages we
expected to finde them as our English ill wishers would make
them, and therefore affraid to build all the weale of our plantation on these peradventures, resolution was made for the
Barbadoes, the granarie of all the Charybbies Iles, which how
be.it it was somewhat about for corne was the surest course.

In this Iland M.ʳ Hierom Hawley his brother was governour,[1] and in his absence M.ʳ Piers his brother in law was
deputie.[2]   Here we arrived Januar: the 3 hopeinge for some
refreshinge by convenient good dyet some few dayes, but in
part we were deceived for every thing bore so high price, that
nothing could be had, but it Cost us our eies.   A pigge six
weekes old was at 5¹ sterling a turke 50.ˢ and a chicken at 6.ˢ.
Beefe or mutton they have none, and the inhabitants live
wholy upon poane (that Indian bread) and homine, and potato roote which they have in such plentie as they will give
Cart loades to almost any for the fetching.   The governour
told us at first, corne was at 1ˢ the bushell, but understanding
that we came for corne he called a Counsell and decreed there
should none be sould us under 2.ˢ a bushell, and soe we found
him a kinde kinsman of M.ʳ Hawleyes.   Other poore passages
we had from [him] not worth recountinge.

At our arrivall here we understood the Spanish fleet was
at Bonavista to hinder all strangers from salt, and it being
beyond the tropicke to make prize of them here, therefore we
admired the providence of god in protecting us from that
danger: but from a farre greater at Barbadoes.   The very
day we arrived, we found the Iland all in armes to the number
of about 800 men.   The servants of the Iland had conspired
to kill their masters and make themselves free, and then
handsomely to take the first ship that came, and soe goe to sea.
This first ship was ours and therefore it was the goodnesse of
god to discover the treason by a servant who was affraid to
Joine in the plott with them.   The ringleaders were 2 brothers
named Westons, Westerne men, whereof one was put to death
but the other saved by means of friends, God be praised for
this our deliverance.

[1] Captain Henry Hawley, governor of Barbadoes 1630–1640.
[2] Richard Peers was deputy-governor. In some texts the name has been
misread "Acers."

This is one of the 12 Charybbian Ilands which runne up like a bow in the baye of Mexico, some 30 miles long, and 15 broad, 13 degrees from the line. The clime is so hote as being now winter they can endure to weare noe more then a shirt, a pare of linneing drawers and linnen stockings on them. That time their corne was newly reapt. They use noe bede, but onely hamachoes[1] which are curious blankets of fine cotton neatly wrought and painted on the outside, and hung up a yard or lesse from ground by a rope at each end fastned to two posts when they goe to rest, and on the day time taken away, and carried about with them when they travaile.

Here are many things as well profitable for trade, as full of content to behold. Their trade is chiefely in corne and cotton, which cotton it delighted us much to see grow upon trees in such plentie. The cotton tree is not much higher then a barbara bush, but more treelike. It beares a little bude in bignesse like a wallnut, which at full time opening in the middle into fower quarters, their appeares a knot of cotton white as snow, with six seede in the middle of the bignesse of vetches which with an invention of wheeles they take out and soe keep it till the merchants fetch it from them. Here is a cabbage growes on a tree 180 foot high to be eaten raw or boiled. The stalke of it is for one yard from top good meat, to be eaten raw with pepper. It is in tast like the Spanish Cardo but sweeter. The tree beares but one yearely, and in wood is onely a leguminous substance. Here are also foxe-berrie trees, high as ash, the berrie is of bignesse of a hazell nut with an unctuous skin or cover which washeth scoureth and laddereth passing well, but is (as they say) somewhat too strong for fine linnen. Of these I found and carried a number to Maryland, and have them now in the ground.

There is another tree called palm Christi, with a spongious stalke. It beares a great thorny cluster of ash-coloured seede speckled with blacke whereof is made an excellent oyle. Oranges, lemmons, limes, pomegranade, peaches and such other fruite there are but not in any great plentie as yet; another fruit I saw called guaveos, in taste like quinches, in colour like gould, in figure like the smallest lemmons, a fruit very gratefull to taste. Another there is like unto these called

[1] Bed; hammocks.

Papares,[1] over sweet and luscious, which they use to eat boiled with other meate.

But the rarest of all other that I thinke is in the world, is the Charybbian Pineaple, of the colour of gould, mixed with an orient greene, bigge as three Spanish pineaples, and of the same figure externall to the eie, save that the worke of this is more perfect. It is not hard to peele, but of softe and thinne skinne, of delitious taste not haveing one membranula or kernell, but all, from highest part to lowest, cleane through equally dainty to taste. It beares in the toppe a Crowne of its owne leaves curiously compacte, and well it may, for sure it is the queene of all meat fruits without exception. The taste, as neere as I can expresse it, is an Aromaticall compound of wine and strawberries, and a better thing then this of Soveraigne efficacy to preserve health, and so well tempered to mans bodie as though it would consume a knife put thereing any time. There is nothing more restoritive. It growes from a thing like a Spanish thistle, one onely on every roote, but the leafe hath noe prickles, but a curious peake about its edges. In fine I wish one of them in your hande with this paper, for nothing can express it but it selfe.

There is another speciall fruit called a plantaine, singular for pleasant and delightfull tast, *fructus platani* as in latine they terme it. The tree is but a leguminous substance, to the hight and thicnesse of a tree of thicknesse of ones thigh. The leaves which are onely in the toppe for its ribbats are commonly a yard or more in length, and more than a quarter brood decently seamed with veines runneing like ribbs from the thicke in the middle as from the backe bone. It growes as high as a Cherry tree. In the top from the very middle pith springeth a purple sheath like a sugar loafe full of blossomes, which with its weight turnes the head downward and then comes thereon the fruit in a cluster like an hundred cucumbers together, but being ripe yellow coloured and somewhat bigger. They are of curious taste like Marmalate and much of that temper, very delightfull, fit to preserve, bake, or eat rawe. The potato root is of the very same colour skinne and figure of artichooke rootes, but in taste and temper much like a carrot, but farre more excellent. Here is the

---

[1] Papayas.

Cinnamon tree, the Avalto tree, the rope tree, which from the
top sendeth out long suckers, which take root in the ground
and so spread over large places, the wilde figge tree, the Maw
forest tree which is poison, the monkey tree bearing fruit, a
plaine and perfect munkeys face, and many others.

Foule I see little, save some few pigeons, stocdoves, and
some others. Vines will not grow there. The place is a
plaine ground, growne over wth trees and undershrubs without
passage, except where the planters have cleared. Some few
Catholiques there be both English and Irish.

Here we staied from January 3 to the 24th by which meanes
we came to enjoy againe our pinnace, wch not knowing of our
comeing was guided, to our soe great comfort as if that day we
had beene revived to life againe: for before we saw her in the
harbour we gave her for lost in that hideous storme. Herein
gods mercy was shewed towards us, and noe lesse again in
staying us here till the Spanish ships, in number five, were gone
out of our way: for soe it happened, five great Spanish men of
warre came to scoure the Charybbian Coaste, and make prize
of whomsoever they saw saile, beyond the grave Meridian or
tropicke: and had beene those very dayes before St Christophers, where findeing 2 small english barkes, and 2 or 3
great Hollanders guarded with a man of warre, by way of
Salve gave them a peece of ordinance, or two, (unwilling to
wrong the priviledge of that permisshend plantation, to which
they had given time till one halfe years end to be gone and
provide them elsewhere, or else to expect blowes to enforce
them; this plantation was once afore destroied by the Spaniard, save some few hidden in the mountaines, by whome
with much miserie the place was againe restored.) The holland man of warre for his salute returned a bullet, and weighing anchour made to sea, to enter fight, and withall engaged
the 2 English barkes to doe the like. Of those five English
and Hollands, onely 2 had ordinance; but the Spaniards each
about 30 brasse peeces. The manner of this feight I know
not, but in fine all runne away except the man of warre, who
either fired her selfe or sunke when she could hold out no longer,
for she cannot be heard of. If we had come the whilest, tis
like enough we had beene to forward with the rest, haveing so
perfect a ship soe well gunn'd and man'd, and whether we had

wonne or lost, our ship had certainly spoiled for saile til she had been repared. But god who endeavoreth the spirituall good of Maryland preserved us from danger, *Protector noster et merces nostra magna nimis.*[1]

The 24th of January we weighed from Barba: and by noone next day made S[t] Lucia's, one [of] the Charybbies, divided in it selfe, the servants (being Negroes) against the Salvage maisters. Then about 4 in the evening we came before Matilena[2] where we came to ankor, and 2 Canowes of starknaked Indians came paddleing aboard us, with parvats, pumpkins, callabashes, bonana's, muskmellons, watermellons and the like to exchange with us. They much feared at first the greatnesse of our ship, and though we put out a white flagge of peace, yet they desired we would put forth our nations proper colours, which done, they perceived whence wee were, and then boldly came aboard. This people is bigger than ours, and fatt and tawney coloured with ointments and oiles wherew[th] they be painted. Something wee trucked with them, as knives, bells and the like: and so they returned, saieing if we would ride there till morneing they would bring better trucke, as hammachoes, baskets and the like. They are a fierce nation, feeding on mans flesh, w[th]out all knowledge of god, and have heretofore cut of some English enterprisers. The Iland is all a hill, yet wonderfull fruitfull and florishing. It is the serious report of seamen, upon report of a ffrench wrecke, that here hath beene seene the Carbuncle, haveing in his head a pretious stone, light as a glowinge coale, of infinite valew; *ffides sit penes autorem.*[3]

Next morning by dawneing of the day we made Guadelupe an Ile so called for the similitude it hath with Guadelupe of Spaine, mountainous, almost as the other. By noone we came before Monserat, where is a noble plantation of Irish Catholiques whome the virginians would not suffer to live with them because of their religion. Thence next morne-

---

[1] "Our protector and our exceeding great reward." Gen. xv. 1.

[2] *Martinique,* called by the natives *Madiana.*

[3] "Let the teller of the tale be responsible for it." The reference is probably to the fable that

> "the toad, ugly and venomous,
> Wears yet a precious jewel in his head."

ing wee came to Maevis,[1] an Iland infamous for agues by reason of the bad aire; here haveing staied a day, next morninge we came to S.[t] Christophers hard by, where we staied 10 dayes, nobly enterteined by S.[r] Thomas Waroner, governour,[2] Captaine Jefferson, leiuetennant Coronell, by 2 Catholiques Capt: Caverley and Capt. Pellam, and my selfe in particular by the governour of the ffrench Colonie in the same Iland.[3] Here is beside all the varities of Barbadoes, a hill of brimstone and much more to be admired, here is also the virgin plant, or Parthenia, w.[ch] they terme the sensible tree, which after the least touch of ones hand I see fall downe withered, and then againe revived after a little space. Here is the locust tree which I supposed to be that whereon S[t] John Baptist lived in the wildernesse. It is high as an elme, soe loved of bees as they build their Combes on it. I have seene and tasted the honnie, then w.[ch] settinge aside the name wilde, there is none purer of taste and colour, the fruit is also called a locust, haveing a hard sheath as bigge as six beane codes, conteineing in it a tough substance in taste like meale and honny, with fower or 5 seedes of colour and greatnesse like chestnut. Some of them we have planted.

From this place we came to Virginia ffebruary the 27th, much contrary to My L[rds] instructions.[4] We expected here every hower to be staied by the Councell, desireing noethinge more then our ruine. At this time Captaine Claborne was there from whome we understood the Indians were all in armes to resist us, having heard that 6 Spanish ships were a comeing to destroy them all. The rumour was most like to have begunne from himselfe. We had the kings letters, and my Lord treasurers[5] to the governours, which made him shew to us the best usage the place afforded, with promise to furnish us with all manner of Provistions for our plantation though much against his Councells will, not doubting I suppose to receive noble gratification from my L[rd] by whose helpe he hoped to recover a great summe of money due to him out of the exchequer. Here we staied 8 or 9 daies not w[th]out imminent daunger, under Commande of the Castle, and then on the 3 of

---

[1] Nevis.   [2] Sir Thomas Warner, governor from 1625 to 1649.
[3] From 1625 to 1713 part of the island of St. Christopher was occupied by the French.   [4] See pp. 17, 23, *supra*.   [5] The Earl of Portland.

March came into Chesapeake bay, at the mouth of Patomecke. This baye is the most delightfull water I ever saw, between two sweet landes, with a channell 4 : 5 : 6 : 7: and 8 fathoms deepe, some 10 leagues broad, at time of yeare full of fish, yet it doth yeeld to Patomecke, wch we have made St Gregories. This is the sweetest and greatest river I have seene, so that the Thames is but a little finger to it. There are noe marshes or swampes about it, but solid firme ground, with great variety of woode, not choaked up with undershrubs, but commonly so farre distant from each other as a coach and fower horses may travale without molestation.

At our first comeing we found (as we were told) all in armes; the king of Pascatoway had drawne together 500 bowmen, great fires were made by night over all the Country, and the biggnesse of our ship made the natives reporte, we came in a Canow as bigg as an Iland, with so many men, as trees were in a wood, with great terrour unto them all. Thus we sailed some 20 leagues up the river to Herne-Iland, so called for infinite swarmes of hernes[1] thereon. This we called St Clements,[2] here we first came ashoare; here by the overturning of a shallop we had allmost lost our mades which wee brought along. The linnen they went to wash was much of it lost, which is noe small matter in these partes. The ground is heare, as in very many places, covered with pokiberries, (a little wilde walnut hard of shell, but with a sweet kernell) with ackhornes, black walnut, cedar, saxafras, vines, salladherbes, and such like. It is not above 400 acres, and therefore too little to seat upon for us: therefore they have designed it for a fort to Command the river, meaneing to raise another on the maine land against it, and soe to keep the river from forraigne trade, here being the narrowest of the river.

In this place on our b: Ladies day in lent,[3] we first offered, erected a crosse, and with devotion tooke solemne possession of the Country. Here our governour was advised not to settle himselfe, till he spoake with the emperour[4] of Pascatoway,

---

[1] Herons.

[2] Now called Blackiston's Island. Thomas, *Chronicles of Colonial Maryland*, pp. 13, 14.

[3] March 25, 1634. "Offered" means "offered the sacrifice of the mass."

[4] See pp. 126, 131, *infra*.

and told him the cause of his comeing (to wit) to teach them a divine doctrine, whereby to lead them to heaven, and to enrich with such ornaments of civill life as our owne country abounded withall, not doubting but this emperour beinge satisfied, the other kings would be more peaceable. With this intention he tooke our pinnace and went therein higher up the river. In their way they found still all the Indians fleede from their houses; till comeing to Patomecke towne, he found there the king[1] thereof a Childe, governed by Archihoe, his uncle. Here, by an Interpretour, they had some speech with Archihoe, a grave and considerate man, and shewed his errours in part unto him, which he seemed to acknowledge, bidding them all very welcome. They could proceed but little with him in matters of religion, their interpretor being a protestant of Virginia, but promised shortly to returne to him, some one or other; which he desired they would and promised they should have the best entertainment they could make them and his men should hunt and fish for them, and he and they would devide what soever they got, being (as they all generally be) of a very loveing and kinde nature.

ffrom here they went to Pascatoway, the seat of the Emperour, where 500 bowmen came to meet them at the water side. Here the Emperour, lesse feareing then the rest came privately aboard, where he found kind usage, and perceiveing we came with good meaneing towards them, gave leave to us to sett downe where we pleased. The king being aboard, his men by the water side feared some treason, till by interpretours we assured them otherwise. In this journey our governour tooke Captaine Henrie ffleet, and his 3 barkes, who had beene a firebrand to inflame the Indians against us. This Capt: brought aboard our shipp accepted of a proportion in our beaver trade, for to serve my Lord, excellent in language, love, and experience with the Indians, most of all other. Thus he remained, untill haveing talked with Claborne, another of our chiefe enemies, he revolted, and leaveing us went againe and traded with out leave, and got that time above 200 skins, and as we feared incensed the Indians against us; yet first he had brought us to as noble a seat as could be wished, and as good ground as I suppose is in all Europe.

[1] See pp. 84, 125, *infra*.

Whilest our governour was abroad, the Indians began to loose feare and come to our coart of guarde, and sometimes aboard our shipp, wondering where that tree should grow, out of which so great a canow should be hewen, supposing it all of one peece, as their canows use to be. They trembled to heare our ordinance thinking them fearefuller then any thunder they had ever heard.

The governour being returned from Pascatoway, by ffleets directions, we came some 9 or 10 leagues lower in the river Patomecke, to a lesser river on the north side of it, as bigge as Thames, which we call St Georges. This river makes 2 excellent bayes, wherein might harbour 300 saile of 1000 tunne a peece with very great safetie, the one called St Georges bay,[1] the other, more inward, St Maries. On the one side of this river lives the king of Yoacomaco, on the other our plantation is seated, about halfe a mile from the water, and our towne we call St Maries.

To avoid all occasion of dislike, and Colour of wrong, we bought the space of thirtie miles of ground of them, for axes, hoes, cloth and hatchets, which we call Augusta Carolina. It made them more willing to enterteine us, for that they had warres wth the Sasquasahannockes, who come sometimes upon them, and waste and spoile them and their country, for thus they hope by our meanes to be safe, God disposeing things thus for those which were to come to bring the light of his holy law to these distressed, poore infidels, so that they doe indeed like us better for comeing so well provided, assuring themselves of greater safety, by liveing by us. Is not this miraculous, that a nation a few daies before in generall armes against us and our enterprise should like lambes yeeld themselves, glad of our company, giveing us houses, land, and liveings for a trifle. *Digitus dei est hic*,[2] and some great good is meant toward this people. Some few Indians are here to stay by us till next yeare, and then the land is wholy to be ours alone.

The natives of person be very proper and tall men, by nature swarthy, but much more by art, painting themselves with colours in oile a darke read, especially about the head,

---

[1] Afterward called St. Inigo's Creek.
[2] "This is the finger of God."   Ex. viii. 19.

which they doe to keep away the gnats, wherein I confesse
there is more ease then honesty.[1] As for their faces they use
sometimes other colours, as blew from the nose downeward,
and read upward, and sometimes contrary wise with great
variety, and in gastly manner. They have noe bearde till
they be very old, but insteed thereof sometimes draw long
lines with colours from the sides of their mouth to their
eares. They weare their [hair] diversly some haveing it cut
all short, one halfe of the head, and long on the other; others
have it all long, but generally they weare all a locke at the left
eare, and sometimes at both eares which they fold up with a
string of wampampeake or roanoake about it. Some of their
Caucorouses[2] as they terme them, or great men, weare the
forme of a fish of Copper in their foreheads. They all weare
beade about their neckes, men and women, with otherwhiles
a haukes bill or the talents of an eagles or the teeth of beasts,
or sometimes a pare of great eagles wings linked together and
much more of the like. Their apparell is deere skins and other
furrs, which they weare loose like mantles, under which all
their women, and those which are come to mans stature,
weare perizomata[3] of skins, which keep them decently covered from all offence of sharpe eies. All the rest are naked, and
sometimes the men of the younger sort weare nothing at all.

Their weapons are a bow and a bundle of arrowes, an ell
long, feathered with turkies feathers, and headed with points
of deeres hornes, peeces of glasse, or flints, which they make
fast with an excellent glew which they have for that purpose.
The shaft is a small cane or sticke, wherewith I have seene
them kill at 20 yards distance, little birds of the bignesse of
sparrows, and they use to practise themselves by casting up
small stickes in the aire, and meeting it with an arrow before
it come to ground. Their bow is but weake and shoots level
but a little way. They daily catch partridge, deere, turkies,
squirrels and the like of which there is wonderfull [plenty?], but
as yet we dare not venture ourselves in the woods to seeke
them, nor have we leasure.

Their houses are built in an halfe ovall forme 20 foot long,
and 9 or 10 foot high with a place open in the top, halfe a

---

[1] Honesty in the now obsolete sense of seemliness.
[2] See p. 84, *infra*.   [3] Girdles.

yard square, whereby they admit the light, and let forth the smoake, for they build their fire, after the manner of ancient halls of England, in the middle of the house, about which they lie to sleep upon mats, spread on a low scaffold hafe a yard from ground. In one of these houses we now doe celebrate,[1] haveing it dressed a little better then by the Indians, till we get a better, which shall be shortly as may be.

The naturall wit of these men is good, conceiveing a thing quick to. They excell in smell and taste, and have farre sharper sight than we have. Their diett is poane, made of wheat, and hominie, of the same with pease and beanes together, to which sometimes they add fish, foule, and venison, especially at solemne feasts. They are very temperate from wines and hote waters, and will hardly taste them, save those whome our English have corrupted. For chastity I never see any action in man or woman tendinge to soe much as levity, and yet the poore soules are daily with us and bring us turkie, partridge, oisters, squirells as good as any rabbit, bread and the like, running to us with smileing countenance and will help us in fishing, fouling, hunting, or what we please.

They hold it lawful to have many wives, but all keep the rigour of conjugall faith to their husbands. The very aspect of the women is modest and grave; they are generally so noble, as you can doe them noe favour, but they will returne it. There is small passion amongst them. They use in discourse of great affaires to be silent, after a question asked, and then after a little studdie to answere in few words, and stand constant to their resolution. If these were once christian, they would doubtlesse be a vertuous and renowned nation. They exceedingly desire civill life and Christian apparrell and long since had they beene cloathed, had the covetous English merchants (who would exchange cloath for nought but beaver, which every one could not get) held them from it (God forbid we should do the like).

As for religion we neither have language as yet to finde it out, nor can wee trust therein the protestant interpretours. Mr Altham[2] hath writ somethin thereof, wch himselfe can witnesse; and likewise Mr Thorowgood, who drives trade with the Indians. They acknowledge one god of heaven,

<hr>

[1] Celebrate the mass.   [2] Father John Altham, S. J.

whome they call our god, and crie a 1000 shames on those that so lightly offend soe good a god, but give noe externall honnour to him But use all their might to please an *Okee* which signifies a frantique spirit, for feare of harme from him. I heare also, they adore wheat and fire, as gods very beneficiall to mans nature. In the Matchcomaco, or temple of the Patuxans, this ceremonie was seene by our traders; at a day appointed the townes about mett together, and built a great fire, then standinge all about the same, lifted up their hands to heaven Crieing *Taho Taho*, after this was brought forth a bagge of *Poate*,[1] which is their tobacco, with a great tobacco pipe, and carried about the fire, a young man following it, crieing *Taho Taho*, with great variety of gesture of body, this done they filled the pipe, and gave to every one a draught of smoake from it which they breathed out on all parts of their bodies, as it were to sanctifie them to the service of their god. This is all I can say, save that we perceive they have notice by tradition of Noah his flood. Wee have not beene above one moneth Conversant amongest them and therefore must reserve further particulars to the next ship.

I will end therefore with the soyle, which is excellent so that we cannot sett downe a foot, but tread on Strawberries, raspires, fallen mulberrie vines, acchorns, walnutts, saxafras etc: and those in the wildest woods. The ground is commonly a blacke mould above, and a foot within ground of a readish colour. All is high woods except where the Indians have cleared for corne. It abounds with delicate springs which are our best drinke. Birds diversely feathered there are infinite, as eagles, swans, hernes, geese, bitters, duckes, partridge read, blew, partie coloured, and the like, by which will appeare, the place abounds not alone with profit, but also with pleasure +

Laus Deo

[1]Spelled *Potu* in the Latin version. Md. Hist. Soc., *Fund Publication* no. 7, p. 42. See p. 136, *infra*.

EXTRACT FROM A LETTER OF CAPTAIN
THOMAS YONG TO SIR TOBY MATTHEW,
1634

INTRODUCTION

THE letter of Captain Thomas Yong to Sir Toby Matthew was written from Jamestown, Virginia, in July, 1634. It was published in volume IX. of the fourth series of the *Collections of the Massachusetts Historical Society*, in Weston's *Documents connected with the History of South Carolina*, and again in Streeter's *Papers relating to the Early History of Maryland*, but the original manuscript is in the Virginia State Library. It is written in a hand very difficult to decipher, which is said to have led to some inaccuracies in the former publications. Special care has been taken by collating with the original manuscript, to make the following text an accurate reproduction of the original.

Captain Yong, as the letter shows, was in chief command of certain trading vessels sailing together to Maryland. Sir Toby Matthew was the son of an Anglican bishop of Durham and archbishop of York, but had become reconciled to the Roman Catholic Church. He was a schoolmate and life-long friend of George, the first Lord Baltimore (father of Cecilius), and one of the witnesses to his will.

This letter is specially valuable as giving us, from the hand of one who had no interest in the matters in controversy, except such as arose from a feeling of loyalty to his employers, evidence as to the early features of the long contention between Lord Baltimore and William Claiborne concerning Kent Island in Maryland. Captain Yong appears to have talked with those interested on both sides of the controversy, and to have reported faithfully the information and impressions received.

The careful directions which Lord Baltimore gave to his brother, Leonard Calvert, and the other commissioners for the founding of Maryland, as to their negotiations with Claiborne, and the terms to be offered to him for conducting trade with the Indians under license from the proprietary government, are contained in Lord Baltimore's Letter of Instructions to the Colonists (p. 19, *supra*).

As references to this controversy in its various stages occur in several of the documents printed in this volume, a brief statement of the grounds of dispute, inserted here, will afford a better understanding of the subject.

The territory of Maryland was originally included in the grant to the old Virginia Company, the northern boundary of which touched the southern boundary of New England. But the charter of that company having been annulled in 1624, the grant to it had become void, and this territory, in which no private titles had been created, was again at the disposal of the Crown.

In June, 1632, the King, Charles I., made a grant, under the name of Maryland, of the territory lying between the Potomac River and the fortieth degree of north latitude to Cecilius Lord Baltimore, as absolute lord and Proprietary. He was thus constituted both lord of the soil and political ruler.[1]

Shortly prior to this grant to Lord Baltimore, William Claiborne, who was a member of the Council of Virginia, had established a post for trading with the Indians in peltries, etc., upon Kent Island, which lay within the boundaries of Maryland as defined in its charter.

Upon the establishment of his government in Maryland, Lord Baltimore sought to obtain from Claiborne recognition of his title, promising to him authority to trade under his license. This Claiborne refused to accept, claiming proprie-

[1] See charter, p. 103, *infra*.

tary rights in Kent Island. Upon investigation it proved that what he had was merely a license, dated in 1631, from Sir William Alexander, Secretary of State for Scotland, to trade with New England and Nova Scotia,[1] and no grant of land whatever.

In the preamble to the Charter of Maryland it is recited that Lord Baltimore had sought leave to transport a colony to a region hitherto uncultivated[2] (*hactenus inculta*) and partly occupied by savages. While the grant itself of the territory described is absolute in terms, it was maintained by Claiborne that the words *hactenus inculta* showed that there was no intention to grant any land already occupied by English colonists, and that Kent Island having been occupied by him prior to the date of Lord Baltimore's patent was excluded from its operation. It is to be noted that the grant of Maryland was sought by and promised to George Lord Baltimore, who had visited Virginia and the Chesapeake Bay in 1629, and at that time there was no settlement at Kent Island. By reason of the death of the first Lord Baltimore shortly before the charter of Maryland was signed, the grant was actually made to Cecilius, his son and successor in title.

Claiborne addressed a petition to the King setting forth his claims and grievances, which was referred to the Lords Commissioners of Plantations, who rendered their decision in April, 1638,[3] in favor of Lord Baltimore, holding that the lands in question belonged absolutely to him, that no trade or plantation should be allowed within their limits without his permission, and that, with regard to the violences complained of, the parties should be left to their remedies at law.

There had been both violence and strife over the possession of Kent Island, and contests with bloodshed both on land

[1] *Archives of Maryland*, III. 19, 20.
[2] Rendered "not yet cultivated and planted" in the version of the charter contained in this volume (p. 101).
[3] *Archives of Maryland*, III. 71.

and water. Finally Governor Calvert succeeded in obtaining the submission of the settlers upon the island and the recognition by them of the authority of the Proprietary.[1] But the strife went on and Claiborne continued for many years to take advantage of every disturbance in the colony or of political change in England, to reassert his claims, and to seek the defeat of Lord Baltimore's grant.

Captain Yong's letter discloses the temper in which the controversy was conducted at the beginning of negotiations between the parties.

C. C. H.

[1] See p. 152, *infra*.

EXTRACT FROM A LETTER OF CAPTAIN THOMAS YONG TO SIR TOBY MATTHEW, 1634

. . . the third of July towards sunsett we arrived between the Capes wch are called Cape Charles and Cape Henry. About one of the clock we came to an Anchor, the tide being spent, within three miles of Point Comfort, wch is some seven leagues from the Capes and lieth upon the very mouth of James River (whereon standeth a new erected fort, wch commandeth that river).

All my men in my owne ship are, God be praysed, in very good health, tho' my Vice Admirall hath bene shrewdly visited with a pestilentiall feavor, whereof about 60 have bene sicke and twelve dead thereof, but they are now most of them recovered.

As soone as we were now come to an anchor we descried a small barke coming out from Point Comfort, wch bare wth us, and about half an hower after she came to an Anchor cloase aboard oʳ vice admirall. We thought she had bene some vessell bound from Virginia to New England, whither the Inhabitants of Virginia drive a great trade for Indian Corne. I sent my Leiutenant aboard her to enquire whence she was and whither she was bound, and withall to learne what he could both concerning the State of Virginia and Maryland, wch is my Lord of Baltimores Collony, as likewise on what tearmes those two Collonyes were, and what correspondence they had one wth another and wth the Indians also. When he came aboard he found this Barke to be a vessell of Virginia belonging to one Captayne Cleyborne, who liveth upon an Island within my Lord of Baltimores Territory called the Ile of Kent. But the Captayne was gone aboard oʳ vice admirall, and thither my Leiuetenant went to him. Where after salutations and some discourse passed to and fro, they fell in talke concerning my Lord of Baltimores Company, who arrived heere in March last. He discovered that there was growne great discontents between my Lords company and him wch he seemed to excuse as well as he could though even by some words that now and then fell from him unawares my Leiuetenant saith a man might read much malice in his heart towards them. After some two houres, my Leiuetenant brought Captayne Cleyborne wth him aboard my ship where he remayned till the morning.

By him I understand that the Governour of Virginia, Sr John Harvie, had bene in Maryland at the Plantation there wch is called St Maries, there to have heard and composed the differents which were growne between those of my Lords Collony and this Cleyburnes; and that, that night he was arrived at Point Comfort: That in his company also were Captayne Calvert Governour of Maryland, Captayne Cornewallis, Mr Hawley,[1] and other principall gentlemen of Maryland, and that they were come thither purposely for the composing of those differents, but that he for his part purposed not to be there, but to retire himself to his own Plantation, under pretence that he went thither to take order for the securing thereof against certayne Indians, who had lately as he understood killed a man and a Boy of his, but I playnly perceaved that the principall and mayne reason of his retreat was to absent himself from that meeting. I found the man subtle and fayre spoken but extreamely averse from the prosperity of that Plantation. He alleaged that my Lords company had accused him to the Governour of Virginia for animating, practizing and conspiring wth the Indians to supplant and cutt them off: that the Governour had appointed certayne comm^{rs} of this Collony to joyne wth certayn other Comm^{rs} of my Lords Collony to examine the truth of that accusation and that upon their information he purposed to proceed herein according to Justice. That accordingly they had examined the matter and had found no grounds for those accusations and so he conceaved that the purpose of their comming was now only to make a reconciliation, but that for his part he purposed not to be there. On the other side, he

---

[1] Thomas Cornwallis and Jerome Hawley, commissioners for governing the province of Maryland. See Lord Baltimore's instructions, p. 16, *supra.*

pretended that heeretofore he had borne very good corre-
spondense with them and that he had furnished them with
hoggs and other provisions and done them what curtesies were
in his power, till my Lords people had given directions for the
taking and surprizing his boates, that went to trade, and likewise of his owne person. After wch discourse he parted from
me, telling me, though I perceaved afterwards he ment it not,
he would meet me at Point Comfort, but he came no more to
me. The next morning I weighed as soone as the tide served
and about eleven of the clocke I came to an anchor within
Point Comfort, where now I ride. Heere I understood that
the Governor was hard by, and as soone as I had fitted my
dress I tooke boate with intention to have awaited upon the
Governor on shoare, but as soone as I was in my boate I descried his Barge on the River making towards our shipp, soe
I stood in wth him to meet him, but he perceaving me row
towards him stood towards my vice admirall, whither also I
stood and gott into the ship before him, who as soone as he
perceaved me aboard presently entered therein. After I had
saluted him he was pleased to treat me wth much curtesy and
great affection; to whome I presented his Maties l^{res} [letters].
After he had read them, he assured me that he would in all
things most willingly and observantly obey his Maties commands, wch I have also found him most effectually and affec-
tionately observe, on all occasions, wherein I had cause to require his assistance.

In his company, of my Lord of Baltimores Plantation, I
mett only wth Captayne Cornewallis, (for Captayne Calvert
fell sicke by the way, and returned,) who was come thither
purposely to meet wth Cleyborne, whom I mentioned before.

After some time I took Captayne Cornewallis aside and
told him what discourse had passed between Cleyborne and
me. He answered me that this Cleybourne had dealt very
unworthyly and falsely with them. That he had also labored
to procure the Indians to supplant them by informing them
that they were Spaniards and that they had a purpose to destroy them and take their Country from them. That the
Indians had a purpose to have attempted it, had they not
bene dissuaded by one Captayne Fleet,[1] who had in former

[1] See p. 41, *supra.*

times lived amongst them, and is now in good creditt wth them. That Cleyborne had contrived divers other malitious plotts and conspiracies against them. That some others also of the principall Councellors of Virginia might justly be suspected to have animated Cleyborne to his foule practises. That his conspiracy and practises was proved against Cleyborne, both by the confession of the Indians and likewise by the confession of Christians taken upon oath. That he himself publikely protested that if my lords plantation should surprize or take any of his boates, he would be revenged though he joined with the Indians in a canoa. That heerupon the Governour of Maryland complayned thereof to Sr John Harvie, the Govern^r of Virginia, who forthwth tooke the matter into his consideration. Upon hearing the accusation of the one and the defence of the other, it was ordered that Cleyborne should remayne confined in the hands of one Captayne Matthews and Captayne Utie,[1] two councellors of State in Virginia, though both of them private friends to Cleyborne, whome he ordered to keep Cleyborne from any conferences or messages to the Indians, and that they two should forthwith, taking Cleyborne along with them, repaire to my Lords Plantation in Maryland, where also two Com^{rs}, namely Captayne Cornewallis and Mr Hawley, chosen for that Colony, should be joined with them, and that they should take on both sides interpretors and from thence goe in company together to the Indians and examine the truth of this examination, but that Cleyborne was not to be present at the examination. And that they should make a true relation of the state of the buisiness to the two Governo^{rs} who would expect them in this plantation at Maryland. But precisely and expressly ordering them that they should be carefull in no case to suffer any conference to be had wth the Indians, on either side, either directly or indirectly.

But these two Captaynes, taking along with them Cleyborne, went towards Maryland, not with any purpose (as it afterwards appeared by the sequelle) to comply with the Governors order of Virginia, having subtlely and sinisterly inveigled into their company two very yong gentlemen of my

---

[1] Samuel Mathews and John Utie. In reference to Mathews see pp. 59, 61, *infra*. In 1635 they led in the deposition of Governor Harvey.

Lords Collony (whereof the one was a younger Brother[1] of my Lords, the other of Sr John Winters), wth faire words, finding them in a joviall humor, perswaded them to accompany them to the examination of these Indians, and so taking these for my Lord Com^{rs}, instead of going to my Lords plantation at Maryland or giving any notice of their arrivall in those parts, they take this advantage and, with these young gentlemen wch themselves tooke and chose in place of Comm^{srs}, they goe directly to the Indians, taking with them also Cleyborne and a servant of his for their Interpreter, and there, in the presence of Cleyborne, examine the Indians upon such Articles and with such Intergatories as they thought would best serve for Cleybornes advantage, using also the helpe of the Interpreter to frame such answerres from the Indians as would best suit with their purpose. When they had done they putt this examination in writing, and after they had themselves signed it, they procured also these two young gentlemen to putt their hands also thereunto as taken before them.

This examination they sent to my Lords plantation at Maryland by one of the Councell of Virginia, for I should have told you that there went also two other Councello^{rs} of Virginia with them (who went without or rather contrary to the order, only to countenance the carriage of this plott the better) to my Lords plantation at Maryland (where all this while both the Governo^{rs} remayned expecting their coming) and in his company came also one of the Indian Kings called the King of Pattuxunt, procured by them to come thither to justifie the truth and impartiality of their proceedings, Laboring by their indirect proceeding to cleerr Cleyborne from his crimes and also to incense and exasperate the Indians both against my Lords people and against those other Christians also who had informed them thereof, suggesting and intimating to them that my Lords were turbulent people, who cared not what false pretenses and suggestions they framed to deprive others of their estate, wch it was evident they labored to wring out of the hands both of Indians and Christians also, that so in Fine they might become Lords of that Country. The Gov-

---

[1] George Calvert. He accompanied the first colonists to Maryland, but appears shortly afterward to have removed to Virginia. He does not figure in Maryland history.

ernor of Virginia not finding himself well intreated by them returned to Virginia, where he made account to finde them expecting him, as they sent him word by the messenger I spake of before, they would at Kecoughtan,[1] but when he came thither he found them all gone, soe as he could at that time doe nothing therein. But he had appointed them a new time for their appearance at James Towne.

Concerning his complaint that my Lords company would have surprized his boates and him, Capt[e] Cornewallis told me that Cleyborne had bene offered all faire correspondence, with as free liberty to trade as themselves, but he refused it, wherefore the Governor gave order to forbid him to trade. That concerning the surprizall of his person (though his carriage towards them very well deserved it) yet it was only a meere supposition and jealousy of his owne, without any grounds.

This, so farre as I can learne, is the true state wherein my Lord of Baltimores plantation stands wth those of Virginia, wch perhaps may prove dangerous enough for them if there be not some present order taken in England for the suppressing the insolence of Cleyborne and force his complines[2] and for disjoynting this faction, wch is soe fast linked and united as I am perswaded will not by the Governor be easily dissevered or over ruled with[out] some strong and powerful addition to his present authority by some new power from England, and it will be to little purpose for my Lord to proceed in his colony against which they have so exasperated and incensed all the English Colony of Virginia as heere it is accounted a crime almost as heynous as treason to favor, nay allmost to speak well of that Colony of my Lords. And I have observed myself a palpable kind of strangenesse and distance between those of the best sort in the country who have formerly bene very familiar and loving one to another, only because the one hath bene suspected but to have bene a well wisher to the Plantation in Maryland.

The Governor only of Virginia (a gentleman in good faith in my judgment of a noble mynde and worthy heart) out of

---

[1] An Indian town at the mouth of Hampton River, on the east side, three miles from Point Comfort.

[2] Compliance.

his care to observe his Maties commands signified to him by his Royall l^res [letters] and also out of his own good inclinations hath carried himself very worthily and respectively towards them and is ready on all occasions to give them all the assistance and furtherance that possibly he can, though thereby he hath acquired to himself extreame hatred and malice from all the rest of the country, to whom I can find only two of his councell indifferent, the one of them called Captaine Purfree a souldier and a man of an open heart, honest and free, hating for ought I can [see?] all kinds of dissimulation and basenesse, the other an honest playne man but of small capacity and lesse power.[1]

The person on whom the strength and sinewes of this faction depends is one Captayne Mathews an ancient planter heere, a man of a bold spiritt, turbulent and strong in the faction of the more refractory sort of the countrey, and as I have bene informed by persons of good creditt a great opposer and interpreter of all letters and commands that come from the King and state of England, apt also to possesse and preoccupate the judgments of the rest of his fellow councellors, that letters from the King and from the Lords are surreptitiously gotten and that the obedience to them may and ought to be suspended till they be warranted by second commands from England, which may issue from them after the Lords have bene informed by them, for that many times the Lords are not sufficiently instructed in the necessities and conveniencies of this Government heere, pretending and making them beleeve that evry kind of disobedience doe oftentimes become gratefull to the State. This gentleman as I heare is lately married to the daughter of one Sir Thomas Hinton, who is lately retired hither into these parts,[2] and he grows, as is conceaved, much bolder by this alliance, as hoping by his power to find great strength in England, though for my part I conceave he hath but small grounds for those hopes, yet heere we have it very confidently and very frequently reported that a sonne of Sr Thomas Hintons, who is a gentleman of the Privie Chamber, is to come over hither Governor.

[1] Sir John Harvey continued to be the stanch friend of Lord Baltimore and the Maryland Colony and to entertain suspicions as to the loyalty of Claiborne.

[2] Sir Thomas Hinton, M. P. 1620–1626.

S[r] John Harvye invited me very earnestly that during the time that my ship was making ready and my shallopp building I would accompany him to James Towne, whither he was then going, wch I accepted as a favor, partly led thereunto with desire to see the country, partly also to see the event of my Lords buisnesse, and likewise a little to recreate myself after my long voyage, wherein I thank God I have yet had my health very well. We lay two nights by the way, at a gentlemans house a planter of the country one night, and the other most parte of it aboard S[r] Johns barge. This countrey aboundeth with very great plentie insomuch as in ordinary planters houses of the better sort we found tables fournished wth porke, kidd, chickens, turkeyes, young geese, Caponetts and such other foules as the season of the yeare affords, besides plentie of milk, cheese, butter and corne, wch latter almost every planter in the country hath.

The country is very good and fertill, the climate pleasant and wholesome, the land fertile enough and with good husbandry will soone grow into great abundance, and a great Trade may quickly be driven heere, if good providence and care be taken, wch will much advance his Ma[ties] customes.

While I stay heere at James Towne, where Now I am, I meet dayly with severall of the best and most understanding sort of the Inhabitants of this place, by whome I enforme myself as much as I can of the State of this countrey and I find really that the present Governor hath carried himselfe heere with very great prudence, hath bene extraordinary dilligent in advancing and furthering the Colony, a great reformer of the abuses in the Governement, especially in point of justice, wch at his first entrance was full of corruption and partiality, the richest and most powerfull oppressing and swallowing up the poorer, though now much amended by his care and zeale to justice, though even in that also he is sometimes overborne by the strength and power of some factious and turbulent spiritts of his councell, for heere in this place all things are carried by the most voyces of the Councell, and they are for the most part united in a kind of faction against the Governor, insomuch as they make their publike consultations give strength and authority to their faction, and it is hard for the Governors to determine or order any thing heere con-

trary to their dreaming, for they come all hither preoccu-
pated and resolved to follow and concurr with the votes of
their leaders.   Of this faction Captain Mathews, of whom
before I spake, is the head and cheefe supporte.   This gentleman, as I am told, tooke the boldenesse publikely when the
kings letter was delivered and read in favor of my Lord of
Baltimore was there read, to question whether they were not
surreptitiously procured, and it is vehemently suspected, and
they say not without reason, that he hath bene the incendiary
of all this wicked plott of Cleybourne's and yet continues to
bee the supporter and upholder of him, and except my Lord
finde some meanes speedily and in a very exemplar manner
to curb and suppresse this mans insolencies, he will dayly find
more and more practizes and treacherous conspiracies contrived against him, and veryly I beleeve if my Lord could
finde meanes over heere to ecclipse his power and greatnesse,
or to remove him from hence, the backe of this faction would
soone be broken and this strong knot would untie of itselfe.
Nor is that other instrument of his of whome I spake before,
namely Cleybourne, lesse carefully to be lookt unto, since his
practizes, though they be not so publike as the others insolencies, yet are they not lesse dangerous to that Colony, yea and
to the security of the peace of this very land and governement
of Virginia, where I have bene informed that some of the Councellors have bene bold enough in a presumptuous manner to
say, to such as told them that perhaps their disobedience
might cause them to be sent for into England,   That if the
King would have them he must come himself and fetch them.

A RELATION OF MARYLAND, 1635

INTRODUCTION

THE ensuing document, *A Relation of Maryland*, published originally as a pamphlet in London in 1635, for the information of persons contemplating emigration to the new colony, is practically of the nature of a prospectus. The William Peaseley mentioned on the title-page, from whom copies and further information and advice could be obtained, was the brother-in-law of Lord Baltimore, having married the latter's eldest sister, Anne.

This *Relation* reproduces much concerning Maryland and its settlement that is contained in Father White's narrative of the voyage over, and the remainder is no doubt derived from the reports which the commissioners for the colony were, under their instructions from the Proprietary, required to send by every ship departing from the province, as well as from the publications of Captain John Smith in relation to Virginia, and William Wood's treatise of New England referred to in the text.

The account does full justice to the advantages of the new settlement and the attractiveness of the country, its climate, etc. If there were any disadvantages or hardships, other than those which necessarily attend a pioneer settlement in the wilderness, they are not mentioned. It is true that in contrast with the suffering and disastrous loss of life which attended the first settlement of Virginia at Jamestown, and of New England at Plymouth, the Maryland colonists had no such experience. This, as is acknowledged in the pamphlet, was partly due to the fact that for their immediate wants they were able to obtain supplies from the older settlements; but in a greater measure probably it was due to a mild winter as compared with the rigors of the New England coast, and to the salubrious situation of St. Mary's upon a high bluff overlooking the river, as contrasted with the low and malarious spot which in ignorance of the climate the Virginia colonists had selected as the site of Jamestown. The lot of the Marylanders was moreover cast among the Pascataways, a gentle and peaceful tribe of Indians, who received them with hospitality and gladly furnished them with shelter and provisions. These people, it appears, were not nomadic and had made some progress in agriculture.[1] It is a pleasant fact to note that these friendly relations were never broken; and that when in after years (1670) the Indians, being reduced in number and wasted by sickness, reported that they were unable through weakness and poverty to bring their annual gift, the Deputy Governors, Philip and William Calvert, promptly replied that they desired to continue in amity with them and would not scorn or cast off the meanest of them.[2]

Appended to the *Relation* (Chapter VI.) are the Conditions of Plantation which Lord Baltimore offered to adventurers to Maryland, and suggestions (Chapter VII.) as to suitable equipment in victuals, apparel, household effects, arms, implements, etc., with which emigrants should provide themselves, wisely using for this purpose the experience of others. The first part of this list of necessary articles is very nearly a copy from that contained in Captain Smith's *Generall Historie of Virginia* (*Narratives of Early Virginia*, pp. 393 *et seq.*). Prescribed forms for contracts to be made with indentured servants, and for bills of lading for shipment of goods, are also given.

Then follows an English translation of the letters patent issued to Cecilius Lord Baltimore, or the Charter of Maryland. This charter has been pronounced by John V. L. McMahon, in his *History of the Government of Maryland* (I. 155), to be more

---

[1] See p. 73, *infra*. [2] *Archives of Maryland*, V. 65.

ample in its terms than any similar charter ever granted by an English king.

As a political or constitutional document it is well worthy of study, especially on account of the palatine authority given to the Proprietary, the feudal character of his tenure, and the provision for a legislative body or General Assembly composed of the freemen or their delegates. The charter is modelled closely after that of Avalon in Newfoundland which had been granted to George, the first Lord Baltimore, by James I., and which is supposed to have been drafted by the grantee. His death occurring in April, 1632, before the grant had passed the seals, it was made in the following June to his son and heir Cecilius.

The following is a brief summary of the more salient features of the instrument:

In order that Maryland might be eminently distinguished above all other regions in that territory (America), and decorated with more ample titles, it was erected into a province, of which the Baron of Baltimore and his heirs were constituted the true and absolute Lords and Proprietaries, with all the powers, prerogatives, and royal rights which any bishop of Durham in the bishopric or county palatine of Durham ever had used or enjoyed or of right could have held and enjoyed.

The proprietaries were given the patronage and advowsons of churches with authority to have them consecrated according to the ecclesiastical law of England. They were given power to enact laws with the advice and assent of the freemen or their representatives, and to enforce the same through courts of their own creation; to punish violations of law, whether committed in the province or on the high seas, even to the taking of life or limb, and, when the freemen could not conveniently be convened, to make ordinances which should have the force of law, except that under such ordinances no one could be deprived of life, limb, or property. They were given authority to confer dignities and titles, to raise and maintain a military force, to wage war, to pursue enemies beyond the borders of the province, and in the event of sedition or rebellion to proclaim martial law; to establish ports of entry, and, upon occasion, to impose taxes and subsidies upon merchandise; to alienate land in fee, fee-tail, or upon lease; to constitute manors and establish courts baron. It was in the charter provided that all subjects of the Crown going to Maryland and their descendants born there, should be esteemed to be natives of England, with power to own land and other estates of inheritance in England. They were given authority to trade not only with the mother country, but also with foreign nations with which England was at peace. The power of the Crown to impose any customs, taxations, or contributions within the province was distinctly renounced, though the payment of the customary duties on wares and merchandise brought into England or exported therefrom was reserved; and it was finally declared that the territory described should not thereafter be considered as part of Virginia, and that in the case of doubt as to the meaning of any word, clause, or sentence in the charter, it should always be interpreted in the manner most beneficial, profitable, and favorable to Lord Baltimore his heirs and assigns. There was reserved to the Crown and to all the King's subjects of England and Ireland the liberty of fishing for sea-fish in the waters of the province, with the privilege of landing for salting and drying the same, and, for that purpose, of cutting underwood and twigs for building huts, so that the same were done without notable injury to the Proprietary or the residents.

This province was granted to Lord Baltimore and his heirs to be held in feudal tenure in free and common socage only, the tribute reserved being two Indian arrows to be delivered yearly in Easter week at Windsor Castle, and the fifth part of the gold and silver ore to be found within the province. As no precious metals were discovered, this last was a barren provision.

The Latin text of the charter, together with an English translation, is contained in Bacon's compilation of the *Laws of Maryland*, published in 1765. A Latin text obtained from the records of the Public Record Office in London (Pat. Roll 8 Car. I.) was printed in *Maryland Archives*, III. 3, and prefixed to it is a table of all variations between that text and the version in Bacon's *Laws*. The differences are unimportant and are chiefly grammatical, such as the use of singular or plural number. According to a foot-note in Bacon's *Laws* it appears that the certified Latin copy which he used, though presenting verbal differences, was procured from the same source.

In the collection of Calvert Papers belonging to the Maryland Historical Society there are two manuscript copies of the charter in Latin, and one in English. There have been numerous reprints of the charter of Maryland in both English and Latin, but the text here given, originally printed three years after the grant, and that contained in Bacon's *Laws* may be regarded as authoritative English versions. It is noted in Bacon's *Laws* that the *old translation* of the charter (the one here given) had been republished by order of the Lower House of the Assembly of Maryland, in 1725.

The following pamphlet was reprinted in close imitation of the typography of the original in 1865, by Joseph Sabin, New York. There is a copy of the original edition, which has become very rare, in the library of the Maryland Historical Society.

C. C. H.

A RELATION OF MARYLAND, 1635

*A Relation of Maryland; together with a Map of the Countrey,
the Conditions of Plantation, with His Majesties Charter to
the Lord Baltemore, translated into English.*
*These Bookes are to bee had, at Master william Peasley Esq; his
house, on the back-side of Drury-Lane, neere the Cock-pit
Playhouse; or in his absence, at Master John Morgans house
in high Holbourne, over against the Dolphin.   London.
September the 8. Anno Dom. 1635.*[1]

CHAP. I

A Relation of the Lord Baltemore's Plantation in Maryland.

HIS most Excellent Majestie having by his Letters Patent,
under the Great Seale of England, granted a certaine Countrey
in America (now called Maryland, in honour of our gratious
Queene) unto the Lord Baltemore, with divers Priviledges,
and encouragements to all those that should adventure with
his Lordship in the Planting of that Countrey: the benefit
and honour of such an action was readily apprehended by
divers Gentlemen, of good birth and qualitie, who thereupon
resolved to adventure their Persons, and a good part of their
fortunes with his Lordship, in the pursuite of so noble and
(in all likelihood) so advantagious an enterprize.   His Lordship was at first resolved to goe in person; but the more important reasons perswading his stay at home, hee appointed his
brother, Mr. Leonard Calvert to goe Governour in his stead,
with whom he joyned in Commission, Mr. Jerome Hawley, and
Mr. Thomas Cornwallis (two worthy and able Gentlemen.)
These with the other Gentlemen adventurers, and their servants to the number of neere 200. people, imbarked themselves
for the voyage, in the good ship called the *Arke*, of 300. tunne

---

[1] The italic words reproduce the title-page of the original.

A
RELATION
OF
MARYLAND;

Together,

With {
A Map of the Countrey,
The Conditions of Plantation,
His Majesties Charter to the
Lord *Baltemore*, translated
into English.

These Bookes are to bee had, at Master *William
Peasley* Esq; his house, on the back-side of *Drury-Lane*, neere the *Cock-pit* Playhouse; or in
his absence, at Master *Iohn Morgans* house in
high *Holbourne,* over against the *Dolphin,*
London.

September the 8. *Anno Dom.* 1635.

TITLE-PAGE OF "A RELATION OF MARYLAND," 1635
From a copy of the original in the New York
Public Library (Lenox Building)

and upward, which was attended by his Lordships Pinnace, called the *Dove*, of about 50. tunne. And so on Friday, the 22. of November, 1633. a small gale of winde comming gently from the Northwest, they weighed from the Cowes in the Isle of Wight, about ten in the morning; And having stayed by the way Twenty dayes at the Barbada's, and Fourteene dayes at Saint Christophers (upon some necessary occasions) they arrived at Point Comfort in Virginia, on the foure and twentyeth of February following. They had Letters from his Majesty, in favor of them, to the Governour of Virginia, in obedience whereunto, he used them with much courtesie and humanitie. At this time, one Captaine Cleyborne (one of the Councel of Virginia) comming from the parts whether they intended to goe, told them that all the Natives were in preparation of defence by reason of a rumor some had raised amongst them, that 6. shippes were to come with many people, who would drive all the inhabitants out of the Countrey.[1]

On the 3. of March, they left Point-Comfort, and 2. dayes after, they came to Patowmeck river, which is about 24. leagues distant, there they began to give names to places, and called the Southerne point of that River, Saint Gregories; and the Northerne point, Saint Michaels.

They sayled up the River, till they came to Heron Island, which is about 14. leagues, and there came to an Anchor under an Island neere unto it, which they called S. Clements.[2] Where they set up a Crosse, and tooke possession of this Countrey for our Saviour, and for our Soveraigne Lord the King of England.

Heere the Governor thought fit for the ship to stay, until hee had discovered more of the Countrey: and so hee tooke two Pinnaces,[3] and went up the River some 4. leagues, and landed on the South side, where he found the Indians fled for feare, from thence hee sayled some 9. leagues higher to Patowmeck Towne where the *Werowance*[4] being a child, Archihau his unckle (who governed him and his Countrey for him) gave all the

---

[1] See pp. 39, 40, *supra*.

[2] Now called Blackistone's Island. Situated in the Potomac River opposite the mouth of St. Clement's Bay. Against "Heron Island" stands in the original a marginal note reading: "So called from the abundance of that Fowle there."

[3] "The *Dove*, and one hyred in Virginia," says the margin.

[4] "So they call their Princes," says the margin.

company good wellcome, and one[1] of the company having entered into a little discourse with him, touching the errours of their religion, hee seemed well pleased therewith; and at his going away, desired him to returne thither againe, saying he should live with him, his men should hunt for him, and hee would divide all with him.

From hence the Governor went to Paschatoway, about 20. leagues higher,[2] where he found many Indians assembled, and heere he met with one Captaine Henry Fleete an English-man, who had lived many yeeres among the Indians, and by that meanes spake the Countrey language very well, and was much esteemed of by the natives. Him our Governour sent a shore to invite the Werowance to a parley, who thereupon came with him aboard privately, where he was courteously entertained, and after some parley being demanded by the Governour, whether hee would be content that he and his people should set downe in his Countrey, in case he should find a place convenient for him, his answer was, "that he would not bid him goe, neither would hee bid him stay, but that he might use his owne discretion."

While this Werowance was aboard, many of his people came to the water side, fearing that he might be surprised, whereupon the Werowance commanded two Indians that came with him, to goe on shore, to quit them of this feare, but they answered, they feared they would kill them; The Werowance therefore shewed himselfe upon the decke, and told them hee was in safety, wherewith they were satisfied.

Whilest the Governour was abroad, the neighbouring Indians, where the ship lay, began to cast off feare, and to come to their Court of guard, which they kept night and day upon Saint Clements Ile, partly to defend their barge, which was brought in pieces out of England, and there made up; and partly to defend their men which were imployed in felling of trees, and cleaving pales for a Palizado, and at last they ventured to come aboard the ship.

The Governour finding it not fit, for many reasons, to seate himselfe as yet so high in the River, resolved to returne backe againe, and to take a more exact view of the lower part, and so

---

[1] Father Altham.

[2] Piscataway, in the southwest corner of Prince George County.

leaving the Ship and Pinnaces there, he tooke his Barge (as most fit to search the Creekes, and small rivers) and was conducted by Captaine Fleete (who knew well the Countrey) to a River on the North-side of Patomeck river, within 4. or 5. leagues from the mouth thereof, which they called Saint Georges River.[1] They went up this river about 4. Leagues, and anchored at the Towne of Yoacomaco: from whence the Indians of that part of the Countrey, are called Yoacomacoes:

At their comming to this place, the Governour went on shoare, and treated friendly with the Werowance there, and acquainted him with the intent of his comming thither, to which hee made little answere (as it is their manner, to any new or suddane question) but entertained him, and his company that night in his house, and gave him his owne bed to lie on (which is a matt layd on boords) and the next day, went to shew him the country, and that day being spent in viewing the places about that towne, and the fresh waters, which there are very plentifull, and excellent good (but the maine rivers are salt) the Governor determined to make the first Colony there, and so gave order for the Ship and Pinnaces to come thither.

This place he found to be a very commodious situation for a Towne, in regard the land is good, the ayre wholsome and pleasant, the River affords a safe harbour for ships of any burthen, and a very bould shoare; fresh water, and wood there is in great plenty, and the place so naturally fortified, as with little difficultie, it will be defended from any enemie.

To make his entry peaceable and safe, hee thought fit to present the Werowance and the *Wisoes*[2] of the Towne with some English Cloth, (such as is used in trade with the Indians) Axes, Howes, and Knives, which they accepted very kindly, and freely gave consent that hee and his company should dwell in one part of their Towne, and reserved the other for themselves; and those Indians that dwelt in that part of the Towne, which was allotted for the English, freely left them their houses, and some corne that they had begun to plant: It was also agreed between them, that at the end of harvest they

[1] Now St. Mary's. The site of the town is a little over six miles from the mouth of the river, which in turn is distant about eight miles from Point Lookout at the mouth of the Potomac.

[2] "So they call the chiefe men of accompt among them." (Marginal note.)

should leave the whole towne; which they did accordingly:
And they made mutuall promises to each other, to live friendly
and peaceably together, and if any injury should happen to be
done on any part, that satisfaction should be made for the
same, and thus upon the 27. day of March, Anno Domini, 1634.
the Governour tooke possession of the place, and named the
Towne Saint Maries.

There was an occasion that much facilitated their treaty
with these Indians, which was this: The Sasquehanocks (a
warlike people that inhabite betweene Chesopeack bay, and
Delaware bay) did usually make warres, and incursions upon
the neighbouring Indians, partly for superiority, partly for
to get their Women, and what other purchase they could meet
with, which these Indians of Yocomaco fearing, had the yeere
before our arivall there, made a resolution, for their safety,
to remove themselves higher into the Countrey where it was
more populous, and many of them were gone thither before the
English arrived.

Three dayes after their comming to Yoacomaco the *Arke*
with the two Pinaces arived there. The Indians much won-
dred to see such ships, and at the thundering of the Ordnance
when they came to an Anchor.

The next day they began to prepare for their houses, and
first of all a Court of Guard,[1] and a Store-house; in the meane
time they lay abord the ship: They had not beene there many
dayes before Sir John Harvie the governor of Virginea came
thither to visit them; Also some Indian Werowances, and
many other Indians from severall parts came to see them,
amongst others the Werowance of Patuxent came to visit
the Governour, and being brought into the great Cabin of the
ship, was placed betweene the Governour of Virginea, and the
Governour of Mary-land; and a Patuxent Indian that came
with him, comming into the Cabin, and finding the Werowance
thus sitting betweene the two Governours, started backe, fearing the Werowance was surprised, and was ready to have
leapt overboard, and could not be perswaded to come into the
Cabin, untill the Werowance came himselfe unto him; for he
remembered how the said Werowance had formerly beene
taken prisoner by the English of Virginia.

[1] Guard-house.

After they had finished the store-house, and unladed the ship, the Governour thought fit to bring the Colours on shore, which were attended by all the Gentlemen, and the rest of the servants in armes; who received the Colours with a volley of shot, which was answered by the Ordnance from the ships; At this Ceremony were present, the Werowances of Patuxent, and Yoacomaco, with many other Indians; and the Werowance of Patuxent hereupon tooke occasion to advise the Indians of Yoacomaco to be carefull to keepe the league that they had made with the English. He stayed with them divers dayes, and used many Indian Complements, and at his departure hee said to the Governour. "I love the English so well, that if they should goe about to kill me, if I had but so much breath as to speake; I would command the people, not to revenge my death; for I know they would not doe such a thing, except it were through mine owne default."

They brought thither with them some store of Indian Corne, from the Barbado's, which at their first arivall they began to use (thinking fit to reserve their English provision of Meale and Oatemeale) and the Indian women seeing their servants to bee unacquainted with the manner of dressing it, would make bread thereof for them, and teach them how to doe the like: They found also the countrey well stored with Corne (which they bought with truck, such as there is desired, the Natives having no knowledge of the use of money) whereof they sold them such plenty, as that they sent 1000. bushells of it to New-England, to provide them some salt-fish, and other commodities which they wanted.[1]

During the time that the Indians stai'd by the English at Yoacomaco, they went dayly to hunt with them for Deere and Turkies, whereof some they gave them for Presents, and the meaner sort would sell them to them, for knives, beades and the like: Also of Fish, the natives brought them great store, and in all things dealt very friendly with them; their women and children came very frequently amongst them, which was a certaine signe of their confidence of them, it being found by

---

[1] Winthrop, in his *Journal*, I. 131, under date of August 29, 1634, notes the arrival of the *Dove* from Maryland, laden with corn, and bringing letters from Governor Calvert, the other two commissioners, the governor of Virginia, and Captain Yong.

experience, that they never attempt any ill, where the women are, or may be in danger.

Their comming thus to seate upon an Indian Towne, where they found ground cleered to their hands, gave them opportunity (although they came late in the yeere) to plant some Corne, and to make them gardens, which they sowed with English seeds of all sorts, and they prospered exceeding well. They also made what haste they could to finish their houses; but before they could accomplish all these things, one Captaine Cleyborne (who had a desire to appropriate the trade of those parts unto himselfe) began to cast out words amongst the Indians, saying, That those of Yoacomaco were Spaniards and his enemies; and by this meanes endeavoured to alienate the mindes of the Natives from them, so that they did not receive them so friendly as formerly they had done. This caused them to lay aside all other workes, and to finish their Fort, which they did within the space of one moneth; where they mounted some Ordnance, and furnished it with some mur-therers,[1] and such other meanes of defence as they thought fit for their safeties: which being done, they proceeded with their Houses and finished them, with convenient accommodations belonging thereto: And although they had thus put themselves in safety, yet they ceased not to procure to put these jealousies out of the Natives minds, by treating and using them in the most courteous manner they could, and at last prevailed therein, and setled a very firme peace and friendship with them. They procured from Virginia, Hogges, Poultrey, and some Cowes, and some male cattell, which hath given them a foundation for breed and increase; and whoso desires it, may furnish himselfe with store of Cattell from thence, but the hogges and Poultrey are already increased in Maryland, to a great stocke, sufficient to serve the Colonie very plentifully. They have also set up a Water-mill for the grinding of Corne, adjoyning to the Towne.[2]

Thus within the space of six moneths, was laid the foundation of the Colonie in Maryland; and whosoever intends now to goe thither, shall finde the way so troden, that hee may proceed with much more ease and confidence then these first ad-

---

[1] Small cannon.
[2] Mill Creek lay at the north side of St. Mary's.

venturers could, who were ignorant both of Place, People, and all things else, and could expect to find nothing but what nature produced: besides, they could not in reason but thinke, the Natives would oppose them; whereas now the Countrey is discovered, and friendship with the natives is assured, houses built, and many other accommodations, as Cattell, Hogges, Poultry, Fruits and the like brought thither from England, Virginea, and other places, which are usefull, both for profit and Pleasure: and without boasting it may be said, that this Colony hath arived to more in sixe moneths, then Virginia did in as many yeeres. If any man say, they are beholding to Virginea for so speedy a supply of many of those things which they of Virginia were forced to fetch from England and other remote places, they will confess it, and acknowledge themselves glad that Virginea is so neere a neighbour, and that it is so well stored of all necessaries for to make those parts happy, and the people to live as plentifully as in any other part of the world, only they wish that they would be content their neighbours might live in peace by them, and then no doubt they should find a great comfort each in other.

CHAP. II

A description of the Countrey.

The precedent discourse gives you to understand, how the first Colony sate downe in Maryland, what progresse they made, and in what estate it is at this present: Now my purpose is to speake of the Countrey in generall, that who so lookes that way, may beforehand know something thereof. It is seated betweene the degrees of 38 and 40 of North-Latitude, Virginia bounds it on the South, New-England on the North, and the Ocean on the East, but the Westerne parts are not yet discovered.

The temper of the Ayre is very good, and agrees well with the English, as appeared at their first comming thither, when they had no houses to shelter them, and their people were enforced, not onely to labour in the day, but to watch in their turnes at night, yet had their healths exceeding well: In Summer its hot as in Spaine, and in Winter there is frost and snow, but it seldome lasts long; this last Winter was the coldest that had beene knowne in many yeeres: but the yeere before, there was scarce any signe of Winter, onely that the leaves fell from the trees, in all other things it appeared to be Summer; and yet the last Winter, both their Cattell and Hoggs kept themselves in the woods, without any fodder, or other helpe, and the Hoggs thrived so well, that some of them were killed out of the woods for Porke and Bacon, which was excellent good and fat.

The Windes there are variable; from the South comes Heat, Gusts, and Thunder; from the North, or North-west, cold-weather, and in winter, Frost and Snow; from the East and South-east, Raine.

The ordinary entrance by Sea into this Countrey, is betweene two Capes, which are distant each from other, about 7 or 8 leagues, the South-Cape is called Cape-Henry, the North, Cape-Charles, When you are come within the Capes, you enter into a faire Bay, which is navigable for at least 200 miles, and is called Chesopeack Bay, and runneth Northerly: Into this Bay fall many goodly navigable Rivers, the chiefe whereof is Patomack, where the Colony is now seated. It's navigable for 140 miles, it begins to be fresh about 2 leagues above Patomack Towne. The next River Northward is Patuxent, which at the entrance is distant from the other, about 20 miles, and is a very pleasant and commodious River; It's fit for habitation, and easie to be defended, by reason of the Ilands, and other places of advantage, that may command it; from thence, untill you come to the head of the Bay, there are no more Rivers that are inhabited: There dwell the Sasquehanocks, upon a River[1] that is not navigable for our Boates, by reason of Sholes and Rockes; but they passe it in *Canoos*;[2] At the entrance thereof, there is an Iland which will command that River. Upon the East side of this Bay lie very many Ilands which are not inhabited, where are store of Deere.

On the Easterne shore of the Country, which lieth upon the maine Ocean, are sundry small Creekes, and one likely to proove a very commodious harbour, called Matsopongue;[3] neere the mouth whereof, lieth an Iland of about 20 miles in

---

[1] The Susquehanna River.

[2] "A tearme they use for their Boates." (Marginal note.)

[3] Machepongo Inlet. This is in Northampton County, Virginia.

length, and thence about 6 leagues more Northerly, another Iland called Chingoto;[1] and about seaven leagues beyond that, to the North, opens another very large faire Bay, called Delaware Bay. This Bay is about 8 leagues wide at the entrance, and into it, there falls a very faire navigable River.

The Countrey is generally plaine and even, and yet hath some pritty small hills and risings; It's full of Rivers and Creekes and hath store of Springs and small Brookes: The Woods for the most part are free from underwood, so that a man may travell on horsebacke, almost any-where, or hunt for his recreation.

CHAP. III

The Commodities which this Countrey affords naturally.

This Countrey affords naturally, many excellent things for Physicke and Surgery, the perfect use of which, the English cannot yet learne from the Natives: They have a roote which is an excellent preservative against Poyson, called by the English, the Snake roote. Other herbes and rootes they have, wherewith they cure all manner of woundes; also Saxafras, Gummes, and Balsum. An Indian seeing one of the English, much troubled with the tooth-ake, fetched of the roote of a tree, and gave the party some of it to hold in his mouth, and it eased the paine presently. They have other rootes fit for dyes, wherewith they make colours to paint themselves.

The Timber of these parts is very good, and in aboundance, it is usefull for building of houses, and shippes; the white Oake is good for Pipe-staves, the red Oake for wainescot. There is also Walnut, Cedar, Pine, and Cipresse, Chesnut, Elme, Ashe, and Popler, all which are for Building, and Husbandry. Also there are divers sorts of Fruit-trees, as Mulberries, Persimons, with severall other kind of Plummes, and Vines, in great aboundance. The Mast and the Chesnuts, and what rootes they find in the woods, doe feede the Swine very fat, and will breede great store, both for their owne provision, or for merchandise, and such as is not inferior to the Bacon of Westphalia.

---

[1] Chincoteague. The distance from Chincoteague Inlet to Cape Henlopen at the entrance to Delaware Bay is in fact about 67 miles or 22 leagues.

Of Strawberries, there is plenty, which are ripe in Aprill: Mulberries in May; and Raspices in June; *Maracocks*[1] which is somewhat like a Limon, are ripe in August.

In the Spring, there are severall sorts of herbes, as Corn-sallet, Violets, Sorrell, Purslaine, all which are very good and wholsome, and by the English, used for sallets, and in broth.

In the upper parts of the Countrey, there are Bufeloes, Elkes, Lions, Beares, Wolves, and Deare there are in great store, in all places that are not too much frequented, as also Beavers, Foxes, Otters, and many other sorts of Beasts.

Of Birds, there is the Eagle, Goshawke, Falcon, Lanner, Sparrow-hawke, and Merlin, also wild Turkeys in great abound-ance, whereof many weigh 50. pounds, and upwards; and of Partridge plenty: There are likewise sundry sorts of Birds which sing, whereof some are red, some blew, others blacke and yellow, some like our Black-birds, others like Thrushes, but not of the same kind, with many more, for which wee know no names.

In Winter there is great plenty of Swannes, Cranes, Geese, Herons, Ducke, Teale, Widgeon, Brants, and Pidgeons, with other sorts, whereof there are none in England.

The Sea, the Bayes of Chesopeack, and Delaware, and gen-erally all the Rivers, doe abound with Fish of severall sorts; for many of them we have no English names: There are Whales, Sturgeons very large and good, and in great abound-ance; Grampuses, Porpuses, Mullets, Trouts, Soules, Place, Mackerell, Perch, Crabs, Oysters, Cockles, and Mussles; But above all these, the fish that have no English names, are the best except the Sturgeons: There is also a fish like the Thorne-backe in England, which hath a taile a yard long, wherein are sharpe prickles, with which if it strike a man, it will put him to much paine and torment, but it is very good meate: also the Tode-fish, which will swell till it be ready to burst, if it be taken out of the water.

The Mineralls have not yet beene much searched after, yet there is discovered Iron Oare; and Earth fitt to make Allum, *Terra lemnia*, and a red soile like Bolearmonicke,[2]

---

[1] See Captain John Smith, in *Narratives of Early Virginia*, p. 92.
[2] *Ibid*, p. 87.

with sundry other sorts of Mineralls, which wee have not yet beene able to make any tryall of.

The soil generally is very rich, like that which is about Cheesweeke[1] neere London, where it is worth 20. shillings an Acre yeerely to Tillage in the Common-fields, and in very many places, you shall have two foote of blacke rich mould, wherein you shall scarce find a stone, it is like a sifted Garden-mould, and is so rich that if it be not first planted with Indian corne, Tobacco, Hempe, or some such thing that may take off the ranknesse thereof, it will not be fit for any English graine; and under that, there is found good loame, whereof wee have made as good bricke as any in England; there is great store of Marish ground also, that with good husbandry, will make as rich Medow, as any in the world: There is store of Marle, both blue, and white, and in many places, excellent clay for pots, and tyles; and to conclude, there is nothing that can be reasonably expected in a place lying in the latitude which this doth, but you shall either find it here to grow naturally: or Industry, and good husbandry will produce it.

CHAP. IIII

The commodities that may be procured in Maryland by industry.

Hee that well considers the situation of this Countrey, and findes it placed betweene Virginia and New-England, cannot but, by his owne reason, conclude that it must needs participate of the naturall commodities of both places, and be capable of those which industry brings into either, the distances being so small betweene them: you shall find in the Southerne parts of Maryland, all that Virginia hath naturally; and in the Northerne parts, what New-England produceth: and he that reades Captaine John Smith shall see at large discoursed what is in Virginia, and in Master William Wood, who this yeere hath written a treatise of New-England,[2] he may know what is there to be expected.

[1] Chiswick, where the Royal Horticultural Society now has its experimental garden.

[2] *New England's Prospect* (London, 1634).

Yet to say something of it in particular.

In the first place I name Corne, as the thing most necessary to sustaine man;   That which the Natives use in the
Countrey, makes very good bread, and also a meate which
they call *Omene*,[1] it's like our Furmety, and is very savory
and wholesome; it will Mault and make good Beere; Also the
Natives have a sort of Pulse, which we call Pease and Beanes,
that are very good.   This Corne yeelds a great increase, so
doth the Pease and Beanes: One man may in a season, well
plant so much as will yeeld a hundred bushells of this Corne,
20 bushells of Beanes and Pease, and yet attend a crop of
Tobacco: which according to the goodnesse of the ground may
be more or lesse, but is ordinarily accompted betweene 800
and 1000 pound weight.

They have made tryall of English Pease, and they grow
very well, also Musk-mellons, Water-mellons, Cow-cumbers,
with all sorts of garden Roots and Herbes, as Carrots, Parse-
nips, Turnips, Cabbages, Radish with many more; and in
Virginia they have sowed English Wheate and Barley, and it
yeelds twise as much increase as in England; and although
there be not many that doe apply themselves to plant Gardens
and Orchards, yet those that doe it, find much profit and pleasure thereby: They have Peares, Apples, and severall sorts of
Plummes, Peaches in abundance, and as good as those of Italy;
so are the Mellons and Pumpions: Apricocks, Figgs and Pomegranates prosper exceedingly; they have lately planted Orange
and Limon trees which thrive very wel: and in fine, there
is scarce any fruit that growes in England, France, Spaine or
Italy, but hath been tryed there, and prospers well. You
may there also have hemp and Flax, Pitch and Tarre, with
little labour; it's apt for Rapeseed, and Annis-seed, Woad,
Madder, Saffron, etc.   There may be had Silke-wormes, the
Countrey being stored with Mulberries: and the superfluity
of wood will produce Potashes.

And for Wine, there is no doubt but it will be made there
in plenty, for the ground doth naturally bring foorth Vines, in
such aboundance, that they are as frequent there, as Brambles
are here.   Iron may be made there with little charge; Brave

[1] Hominy.

ships may be built, without requiring any materialls from other parts: Clabboard, Wainscott, Pipe-staves and Masts for ships the woods will afford plentifully. In fine, Butter and Cheese, Porke and Bacon, to transport to other countrys will be no small commodity, which by industry may be quickly had there in great plenty, etc. And if there were no other staple commodities to be hoped for, but Silke and Linnen (the materialls of which, apparantly will grow there) it were sufficient to enrich the inhabitants.

CHAP. V

Of the Naturall disposition of the Indians which inhabite the parts of Maryland where the English are seated: And their manner of living.

Hee that hath a Curiosity to know all that hath beene observed of the Customes and manners of the Indians, may find large discourses thereof in Captaine Smiths Booke of Virginia, and Mr. Woods of New-England: but he that is desirous to goe to Maryland, shall heere find enough to informe him of what is necessary for him to know touching them. By Captaine Smith's, and many other Relations you may be informed, that the People are War-licke, and have done much harme to the English; and thereby are made very terrible. Others say that they are a base and cowardly People, and to be contemned: and it is thought by some who would be esteemed Statesmen, that the only point of pollicie that the English can use, is, to destroy the Indians, or to drive them out of the Countrey, without which, it is not to be hoped that they can be secure. The truth is, if they be injured, they may well be feared, they being People that have able bodies, and generally, taller, and bigger limbed then the English, and want not courage; but the oddes wee have of them in our weapons, keepes them in awe, otherwise they would not flie from the English, as they have done in the time of Warres with those of Virginia, and out of that respect, a small number of our men being armed, will adventure upon a great troope of theirs, and for no other reason, for they are resolute and subtile enough: But from hence to conclude, that there can be no safety to live with them, is a very great errour. Experience hath taught us, that by kind and faire usage, the Natives are not onely become peaceable, but also friendly, and have upon all occasions performed as many friendly Offices to the English in Maryland, and New-England, as any neighbour or friend uses to doe in the most Civill parts of Christendome: Therefore any wise man will hold it a far more just and reasonable way to treat the People of the Countrey well, thereby to induce them to civility, and to teach them the use of husbandry, and Mechanick trades, whereof they are capable, which may in time be very usefull to the English; and the Planters to keepe themselves strong, and united in Townes, at least for a competent number, and then noe man can reasonably doubt, either surprise, or any other ill dealing from them.

But to proceede, hee that sees them, may know how men lived whilest the world was under the Law of Nature; and, as by nature, so amongst them, all men are free, but yet subject to command for the publike defence. Their Government is Monarchicall, he that governs in chiefe, is called the Werowance, and is assisted by some that consult with him of the common affaires, who are called Wisoes: They have no Lawes, but the Law of Nature and discretion, by which all things are ruled, onely Custome hath introduced a law for the Succession of the Government, which is this; when a Werowance dieth, his eldest sonne succeeds, and after him the second, and so the rest, each for their lives, and when all the sonnes are dead, then the sons of the Werowances eldest daughter shall succeede, and so if he have more daughters; for they hold, that the issue of the daughters hath more of his blood in them than the issue of his sonnes. The Wisoes are chosen at the pleasure of the Werowance, yet commonly they are chosen of the same family, if they be of yeeres capable: The yong men generally beare a very great respect to the elder.

They have also *Cockorooses*[1] that are their Captains in time of war, to whom they are very obedient: But the Werowance himselfe plants Corne, makes his owne Bow and Arrowes, his Canoo, his Mantle, Shooes, and what ever else belongs unto him, as any other common Indian; and commonly the Commanders are the best and most ingenious and active in all those

---

[1] *Cawcawaassough*, adviser.

things which are in esteeme amongst them. The women serve their husbands, make their bread, dress their meate, such as they kill in hunting, or get by fishing; and if they have more wives than one, as some of them have (but that is not generall) then the best beloved wife performes all the offices of the house, and they take great content therein. The women also (beside the household businesse) use to make Matts, which serve to cover their houses, and for beds; also they make baskets, some of Rushes, others of Silke-grasse, which are very handsom.

The Children live with their Parents; the Boyes untill they come to the full growth of men; (for they reckon not by yeeres, as we doe) then they are put into the number of Bow-men, and are called Blacke-boyes (and so continue untill they take them wives) When they are to be made Black-boyes, the ancient men that governe the yonger, tell them, That if they will be valiant and obedient to the Werowance, Wisos, and Cockorooses, then their god will love them, all men will esteeme of them, and they shall kill Deere, and Turkies, catch Fish, and all things shall goe well with them; but if otherwise, then shall all goe contrary: which perswasion mooves in them an incredible obedience to their commands; If they bid them take fire in their hands or mouthes, they will doe it, or any other desperate thing, although with the apparant danger of their lives.

The women remaine with their Parents untill they have husbands, and if the Parents bee dead, then with some other of their friends. If the husband die, he leaves all that he hath to his wife, except his bow and arrowes, and some Beades (which they usually bury with them) and she is to keepe the children untill the sons come to be men, and then they live where they please, for all mens houses are free unto them; and the daughters untill they have husbands. The manner of their marriages is thus; he that would have a wife, treates with the father, or if he be dead, with the friend that take care of her whom he desires to have to wife, and agrees with him for a quantity of Beades, or some such other thing which is accepted amongst them; which he is to give for her, and must be payed at the day of their marriage; and then the day being appointed, all the friends of both parts meet at the mans house that is to have the wife, and each one brings a present of meate, and the woman that is to be married also brings her present: when the company is all come, the man he sits at the upper end of the house, and the womans friends leade her up, and place her by him, then all the company sit down upon mats, on the ground (as their manner is) and the woman riseth and serves dinner, First to her husband, then to all the company. The rest of the day they spend in singing and dancing (which is not unpleasant) at night the company leaves them, and comonly they live very peaceably and lovingly together; Yet it falls out sometimes, that a man puts away one wife and takes another: then she and her children returne to her friends again. They are generally very obedient to their husbands, and you shal seldome heare a woman speake in the presence of her husband, except he aske her some question.

This people live to a great age, which appeares, in that although they marry not so yong as we doe in England, yet you may see many of them great-grandfathers to children of good bignesse; and continue at that age, very able and strong men: The Men and Women have all blacke haire, which is much bigger and harsher then ours, it is rare to see any of them to waxe gray, although they be very old, but never bauld: It is seldome seene that any of the men have beards, but they weare long locks, which reach to their shoulders, and some of them to their wasts: they are of a comely stature, well favoured, and excellently well limbed, and seldome any deformed. In their warres, and hunting, they use Bowes and Arrowes (but the Arrowes are not poysoned, as in other places.) The Arrow-heads are made of a Flint-stone, the top of a Deares horn, or some Fish-bone, which they fasten with a sort of glew, which they make. They also use in warres, a short club of a cubite long, which they call a *Tomahawk.*

They live for the most part in Townes, like Countrey Villages in England; Their houses are made like our Arboures, covered some with matts, others with barke of trees, which defend them from the injury of the weather: The fiers are in the midst of the house, and a hole in the top for the smoake to goe out at. In length, some of them are 30. others 40. some a 100. foote; and in breadth about 12. foote.[1]

---

[1] Their form may be seen from an interior view in a corner of the map facing p. 76 of *Narratives of Early Virginia.*

They have some things amongst them which may well become Christians to imitate, as their temperance in eating and drinking, their Justice each to other, for it is never heard of, that those of a Nation will rob or steale one from another; and the English doe often trust them with truck, to deale for them as factors, and they have performed it very justly: Also they have sent letters by them to Virginia, and into other parts of the Countrey, unto their servants that have beene trading abroad, and they have delivered them, and brought backe answere thereof unto those that sent them; Also their conversation each with other, is peaceable, and free from all scurrulous words, which may give offence; They are very hospitable to their owne people, and to strangers; they are also of a grave comportment: Some of the Adventurers at a time, was at one of their feasts, when Two hundred of them did meet together; they eate of but one dish at a meale, and every man, although there be never so many, is served in a a dish by himselfe; their dishes are made of wood, but handsomely wrought; The dinner lasted two houres; and after dinner, they sung and danced about two houres more, in all which time, not one word or action past amongst them that could give the least disturbance to the company; In the most grave assembly, no man can expect to find so much time past with more silence and gravitie: Some Indians comming on a time to James Towne in Virginia, it happened, that there then sate the Councell to heare causes, and the Indians seeing such an assembly, asked what it meant? Answer was made, there was held a *Match-comaco* (which the Indians call their place of Councell) the Indian replyed, that they all talke at once, but wee doe not so in our *Match-comaco*.

Their attire is decent and modest; about their wasts, they weare a covering of Deares skinnes, which reacheth to their knees, and upon their shoulders a large mantle of skinnes, which comes downe to the middle of the legge, and some to the heele; in winter they weare it furred, in summer without; When men hunt they put off their Mantles, so doe the women when they worke, if the weather be hot: The women affect to weare chaines and bracelets of beades, some of the better sort of them, weare ropes of Pearle about their necks, and some hanging in their eares, which are of a large sort, but spoyled with burning the Oysters in the fire, and the rude boaring of them. And they and the young men use to paint their faces with severall colours, but since the English came thither, those about them have quite left it; and in many things shew a great inclination to conforme themselves to the English manner of living. The Werowance of Paschatoway desired the Governor to send him a man that could build him a house like the English, and in sundry respects, commended our manner of living, as much better then their owne: The Werowance of Patuxent, goes frequently in English Attire, so doth he of Portoback,[1] and many others that have bought Clothes of the English: These Werowances have made request, that some of their children may be brought up amongst the English, and every way, shew great demonstrations of friendship, and good affection unto them.

These People acknowledge a God, who is the giver of al the good things, wherewith their life is maintained; and to him they sacrifice of the first fruits of their Corne, and of that which they get by hunting and fishing: The sacrifice is performed by an Ancient man, who makes a speech unto their God (not without something of Barbarisme) which being ended, hee burnes part of the sacrifice, and then eates of the rest, then the People that are present, eate also, and untill the Ceremony be performed, they will not touch one bit thereof: They hold the Immortalitie of the soule, and that there is a place of Joy, and another of torment after death, and that those which kill, steale, or lye, shall goe to the place of torment, but those which doe no harme, to the good place; where they shall have all sorts of pleasure.

It happened the last yeere, that some of the Sasquehanocks and the Wicomesses (who are enemies) met at the Iland of Monoponson,[2] where Captaine Cleyborne liveth, they all came to trade, and one of the Sasquehanocks did an Injury to a Wicomesse, whereat some of Cleybornes people that saw it, did laugh. The Wicomesses seeing themselves

---

[1] Now Port Tobacco, in Charles County. For probable origin of this name, see p. 136, note 1, infra.

[2] Probably the Indian name for Kent Island, where Claiborne had a residence. Cf. Archives of Maryland, III. 363, 364.

thus injured and despised (as they thought) went away, and
lay in ambush for the returne of the Sasquehanocks, and
killed five of them, onely two escaped; and then they returned againe, and killed three of Cleybornes People, and
some of his Cattle; about two moneths after this was done,
the Wicomesses sent a messenger unto his Lordships Governor, to excuse the fact, and to offer satisfaction for the
harme that was done to the English: The Wicomesse that
came with the message, brought in his company an Indian,
of the Towne of Patuxent, which is the next neighbouring
Towne unto the English at Saint Maries, with whom they
have good correspondence, and hee spake to the Governour
in this manner.

I Am a Native of Patuxent, as this man (whom you know) can
tell you, true it is, I married a wife amongst the Wicomesses, where
I have lived ever since, and they have sent me to tell you, that they
are sorry for the harme, which was lately done by some of their
people, to the English at Monaponson; and hope you will not make
the rash act of a few young men (which was done in heate) a quarrell to their Nation, who desire to live in peace and love with you,
and are ready to make satisfaction for the Injury, desiring to know
what will give you content, and that they will returne such things
as were then taken from thence; But withall, they desire you not to
thinke that they doe this for feare, for they have warres with the
Sasquehanocks, who have by a surprise, lately killed many of their
men, but they would not sue to them for peace, intending to revenge
the injuries, as they could find opportunitie, yet their desire was to
have peace with the English.

The Governour returned answere to the Wicomesse;

Since you acknowledge the Injury, and are sorry for it, and
onely desire to know what I expect for satisfaction; I tell you I expect that those men, who have done this out-rage, should be delivered unto me, to do with them as I shall thinke fit, and likewise
that you restore all such things as you then tooke from the English;
and withall, charged him with a second Injury attempted upon
some of his owne People, since that time, by the Wicomesses.

The Wicomesse after a little pause, replyed;

It is the manner amongst us Indians, that if any such like accident happen, wee doe redeeme the life of a man that is so slaine,

with a 100. armes length of *Roanoke* (which is a sort of Beades that they make, and use for money) and since that you are heere strangers, and come into our Countrey, you should rather conforme your selves to the Customes of our Countrey, then impose yours upon us; But as for the second matter, I know nothing of it, nor can give any answere thereunto.

The Governour then told him;

It seemes you come not sufficiently instructed in the businesse which wee have with the Wicomesses, therefore tell them what I have said; and that I expect a speedy answere; and so dismist him.

It fell in the way of my discourse, to speake of the Indian money of those parts, It is of two sorts, *Wompompeag* and *Roanoake;* both of them are made of a fish-shell, that they gather by the Sea side. Wompompeag is of the greater sort, and Roanoake of the lesser, and the Wompompeag is three times the value of Roanoake; and these serve as Gold and Silver doe heere; they barter also one commoditie for another, and are very glad of trafficke and commerce, so farre as to supply their necessities: They shew no great desire of heaping wealth, yet some they will have to be buryed with them; If they were Christians, and would live so free from covetousnesse, and many other vices which abound in Christendome, they would be a brave people.

I therefore conclude, that since God Almighty hath made this Countrey so large and fruitfull, and that the people be such as you have heard them described; It is much more Prudence, and Charity, to Civilize, and make them Christians, then to kill, robbe, and hunt them from place to place, as you would doe a wolfe. By reducing of them, God shall be served, his Majesties Empire enlarged by the addition of many thousand Subjects, as well as of large Territories, our Nation honoured, and the Planters themselves enriched by the trafficke and commerce which may be had with them; and in many other things, they may be usefull, but prejudiciall they cannot be, if it be not through their owne faults, by negligence of fortifying themselves, and not conserving military discipline.

CHAP. VI

Conditions propounded by the Lord Baltemore, to such as shall goe, or adventure into Maryland.[1]

I

What person soever, subject to our soveraigne Lord the King of England, shal be at the charge to transport into the Province of Maryland, himselfe or his deputy, with any number of able men, betweene the ages of 16 and 50, each man being provided in all things necessary for a Plantatio (which, together with their transportation, will amount to about 20 *l.* a man, as by an æstimate hereafter following may appeare) there shalbe assigned unto every such adventurer, for every five men which he shall so transport thither, a proportion of good land within the said Province, containing in quantity 1000 acres of English measure, which shall be erected into a Mannor, and be conveyed to him, his heires, and assignes for ever, with all such royalties and priviledges, as are usually belonging to Mannors in England; rendring and paying yerely unto his Lordship, and his heires for every such Mannor, a quit rent of 20 shillings, (to be paid in the Commodities of the Countrey) and such other services as shall be generally agreed upon for publike uses, and the common good.

II

What person soever, as aforesaid, shall transport himselfe, or any less number of servants then five, (aged, and provided as aforesaid) he shall have assigned to him, his heires and assignes for ever, for himselfe, 100 acres of good land within the said Province; and for and in respect of every such servant, 100 acres more, he be holden of his Lordship in freehold, paying therefore, a yeerely quit rent of 2 shillings for every hundred acres, in the Commodities of the Countrey.

[1] In after years the conditions offered to settlers were more than once modified, the later comers receiving less favorable terms than those offered as inducements to the first adventurers.

III

Any married man that shall transport himselfe, his wife and children; shall have assigned unto him, his heires and assignes for ever, in freehold, (as aforesaid) for himselfe 100 acres; and for his wife 100 acres; and for every child that he shall carry over, under the age of 16 yeeres, 50 acres; paying for a quit rent 12 pence for every fifty acres.

IIII

Any woman that shall transport herselfe or any children, under the age of sixe yeeres, shall have the like Conditions as aforesaid.

V

Any woman that shall carry over any women servants, under the age of fourty yeeres, shall have for and in respect of every such woman servant, 50 acres; paying onely a quit rent as aforesaid.

CHAP. VII

Instructions and advertisements, for such as shall intend to goe, or send, to plant in Maryland.

This Countrey of Maryland, lieth from England to the Southwest, about 1200 leagues by Sea: the voyage is sometimes performed thither in 5 or 6 weekes, but ordinarily it is two moneths voyage, and oftner, within that time then beyond it. The returne from thence to England, is ordinarily made in a moneth, and seldome exceeds sixe weekes.

The best time of the yeere for going thither is to be there by Michaelmas, or at furthest by Christmas, for he that comes by that time shall have time enough to build him a house, and to prepare ground sufficient to plant in the spring following. But there is conveniency of passage thither in most moneths of the yeere; and any one that will send unto Mr. Peasleys,[1] or Master Morgans house, may there be informed of the certaine time when any of his Lordships company is to goe away, and so save the charge of unnecessary attendance here in London.

[1] See the Introduction, p. 65, *supra*.

A particular of such necessary provisions as every Adventurer must carry, according to the number of his servants: together with an estimate of their prices.[1]

In Victualls.

For one man, for a yeere,

	l.—s—d
Imprimis, eight bushells of meale - - - - - -	2—8—0
Item, two bushells of Oatmeale - - - - - - -	0—9—0
Item, one bushell of Pease - - - - - - - -	0—4—0
Item, one gallon of Oyle - - - - - - - - -	0—3—6
Item, two gallons of Vinegar - - - - - - - -	0—2—0
Item, one gallon of Aquavitæ - - - - - - -	0—2—6
Item, one bushell of Bay-salt - - - - - - - -	0—2—0
Item, in Sugar, Spice and Fruit - - - - - - -	0—6—8
Summ. - - -	3—17-8

In Apparrell.

For one man,

	l—s—d
Item, two Munmoth caps or hats - - - - - -	0—4—0
Item, three falling Bands - - - - - - - - -	0—1—3
Item, three shirts - - - - - - - - - - -	0—7—6
Item, one Wastcoate - - - - - - - - - -	0—2—2
Item, one suite of Canvas - - - - - - - -	0—7—6
Item, one suite of Frize - - - - - - - - -	0–10—0
Item, one suite of Cloth - - - - - - - - -	0—16—0
Item, one course cloth, or frize coate - - - -	0–15—0
Item, three paire of stockings - - - - - -	0—4—0
Item, sixe paire of shooes - - - - - - - -	0–13—0
Item, Inkle[2] for garters - - - - - - - -	0—0—2
Item, one dozen of points [3] - - - - - - -	0—0—3
Summ. - - -	4—0-10

---

[1] This list is copied closely from Captain John Smith's *Generall Historie of Virginia* (see *Narratives of Early Virginia*, pp. 393 *et seq.*).

[2] Broad tape.

[3] Laces for fastening the clothing.

In Bedding.

For two men,

	l—s—d
Item, two paire of Canvas sheets - - - - - - -	0–16—0
Item, seven ells of Canvas to make a bed and boulster to be fill'd in the country - - - - - - - - -	0—8—0
Item, one Rugg for a bed - - - - - - - - - -	0—8—0
Item, five ells of course Canvas to make a bed at Sea, to bee fill'd with straw - - - - - - - - -	0—4—0
Item, one course Rugg at Sea - - - - - - - -	0—6—0
Summ. - - - -	2—2—0
whereof one mans part is, - - - - - - - -	1—1—0

In Armes.

For one man,

	l—s—d
Item, one musket - - - - - - - - - - - -	1—0—0
Item, 10 pound of Powder - - - - - - - -	0–11—0
Item, 40 pound of Lead, Bullets, Pistoll and Goose shot, of each sort some. - - - - - - - - -	0—4—0
Item, one sword - - - - - - - - - - - - -	0—5—0
Item, one belt - - - - - - - - - - - - - -	0—1—0
Item, one bandeleere and flaske - - - - - - -	0—2—0
Item, in Match - - - - - - - - - - - - -	0—2—6
Summ. - - - -	2—5—6

In Tooles.

For five persons, and so after the rate for more or lesse.

	l—s—d
Item, 5 broad Howes, at 2 s. a piece - - - - -	0–10—0
Item, 5 narrow Howes, at 16 d. a piece - - - -	0—6—8
Item, 2 broad Axes, at 3 s. 8 d. a piece - - - -	0—7—4
Item, 5 felling Axes, at 1 s. 6 d. a piece - - - -	0—7—6
Item, 2 steele Hand-sawes, at 1 s. 4 d. - - - -	0—2—8
Item, Two-handsawes at 5 s. - - - - - - -	0–10—0
Item, a Whip-saw set and filed, with boxe, file and wrest - - - - - - - - - - - - - - - - -	0–10—0
Item, 2 Hammers, at 12 d. - - - - - - - - -	0—2—0

Item, 3 Shovells, at 1 s. 6 d. - - - - - - - - - 0—4—6
Item, 3 Spades, at 1 s. 6 d. - - - - - - - - - 0—4—6
Item, 2 Awgurs, at 6 d. - - - - - - - - - - 0—1—0
Item, 6 Chissells at 6 d. - - - - - - - - - 0—3—0
Item, 2 Piercers stocked, at 4 d. - - - - - 0—0—8
Item, 3 Gimlets, at 2 d. - - - - - - - - - 0—0—6
Item, 2 Hatchets, at 1 s. 9 d. - - - - - - - 0—3—6
Item, 2 Frowes[1] to cleave Pales, at 1 s. 6 d. - - - 0—3—0
Item, 2 Hand-bills, at 1 s. 8 d. - - - - - - 0—3—4
Item, one Grindstone - - - - - - - - - - 0—4—0
Item, Nailes of all sorts - - - - - - - - - 2—0—0
Item, 2 Pickaxes, at 1 s. 6 d. - - - - - - 0—3—0

Summ. - - - - 6—7—2
whereof one mans part is - - - - - - - - 1—5—8

Houshold Implements.

For 6 persons, and so after the rate, for more

	l—s—d
Item, one Iron pot - - - - - - - - - - - -	0—7—0
Item, one Iron kettle - - - - - - - - - -	0—6—0
Item, one large Frying-pan - - - - - - -	0—2—6
Item, one Gridiron - - - - - - - - - - -	0—1—6
Item, two Skillets - - - - - - - - - -	0—5—0
Item, one Spit - - - - - - - - - - - -	0—2—0
Item, Platters, Dishes, and spoones of wood - - -	0—4—0

Summ. - - - - - 1—8—0
whereof one mans part is, - - - - - - - 0—4—8

*An estimate of the whole charge of transporting one ser-
vant, and providing him of all necessaries for one
yeere.*

	l. s. d.
Inprimis, In Victualls - - - - - - - - -	3-17—8
Item, In apparell - - - - - - - - - - -	4—0-10
Item, In bedding - - - - - - - - - - - -	1—1—0
Item, In Armes - - - - - - - - - - - -	2—5—6
Item, In tooles - - - - - - - - - - - -	1—5—8

[1] A frow was a wedge-shaped tool for splitting rails or staves.

Item, In houshold Implements - - - - - - - 0—4—8
Item, Caske to put his goods in - - - - - - - 0–10—0
Item, fraight for his goods at halfe a tunne - - - 1–10—0
Item, For his Victuall, and passage by Sea - - - - 6—0—0

                                                                                20.–15.–4

Of which charge, the Adventurer having the greatest part of it in provision and goods; in case any servant die by the way, or shortly after his comming thither, the goods of that servant being sold in the Countrey, will returne all his charge againe, with advantage.

A Computation of a servants labour, and the profit that may arise by it, by instance in some particulars, which may be put in practise the first yeere.

                                                                                l.—s.—d.

One man may at the season plant so much corne, as
    ordinarily yeelds of Wheate 100. bushels, worth
    upon the place, at Two shillings a Bushell, - -   10-0—0
Of Beanes and Pease, 20. bushels, worth at three
    shillings a bushell, - - - - - - - - - - -   3—0—0
The same man will plant of Tobacco, betweene 800.
    and a 1000. weight, which at the lowest rate, at
    two pound 10. shil. the hundred, is worth, - - -   20-0—0
The same man may within the same yere, in the
    winter, make 4000. of Pipe-staves, worth upon
    the place foure pound the thousand. - - - - -   16-0—0

                                                                                49.——00——00.

Beside all their other labours in building, fencing, clearing of ground, raising of Cattell, gardening, etc.

If a mans labour be imployed in Hempe and Flaxe, it will yeeld him as much profit, as Tobacco at this rate; and so in many other Commodities, whereof this Countrey is capable.

No man neede to doubt of the vent of these Commodities, for Merchants send shipping to those parts, who will buy off these Commodities at the aforesaid rates, in as great a quantitie, as they shalbe able to make ready for them; because they yeeld a great encrease of profit in other Countreys, which the Planters themselves may make advantage of to themselves, if they have shipping, and thinke fit to deale in such a kind of trade. As for instance, a 1000. of Pipe-staves, which are rated upon the place at foure pound, being carried to the Canaries, will yeeld 15. or 20. *l.* Where likewise, and at the Westerne Islands, the Indian Corne will yeeld a great increase of benefit. The benefit also which may be raised by trade out of Swine onely, may easily be conceived to be very great, seeing they multiplie exceedingly, aske little tendance, and lesse charge of keeping in that Countrey, so abounding with Mast, Chestnuts, etc. For Porke being transported into Spaine, or the Westerne Islands will yeeld about 6. pence a pound, and Bacon, 8. pence. or 9. pence.

A note for the Adventurers memory, of such things as hee may (if he please) carry with him, either for his owne better accommodation (on Ship-board, or for some time after his arrivall in Maryland) or for trade, according to his abilitie.

Provision for Ship-board.

Fine Wheate-flower, close and well packed, to make puddings, etc. Clarret-wine burnt. Canary Sacke. Conserves, Marmalades, Suckets, and Spices. Sallet Oyle. Prunes to stew. Live Poultry. Rice, Butter, Holland-cheese, or old Cheshire, gammons of Bacon, Porke, dried Neates-tongues, Beefe packed up in Vinegar, some Weather-sheepe, meats baked in earthen potts, Leggs of Mutton minced, and stewed, and close packed up in tried Sewet, or Butter, in earthen pots: Juyce of Limons, etc.

Provision for trade in Virginia or Maryland.

If he be minded to furnish himselfe with Cattell in Virginia, his best way is to carry a superfluitie of wollen, or linnen cloth, callicoes, sayes, hatts, shooes, stockings, and all sorts of clothing; of Wine, Sugar, Prunes, Rasins, Currance, Honey, Spice, and Grocery wares, with which hee may procure himselfe cattell there, according to the stocke he dealeth withall.   About 4. or 5. Pound laid out heere in commodities, will there buy a Cow; and betweene 20. and 30. shillings, a breeding Sow.   The like Commodities will furnish him either there, or in Maryland, with Hogges, Poultry, and Corne.   Hee may doe well also to carry a superfluity of Knives, Combes, and Bracelets, to trade with the women Natives; and some Hatchets, Howes, and Axes, to trade with the men for Venison, Fish, Turkies, Corne, Fawnes to store a Parke, etc.

Provision for his House.

Iron, and Locks, and Hinges, and bolts; etc.   Mustardseede, Glasse and Leade for his windowes, Mault for beere, a Hogshead of Beefe or Porke: Two or three Firkins of Butter, a hundred or two of old Cheeses; a gallon of honey, Soape and Candles, Iron wedges, Pookes[1] for Rennet to make cheese: a good Mastiffe, etc.

Provision for Husbandry.

Seede Wheate, Rie, Barley, and Oates (the best way to preserve it from heating at sea, is to carry it in the eare) Kernells of Peares and Apples (especially of Pepins, Pearemaines, and Dusons)[2] for the making hereafter of Cider, and Perry; the stones and seedes of all those fruits and rootes, and herbes, which he desireth to have.   Good store of claver grasse seede, to make good meadow.

Provision for Fishing and Fowling.

Inprimis, necessaries for a boate of 3. or 4. Tunne; as Spikes, Nayles, Pitch, Tarre, Ocome, Canvis for a sayle, Ropes, Anchor, Iron for the Ruther: Fishing-lines for Cod and Macrills, etc.   Cod-hookes, and Macrill-hookes, a Seane or Basse-net, Herring-netts, Leade, Fowling-pieces of sixe foote; Powder and Shott, and Flint Stones; a good Water-Spaniell, etc.

A direction for choice of servants.

In the taking of servants, he may doe well to furnish himselfe with as many as he can, of usefull and necessary Arts:

---

[1] Ferments used in place of rennet for curdling the milk.
[2] Pippins, pearmains, and deuzans—varieties of apple.

A Carpenter, of all others the most necessary; A Mill-wright, Ship-wright, Boate-wright, Wheele-wright, Brick-maker, Bricklayer, Potter: one that can cleave Lath and Pale, and make Pipe-staves, etc. A Joyner, Cooper, Turner, Sawyer, Smith, Cutler, Leather-dresser, Miller, Fisherman, and Gardiner. These will be of most use; but any lusty young able man, that is willing to labour and take paines, although he have no particular trade, will be beneficiall enough to his Master.

And in case any Adventurer shall be unprovided of such men to supply his number, hee may have directions at the place where these bookes are to bee had, how and where hee may provide himselfe of as many as hee please.

The forme of binding a servant.

This Indenture made the   day of
          in the   yeere of our Soveraigne Lord King Charles, etc. betweene
          of the one party, and   on
the other party, Witnesseth, that the said
          doth hereby covenant promise, and grant, to
and with the said   his Executors
and Assignes, to serve him from the day of the date hereof, untill his first and next arrivall in Maryland; and after for and during the tearme of   yeeres, in such service and imployment, as the said   or his
assignes shall there imploy him, according to the custome of the Countrey in the like kind. In consideration whereof, the said   doth promise and grant, to
and with the said   to pay for his
passing, and to find him with Meat, Drinke, Apparell and Lodging, with other necessaries during the said terme; and at the end of the said terme, to give him one whole yeeres provision of Corne, and fifty acres of Land, according to the order of the countrey. In witnesse whereof, the said
                                                   hath
hereunto put his hand and seale, the day and yeere above written.

          Sealed and delivered in
               the presence of

The usuall terme of binding a servant, is for five yeers; but for any artificer, or one that shall deserve more then ordinary, the Adventurer shall doe well to shorten that time, and adde encouragements of another nature (as he shall see cause) rather then to want such usefull men.

A Forme of a Bill of Lading, to be taken from the Master of the Ship, by every Adventurer, for the better securing of the transportation of his goods.

Shipped by the grace of God in good order and well conditioned   by   in and upon the good Ship, called the
whereof is master, under God, for this present voyage
                                        and   now   riding   at
anker in the   and by Gods grace,
bound for   to say being marked and numbred, as in the margent, and are to be delivered in the like good order and well conditioned, at the Port of Saint Maries in Maryland (the danger of the Seas onely excepted) unto   or to   assignes.
                                paying fraught for the said goods
                                with primage and avarage accustomed.[1] In witnesse whereof, the Master or Purser of the said ship hath affirmed to three Bills of Lading, all of this tenor and date, the one of which three bills being accomplished, the other two to stand void.   And so God send the good Ship to her desired Port in safety.   Amen.   Dated in

There is order taken for convenient houses to be set up at Saint Maries, where all strangers may at their first comming bee entertained, with lodging and other fitting accommodations, for themselves and their goods, till they can better provide for themselves.

---

[1] Primage and average were small customary additional payments to the master of the ship, for his care of the goods.

The names of the Gentlemen adventurers that are gone in person to this Plantation.

Mr.
{
Leonard Calvert, the governor } his Lordships
George Calvert,   } brothers.
Jerome Hawley,   Esq; } Commissioners.
Thomas Cornewallis, Esq; }
Richard Gerard, son to Sir Thomas Gerard Knight and Baronet.
Edward Wintour, } sonnes of the Lady Anne Wintour.
Freder: Wintour, }
Henry Wiseman, son to Sir Thomas Wiseman Knight.
John Saunders.
Edward Cranfield.
Henry Greene.
Nicholas Ferfax.
John Baxter.
Thomas Dorrell.
Captaine John Hill.
John Medcalfe.
William Saire.
}

THE CHARTER OF MARY LAND

CHARLES by the Grace of God, King of England, Scotland, France, and Ireland, Defender of the Faith, etc. To all to whom these Presents shall come greeting.

WHEREAS Our right Trusty and Wellbeloved Subject Cecilius Calvert, Baron of Baltemore in our Kingdom of Ireland, Sonne and heire of Sir George Calvert Knight, late Baron of Baltemore in the same Kingdome of Ireland, pursuing his Fathers intentions, being excited with a laudable and pious zeale for the propagation of the Christian Faith, and the enlargement of our Empire and Dominion, hath humbly besought leave of Us, by his industry and charge, to transport an ample Colony of the English Nation unto a certaine Countrey hereafter described, in the parts of America, not yet culti-vated and planted, though in some parts thereof inhabited by cer-taine barbarous people, having no knowledge of Almighty God, and hath humbly besought our Royall Majestie to give, grant, and con-firme all the said Countrey, with certaine Priviledges and Jurisdictions, requisite for the good government, and state of his Colony, and Countrey aforesaid, to him and his heires for ever.

KNOW YEE therefore, that Wee favouring the Pious, and Noble purpose of the said Barons of Baltemore, of our speciall grace, certaine knowledge, and meere motion, have given, granted, and confirmed, and by this our present Charter, for Us, Our Heires, and Successors, doe give, grant and confirme unto the said Cecilius, now Baron of Baltemore, his heires and Assignes, all that part of a Peninsula, lying in the parts of America, betweene the Ocean on the East, and the Bay of Chesopeack on the West, and divided from the other part thereof, by a right line drawne from the Promontory or Cape of Land called Watkins Point (situate in the foresaid Bay, neere the river of Wighco)[1] on the West, unto the maine Ocean on the East; and betweene that bound on the South, unto that part of Delaware Bay on the North, which lieth under the fortieth degree of Northerly Latitude from the Equinoctiall, where New-England ends; And all that tract of land betweene the bounds aforesaid; that is to say, passing from the foresaid Bay, called Delaware Bay, in a right line by the degree aforesaid, unto the true Meridian of the first fountaine of the River of Pattowmeck, and from thence trending toward the South unto the farther banke of the fore-said River, and following the West and South side thereof unto a certaine place called Cinquack,[2] situate neere the mouth of the said River, where it falls into the Bay of Chesopeack, and from thence by a straight line unto the foresaid Promontory, and place called Watkins Point, (So that all that tract of land divided by the line aforesaid, drawne betweene the maine Ocean, and Watkins Point unto the Promontory called Cape Charles, and all its apurtenances, doe remaine intirely excepted to us, our heires, and Successors for ever.)

Wee doe also grant and confirme unto the said now Lord Baltemore, his heires and Assignes, all Ilands, and Iletts within the limitts aforesaid, and all and singular the Ilands and Iletts, which are, or shall be in the Ocean, within 10. Leagues from the Easterne shoare of the said Countrey, towards the East, with all and singular Ports, Harbors, Bayes, Rivers, and Inletts, belonging unto the Countrey, or

---

[1] Now called Pocomoke River.

[2] Uncertainty as to the exact location of the points named and changes in the shore line from the action of the tides led to long disputes with Virginia as to the position of the boundary across the Chesapeake Bay and on its eastern shore. The matter was finally determined in 1877 by arbitrators appointed on behalf of the two states. The agreement thus reached was ratified by the General Assembly of Maryland, subject to ratification by Virginia and the Congress of the United States, in 1878 (acts of Assembly, chapter 374), and provision made for surveying and marking the boundary.

Ilands aforesaid: And all the Soile, lands, Fields, Woods, Mountaines, Fennes, Lakes, Rivers Bayes, and Inletts, situate, or being within the bounds, and limits aforesaid, with the fishing of all sorts of fish, Whales, Sturgeons, and all other royal fishes in the Sea, Bays, Inletts, or Rivers, within the premises: and the fish therein taken: and moreover all Veines, Mines, and Quarries, as well discovered, as not discovered, of Gold, Silver, Gemmes, and pretious stones, and all other whatsoever, be it of Stones, Mettalls, or of any other thing, or matter whatsoever, found, or to bee found within the Countrey, Iles, and limits aforesaid. And Furthermore the Patronages and Advowsons of all Churches, which (as Christian Religion shall encrease within the Countrey, Iles, Iletts, and limits aforesaid) shall happen hereafter to bee erected: together with licence and power, to build and found Churches, Chappells, and Oratories, in convenient and fit places within the premises, and to cause them to be dedicated, and consecrated according to the Ecclesiasticall Lawes of our Kingdome of England: Together with all and singular the like, and as ample rights, Jurisdictions, Priviledges, Prerogatives, Royalties, Liberties Immunities, Royall rights, and franchises of what kind soever temporall, as well by Sea, as by land, within the Countrey, Iles, Iletts, and limits aforesaid; To have, exercise, use and enjoy the same, as amply as any Bishop of Durham, within the Bishoprick, or County Palatine of Durham,[1] in our Kingdome of England, hath at any time heretofore had, held, used, or enjoyed, or of right ought, or might have had, held, used, or enjoyed.

And him the said now Lord Baltemore, his Heires and Assignes, Wee doe by these Presents for Us, Our Heires and Successors, make, create, and constitute the true and absolute Lords, and Proprietaries of the Countrey aforesaid, and of all other the Premises, (except before excepted) saving alwayes, the faith and allegeance, and Soveraigne dominion due unto Us, Our Heires and Successors.

To have, hold, possesse, and enjoy the sayd Countrey, Iles, Iletts, and other the Premises, unto the said now Lord Baltemore,

---

[1] Durham was erected into a county palatine by William the Conqueror. It was specially referred to in the text as a means of defining the authority conferred upon the Lord Baltimore in Maryland for the reason that it was the sole one of the ancient palatinates in England remaining, the others, Chester and Lancaster, having been united to the Crown. Special power and almost independent authority as counts palatine were bestowed upon lords occupying frontier positions, so that they might act quickly for defense. For this reason William of Normandy conferred palatine rank upon the Bishop of Durham, near the border of Scotland, and upon the Earl of Chester, near the border of Wales. The palatine jurisdiction of the Bishop of Durham was not wholly abrogated until 1836.

his heires and assignes, to the sole and proper use and behoofe of him the said now Lord Baltemore, his heires and assignes for ever.

To bee holden of Us, Our Heires, and Successors, Kings of England, as of Our Castle of Windsor, in Our County of Berkshire, in free and common soccage,[1] by fealty onely, for all services, and not in Capite, or by Knights Service: Yeelding and paying therefore to Us, our Heires and Successors, two Indian Arrowes of those parts, to be delivered at Our said Castle of Windsor, every yeere on the Tuesday in Easter weeke; and also the fifth part of all Gold and Silver Oare within the limits aforesaid, which shall from time to time happen to be found.

Now that the said Countrey thus by Us granted, and described, may be eminent above all other parts of the said territory, and dignified with larger titles: Know yee that wee of our further grace, certaine knowledge, and meere motion, have thought fit to erect the same Countrey and Ilands into a Province, as out of the fullnesse of Our royall Power, and Prerogative, Wee doe, for Us, Our Heires, and Successors, erect, and incorporate them into a Province, and doe call it *Mary land*, and So from henceforth will have it called.

And forasmuch as Wee have hereby made, and ordained the foresaid now Lord Baltemore, the true Lord, and Proprietary of all the Province aforesaid: Know yee therefore moreover, that Wee, reposing especiall trust and confidence in the fidelitie, wisedome, Justice, and Provident circumspection of the said now Lord Baltemore, for Us, Our Heires and Successors, doe grant free, full, and absolute power, by vertue of these Presents, to him and his heires, for the good and happy government of the said Province, to ordaine, make, enact, and under his and their seales to publish any Lawes whatsoever, appertaining either unto the publike State of the said Province, or unto the private utility of particular Persons, according unto their best discretions, of and with the advise assent and approbation of the Free-men of the said Province, or the greater part of them, or of their delegates or deputies, whom for the enacting of the said Lawes, when, and as often as neede shall require, We will that the said now Lord Baltemore, and his heires, shall assemble in such sort and forme, as to him or them shall seeme best: And the same

---

[1] Free and common socage is a feudal tenure and differs from a tenure *in capite* by knights' service only in that the uncertain military service required by the latter is, under the former, commuted for a fixed tribute, which in this case consisted only of the two Indian arrows, annually, as mentioned above, and one-fifth part of the precious metals mined should any be discovered. A number of receipts for the Indian arrows delivered from year to year at Windsor Castle are now in the possession of the Maryland Historical Society. The province of Avalon in Newfoundland was held by Lord Baltimore *in capite*.

lawes duly to execute upon all people, within the said Province, and limits thereof, for the time being, or that shall be constituted under the government, and power of him or them, either sayling towards Mary-land, or returning from thence toward England, or any other of Ours, or forraine Dominions, by imposition of Penalties, Imprisonment, or any other punishment; yea, if it shall be needfull, and that the quality of the offence require it, by taking away member or life, either by him the said now Lord Baltemore, and his heires, or by his or their Deputies, Lieutenants, Judges, Justices, Magistrates, Officers, and Ministers to be ordained or appointed, according to the Tenor, and true intention of these Presents: And likewise to appoint and establish any Judges and Justices, Magistrates and Officers whatsoever, at sea and Land, for what causes soever, and with what power soever, and in such forme, as to the said now Lord Baltemore, or his heires, shall seeme most convenient: Also to remit, release, pardon, and abolish, whether before Judgment, or after, all crimes or offences whatsoever, against the said Lawes: and to doe all and every other thing or things, which unto the compleate establishment of Justice, unto Courts, Prætories, and Tribunals, formes of Judicature and maners of proceeding, do belong: although in these Presents expresse mention be not made thereof, and by Judges by them delegated, to award Processe, hold Pleas, and determine in all the said Courts and Tribunalls, all actions, suits, and causes whatsoever, as well criminall as civill, personall, reall, mixt, and prætoriall; which laws, so as aforesaid to be published, Our pleasure is, and so We enjoyne, require, and command, shall be most absolute and available in Law, and that all the Liege people, and subjects of Us, Our Heires and Successors, doe observe and keepe the same inviolably, in those parts, so farre as they concerne them, under the paines therein expressed, or to be expressed: Provided neverthelesse, that the said Lawes be consonant to reason, and be not repugnant or contrary, but as neere as conveniently may be, agreeable to the Lawes, Statutes, Customes, and Rights of this our Kingdome of England.

And forasmuch, as in the Government of so great a Province, suddaine accidents doe often happen, whereunto it will be necessary to apply a remedy, before the Free-holders of the said Province, their Delegates, or Deputies, can be assembled to the making of Lawes, neither will it be convenient, that instantly upon every such emergent occasion, so great a multitude should be called together: Therefore for the better government of the said Province, Wee will and ordaine, and by these Presents for Us, Our Heires and Successors, doe grant unto the said now Lord Baltemore, and his heires, that the said now Lord Baltemore and his heires, by themselves, or by their Magistrates and Officers in that behalfe duely to be or-

dained as aforesaid, may make and constitute, fit and wholesome
Ordinances, from time to time, within the said Province, to be kept
and observed, as well for the preservation of the Peace, as for the
better government of the people there inhabiting, and publikely to
notice the same to all persons, whom the same doth, or any way
may concerne; which Ordinances, Our pleasure is, shall be observed inviolably within the said Province, under the paines therein
to bee expressed. So as the said Ordinances be consonant to reason,
and be not repugnant nor contrary, but so farre as conveniently may
be, agreeable with the Lawes and Statutes of Our Kingdome of
England, and so as the said Ordinances be not extended, in any sort
to bind, charge, or take away the right or interest of any person, or
persons, of, or in their Life, Member, Free-hold, Goods, or Chattells.

Furthermore, that this new Colony may the more happily encrease by the multitude of people resorting thither, and may likewise be the more strongly defended from the incursions of Salvages,
or other enemies, Pyrates and Robbers: Therefore Wee, for Us,
Our Heires and Successors, doe give and grant by the Presents,
Power, licence, and liberty unto all the liege people, and subjects,
both present, and future, of Us, Our Heires, and Successors (excepting those who shall be specially forbidden) to transport themselves
and families unto the said Province, with convenient shipping, and
fitting provisions, and there to settle themselves, dwell and inhabite,
and to build, and fortifie Castles, Forts, and other places of strength,
for the publike, and their owne private defence, at the appointment of
the said now Lord Baltemore, and his heires, the Statute of fugitives, or any other whatsoever, to the contrary of the premises, in
any wise notwithstanding.

And wee will also, and of Our more speciall grace, for Us, Our
Heires, and Successors, wee doe straightly enjoyne, constitute, ordaine, and command, that the said Province shall be of Our Allegiance, and that all and singular the Subjects, and Liege people of
Us, Our Heires, and Successors, transported, or to be transported
into the said Province, and the children of them, and of such as shall
descend from them, there already borne, or hereafter to be borne, bee,
and shall be Denizens, and Lieges of Us, Our Heires, and Successors, of Our Kingdome of England, and Ireland, and be in all things
held, treated, reputed, and esteemed as the liege faithfull people of
Us, Our Heires, and Successors, borne within Our Kingdome of
England: and likewise any Lands, Tenements, Revenues, Services,
and other hereditaments whatsoever, within Our Kingdome of England, and other Our Dominions, may inherite, or otherwise purchase,
receive, take, have, hold, buy, and possesse, and them may occupy,
and enjoy, give, sell, aliene, and bequeath, as likewise, all Liberties,

Franchises, and Priviledges, of this Our Kingdome of England, freely, quietly, and peaceably, have and possesse, occupy and enjoy, as Our liege people, borne, or to be borne, within Our said Kingdome of England without the let, molestation, vexation, trouble, or grievance of Us, Our Heires and Successors: any Statute, Act, Ordinance, or Provision to the contrary hereof notwithstanding.

And furthermore, That Our Subjects may be the rather encouraged to undertake this expedition, with ready and cheerfull minds; KNOW YEE, that We of Our speciall grace, certaine knowledge, and meere motion, doe give and grant, by vertue of these presents, as well unto the said now Lord Baltemore and his Heires, as to all other that shall from time to time repaire unto that province, with a purpose to inhabite there, or to trade with the Natives of the said Province, full licence to Lade and Fraight in any Ports whatsoever, of Us, Our Heires and Successors, and into the said Province of Mary land, by them, their servants or assignes, to transport, all and singular, their Goods, Wares, and Merchandize; as likewise all sorts of graine whatsoever, and any other things whatsoever, necessary for food or clothing (not prohibited by the Laws and Statutes of our Kingdomes and Dominions to bee carried out of the said kingdomes) without any lett, or molestation of Us, Our Heires, or Successors, or of any of the officers of Us, Our Heires, or Successors; (saving alwayes, to Us, Our Heires and Successors, the Impositions, Customes, and other duties and payments for the said Wares and Merchandise) any Statute, Act, Ordinance or other thing whatsoever to the contrary notwithstanding.

And because in so remote a Countrey, and situate amongst so many barbarous nations, the incursions as well of the Salvages themselves, as of other enimies, pyrates and robbers, may probably be feared: Therefore Wee have given, and for Us, Our Heires, and Successors, doe give power by these presents, unto the now Lord Baltemore, his heires and assignes, by themselves, or their Captaines, or other their officers, to Leavy, Muster and Traine, all sorts of men, of what condition, or wheresoever borne, in the said Province of Mary-land for the time being, and to make warre, and to pursue the Enemies and Robbers aforesaid, as well by sea as by land, yea, even without the limits of the said Province, and (by Gods assistance) to vanquish and take them, and being taken, to put them to death by the Law of warre, or to save them at their pleasure, and to doe all and every other thing which unto the charge and office of a Captaine Generall of an Army belongeth, or hath accustomed to belong, as fully and freely as any Captaine Generall of any army hath ever had the same.

Also, Our Will and Pleasure is, and by this Our Charter, We

doe give unto the said now Lord Baltemore, his heires, and assignes, full power, liberty, and authority, in case of Rebellion, Tu-
mult, or Sedition, if any should happen (which God forbid) either
upon the land within the Province aforesaid, or upon the maine sea,
in making a voyage thither, or returning from thence, by themselves,
or their captaines, deputies, or other officers, to be authorized under
their seales for that purpose (to whom we also, for Us, Our Heires and
Successors doe give and grant by these presents, full power and authority) to exercise Martiall Law against mutinous and seditious
persons of those parts, such as shall refuse to submit themselves to
his, or their government, or shall refuse to serve in the warres, or
shall flie to the Enemy, or forsake their Ensignes, or be loyterers, or
straglers, or otherwise howsoever offending against the Law, Custome, and Discipline military, as freely, and in as ample manner and
forme, as any Captaine generall of an army by vertue of his office
might, or hath accustomed to use the same.

Furthermore, That the way to honors and dignities, may not
seeme to be altogether precluded and shut up, to men well borne,
and such as shall prepare themselves unto this present Plantation,
and shall desire to deserve well of Us, and Our Kingdomes, both in
peace and war, in so farre distant and remote a Countrey: Therefore Wee, for Us, Our Heires and Successors, doe give free, and absolute power,unto the said now Lord Baltemore, his heires and assignes,
to conferre favours, rewards, and honors, upon such inhabitants
within the Province aforesaid, as shall deserve the same; and to
invest them, with what titles and dignities soever, as he shall thinke
fit (so as they be not such as are now used in England). As likewise
to erect and incorporate, Townes into Boroughes, and Boroughs
into Cities, with convenient priviledges and immunities, according to
the merit of the inhabitants, and the fitnesse of the places, and to doe
all and every other thing or things, touching the premises, which to
him, or them, shall seeme meete and requisite; albeit they be such as
of their owne nature might otherwise require a more speciall com-
mandement and warrant, then in these Presents is expressed.

Wee will also, and by these Presents, for Us Our Heires and
Successors, Wee doe give and grant licence, and by this Our Charter,
unto the said now Lord Baltemore, his heires and assignes, and to all
the inhabitants and dwellers in the Province aforesaid, both present
and to come, to import, or unlade, by themselves, or their servants,
factors, or assignes, all Merchandizes and Goods whatsoever, that
shall arise of the fruits and commodities of the said Province, eithec
by land or sea, into any of the ports of Us, Our Heires and Successors, in Our kingdomes of England, or Ireland, or otherwise to dispose of the said goods, in the said Ports, and if need be, within one

yeere next after the unlading of the same, to lade the said merchandizes and goods againe, into the same or other ships, and to export the same into any other Countreys, either of our Dominion or forreigne, (being in Amity with Us, Our Heires and Successors) Provided alwayes, that they pay such Customes, Impositions Subsidies and Duties for the same, to Us, Our Heires and Successors, as the rest of Our Subjects of Our Kingdome of England, for the time being, shall be bound to pay: beyond which, We will not that the inhabitants of the foresaid Province of Mary-land, all be any way charged.

And furthermore, of Our more ample and speciall Grace, certaine knowledge, and meere motion, Wee doe, for Us, Our Heires and Successors, grant unto the said now Lord Baltemore, his heires and assignes, full and absolute power and authority to make, erect, and constitute, within the Province of Mary-land, and the Iles and Iletts aforesaid, such, and so many Seaports, Harbours, Creekes, and other places, for discharge and unlading of goods and merchandises, out of Ships, Boates, and other vessells—and lading them, and in such and so many places, and with such Rights, Jurisdictions, Liberties and Priviledges unto the said ports belonging, as to him or them shall seeme most expedient. And that all and singular the Ships, Boats, and other Vessells, which shall come for merchandize and trade unto the said Province, or out of the same shall depart; shall be laden and unladen only at such Ports as shall be so erected and constituted by the said now Lord Baltemore, his heires or assignes, any Use, Custome, or other thing to the contrary notwithstanding; saving alwayes unto Us, Our heires and Successors, and to all the Subjects (of Our Kingdome of England and Ireland) of Us, Our Heires and Successors, free liberty of fishing for Sea-fish, as well in the Sea, Bayes, Inletts, and navigable Rivers as in the Harbours, Bayes and Creekes of the Province aforesaid, and the Priviledges of salting and drying their fish on the shore of the said Province; and for the same cause, to cut and take underwood, or twiggs there growing, and to build Cottages and Shedds necessary in this behalfe, as they heretofore have, or might reasonably have used; which Liberties and Priviledges, neverthelesse, the Subjects aforesaid, of Us, Our Heires and Successors, shall enjoy without any notable dammage, or injury, to be done to the said now Lord Baltemore, his heires, or assignes, or to the dwellers and inhabitants of the said Province, in the Ports, Creekes and shores aforesaid, and especially in the woods and Copses growing within the said Province: And if any shall doe any such dammage, or injury, he shall incurre the heavy displeasure of Us, Our Heires and Successors, the punishment of the Lawes; and shall moreover make satisfaction.

Wee doe furthermore, will, appoint, and ordaine, and by these

Presents, for Us, Our Heires and Successors, Wee doe grant unto the said now Lord Baltemore, his heires and assignes, that he the said Lord Baltemore, his heires and assignes, may from time to time for ever, have and enjoy, the Customes and Subsidies, in the Ports, Harbours, and other Creekes and places aforesaid, within the Province aforesaid; payable, or due for Merchandizes and wares, there to be laded or unladed, the said Customes and Subsidies to be reasonably assessed (upon any occasion) by themselves and the people there, as aforesaid; to whom we give power by these Presents, for Us, Our Heires and Successors upon just cause, and in due proportion, to assesse and impose the same.

And further, of Our speciall grace, and of Our certaine knowledge, and meere motion, Wee have given granted, and confirmed, and by these Presents for Us, Our Heires and Successors, doe give, grant, and confirme unto the said now Lord Baltemore, his heires and assignes, full and absolute licence, power, and authoritie, that hee the said now Lord Baltemore, his heires and assignes, from time to time hereafter for ever, at his, or their will, and pleasure, may assigne, aliene, grant, demise, or enfeoffe of the Premises so many, and such parts and parcells, to him or them that shall be willing to purchase the same, as they shall thinke fit, to have and to hold to them the sayd person, or persons, willing to take or purchase the same, their heirs and assignes in fee simple, or fee taile, or for terme of life, or lives, or yeeres, to bee held of the said now Lord Baltemore, his heires, and assignes, by such services, customes, and rents, as shall seeme fit to the said now Lord Baltemore, his heires and assignes; and not immediately of Us, Our Heires or Successors: and to the same person or persons, and to all and every of them, Wee doe give and grant by these Presents for Us, Our Heires and Successors, licence, authoritie, and power, that such person or persons, may take the premises, or any parcell thereof, of the foresaid now Lord Baltemore, his heires or assignes, and the same hold to themselves, their heirs, or assignes, (in what estate of inheritance soever, in fee simple, or in fee taile, or otherwise, as to them, and the now Lord Baltemore, his heires and assignes, shall seeme expedient) of the said now Lord Baltemore, his heires and assignes; the statute made in the Parliament of Edward, Sonne of King Henry, late King of England, Our Predecessor, commonly called the Statute *Quia emptores terrarum*,[1] lately published in Our Kingdome of England, or any other Statute, Acte, Ordinance, Use, Law, or Custome, or any other thing, cause, or matter thereupon heretofore had, done, published, ordained, or provided to the contrary, in any wise notwithstanding; And by these Presents, We give, and grant licence unto the said now Lord Baltemore, and his heires,

[1] Statute of Edward I., A. D. 1290, to prevent further sub-infeudation.

to erect any parcells of land within the Province aforesaid, into Mannors and in every of the said Mannors, to have, and to hold a Court
Baron, with all things whatsoever, which to a Court Baron doe belong,
and to have and hold viewe of Franck-pledge, (for the conservation
of the peace, and the better government of those Parts,) by themselves or their stewards, or by the Lords for the time being of other
Mannors, to bee deputed when they shall bee erected: and in the
same, to use all things belonging to View of Franck-Pledge.

And further, Our pleasure is, and by these Presents, for Us, Our
Heires, and Successors, wee doe covenant and grant to and with the
said now Lord Baltemore, his heires and assignes; That Wee, Our
Heires and Successors, shall at no time hereafter, set, or make, or
cause to be set, any Imposition, Custome, or other Taxation, Rate,
or Contribution whatsoever, in or upon the dwellers and inhabitants
of the foresaid Province, for their Lands, Tenements, goods or Chattells within the said Province, or in or upon any goods or merchandizes, within the said Province, or to be laden, or unladen within any
the Ports or harbours of the said Province: And Our pleasure is,
and for Us, Our Heires, and Successors, Wee charge and command,
that this Our Declaration shall be henceforward from time to time
received, and allowed in all Our Courts, and before all the Judges
of Us Our Heires and Successors, for a sufficient and lawfull discharge, payment, and acquittance; Commanding all and singular,
our Officers and Ministers of Us, Our Heires and Successors, and
enjoyning them upon paine of Our high displeasure, that they doe
not presume at any time to attempt any thing to the contrary of the
premises, or that they doe in any sort, withstand the same, but that they
be at all times ayding and assisting, as is fitting, unto the said now
Lord Baltemore, and his heires, and to the Inhabitants, and Merchants of Mary-land aforesaid, their servants, ministers, factors and assignees, in the full use and fruition of the benefit of this Our Charter.

And further, Our pleasure is, and by these Presents for Us,
Our Heires and Successors Wee doe grant unto the said now Lord
Baltemore, his heires and assignes, and to the Tenants, and Inhabitants of the said Province of Mary-land, both present, and to come,
and to every of them, that the said Province, Tenants, and Inhabitants of the said Colony or Countrey, shall not from henceforth bee
held or reputed as a member, or a part of the land of Virginia, or
of any other Colony whatsoever, now transported or hereafter to be
transported, nor shall be depending on, or subject to their government in any thing, from whom Wee doe separate that, and them, and
Our pleasure is, by these Presents that they bee separated, and that
they be subject immediately to Our Crowne of England, as depending
thereof for ever.

And if perchance hereafter it should happen, that any doubts or questions should arise, concerning the true sence and understanding of any word, clause, or sentence contained in this Our present Charter, Wee will, ordaine, and command, that at all times, and in all things, such Interpretation bee made thereof, and allowed in any of Our Courts whatsoever, as shall be judged most advantagious, and favourable unto the said now Lord Baltemore, his heires and assignes. Provided alwayes, that no Interpretation bee admitted thereof, by which Gods Holy and Truely Christian Religion, or the allegiance due unto Us, Our Heires and Successors, may in any thing suffer any prejudice, or diminution.

Although expresse mention bee not made in these Presents, of the true yeerely value, or certainty of the premises, or of any part thereof, or of other gifts and grants, made by Us, Our Heires, and Predecessors, unto the said now Lord Baltemore, or any Statute, Acte, Ordinance, Provision, Proclamation, or restraint heretofore had, made, published, ordained, or provided, or any other thing, cause, or matter whatsoever to the contrary thereof in any wise notwithstanding.

In witnesse whereof, Wee have caused these Our Letters to bee made Pattents. Witnesse Our selfe at Westminster, the Twentieth day of June, in the Eighth yeere of Our Reigne.[1]

[1] *I. e.*, June 20, 1632.

EXTRACTS FROM THE ANNUAL LETTERS OF THE ENGLISH PROVINCE OF THE SOCIETY OF JESUS, 1634, 1638, 1639, 1640, 1642, 1654, 1656, 1681

INTRODUCTION

THE *Annual Letters* of the Provincials of the Society of Jesus are the reports which they were required to make to the General of the Society at Rome of the chief events of the province during the preceding year, and in particular of the results accomplished by the Jesuit fathers in the missionary fields. The letters of the Provincials are compilations from the reports which they themselves received from those under their jurisdiction. The Maryland mission was included in the English province, and therefore reports concerning it are contained in the letters of the English Provincial. The extracts which follow are the portions of the letters for the years indicated which relate to Maryland.

In view of the intolerant spirit of the age, great caution was observed in the preparation of these letters to avoid the designation of individuals by their proper names, lest they should be brought into trouble if the letters should go astray. In the letter of 1634, for instance, Lord Baltimore is referred to merely as "a certain Catholic Baron"; and throughout these extracts the names of converts, except those of Indians, are uniformly omitted. For the same reason the letters are without signature. The Jesuit fathers usually travelled under fictitious names, and were often known by different names in different localities. When proper names of persons appear in the letters they are generally assumed, the correct names, as a sort of key to the letter, being sent in a separate communication.[1] The Father Philip Fisher men-

[1] Hughes, *History of the Society of Jesus in North America, Text*, I. 52.

tioned in the letters was known in Maryland as Thomas Copley. The real name of Father John Brock was Morgan; and Father John Gravener is believed to be the same as Father John Altham, who was the companion of Father White in the first voyage.

In the letter of 1639, mention is made of the gift to the Jesuit fathers by the King of Patuxent of the plantation of Metapannay,[1] afterward referred to as a farm. This and other gifts or cessions of land by the Indians to the missionaries, or rather to the Society of Jesus, led to a sharp contention between them and Lord Baltimore, who as absolute lord and proprietary of the province, under letters patent from the King of England, maintained that no one could hold title to land in Maryland except under grant from him. The contention of the clergy, or their view of the question involved, is expressed in the letter of 1642 where it is complained that there were those who "have not feared to violate the immunities of the Church, by using their endeavors that laws of the kind formerly passed in England and unjustly observed there, may obtain like force here, to wit: that it shall not be lawful for any person or community, even ecclesiastical, in anywise, even by gift, to acquire or possess any land unless the permission of the Civil Magistrate first be obtained."

Lord Baltimore was so much in earnest in the matter, and in his apprehensions as to the possible results of encroachment upon his rights by a religious corporation or community, that he went so far as to appeal to the *Congregatio de Propaganda Fide* at Rome for the recall of the Jesuit missionaries and the sending of secular priests in their stead.[2] But the matter being referred to Father Henry More (great-grandson of Sir Thomas More, Lord High Chancellor of England), who was then Provincial of the English province, he conceded the

[1] Mattapany.
[2] Foley, *Records of the English Province S. J.*, III. 366.

justice of Lord Baltimore's contention, caused to be released all lands obtained from the Indians, and directed that grants from the Lord Proprietary be accepted by the priests as tenants under him.[1] This question being thus settled, the missions in Maryland continued to be served by the Jesuit fathers.

In the letter of 1654 there is mention of the hanging of a woman, accused of sorcery on account of the disablement of a vessel bound to Maryland upon which she was a passenger. This occurred near Barbados, outside the jurisdiction of Maryland. Existing records do not show that any one was ever executed for sorcery or witchcraft in the province, though there are records of two trials of persons accused of being guilty of executions for these causes on the high seas.

All of the extracts here printed, except those from the letters of 1634 and 1681, were published from transcripts made in Rome by Father McSherry, S. J., in 1832, both the Latin text and a translation thereof, by the Maryland Historical Society in *Fund Publication* no. 7 and the supplement thereto. The Latin text of the extract from the letter of 1634, and a portion of that of 1681, were printed by the same society in its *Fund Publication* no. 35 (*Calvert Papers* no. 3), Appendix A, from notes furnished by Father Thomas Hughes, S. J. English translations of them all are contained in *Records of the English Province of the Society of Jesus,* by Brother Henry Foley, S. J. (vol. III., London, 1878). The translations in this volume have been carefully revised throughout by collating with the Latin text given in the *History of the Society of Jesus in North America,* by Father Thomas Hughes, S. J. (1907), *Documents,* I., pt. I., 107–136.

C. C. H.

---

[1] Stonyhurst MSS. Anglia, IV. 108 f, 108 g, printed in Johnson's *Foundation of Maryland* (Maryland Historical Society, *Fund Publication* no. 18, pp. 84, 87).

EXTRACTS FROM THE ANNUAL LETTERS OF THE ENGLISH PROVINCE OF THE SOCIETY OF JESUS, 1634, 1638, 1639, 1640, 1642, 1654, 1656, 1681

From the Annual Letter of 1634.

LAST year, by the good grace and authority of the King, and under the auspices of a certain Catholic baron, a considerable colony of Englishmen, largely Catholics, was taken out to the hither shores of America. With them went two priests of Ours, with a coadjutor; another priest and another coadjutor followed. Their purpose was, not only to work among the colonists, but also to devote themselves to procuring the conversion and salvation of the barbarians. For the promotion of this pious undertaking, many Catholics showed great liberality, and contributed money as well as servants, these latter being of the first necessity there. In the case of a certain servant it seems to have happened not without divine providence that he was found by those of Ours who sailed last. Our lay-brother had known him in Belgium, and had found him an industrious and faithful man. Therefore, while preparing himself for departure, he used all diligence to seek him out. But when there seemed now to be no further hope of finding the man, going on board a ship which was carrying fresh supplies to several colonies, he unexpectedly came upon the man. This person, on account of the open profession of his faith, had fallen into extreme misery, chiefly because he would by no means bind himself by the oath which they call that of allegiance. So he was being sent out of the country, according to the usual course in the charge of a certain heretical merchant, to be sold at his will in some heretical colony. Recognizing him, our brother redeems him, and takes him with him as a companion upon his voyage, as one rescued from the very jaws of hell and filled with extreme joy.

Furthermore two priests of Ours were assigned this year as companions to a certain gentleman who went to explore unknown lands. They with great courage performed an uncomfortable voyage of about eight months, both much shaken in health, with spells of illness, and gave us no slight hope of reaping ultimately an abundant harvest, in ample and excellent regions.[1]

From the Annual Letter of 1638.[2]

Four fathers belonged to this mission, with one coadjutor in temporal concerns. And he indeed, after enduring severe toils for the space of five years with the greatest patience, humility and ardent love, chanced to be seized by the disease prevailing at the time, and happily exchanged this wretched life for an immortal one.

He was also shortly followed by one of the fathers, who was young indeed, but on account of his remarkable qualities of mind, evidently of great promise. He had scarcely spent two months in this mission, when, to the great grief of all, he was carried off by the common sickness prevailing in the colony, from which no one of the three remaining priests has escaped unharmed; yet we have not ceased to labor, to the best of our ability, among the neighboring people.

And though the rulers of this colony have not yet allowed us to dwell among the savages, both on account of the prevailing sicknesses, and also because of the hostile acts which the barbarians commit against the English, they having slain a man from this colony, who was staying among them for the sake of trading, and having also entered into a conspiracy against our whole nation; yet we hope that one of Ours will shortly secure a station among the barbarians. Meanwhile, we devote ourselves more zealously to the English; and since

---

[1] This expedition was probably to Virginia, and the gentleman referred to is supposed to be George Calvert, the brother of Lord Baltimore. The time mentioned apparently included that required for the return voyage to England. Hughes, *History of the Society of Jesus in North America, Text*, I. 272.

[2] By Father Edward Knott, Provincial of the English Province, S. J.

there are Protestants as well as Catholics in the colony, we have labored for both, and God has blessed our labors.

For, among the Protestants, nearly all who have come from England in this year 1638, and many others, have been converted to the faith, together with four servants, whom we purchased in Virginia, (another colony of our kingdom,) for necessary services, and five mechanics, whom we hired for a month, and have in the meantime won to God. Not long afterwards, one of these, after being duly prepared for death, by receiving the sacraments, departed this life. And among these persons hardly anything else worth mentioning has occurred. The following occurrences are more remarkable.

A certain man, entirely unknown to us, but a zealous disciple of the Protestant religion, was staying with a friend who was still more zealous; and having been bitten by one of the snakes which abound in these parts, was expecting immediate death. One of Ours, finding this out, took with him a surgeon, and hurried to the sick man, who, it was reported, had already lost his senses, with the intention of ministering to his soul in any way that he could. But the host, divining his intention, tried to thwart his pious efforts. And the priest, as he could find no other opportunity, determined to stay all night with the sick man. But the host prevented this too, and, lest the Father should be admitted at night, he appointed a guard to sleep on a bed, laid across the door of the chamber occupied by his friend. Nevertheless, the priest kept on the watch for every opportunity of approach; and going at the dead of night, when he supposed the guard would be especially overcome by sleep, he contrived, without disturbing him, to pass in to the sick man; and, at his own desire, received him into the Church. And although, under the circumstances, it was impossible that the sick man should be taught much, or be firmly established in his belief, yet when, contrary to all expectation, he had been cured by our surgeon, the grace of God prevailed with him, and he chose rather to be put out of his friend's house than to retract what he had done; nay, he even came to us of his own accord, and happily completed the work he had begun.

Another man, when one of Ours tried to bring him to the orthodox faith, repulsed him with the answer, "that he had vowed that he never would embrace that faith." A short time afterwards this wretched man was attacked by disease, and brought to the last extremity, before the Father was advised of his sickness. He, however, hastens to the sick man with all speed, and finds him entirely insensible, yet still breathing. Accordingly he instructs the attendants to put some nourishment into the mouth of the sick man, every now and then, and to summon him if at any time he returned to consciousness. This was done early the next morning, and the Father runs to him, and, while talking to him, perceives that he is in some measure recognized by him, and receives from him, at times, an answer to a short question, (for he could not take in too long a discourse at once.) The Father therefore determined to make use of the present opportunity, inasmuch as he could not hope for another one afterwards. And when by various communications he had obtained (as he judged) the consent of the sick man, understanding from him that he wished to be made a Catholic, that he was sorry for his sins, and that he wished to be absolved from them, he absolved him from his sins and anointed him with the sacred oil. After this had been done, the sick man, in a day or two, was perfectly restored to his senses. And when he was asked what he had done, or what he had perceived to have been done around him, he answered with so great joy and such heart-felt emotion, that he had been admitted into the Catholic Church, and that he intended to remain in it even to his last breath, that all who were present were affected with no small admiration. Afterwards, when the Father came again, he expressed the same joy to him; and to his great satisfaction performed the other things necessary for completing the work he had begun. From that time he gradually recovered; but, since he had scarcely any proper remedies, and lay for a long time on his back, a dreadful ulcer broke out over his whole body. Wherefore we procured necessaries for him, as far as we could, at our own expense, and sent a surgeon to cure his malady. And although the surgeon removed a great many worms from the ulcer, yet by his skilful attention and the watchful care of others the sick man was cured, and now he is a strong servant, sound, as we trust, both in mind and body.

Another man, who was of noble birth, had been reduced to such poverty by his own unrestrained licentiousness, that he sold himself into this colony.[1] Here, when he had been recalled by one of Ours, to the right faith and the fruit of good living, he always anxiously doubted whether he had entered upon the safe road; and on one occasion, when he had intrusted himself to the sea in a small skiff, and a frightful storm arose, such as he had never seen, although he had often met with storms at sea, and certain shipwreck seemed already at hand, he earnestly prayed to God, that in confirmation of the faith he had lately received—if it was really true—he would ward off the impending danger. God heard his prayer, and turning the storm in another direction, confirmed his wavering mind with tranquil peace. Not long afterwards, this man was brought to the last extremity by a severe disease, and after taking all the sacraments, about an hour before his death asked his Catholic attendant to pray for him. It is probable that an evil angel presented himself to his sight; for almost at the very point of death he called the same attendant and said, with a cheerful voice: "Don't you see my good angel? behold him standing near to carry me away; I must depart;" and thus, happily (as we are permitted to hope) he breathed his last. Since his burial, a very bright light has often been seen at night around his tomb, even by Protestants.

Besides these, one of Ours, going out of the colony, found two Frenchmen, one of whom had been without the sacraments of the Catholic Church for three entire years; the other, who was already near death, having spent fifteen whole years among heretics, had lived just as they do. The Father aided the former with the sacraments and confirmed him in the Catholic faith as much as he could. The latter he restored to the Catholic Church, and, administering all the sacraments, prepared him for dying happily.

As for the Catholics, the attendance on the sacraments here is so large, that it is not greater among the Europeans, in proportion to the number of Catholics. The more ignorant have been catechised, and catechetical lectures have been delivered for the more advanced every Sunday; and

---

[1] That is, as an indented servant. See pp. 99, 100, *supra.*

on feast days sermons have been rarely neglected. The sick and the dying, who have been very numerous this year, and who dwelt far apart, we have assisted in every way, so that not even a single one has died without the sacraments. We have buried very many, and baptized various persons. And, although there are not wanting frequent occasions of dissension, yet none of any importance has arisen here in the last nine months, which we have not immediately allayed. By the blessing of God, we have this consolation, that no vices spring up among the new Catholics, although settlements of this kind are not usually supplied from the best class of men.

We bought off in Virginia two Catholics who had sold themselves into bondage, nor was the money ill-spent, for both are showing themselves good Christians: one, indeed, surpasses the ordinary standard. Some others have performed the same duty of charity, buying thence Catholic servants, who are very numerous in that country. For every year very many sell themselves thither into bondage, and living among men of the worst example and being destitute of all spiritual aid, they generally make shipwreck of their souls.

Several of the chief men by spiritual exercises have been formed by us to piety, a fruit not to be repented of. In the case of one, we adore the remarkable providence and mercy of God, which brought a man encompassed in the world with very many difficulties, and now at length living in Virginia, almost continually without any aid to his soul, to undertake these exercises, not long before his death; by which he profited so much that he determined on the very best mode of spending his life thenceforth. This design a severe sickness prevented, which he bore with the greatest patience, with a mind generally fixed on God; and at length having properly received all the sacraments, in the most peaceful manner, contrary to the usual course of his life, which had been so full of troubles and disquietudes, renders back his soul to his Creator.

A noble matron also has died, who, coming with the first settlers into the colony, with more than woman's courage bore all difficulties and inconveniences. She was given to much prayer, and most anxious for the salvation of her neighbors—a perfect example of right management as well in her self as in her domestic concerns—she was fond of our society while living, and a benefactor to it when dying—of blessed memory with all, for her notable examples, especially of charity to the sick, as well as of other virtues.

From the Annual Letter of 1639.

There are in this mission four priests and one coadjutor. All are in places far distant—doubtless, because they expect thus to obtain an earlier acquaintance with the barbarian language, and propagate more widely the sacred faith of the Gospel. Father John Brock, the Superior, with a coadjutor brother, remains in the plantation of Metapannayen, which was given us by Maquacomen,[1] the King of Patuxent, and is a sort of storehouse of this mission, whence most of our bodily supplies are obtained. Father Philip Fisher[2] lives in the principal town of the colony, to which the name of St. Mary's is given. Father John Gravener[3] lives in Kent Island, sixty miles distant. Father Andrew White is distant still farther, one hundred and twenty miles, to wit: at Kittamaquund, the metropolis of Pascatoa,[4] having lived in the palace with the Emperor himself of the place, whom they call the Tayac, from the month of June, 1639.

The cause of the father's going there was on this wise. He had bestowed much labor and time for the conversion of the King of Patuxent, which indeed was prayed for by all, both on account of the recollection of kindness received, for he had given to the society, as has been said, a farm; and because he was said to be very powerful among the barbarians, on account of his reputation for wisdom and his influence. And now, such had been the beginnings, the desired event was shortly expected; for some of the people of the king had connected themselves with the fold of Christ; and he himself appeared abundantly instructed in the first principles of the faith, when lo! unhappy man, he first begins to procrasti-

---

[1] This gift or grant led to controversy between the Proprietary and the missionaries as to their respective rights. See pp. 116, 117, *supra*.

[2] *Alias*, Father Thomas Copley.

[3] *Alias*, Father John Altham.

[4] Pascataway.

nate, then by degrees to grow indifferent, and lastly, in an open manner, to break off altogether from the design he had commenced. Nor this only, but he also gave indications, not to be misunderstood, of a mind entirely alienated from the whole colony. The Governor, after prudently sounding, determined, by the advice of his friends, that the father should be recalled from the hospitality of the King, lest, unexpectedly, the barbarian should give some example of his perfidy and cruelty against an innocent man; or indeed lest, this hostage, as it were, being left with the King, he himself might be hindered from being able to revenge injuries, if at any time the Patuxent should discover himself an enemy.

When rulers and kings are spoken of, let no one in his mind form an august idea of men, such as of the different princes in Europe. For these Indian kings, though they have absolute power of life and death over their people, and in certain prerogatives of honor and wealth excel others, nevertheless in personal appearances are scarcely anything removed from the multitude. The only peculiarity by which you can distinguish a chief from the common people is some badge; either a collar made of a rude jewel, or a belt, or a cloak, oftentimes ornamented with shells in circular rows. Their kingdoms are generally circumscribed by the narrow confines of a single village and the adjacent country; though the Tayac has a much more extensive dominion, stretching about one hundred and thirty miles, to whose empire also other inferior chieftains are subject.

To him therefore, the salvation of Maquacomen being despaired of, Father Andrew betook himself, and being treated by him very kindly at the first interview, so attached the man to him, that he was afterwards held by him in the greatest love and veneration; of which thing this is the strongest proof, that he was unwilling that the Father should use any other hospitality than that of his palace. Nor was the queen inferior to her husband in benevolence to their guest, for with her own hands, (which thing the wife of our treasurer also does willingly) she is accustomed to prepare meat for him and bake bread, with no less care than labor.

The cause of this remarkable affection for the Father, is to be referred to two dreams which he had, unless you may deem it proper to honor them with another name. One dream appeared to the mind of Uwanno, the brother-german of the Emperor, who reigned before him, and whom he slew. For in his sleep he appeared to see Father White and Father Gravener before him, and moreover to hear a voice admonishing him, "Finally these are the men, who from their soul loved him with all his tribe, and had brought with them those blessings, by which he could be happy, if he desired it." Hence so lively an impression of these unknown men remained in his mind, that even at the first sight, he recognized them when coming to him, whom afterwards he embraced with remarkable affection. He was accustomed also to call Father White his parent, to whose instruction also he wished to give up for seven years his son, who was very dear to him, as the whole tribe is very fond of children, and seldom let them go from their embrace. The other dream, which he is accustomed to relate in frequent conversations, occurred to the Tayac as he slept, to wit: That his father, deceased some time before, appeared to be present before his eyes, accompanied by a god of a dim color, whom he worshipped, and who was beseeching him that he would not desert him. At a short distance stood, accompanied by a most hideous god, one Snow, an obstinate heretic from England; and finally, in another direction, the Governor of the colony and Father White appeared, a god also being his companion, but much more beautiful, who excelled the unstained snow in whiteness, seeming gently to beckon the Emperor to him. From that time, he treated both the Governor and the Father with the greatest affection.

Not long after the coming of Father White to his court, the Tayac was in danger from a severe disease; and when forty conjurers had in vain tried every remedy, the Father, by permission of the sick man, administered medicine, to wit: a certain powder of known efficacy mixed with holy water, and took care the day after, by the assistance of the boy, whom he had with him, to open one of his veins for bloodletting. After this, the sick man began daily to grow better, and not long after became altogether well. Restored from the disease entirely, of himself he resolved as soon as possible to be initiated in the Christian rites; nor himself only, but his wife also and two daughters—for as yet he has no male offspring. Father White is now diligently engaged in their instruction; nor do they slothfully receive the heavenly doctrine, for by the light of heaven poured upon them, they have long since found out the errors of their former life. The Emperor has exchanged the skins, with which he was heretofore clothed, for a garment made in our fashion; he makes also a little endeavor to learn our language.

Having put away his concubines from him, he lives content with one wife, that he may the more freely (as he says) have leisure to pray to God. He abstains from meat on the days in which it is forbidden by the Christian laws; and men that are heretics who do otherwise, he for that very reason thinks ought to be called bad Christians. He is greatly delighted with spiritual conversation, and indeed seems to esteem earthly wealth as nothing, in comparison with heavenly, as he once told the Governor, when explaining to him what great advantages from the English could be enjoyed by a mutual exchange of wares—"Verily, I consider these trifling when compared with this one advantage—that through their testimony I have arrived at the true knowledge of the one God, than which there is nothing greater, or which ought to be greater, in my wishes."

Not long since, when he held a convention of the empire, in a crowded assembly of the chiefs and a circle of the common people, Father White and some of the English being present, he publicly attested it was his determination, together with that of his wife and children, abjuring the superstition of the country, to take the part of Christ; for that no other true deity is anywhere else had than among the Christians, nor otherwise can the immortal soul of man be saved from death —but that stones and herbs, to which, through blindness of mind, he and they had hitherto given divine honors, are the humblest things created by the Almighty God for the use and relief of human life. Which being spoken, he spurned far away from him with his foot a stone which happened to be near. A murmur of applause from the people sufficiently indicated that they did not hear these things with unfavorable ears. But the greatest hope is, that when the family of the Emperor is purified by baptism, the conversion of the whole empire will speedily take place. In the meantime, we heartily thank God for so joyful a commencement of affairs, and are especially encouraged when we daily behold those idols to be the contempt of the natives, which were lately reckoned in the number of deities.

Another thing not unworthy of mention, the more inflamed the Emperor, long since enkindled with the desire of baptism. A certain Indian having slain an Englishman, on account of an injury, was found guilty of the homicide, and was also sentenced to death, at just the time when the Tayac, with Father White, was coming to the colony. We exhorted the miserable man, devoted to death, that by receiving solemnly the Christian sacraments he should provide for the salvation of his immortal soul. When in this thing he appeared to show himself not at all obdurate, we endeavored, as far as we could, by the power of speech, to move the mind of the man in some measure inclined to our advice. The pious Emperor perceived us to labor for language; wherefore, of his own accord, he added his assistance to accomplish the end. He not only did not refuse to perform the office of a faithful interpreter, conveying to the man the things, which he had received from Father White, to be impressed; but also of himself added some things so apposite and efficacious, that he was the admiration of those present, and at length drew over the Indian himself to the Catholic side; who, imbued with the necessary knowledge and washed in the sacred font, prepared himself for death, for the most part in the very way which was prescribed to him. And indeed he appeared to be possessed with so vehement a desire of seeing God, that you would have thought him almost too eager to have the execution hastened. A remarkable eagerness appeared in his countenance; he fortified himself by·the frequent and salutary sign of the cross; he often repeated submissively; and whatever things he did or said, did not seem feigned for show only, but to come from the inmost senses and recesses of the soul. When he came to the place of execution, he inquired, with cheerful countenance, if he was to sing at his departure;[1] and when answer was given, that rather by piously taking the holy names of the blessed Jesus and Mary he should propitiate them in his

[1] *Cf.* pp. 368, 369, *infra.*

last conflict, he cheerfully obeyed those who advised him, and almost at the same moment closed his life and pious voice, by the cord that stopped his breath. When dead, he was buried in our cemetery, in the most solemn manner, that even from this, the barbarians might understand, that although, execrating the crimes of malefactors, Christians may avenge them by merited punishment, nevertheless they hold their souls dear, and are easily reconciled to them, if they repent. And surely such an example of clemency and charity to the deceased, struck them so much the more forcibly, the more it differed from their customs—who indeed are accustomed to serve up their enemies, slain in the most cruel manner, to be feasted on by their friends.

No one, however, was more vehemently moved at the sight of the dying neophyte than the Tayac, who afterwards earnestly insisted that he too should receive the gift of baptism. But the thing being considered in council, it appeared that it would be for the greater glory of God, if it be deferred a little, until it could be performed with splendid display, in the greatest solemnity, and in the sight of his countrymen; his wife also, and his children coming to a participation of his joy and gladness.

The Emperor, at length, won over by the attentions of the Catholics, and greatly delighted with their prolonged hospitality, returned home, the same Father White being his attendant; whither as soon as he came, he gave command to his people to prepare the church by next Pentecost, the time appointed for the baptism. On that day, at Kittamaquund, the Governor and other distinguished men of the colony contemplate honoring, by their presence, and by whatever other means they can, the Christian sacraments and the second and better birth of the Tayac. May the merciful God cause this thing to turn out to the good of all—to his glory, to our reward, and to the salvation of the whole tribe.

Whoever shall contemplate in thought the whole earth, will perhaps nowhere find men more abject in appearance than these Indians; who nevertheless have souls (if you consider the ransom paid by Christ,) no less precious than the most cultivated Europeans. They are inclined indeed to vices, though not very many, in such darkness of ignorance, such barbarism, and in so unrestrained and wandering a mode of life; nevertheless in their disposition they are docile, nor will you perceive in them, except rarely, the passions of the mind transported in an extraordinary manner. They are most patient of troubles, and easily endure contumely and injuries, if they do not involve danger of life. Idols they have few or none, to whose worship they are greatly addicted; nor are there any priests or mystae, to whom the administration of sacrifices appertains by appointment; though there are not wanting those who interpret superstitions, and sell them to the people; but even these are commonly not at all numerous. They acknowledge one God of heaven; notwithstanding, they distrust that they know in what way he is to be worshipped, in what way to be honored; from which it happens that they give willing ear to those that teach this knowledge. They rarely think of the immortality of the soul, or of the things that are to be after death. If at any time they meet a teacher clearly explaining these things, they show themselves very attentive as well as docile, and by and by are seriously turned to think of their souls, so as to be ready to obtain those things, which, they perceive, conduce to the salvation of the same. They are readily swayed by reason, nor do they withhold their assent obstinately from the truth set forth in a credible manner. This natural disposition of the tribe, aided by the seasonable assistance of divine grace, gives us hope of a most desirable harvest hereafter, and animates us in the highest degree to continue our labors in this vineyard. And the same ought to be an incitement to all those who in future, by the will of God, may come hither to us for supply or assistance.

To the hope of the Indian harvest, are to be added also no mean fruits reaped from the colony and its inhabitants, to whom, on the principal festival days of the year, sermons are preached, and the expositions of the catechism given on the Lord's day. Not only Catholics come in crowds, but also very many heretics—not without the reward of our labors; for this year twelve in all, wearied of former errors, have returned to favor with God and the Church. Our people cease not daily to engage in their divine employment, and to dispense the sacraments to those that come, as often as circumstances demand. In fine, to those in health, to the sick, to the afflicted and the dying, we strive to be in season for counsel, for relief, and assistance of every kind whatsoever.

College of Liège, etc.

From the Annual Letter of 1640.

In this mission this year we have been four priests and one coadjutor. We stated last year what hope we had conceived of converting the Tayac, or the Emperor, as they call him, of Pascatoa. From that time, such is the kindness of God, the event has not disappointed the expectation; for he has joined our faith, some others also being brought over with him; and on the 5th of July, 1640, when he was sufficiently instructed in the mysteries of the faith, in a solemn manner he received the sacramental waters in a little chapel, which, for that purpose and for divine worship, he had erected out of bark, after the manner of the Indians. At the same time the queen, with an infant at the breast, and another of the principal men, whom he especially admitted to his counsels, together with his little son, were regenerated in the baptismal font. To the Emperor, who was called Chitomachon[1] before, was given the name of Charles; to his wife that of Mary. The others, in receiving the Christian faith, had Christian names allotted to them. The Governor was present at the ceremony, together with his secretary and many others; nor was anything wanting in display which our means could supply.

In the afternoon, the Tayac and his queen were united in matrimony in the Christian manner; then a great holy cross was erected, in carrying which to its destined place the king, governor, secretary, and others, lent their shoulders and hands; two of Ours in the meantime chanting before them the litany in honor of the Blessed Virgin. And not long after, Father Andrew White and Father John Gravener had to bear their own crosses by no means light; for Father White, in performing the ceremonies of the sacred rite of baptism, which were somewhat long, had contracted a fever and became dangerously sick with chills; and though he grew better of that illness, he again suffered a relapse, which held him even till the

---

[1] Kittamaquund. This was the name also of the principal settlement or town of the tribe. See p. 124, *supra*.

winter. But Father Gravener was so deprived of the use of his feet, that he could not even put a foot to the ground. Nevertheless he became well, though afterwards, affected with an abcess, he was carried off in the space of a few days, upon the 5th of November.

When famine prevailed among the Indians, on account of the excessive drought of the past summer, that we might not appear to neglect their bodies, for the care of whose souls we had made so great a voyage, though corn was sold at a great price, nevertheless we considered it necessary to relieve their want of bread by assisting them. Amidst these cares, intent also on settling the affairs of the mission, we passed the greater part of the winter.

On the 15th of February we came to Pascatoa, not without the great gratulation and joy of the inhabitants, who indeed seem well inclined to receive the Christian faith. Not long after, the King brought his daughter, seven years old, (whom he loves with great affection,) to be educated among the English at St. Mary's, and, when she shall well understand the Christian mysteries, to be washed in the sacred font of baptism. His counsellor, also, of whom we have spoken above, desiring the goodness of God, which he had experienced in his own case, to be brought also to his people, has nothing more earnest in his prayers, than that his wife and children may be brought to the waters of salvation; which most proper desire, after suitable instruction, by the favor of God, shall be gratified.

The King also of the Anacostans, whose territory is not far distant, has expressed a desire that one of Ours should sojourn with him; from which it is plainly evident that a harvest will by no means be wanting to Ours, on which they may bestow labor with advantage; but rather it is to be feared that there will not be laborers for gathering so abundant a harvest. There are also other villages lying near, which, I doubt not, would run promptly and joyfully to the light of gospel truth, if any one would impart to them the word of eternal life. But it is not right for Ours here to be too anxious for bringing the others to the truth, lest they may seem to abandon prematurely our present tender flock. Nor need those who are sent for assisting them fear lest the means of life be wanting, since He who clothes the lilies and feeds the fowls of the air will not suffer those, who are laboring to extend His kingdom, to be destitute of necessary sustenance.

To Father Philip Fisher, who now resides in the colony of St. Mary, nothing could have happened more agreeable, than to labor in the Indian harvest, if he had been permitted by his own people, who could not do without his services. His reward, however, has been correspondent to his will; for while those five of whom we have spoken above, among the Indians, are cleansed by the water of baptism, as many at the same time by his active industry are brought back from heretical depravity into the bosom of the Church. The Catholics who live in the colony are not inferior in piety to those who live in other countries; but in urbanity of manners, according to the judgment of those who have visited the other colonies, are considered far superior to them. Everywhere the hope of harvest has dawned; and while each one of us is anxious by his own efforts to help now these, now those, various things happen worthy of recital—of which, (others being omitted for purpose of avoiding prolixity,) two of the most prominent shall be stated here, in one of which the divine mercy was manifest, in the other the divine justice.

On the day, upon which a certain man was about to abjure heresy, and expiate the sins of his past life by confession, a flame having caught in the interior part of his house during his absence, running up the door-post, had burst out at the top; when he had perceived the thing, for he was not far distant, he suddenly called to a neighbor, but finds no assistance; he runs then to another, when he finds only two who will go with him; and although all this time the fire was burning, and the house was built of dry logs, nevertheless relief arrived before any great injury had happened. Some feared lest by this unexpected occurrence he might be deterred from conversion. It happened far otherwise however; for his house being almost uninjured, he thence drew the conclusion that God was propitious to him and approved his design by a manifest token. Wherefore, uniting a great reformation in morals with the faith he professed, he now sheds abroad the very sweet savor of a good example upon all who are acquainted with him.

The other man, though he had felt some internal drawings of God, and had for some time made use of means which seemed to lead toward conversion, yet on a certain day determined to cast aside all such thoughts, and go back to the customary paths of his earlier life. In the time when he meditated better thoughts he had obtained prayer-beads for himself; but afterwards, having changed his mind, he was accustomed to smoke them in his pipe with tobacco, after grinding them to powder, often boasting that he was eating up his "Ave Marias"; for so he called the beads by telling of which the salutation of the angel is recited. But the divine vengeance did not let the wicked crime go long unpunished; for scarcely a year having passed, on the returning vigil of the day on which he had abandoned his purpose of embracing the Catholic faith, a more sacrilegious playfulness possessed him, as was noticed by his companions. Therefore, in the afternoon, when he had betaken himself to the river for the purpose of swimming, scarcely had he touched the water when a huge fish having suddenly seized the wicked man, before he could retreat to the bank, tore away, at a bite, a large portion of his thigh, by the pain of which most merited laceration, the unhappy wretch was in a short time hurried away from the living—the divine justice bringing it about that he, who a little while before boasted that he had eaten up his "Ave Maria beads," should see his own flesh devoured, even while he was yet living.

College of the English at Liège, etc.

A Narrative derived from the Letters of Ours, out of Maryland, [1642].

In the mission of Maryland for the year 1642, just elapsed, we have had only three companions and those three priests, one of whom too was confined by sickness of three months' duration. This was Father Roger Rigby. The other two were Father Philip Fisher, superior of the mission, and Father Andrew White, who separated themselves in different places for the purpose of collecting more fruit. The superior, Father Philip, remained for the most part at St. Mary's, the chief town of the colony, in order that he might take care of the

English, who live there in greater numbers, and also of the
Indians not living far distant, as well as those going and
coming backwards and forwards. Father Andrew betook
himself to his former station at Pascataway; but Father Roger
went to a new residence, which in the vulgar idiom they call
Patuxen, where he could learn the more easily the Indian language, and so better instruct and strengthen in the faith certain neophytes, and scatter more widely along the bank of
that great river the seed of faith.

The following was in substance the fruit of their labors.

Father Andrew suffered no little inconvenience, from a
hard-hearted and troublesome sea-captain of New England,
whom he had engaged for the purpose of taking him and his
effects, from whom he was in fear a little while after, not
without cause, that he would either be cast into the sea, or be
carried with his property to New England, to the Puritan
Calvinists—that is, the very dregs of all Calvinist heresy.
Silently committing the thing to God, at length in safety he
reached Potomac—which in the vernacular is called Patomake
—in which harbor, when they had cast anchor, the ship stuck
so fast, bound by a great quantity of ice, that for the space of
seventeen days it could not be moved. Walking on the ice,
as if on land, the Father departed for the town; and when the
ice was broken up, the ship, driven and jammed by the force
and violence of the ice, sunk, the cargo however being in a
great measure recovered.

By this misfortune the Father was detained longer in his
visit, to wit, seven weeks; for he found it necessary to bring
another ship from St. Mary's. But the spiritual advantage
of souls readily compensated for that delay; for during that
time was added to the Church the ruler of that little village,
with the other principal men of its inhabitants, who received
the faith of Christ and baptism. Besides these, also another,
with many of his friends; a third likewise, with his wife, his
son, and a friend; a fourth, in like manner, with another of
no ignoble standing among his people. By their example, the
people are prepared to receive the faith, whenever we shall
have leisure to instruct them by catechism.

Not long after, the young Empress (as they call her) of
Pascataway was baptized in the town of St. Mary's and is

being educated there, and is now a proficient in the English language. Almost at the same time most of the town called Portobacco[1] received the faith with baptism; which town, as it is situated on the river Pamac,[2] (the inhabitants call it Pamake,) almost in the centre of the Indians, and so more convenient for excursions in all directions, we have determined to make our residence; and the more so, because we fear that we may be compelled to abandon Pascataway, on account of its proximity to the Sesquesehanni, which nation is the most savage and warlike of these regions, and hostile to the Christians. An attack having been recently made on a place of ours, they slew the men whom we had there, and carried away the goods, to our great loss. And unless they be restrained by force of arms, which we little expect from the counsels of the English, who disagree among themselves, we shall not be safe there.

Wherefore, we have to be content with excursions, many of which we have made this year in ascending the river, which they call Patuxen. Out of these this fruit has arisen, namely the conversion of the young queen of that place, namely of the town having the same name with the river there, and her mother; also of the young queen of Portobacco; of the wife and two sons of the great Tayac, as they call him—that is the Emperor, who died last year; and of one hundred and thirty others besides. The following is our manner of making an excursion. We are carried in a pinnace or galley, to wit: the Father, the interpreter, and a servant—for we use an interpreter, as will be stated hereafter. Two of them propel the boat with oars, when the wind is adverse or fails; the third steers with the helm. We take with us a little chest of bread, butter, cheese, corn, cut and dried before it is ripe, beans and a little flour—another chest, also, for carrying bottles, one of which contains wine for religious purposes, six others holy water for the purpose of baptism; a box with the

---

[1] Now known as Port Tobacco. The name is said to come from the Indian words Potu-bago, meaning *tobacco-leaves* (Maryland Historical Society, *Fund Publication* no. 7, supplement, p. 44).

[2] Now called Port Tobacco Creek. From filling up of the channel, vessels of even moderate draft can now (1910) come up only to within four miles of the town.

sacred vessels, and a slab as an altar for the sacred function; and another casket full of trifles, which we give the Indians to conciliate their affection—such as little bells, combs, knives, fish-hooks, needles, thread and other things of this kind. We have, besides, a little tent, when we are obliged to lie out in the open air, which is frequently the case; also a larger one, which is adapted to keep out the rain. The servants also bring other things, which are necessary for hunting, and preparing for food whatever they have taken in hunting.

In our excursions we endeavor, as much as we can, to reach by evening some English house, or Indian village, but if not, we land and to the Father falls the care of mooring the boat fast to the shore, then of collecting wood and making a fire, while in the meantime the two others go to hunt—so that if they take anything it may be prepared. But if not, having refreshed ourselves with our provisions, we lie down by the fire and sleep. If fear of rain threatens, we erect our hut and cover it with a larger mat spread over; and, praise be to God, we enjoy this humble fare and hard couch with a not less joyful mind, than more luxurious provisions in Europe, with this present comfort that God now imparts to us a foretaste of what he will give to those who labor faithfully in this life, and mitigates all hardships with a degree of pleasantness; especially because His Divine Majesty appears to be present with us, in an extraordinary manner. For, considering that the difficulty of this language is so great, that none of us can yet converse with the Indians without an interpreter (though Father Rigby has made a little progress, so that he hopes he will be able by a short time to converse with them upon things of ordinary importance, and to instruct them as far as may be necessary for admission to baptism; for he has composed a short catechism, by the aid of an interpreter), these things, I say, being considered, it appears miraculous that we have been able to effect anything with them; especially when we have no interpreter except a young man who is not himself so well acquainted with their language but that he sometimes excites their laughter; so that for a time we seemed almost to despair in mind, but by patience we are succeeding, and in a gradual way are bringing them over to what we desire.

It has also pleased the Divine Goodness, by the virtue of

His Holy Cross, to effect something beyond mere human power. The circumstances are these: a certain Indian, called an Ana- costian, from his country, but now a Christian, whilst he was making his way with others through a wood, fell behind his companions a little, when some savages of the tribe of the Susquesehanni, which I have mentioned before, attacked him suddenly from an ambuscade, and with a strong and light spear of locust wood, (from which they make their bows), with an oblong iron point, pierced him through from the right side to the left, at a hand's breadth below the armpit near the heart itself with a wound two fingers broad at each side. From the effect of this when the man had suddenly fallen, his ene- mies fly with the utmost precipitation; but his friends who had gone on before, recalled by the sudden noise and shout, return and carry the man from the land to the boat, which was not far distant, and thence to his home at Pascataway, and leave him speechless and out of his senses. The occur- rence being reported to Father White, who by chance was but a short distance away, he hastened to him the following morn- ing, and found the man before the doors, lying on a mat before the fire and enclosed by a circle of his tribe—not indeed alto- gether speechless, or out of his senses, as the day before, but expecting the most certain death almost every moment, and with a mournful voice joining in the song with his friends that stood around, as is the custom in the case of the more dis- tinguished of these men, when they are thought to be certainly about to die. But some of his friends were Christians, and their song, which, musically indeed, but with plaintive inflec- tion of tone, they modulated, was, "May he live, oh God! if it so please thee;" and they repeated it again and again, until the Father attempted to address the dying man, who imme- diately knew the Father, and showed him his wounds. The Father pitied him exceedingly; but since he saw the danger to be most imminent, omitting other things he briefly runs over the principal articles of faith; and repentance of his sins being excited, he received his confession; then elevating his soul with hope and confidence in God, he recited the gospel which is appointed to be read for the sick, as also the Lauretan litanies of the Blessed Virgin,[1] and told him to commend him-

---

[1] Litanies of the Virgin, originally used at the Holy House of Loretto.

self to her most holy intercessions, and to call unceasingly upon the most sacred name of Jesus. Then the Father, applying the sacred relics of the Most Holy Cross, which he carried in a casket hung to his neck, but had now taken off, to the wound on each side, before his departure (for it was necessary to depart, for the purpose of administering baptism to an aged Indian, who was considered about to die before the morrow) directed the bystanders, when he should breathe his last, to carry him to the chapel for the purpose of burial.

It was now noon when the Father departed; and the following day, at the same hour, when by chance he was borne along in his boat, he saw two Indians propelling a boat with oars towards him; and when they had come alongside, one of them put his foot into the boat, in which the Father was sitting. Whilst he gazed on the man with fixed eyes, being in doubt, for in a measure he recognized by his features who he was, but in part recollected in what state he had left him the day before, the man, on a sudden, having thrown open his cloak, and having disclosed the cicatrices of the wounds, or rather a red spot on each side, as a trace of the wound, immediately removed all doubt from him. Moreover, in language of great exultation he exclaims that he is entirely well, nor from the hour at which the Father had left yesterday had he ceased to invoke the most holy name of Jesus, to whom he attributed his recovered health. All who were in the boat with the Father, taking cognizance of the thing both by seeing and hearing, breaking forth into praise of God and thanksgiving, were greatly rejoiced and confirmed in the faith at this miracle.

But the Father advising the man that, always mindful of so great and manifest a blessing, he should return thanks, and persevere to treat that holy name and most holy cross, with love and reverence, dismisses the same from him. Then the man, returning to his own boat together with the other, boldly propelled it with the oar, which he could not have done, unless he had been of sound and entire strength.

This is about the sum of the labor and fruit for this year; one thing, however, remains not altogether to be omitted, though to be touched upon lightly, to wit, that occasion of suffering has not been wanting from those, from whom rather it was natural to expect aid and protection; who, too intent upon their own affairs, have not feared to violate the immunities of the Church, by using their endeavors, that laws of this kind formerly passed in England and unjustly observed there, may obtain like force here, to wit: that it shall not be lawful for any person or community, even ecclesiastical, in any wise, even by gift, to acquire or possess any land, unless the permission of the civil magistrate first be obtained.[1] When Ours declared this to be repugnant to the laws of the Church, two priests were sent from England to teach the contrary. But the reverse of what was expected happened; for our reasons being heard, and the thing itself being more clearly understood, they easily fell in with our opinion, and most of the laity. This I add by way of conclusion, that two other fathers have recently come to us from England, to our great comfort, after an unpleasant voyage of fourteen weeks, whereas it is not generally more than six or eight. But of these and their labors and their fruit, if God grant it, we will speak elsewhere. We hope indeed that it will be abundant, which we may predict from their present zeal and the unanimity of their minds, since that is the most certain sign of the abiding of Him with us, who is in the completest degree one, and the beginning of all unity.

From the Annual Letter of 1654

This year Father Francis Fitzherbert, destined for Maryland, at the first intimation of our superior, without a single companion, with singular magnanimity and alacrity of mind, entered upon an arduous expedition, and a laborious and long journey among unknown men, dissimilar in morals and religion. Nor during his whole journey was there wanting a harvest abundant according to his deserts, from his confidence in God and his patience. Four ships sailed together from England, which a fearful storm overtook, when carried beyond the Western Isles,[2] and the ship in which the Father was carried, the violent waves so shattered, that, springing a leak by the continued violence of the sea, it almost filled its hold. But in carrying away and exhausting the water, the men, four

---

[1] In reference to this controversy see pp. 116, 117, supra.   [2] Azores.

at a time, not only of the ship's crew but of the passengers, every one in his turn, sweated at the great pump in ceaseless labor, day and night.

Wherefore, having changed their course, their intention was to make sail towards the island, which the English call Barbados; but it could be accomplished by no art, by no labor; then the design was, having abandoned the ship and its freight, to commit themselves to the long boat. But the sea, swelling with adverse winds, and the huge mountainous waves, forbade. Many a form of death presenting itself to the minds of all, the habit of terror, now grown familiar, had almost excluded the fear of death. The tempest lasted two months in all, whence the opinion arose, that it was not raised by the violence of the sea or atmosphere, but was occasioned by the malevolence of witches. Forthwith they seize a little old woman suspected of sorcery; and after examining her with the strictest scrutiny, guilty or not guilty, they slay her, suspected of this very heinous sin. The corpse, and whatever belonged to her, they cast into the sea.[1] But the winds did not thus remit their violence, or the raging sea its threatenings. To the troubles of the storm, sickness was added, which having spread to almost every person, carried off not a few. Nevertheless, the Father remained untouched by all the contagion, and unharmed, except that in working and exercising at the pump too laboriously, he contracted a slight fever of a few days' continuance. Having passed through multiplied dangers, at length, by the favor of God, the ship, contrary to the expectation of all, reached the port of Maryland.

From the Annual Letter of 1655 and 1656

In Maryland, during this year and the next preceding, Ours have escaped grievous dangers, but have had to contend with great difficulties and straits, and have suffered many unpleasant things as well from enemies as from our own people. The English who inhabit Virginia made an attack on the colonists, themselves Englishmen too; and safety being guaranteed on certain conditions, received indeed the Governor of Mary-

[1] See p. 117, *supra*, and *Archives of Maryland*, III. 306.

land,[1] with many others, in surrender.   But in treacherous violation of the conditions, four of the captives, and three of them Catholics, out of extreme hatred of our religion were pierced with leaden balls.[2]   Rushing into our houses, they demanded for death the impostors, as they called them, intending inevitable slaughter to those who should be caught.   But the Fathers, by the protection of God, unknown to them, were carried from before their faces in a little boat; their books, furniture, and whatever was in the house, fell a prey to the robbers.   With almost the entire loss of their property, private and domestic, together with great peril of life, they were secretly carried into Virginia; and in the greatest want of necessaries, scarcely and with difficulty do they sustain life.   They live in a mean hut, low and depressed, not much unlike a cistern, or even a tomb, in which that great defender of the faith, St. Athanasius, lay concealed for many years.   To their other miseries this inconvenience was added, that whatever comfort or aid this year, under name of stipend, from pious men in England, was destined for them, had been lost, the ship being intercepted in which it was carried.   But nothing affects them more than that there is not a supply of wine, which is sufficient to perform the sacred mysteries of the altar.   They have no servant, either for domestic use, or for directing their way through unknown and suspected places, or even to row and steer the boat, if at any time there is need.   Often, over spacious and vast rivers, one of them, alone and unaccompanied, passes and repasses long distances, with no other pilot directing his course than Divine Providence.   Even though the enemy should depart and they should return to Maryland, the things which they have already suffered from their people, and the disadvantages which still threaten are not much more tolerable.[3]

---

[1] William Stone.   [2] See p. 305, *infra*.

[3] The occurrences here described, and the expulsion of the Jesuit missionaries, occurred during the sway of the Commissioners appointed by Parliament, by whom the government of the Proprietary was temporarily overthrown. (See pp. 169, 206, *infra*.)   In 1658, when the supreme authority had become vested in Oliver Cromwell as Lord Protector, the authority of Lord Baltimore was restored, and thereupon the Jesuit missionaries returned to their fields of labor.

From the Annual Letter of 1681

The Maryland mission flourishes; the seed which our Fathers sowed there is growing up into a copious crop and promises an abundant harvest hereafter. Four years ago they opened, in the midst of barbarism, a school of humane letters, conducted by two of them, and the youths born there, unusually devoted to letters, are making good progress. This new-born school has sent to St. Omer two students, who are surpassed in intelligence by few Europeans and strive for the palm with the foremost of their class. Hence we infer that these lands, undeservedly called barbarous, are most prolific, not alone of gold and silver and other products of the earth, but also of men made for virtue and the higher education. Two have been sent thither this year to aid those who are laboring in that most ample vineyard of the Lord.

All this year there has been a great contention about property. The enemies of the Society have enviously spread the report that it possessed immense wealth, almost enough to sustain an army, thus turning to the injury of the Society the very beneficence of our Fathers, who to those who have had recourse to them have administered the desired aid promptly, and in proportion to their slender resources generously; and yet it is certain that those who speak thus are either deceived or deceiving, for whatever Ours possess in the island [1] would hardly suffice to support a hundred. And if we take account of what perishes through the ignorance of those in charge of it, of what is lost through the avarice of rustics [2] withholding the annual revenues, of what is spent on lawyers that the estate itself be not filched away, it suffices for far fewer, unless they aid themselves by their own labor. The rest is adequately supplied by the charity of the faithful, for whom we labor strenuously. Much has been brought into jeopardy and preserved with difficulty; some things have been lost. Yet we trust in the goodness of God and the piety of the Catholics that, while we sow spiritual seed, we shall reap carnal things in abundance, and that to those who seek the kingdom of God the other things

---

[1] At that time Europeans not minutely informed were prone to assume that any American ("West Indian") colony was an island. See p. 301, *infra.*

[2] Tenant farmers.

shall be added. Meanwhile having modest and frugal living and proper clothing, we are contented therewith.

In the mean time hearty thanks are to be rendered to the Divine mercy for the occasions whereby it calls into exercise our faith and virtue, and for the singular fortitude from on high with which it indues our Fathers, to bear all things readily and joyfully for Christ. They have taken joyfully the spoiling of their goods, knowing that they have a better and enduring substance. They had trial of mockings and scourgings, yea, moreover of bonds and imprisonment; they were stoned, they were sawn asunder,[1] were tempted, were slain with the halter; they wandered about destitute, tormented, afflicted. Yet, such is the mercy of God, he has not suffered us to be tempted above that we are able to bear, but with the temptation has also made a way to escape, that we may be able to bear it. In Him is placed our assured hope, that He that hath begun this good work will Himself finish it.

[1] The statements as to being sawn asunder and slain with the halter are not to be taken literally, the phrases being borrowed from Hebrews xi. 36, 37. The actual grievances, however real, were not due to those in authority, but were the result rather of lawless violence.

LETTER OF GOVERNOR LEONARD CALVERT TO LORD BALTIMORE, 1638

INTRODUCTION

THE letter of Leonard Calvert, Lieutenant-Governor of Maryland, to his brother the Lord Proprietary, dated April 25, 1638, contains a graphic account of the reduction of Kent Island to obedience, the inhabitants of which, instigated by William Claiborne, had continued during the four years which had elapsed since the founding of the Colony to refuse submission to the authority of Lord Baltimore.

Palmer's Island, mentioned in the narrative as being occupied and fortified by Thomas Smith and others from Kent Island, lies near the head of Chesapeake Bay, within the mouth of the Susquehanna River, and therefore commands the entrance to what was then a great waterway for trade, conducted in canoes, with the Indians. The island is well within the borders of Maryland, and is now generally known as Watson's Island. William Claiborne, who sought to control this trade independently of Lord Baltimore's rights under the charter of Maryland, was the agent of, and in some enterprises a profit-sharer with, the mercantile house of Cloberry and Company, of London. When this firm was informed of Lord Baltimore's authority and of Claiborne's resistance thereto, they revoked his agency, and appointed as his successor George Evelin, with power of attorney to act for them. But so greatly were the inhabitants under the influence of Claiborne that Evelin seems to have been unable to assert his authority until Governor Calvert entered upon the island with an armed force and made prisoners of Thomas Smith and John Butler, who were Claiborne's principal agents, the latter being his brother-in-law. This being done, and a general amnesty offered to all

147

the other inhabitants who should within twenty-four hours submit themselves to the authority of the Lord Proprietary, they with one accord accepted the offer, and gladly received grants of the land which they occupied, to which previously they had no pretence of title.

In this letter Governor Calvert asks his brother to send over, signed in advance, the draft of an act, to be submitted to the Assembly, "censuring" Butler for piracy as Smith had been. The reference here made appears to be the only record extant of the seizure of goods by Butler from a boat belonging to those at St. Mary's. This formal accusation against Butler the Governor wished to have, to hold over his head as a means of securing loyalty and good behavior on his part for the future.

The charge of piracy against Smith, for which he was tried and condemned to death, arose in this wise:

In 1635, a pinnace belonging to the Kent Island station[1] was seized by the Maryland officers for trading without a licence from the proprietary government. Claiborne retaliated by sending out a vessel, the *Cockatrice*, under the command of Ratcliffe Warren,[2] with orders to seize any vessels belonging to St. Mary's. To meet this move, and to maintain his authority, Governor Calvert despatched two pinnaces, the *St. Helen* and the *St. Margaret*, Captain Thomas Cornwaleys being in command. Meeting on April 23, 1635, with Claiborne's vessel in the Pocomoke River, an engagement followed, in which one Marylander was killed and several wounded, while on the other side Lieutenant Warren and two of his men were killed and their boat captured.

On the 10th of May following, there was another conflict in the same river, this time Thomas Smith being in command of Claiborne's vessel. There appears to have been bloodshed

[1] *Calvert Papers*, I. 141, 145 (Maryland Historical Society, *Fund Publication* no. 28).

[2] Bozman, *History of Maryland*, II. 34, 35.

upon this occasion also, and for this occurrence the charge
of piracy was laid against Smith, for which he was arrested,
tried and convicted three years later.[1]

The latter part of the letter is interesting from its personal character, and the account it contains of Governor
Calvert's efforts to send to his brother specimens of the native
birds and animals of America, and to obtain for him Indian
matting, which appears to have been desired as a novelty both
for domestic use and for gifts to friends.

C. C. H.

[1] *Archives of Maryland*, I. 16, 17.   The original manuscript is in the possession of the Maryland Historical Association, by which it was published in
1889 in *Calvert Papers* no. 1 (*Fund Pub.* no. 28).

LETTER OF GOVERNOR LEONARD CALVERT TO LORD BALTIMORE, 1638 [1]

Good Brother: I have endeavored this last winter to bring the Inhabitants of the Ile of Kent[2] willingly to submit themselves to your governement and to incourage them thereunto I wrote unto them a letter in November, where amongst other motives I used to perswade them, I promised to free them from all question of any former contempts they had committed against you, so that they would from thence forward desist from the like and submit themselves to the governmen.t and to shew them greater favor I gave them the choice to name whom they would of the Inhabitants of the Ileand to be theire commaunder; but one Jhon Butler Cleybornes brother in law and one Tho: Smith an agent of Cleybornes upon Kent was of such power amongst them that they perswaded them still to continue in theire former contumacie. Upon notice given me hereof, I presently appointed Cap.t Evelin[3] Commander of the Ileand w.ch formerly I purposely omitted because he was had in a generall dislike amongst them, him they contemned and committed many Insolencies against; wherefore findeing all faire meanes I could use to be in vaine, and that no way but compulsion was left, I gathered togeather about twenty musketteers out of the Colony of S.t Maries and appointing the command of them to Cap.t Cornewallis[4] whome I tooke

---

[1] The original manuscript is endorsed as follows: "25 Aprill 1638. My Bro: Leonard to me. from Virginea. the taking of the Ile of Kent. Palmers Iland. what number of people and catle upon them. Portobacke. Cedar, redd-bird, matts and Lyon."

[2] For a brief statement of the grounds of controversy between Lord Baltimore and William Claiborne concerning Kent Island, see p. 50, *supra.*

[3] Robert Evelin had been appointed by Cloberry and Company of London their attorney in the room of Claiborne, who had been their former agent and representative for trading with the Indians.

[4] One of the commissioners for the colonization of Maryland (see p. 16, *supra*) and for many years the chief military officer of the province.

as my assistant wth. me, I sat saile from S^t. Maries towards Kent
about the latter end of November, intending to apprehend
Smith and Butler if I could, and by the example of theire
punishm^t. to reduce the rest to obedience, but it beeing then
farre in the winter, the windes were so cross and the weather
so fowle in the bay, that after I had remayned a week upon
the water I was forct to returne back and deferre that expedition untill some fitter tyme. Two months affter in the beginning of ffebruarie I was given to understand that the Indians at the head of the bay, called the Sasquahannoughs,
intended in the spring following to make warre upon us at
S^t. Maries pretending revenge for our assisting of our neighbors Indians against them two yeares before (wch we never
did though they will needs thinck so) and that they were incouraged much against us by Thomas Smith who had transplanted himselfe wth other English from the Ile of Kent the
last summer to an Ileand at the head of the bay fower miles
below the falls called Palmers Ileand[1] and understanding likewise that they had planted and fortified themselves there by
directions from Capt Cleybourne wth intent to live there independent of you (because they supposed it out of the limits of
your Province) and that the s^d Smith and Mr Botler whom
I have formerly mentioned was then preparing to carrie a
farther supply from Kent both of men and necessaries to the
s^d Ileand; I thought it expedient to stop theire proceedings
in the beginnings, and for that purpose haveing advised w^{th}
the councell about the busines I sat forth from St Maries for the
Ile of Kent wth thirtie choice musketteers takeing Capt. Cornewalleis and Capt: Evelin in my company. To Capt. Cornew:[2]
I appointed the command of those Soldiers I carried wth me,
and afterward arriving at the s^d Ileand I landed wth my company a little before sunne rise, at the southermost end thereof
where Capt Cleybornes howse is seated w^{th}in a small ffort of
Pallysadoes, but findeing the gate towards the sea at my
comeing fast barred in the inside one of my company beeing
acquainted wth the place quickly fownd passage in at an other
gate and commeing to the gate wch I was at opened unto me,

---

[1] So called from the name of the original grantee. Afterward variously
known by the names of subsequent occupants, and now, generally, as Watson's
Island.   [2] Cornewallis.

so that I was arrived and entered the fort wthout notice taken
by any of the Ileand wch. I did desire, the easilier to apprehend Boteler and Smith the cheife incenduaries of the former
seditions and mutinies upon the Ileand, before they should be
able to make head against me, and understanding that Boteler
and Smith were not then at the fort but at theire severall plantations I sent to all the lodgeings in the fort and caused all the
persons that were fownd in them to be brought unto me thereby to prevent theire giving untymely notice unto Boteler and
Smith of my commeing, and takeing them all alongst wth.
me I marched wth. my company from thence wth. what speed
I could towards Botelers dwelling called the great thicket
some five miles from the fort and appointed my Pinnass to
meet me at an other Place called Craford, and makeing a stand
about halfe a mile short of the place, I sent my Ensigne one
M^r. Clerck (that came once wth M^r. Copley from England) wth.
tenne musketteires to Butler to acquaint him that I was come
upon the Ileand to settle the governement thereof and commaund his present repaire unto me at Craford two miles distant from thence, wch. the Ensigne accordingly did and brought
Boteler unto me before I removed from where he left me.
After I had thus possessed myselfe of him I sent my Serjeant
one Robert Vaugham wth. six musketteires to Thomas Smiths
who lived at a place called beaver neck right against Boteler
on the other side of a Creeck wth. like commands as I had
formerly given for Boteler, and then marching forward wth.
your Ensigne displayed to Craford by the tyme I was come
thither Smith was brought unto me where haveing both the
cheife delinquents against you I first charged them wth theire
crimes and afterward committed them Prisoners aboard the
Pinnass. I came in and appointed a gard over them, after I
caused a proclamation to be made of a generall pardon to all
other the Inhabitants of the Ileand excepting Boteler and
Smith for all former contempts against you that should wthin
fower and twenty howers after the proclaiming of the same
come in and submit themselves to your governement whereupon wthin the time appointed the whole Ileand came in
and submitted themselves. Haveing received theire submission, I exorted them to a faithfull continuance of the same,
and encouraged them thereto by assureing them how ready

you would be alwayes upon theire deserts to condescend to any thing for theire goods. Afterward I gave order for the carrieing of Boteler and Smith to St Maries in the Pinnass I came in, and wth them sent most of the Soldiers as a gard upon them commaunding them to be delivered into the custody of the sheriffe at St Maries untill my returne and my Pinnass to returne to the Ileand to me, where till my Pinnasses returne I held a court and heard and determined diverse causes between the Inhabitants. At the end of the s^d court I assembled all the Inhabitants to make choise of theire delegates to be present for them at a generall assembly then held at St Maries for the makeing of Lawes wch they accordingly did, and before my departure from them I gave them to understand that every man that held or desired to hold any land in the Ileand, it was necessarie they should take pattents of it under the seale of the Province as holding it of you wch they were all very desireous of, so that some tyme this summer I promised to come to the Ileand and bring Mr Lewger wth me to survay and lay out theire lands for them and then to pass grants unto them of it, reserveing onely such rents and services to you as the law of the Province should appoint. There is upon the Ileand about one hundred and twentie men able to beare armes as neer as I could gather; of the women and children I can make no estimate. In conclusion appointing the command of the Ileand to three of them, vist: to Mr Robert Philpot as commaunder and William Cox and Tho: Allen joynt commissioners wth him I departed for St Maries, where after my arrivall I called a grand inquest upon Smith who fownd a bill against him for Pyracie, whereupon he was arraigned before the assembly and by them condemned to suffer death and forfeit, as by a particular act for that purpose assented unto by the whole howse and sent unto you, you will perceive;[1] I have omitted as yet to call Mr Boteler to his tryall, because I am in hopes by shewing favor unto him to make him a good member, but I have not as yet released him, though I have taken him out of the sheriffes custody into my owne howse where I intend to have him remayne untill I have made farther experience of his disposition and if I can win him to a good inclination to your Service, I shall thinck him fittest to take

---

[1] *Archives of Maryland*, I. 16, 17.

the commaund of the Ile of Kent; for those others wch have now that charge from me are very unable for it, nor is there better to be fownd upon the Ileand, but least (Boteler demeaning himselfe otherwise then well and that I should finde cause to thinck him fitter to be punished then pardoned) there should want meanes to give him condigne punishment for all his former offences, I desire you would send over an act the next yeare wth your assent thereto, to be proposed to an assembly in Maryland for theire assent censureing Boteler as Smith was for Pyracie wch he committed at the head of the bay neer Palmers Ileand in the yeare 1635 upon a Pinnasse belonging to St Maries by takeing and a great quantitie of trucking commodities from Jhon Tomkins and serjeant Robert Vaughan who had the charge of her and togeather wth the s^d Pinnass and goodes carried the s^d Tomkins and Vaughan prisoners to Kent.   Smith hath solicited you I suppose by his letters for his pardon but I shall desire you that you would leave it to me to do as I shall finde him to deserve; whereby (if it be possible he should be the better for it) it will take better effect wth him when he shall continue at my mercie under whose eye he is.   Palmers Ileand beeing already seated and fortifyed and a good stock of cattle to the number of thirteen head put upon it, I thought not good to supplant but understanding there were five men inhabiting it servants to Capt Cleyborne and formerly under the command of Smith I sent serjeant Robert Vaugham and two others wth him from St Maries to set downe there and to the sd: Vaugham gave the commaund of all the rest, and by reason Capt Cleyborne hath been attainted of ffelony in the last assembly at St Maries by particular act and sentenced to forfeit all his estate in the Province[1] I gave Vaugham authoritie to take the servants and other goodes and chattles belonging to Cleyborne upon the Ileand into his charge, and to have them forth commeing when they shall be demaunded of him togeather wth what profitt shall be made by the serjeants labors.   I am informed that upon occasion of discourse given before Sr Jhon Harvey Mr Kempe and Mr Hawley[2] by Mr Boteler whether Palmers Ile

---

[1] *Archives of Maryland*, I. 23.

[2] Jerome Hawley, one of the commissioners for the original settlement of Maryland.   See p. 16, *supra*.

were w^th^in the Province of Maryland or no Mr Hawley did so
weackly defend your title to it that Boteler grew more confident of proceeding in planting it for his Brother Cleyborne and
I have some reason to thinck that Mr Hawley did willingly let
your title fall for some designe sake of his owne upon trade
wth the Sasquahannoughs wch he might conceive better hopes
to advance by its depenice on Virginia then on Maryland. for
when I sat in counsell at St Maries about the expedition I
made to Kent to stop the proceedings of that designe of Boteler and Smiths planting it, he earnestly diswaded it by suggesting all the reasons he could to make your title doubtfull
to it the Ileand and then how unlawfull an act it would be to
hinder theire planting it, and though it was made appeare that
theire seating there was most dangerous to the Colony at S.^t^
Maries by reason that they had incouraged the Indians to set
upon us and might hereafter furnish them wth gunns to our
further harme if we should suffer them to proceed, whereas
otherwise Boteler and Smith beeing removed we might hope
to make a peace wth those Indians yet it seemed some designe
he had upon theire setting downe there was so deare unto him
that he preferred it before the safetie of all us and his owne
family beeing included in the daunger, and would needs have
perswaded it to be in Virginia though the express words of
your pattent limits the Province to the northward where New
England ends but it is apparent that the Iland is w^th^in your
Province for the line of fortie by Smiths map[1] by wch the
Lords Refferies[2] lade out the bonds[3] lyeth right over the first
falls and this Ileand is fowre miles to the sowtherd below those
falls as I can witnes for I was there the last summer and observed it. I beleeve the faire promises wch he made you in
England when you procured the preferm.^t^ he hath in Virginia
how usefull he would prove to your Colony by it, will never
be performed by him for nothing moveth him but his owne
ends and those he intendeth wholly to remove from Maryland
and place them in Virginia, and intendeth shortly to remove
his wife and family thither. I am sorry it was your ill fortune to be a meanes of so much good to him who is to ingrate-

---

[1] See in *Narratives of Early Virginia*, opposite p. 76, the reproduction of
Captain John Smith's map of Virginia, 1612, on which "Smiths falls" appear
just south of 40° N. lat.   [2] Referees.   [3] Bounds.

full for it, for he disclaimes that he ever sought your help or
had any from you towards his preferm.ᵗ for he thincketh you
did not so much as know he pretended to the place he hath
nor that you knew he had it untill a long tyme after it was
passed unto him, thus Cap.ᵗ Cornewallis telleth me hath heard
him say, and he is of such greevance unto the Governor and
Secretarie of Virginia that they promise to themselves nothing but ruine by his draweing all the perquisites of theire two
places from them, and do therefore wonder that you would be
the meanes of procureing such a place for him.   They do both
intend by theire letters to solicite your help for the removeing
him and it were well for both Colonies that he were, for he
can not have less power, then too much in that Colony wᶜʰ (by
impoverishing Sᵣ Jhon Harvey and draweing from him and
the secretarie the execution of all the cheife services wᶜʰ the
Kings proffitts and the peoples estates hath dependencie on
he will bring unto himselfe; so that Maryland wherein it shall
have occasion to use Virginia is like shortly to seeck for it
onely to him where there is nothing to be hoped for but what
is unserviceable to his owne ends and nothing scapeth his
designmt though it be never so much beyond his reach to
compass.

    The body of lawes you sent over by Mᵣ Lewger[1] I endeav-
ored to have had passed by the assembly at Maryland but
could not effect it, there was so many things unsuteable to
the peoples good and no way conduceing to your proffitt that
being they could not be exempted from others wᶜʰ they willingly would have passed they were desireous to suspend them
all.   The particular exceptions wᶜʰ were made against them
Mᵣ Lewger hath given you an account of in his dispatches to
you: others have been passed in the same assembly and now
sent unto you wᶜʰ I am perswaded will appear unto you to
provide both for your honor and proffitt as much as those
you sent us did.[2]   The trade wᵗʰ the Indians they wholly
exempted themselves from and leaft it to you, onely Capᵗ
Cornewallis I have promised should not want the most I could
say unto you to procure leave for him that he might rent
three twenty pownds shares in it yearely so long as he is

[1] John Lewger, secretary of the province.
[2] *Archives of Maryland*, I. 619.

a member of your Colony, wch I did as well to decline his
hindrance of passing the whole to you, as also to give him
incouragement for the many services he hath done you in the
Colony, for though it hath been his fortune and myne to have
had some differences formerly yet in many things I have had
his faithfull assistance for your service and in nothing more
then in the expedicion to Kent this last winter.

I would not wish you (now it is in your hands to dispose
of) to intrest too many sharers in it for that hath been hitherto the distruction both of the trade and the traders, for they
never agreeing to trade joyntly did by theire severall trade prevent on an others marcket and by over bidding the prise for
beaver dayly spoyled the trade whereas if it had been in one
hand, or in so many as would have joyned, it might have
made some profit to the adventurers but in the way it hath
been hitherto they that have used it hath reaped nothing
but losse, wherefore if you shall thinck good to let me have
any share in it I desire you would not interest any other besides Capt Cornewalleis, for there is none else in Maryland
that knoweth what belongeth to the trade and therefore are
not like to joyne in the wayes wch are most expedient for the
good of it. If you would let it out to us two for two or three
yeares, rent free, I am perswaded it would be brought to such
a state by the way we should bring it in that it would be farre
more profittable and certaine then ever it was for hereafter
or if you thinck good to use it all yourselfe and send over
truck for it I shalbe ready to do you the best service I can,
but you must cause boates and hands to be procured of your
owne here and not put yourselfe to hyer them for that will
eat you out of all your profitt if not your principall and you
must designe to place ffactories as soone as you can on shore
in some convenient places whereto the trade may be drawne
for the way of boating it though the boates be a mans owne
is very chargeable and uncertaine. I have delivered some
Tobaccoes to Mr Lewger but whether it be sufficient or too
much to ballance the accounts I am to passe I can not yet tell
for I have not had tyme since his commeing to make them up.
it is not for any profitt to myselfe that I have purposely delayed it (as I hope you will do me so much right as to beleeve)
but for want of Leisure from the publike services of the

Colony and the necessarie loockeing after some meanes of my owne subsistance wch is so difficult to compass here as it requireth much tyme and labor. I meane this summer to pass all manner of accounts that are between you and me unto Mr Lewger, for I have disposed of all my other businesses so, as I may have sufficient leisure to do it in. Mr Lewger is a very serviceable and diligent man in his secretaries place in Maryland, and a very faithfull and able assistant to me. The cedar you writt for by him I could not procure to send this yeare by reason there is very few to be fownd that are usefull tymber trees. Two I heard of farre up in Patuxent river, and two others upon popelyes[1] Iland in the bay nere to Kent, and the fraight and other charges for the shipping them will be so deer that I made a question whether you would thinck fitt to undergo it. It will stand in eight or tenne pownds a tunne fraight for England besides other charges of transporting it to shipping from where it is felled neither is there meanes in Maryland to transport it unless it might be split into clapboard, and whether it will not be made unserviceable to y^u by useing it so, I can not tell because I do not know the use you designe it for; by your next letters I pray informe me what you will have done in it. The matts wch you wrot for amounts to such a charge to be bought from the Indians that I had not sufficient meanes to purchase it. It is not lesse then fortie pownds worth of truck out of England will buy 350 yards of matt besides the charge of seecking them in twentie severall indian towns, for unless they be bespocken there is very few to be had but such as are not worth buyeing to give a freind, and besides for the use you intend them it is necessarie they should be all of one make otherwise they cannot flower a roome; and before I shall procure so many yards I must send all the Province over but if you desire to have them and will provide truck to buy the^m upon farther notice from you I will be speack them, to have them all in as few places as I can to avoid charge; I am sure my Brother Porttobacco[2] now Emperor of Paskattaway, will assist me in it as much as he can for he is much your freind and servant and hath expressed himselfe to me to be so and giveth y^u many thancks after his Indian fashion for your guift sent him by Mr Lewger. He hath wthin this two yeares stept

---

[1] Poplar Island.   [2] See above, pp. 126 and 136.

into the Empire of the Indians by killing his eldest brother, the old Emperor, and enjoyeth [it] yet wth peace through the good correspondencie he keepeth wth me wch aweth his Indians from offereing any harme unto him. I had procured a red bird and kept it a good while to have sent it to you but I had the ill fortune to loose it by the negligence of my servant who carelesly let it out of the cage. The beaver wch I sent to you the last yeares belongeth unto the account of the stock of Capt Humber brought over.

The Lyon I had for you is dead, if I can get an other I will and send it you. I have had no leisure all this last winter to Virginia to procure an act to be made by the generall assembly then held there for the secureing of your right in the trade wthin your precincts, and thought it to no purpose to recommend it to Mr Hawleys care after I had understood so much of him concerning Palmers Ileand. Against there next assembly wch will be at the returne of shipping next yeare I will provide a bill drawne as effectuall for that purpose as I can and endeavor what I may to get it passed.

I have sent you herewth a letter from Mr Robert Philpot of Kent (who hath at this present the commaund of the Ileand) to his ffather the keeper of hygh parcke,[1] I pray cause it to be delivered unto him and finde some occasion to commend his sonne unto him for his faire carriage here, as he doth deserve, for he came in at the first claime I made of the Ileanders submission to your Pattent, and incourage his ffather I pray what you can to supply him this yeare, for that I understand is the intent of his letter to him; I have writ unto you concerneing the deer you sent for in an other letter by it selfe sent herewth as you appointed me. Thus wth best love and service to my sister Baltimore and my other two sisters and my Brother Peasely I rest

Your most affectionate

ffrom Virginia   loveing Brother
this 25th of Aprill   LEONARD CALVERT
1638.

Capt Wintor remembreth his
service to you, I left him well
in Maryland.

[1] Hyde Park.

THE LORD BALTEMORE'S CASE, 1653

INTRODUCTION

AFTER the death of the King, Charles I., and the assumption by Parliament of all the functions of government in England, Lord Baltimore recognized the necessity of so constituting the government of Maryland, if he were to retain control of it, as to disarm the oft-repeated charge that it was "a hot-bed of popery." He therefore appointed as Lieutenant Governor, William Stone, a Protestant and friend of the Parliament, and reorganized the Council so that one-half the members were Protestants. He required in the form of oath prescribed for the Governor that he would engage to maintain religious liberty in the province, in accordance with the policy pursued from its founding, and that in making appointments to office, etc., he would not discriminate between persons on account of religious opinion, but "only as they were found faithful and well deserving."[1] About this time a considerable number of Puritans, availing of the broad liberty of conscience secured in Maryland, migrated thither from Virginia, where they had been harshly treated, and settled at a place assigned to them which they called Providence, but upon which the name of Annapolis was afterward bestowed. In 1694, under the administration of Sir Francis Nicholson, royal governor, the seat of government was transferred thither from St. Mary's, and it remains the capital of the state.

Governor Stone, having occasion to visit Virginia in 1651, designated as deputy governor during his absence his predecessor, Thomas Greene,[2] a Roman Catholic and royalist,

[1] *Archives of Maryland*, III. 210.

[2] Leonard Calvert died in 1647, and on his death-bed named Greene as his successor.

and a member of the Governor's Council. Greene took advantage of his brief authority to follow the example of Governor Berkeley in Virginia, and proclaimed Charles II. king, with rejoicings and a general pardon. Stone promptly returned and relieved Greene of his office, but the mischief had been done.

William Claiborne, whose watchful eye appears ever to have been upon Kent Island,[1] saw his opportunity. He had been an ardent royalist and a member of the Council of Virginia; but that did not prevent him from applying to Parliament for a commission to be issued to himself and others to reduce the colonies of Virginia and Maryland to obedience, pointing to the proclamation in each of the accession of Charles II. as evidence of their disaffected condition.

Meanwhile the royalists in Virginia had pointed out to the exiled heir to the throne that large numbers of Puritans, enemies to the Crown, were being received and harbored in Maryland, thus proving the disloyalty of Lord Baltimore to the royal cause. Charles was thereupon led to issue from his court on the island of Jersey a commission to Sir William Davenant as governor of Maryland, to supersede Lord Baltimore in authority, though not to deprive him of his rights as lord of the soil. Sir William was a poet; how efficient a governor he would have proved is unknown, as the vessel upon which he sailed got no further than the English Channel, where it was seized by a cruiser belonging to the Parliament. His mission to Maryland was thus quickly ended.

In this way Lord Baltimore was called upon to defend his charter from attack on both sides. Its annulment was the one thing desired by the members of the old Virginia Company, and title to Kent Island was what Claiborne sought. Each used the arguments they deemed best calculated to serve their purpose.

[1] For a brief statement of Claiborne's relations to Kent Island, see p. 50, supra.

The Lord Baltemore's Case, with the "Reasons of State" which follow, is of the nature of a brief in answer to the contentions of Claiborne and those associated with him. Appended to it as an exhibit is a copy of the commission issued to Sir William Davenant. These documents were printed in pamphlet form so as to be useful apparently in informing the public mind, as well as in presenting the case before the Council of State.

In the opening statement it is represented that the Council, being satisfied that Maryland was never in opposition to the Parliament, had caused the name of Maryland to be stricken out of the Instructions to the Commissioners, which was twice done, but by some mistake or other it was put in again. The commission was eventually issued (as the narrative shows) to apply to "all the Plantations in the Bay of Chesapeake." Maryland, therefore, while omitted by name, was included by geographical description. This "mistake" has been attributed to the ingenuity of Claiborne, who, being perfectly familiar with the country, relied successfully upon ignorance of American geography on the part of members of the Council. It is not evident, however, that he was in England at the time that this commission was issued. At all events he joined the other commissioners after their arrival in Virginia.

The commissioners appointed by Parliament overthrew Lord Baltimore's government, removed Governor Stone from office, and placed the control of affairs in the hands of men of their own selection from among the Puritans who had sought refuge in Maryland and settled at Providence. Lord Baltimore's authority was not restored without bloodshed, and not completely until 1658, after Cromwell had become Lord Protector. Then the government of the province was surrendered to Josias Fendall, whom Lord Baltimore had commissioned as Lieutenant Governor.

Copies of this pamphlet are very rare. The following text was copied from an original in the Lenox Library, New York. There is another copy of the original edition in the library of the Maryland Historical Society, from which a reprint was made in the *Maryland Historical Magazine*, vol. IV., no. 2 (June, 1909). The "Reasons of State concerning Maryland" are to be found in *Archives of Maryland*, III. 280.

C. C. H.

THE LORD BALTEMORE'S CASE, 1653

The Lord Baltemore's Case, Concerning the Province of Maryland, adjoyning to Virginia in America, With full and clear Answers to all material Objections, touching his Rights, Jurisdiction, and Proceedings there, And certaine Reasons of State, why the Parliament should not impeach the same. Unto which is also annexed, a true Copy of a Commission from the late King's Eldest Son, to Mr. William Davenant, to dispossess the Lord Baltemore of the said Province, because of his adherence to this Common-Wealth.
London, Printed in the Yeare, 1653.[1]

IN 1632 the Lord Baltemore had a Patent granted to him and his heirs, of the said Province of Maryland, with divers priviledges and jurisdictions for the Government thereof, the better to incourage him to settle a Colony of English there, whereby to prevent the Dutch and Swedes from incroaching any nearer to Virginia, Maryland being between Virginia, and the Dutch and Swedes Plantation on that Continent, and New-England beyond them, to the Northward.

The Lord Baltemore hereupon in 1633 sent two of his own brothers with above 200 people to begin and seat a Plantation there, wherein, and in the prosecution of the said Plantation, ever since, hee and his friends have disbursed above 40000 *l.* whereof 20000 *l.* at least, was out of his own purse, and his said two brothers died there in the prosecution thereof.

In Septem. 1651, when the Councell of State sent Commissioners from hence, to wit, Captaine Dennis, Captain Steg,[2] and Captain Curtes, to reduce Virginia to the obedience of the Parliament, Maryland was at first inserted in their Instructions to be reduced as wel as Virginia, but the Councel

---

[1] Title-page.   [2] Spelled *Stagge* in the commission.

being afterwards satisfied that that Plantation was never in opposition to the Parliament, that Captain Stone, the Lord Baltemore's Deputy there, was generally knowne to have been always zealously affected to the Parliament, and that divers of the Parliaments friends were, by the Lord Baltemore's speciall direction, received into Maryland, and well treated there, when they were fain to leave Virginia for their good affection to the Parliament; then the Councell thought it not fit at all to disturb that Plantation, and therefore caused Maryland to be struck out of the said Instructions, which was twice done, it being by some mistake or other put in a second time.

In this expedition to Virginia, Captain Dennis and Captain Stegg, the two chiefe Commissioners, were cast away, outward bound in the Admirall of that Fleet, which was sent from hence upon that service, and with them the Originall Commission for that service was lost.

But Cap. Curtes having a copy of the said Commission and Instructions with him in another ship, arrived safe in Virginia, and there being also nominated in the said Commission two other persons resident in Virginia, to wit, Cap. Bennet, and Cap. Cleyborn (known and declared enemies of the L. Baltemore's) they, together with Cap. Curtes, proceeded to the reducement of Virginia, which was effected accordingly upon Articles, among which one was; That the Virginians should injoy the antient bounds and limits of Virginia,[1] and that they should seek a Charter from the Parliament to that purpose.

In the reducement of Virginia, Captain Stone (the L. Baltemore's Deputy of Maryland) sent to the Commissioners at the first arrival of the Fleet in Virginia, to offer them all the assistance he could, and did actually assist them therein, with provision of victuall, and other necessaries, as will be testified (if need be) by Mr. Edward Gibbons Major-Generall of New-England,[2] and divers others who were then there, and eye-witnesses of it, and are now here.

Notwithstanding which, the said Commissioners, after

---

[1] The effect of this would have been to include Maryland within the bounds of Virginia.

[2] See Johnson's *Wonder-working Providence*, in this series, p. 64.

Virginia was reduced, went to Maryland, and upon pretence
of a certaine clause (which it seems was by some meanes or
other, put into their Instructions, after Maryland was struck
out as aforesaid) to wit, that they should reduce all the Plantations in the Bay of Chesapeack[1] to the obedience of the
Parliament, and some part of Maryland, where the L. Baltemore's chief Colony there is seated, being within that Bay, as
well as most of the Plantations of Virginia are; they required
Captaine Stone, and the rest of the Lord Baltemore's Officers
there, first to take the Ingagement, which they all readily
subscribed, and declared, that they did in all humility submit themselves to the Government of the Commonwealth of
England in chief under God; then the Commissioners required them to issue out Writs and Processe out of the L.
Baltemore's Courts there in the name of the Keepers of the
Liberty of England, and not in the name of the Lord Proprietary, as they were wont to doe, wherein they desired to be
excused; because they did not conceive the Parliament intended to divest the Lord Baltemore of his right there, and
that they understood out of England that the Councell of
State intended not that any alteration should be made in
Maryland. That the Kings name was never used heertofore
in the sayd Writs, but that they had alwayes been in the name
of the Lord Proprietary, according to the Priviledges of his
Patent,[2] ever since the beginning of that Plantation; that
the late Act in England for changing of the forms of Writts
declared only, that in such Writs and Process wherein the
Kings name was formerly used, the Keepers of the Liberty
of England, should for the future be put in stead thereof:
that the continuing of the Writs in the Lord Proprietaries
name, was essentiall to his Interest there, and that therefore
they could not without breach of trust, concur to any such
alteration; whereupon the Commissioners demanded of Captain Stone the Lord Baltemore's Commission to him, which
he delivered, and then without any other cause at all, they
removed the sayd Captain Stone, and the Lord Baltemore's
other Officers out of their Imployment there under him, and

---

[1] For the text of these instructions see pp. 206-208, infra, and *Archives of
Maryland*, III. 264. In the caption Virginia only is mentioned.

[2] See charter of Maryland, p. 105, *supra*.

appointed others to manage the government of that Plantation, till the pleasure of the Councell of State and Parliament should be further known therein; seized upon all the Records of the Place, and sent divers of them hither into England, all which they did without any opposition at all from Cap. Stone, or any other of the Lord Baltemore's Officers, in regard of their respect and reverence to the Commissioners of the Parliament.

The Colony of Virginia, not long after, sent one Colonell Mathews[1] hither into England to get their Articles confirmed by the Parliament, which were read in the House on the 31. August 1652. Upon the reading whereof a Petition of the Lord Baltimores, and of about twenty more considerable Protestant Adventurers and Planters to and in Maryland, who are known by divers Members of the House to have been well affected alwayes to the Parliament, and who signed the said Petition, was also read; whereby it was humbly desired that before the House passed that Article concerning the old limits of Virginia, the said Petitioners might be heard by their Councell, in regard Maryland was long since esteemed part of Virginia, and therefore they were concerned in that Article; and they further humbly desired in the sayd Petition, that the Lord Baltemore's Officers might be restored to their places in Maryland under him, and that the Petitioners might quietly enjoy the Priviledges of the sayd Patent of Maryland, upon confidence whereof, they had Adventured so much of their fortunes thither as aforesayd.

Whereupon divers Parchments under the Lord Baltemore's hand and seale, which were sent out of Maryland, by the sayd Capt. Bennet, and Capt. Cleyborn, were at that time produced to the House by a Member thereof, who it seems conceived that there would appear something in them, whereby the Lord Baltemore had forfeited his said Patent, or at least that his Authority in Maryland was not fit to be allowed of by the Parliament.

The House on the 31. August 1652[2] referred the sayd Article concerning the old Limits of Virginia, to the Committee of the Navy to consider what Patent was fit to be

---

[1] See Letter of Thomas Yong, pp. 59, 61, *supra.*
[2] *Commons Journals*, VII. 173.

granted to the Inhabitants of Virginia, and to hear all Parties, and consider of their particular Claims, and report the same, with their Opinions to the Parliament, and the sayd Parchments delivered in concerning Maryland, were also referred to the same Committee.

The Lord Baltemore accordingly made his claim before the said Committee, unto whom he delivered a true Copy of his said Patent, and desired therefore that the Patent which the Virginians were Suitors for, might not extend to any part of Maryland, it being made appear to the said Committee, that that Province had not been for these 20 years last past accounted any part of Virginia, and that the Virginians had neither possession of any part thereof, at the time of the making of the said Articles, nor for 20 years before, nor that the present Inhabitants of Virginia had ever at all any right unto it.[1]

Then, upon the suggestion of a Member of that Committee, certain Exceptions against the Lord Baltimores Patent, and his Proceedings thereupon in Maryland, were shortly after presented in writing to the said Committee, unto which the Lord Baltemore put in his Answer also in writing, which was read, and the Committee upon debate thereof (it seems) thought not fit to deliver any Opinion in the business, but Ordered, that the whole matter of fact should be stated by a Sub-Committee, and reported first to the said Grand Committee, and afterwards to the House.

The Exceptions aforesaid were many, but the substance of them are reduceable to these heads following, which are set down by way of Objections, with Answers to them.

1. *Object.* A pretended injury done to the Virginians by the said Patent, in regard Maryland was heretofore part of Virginia.

Answ. The present Inhabitants of Virginia had never any right to Maryland, no more then[2] to New-England, which was part of that Country heretofore called Virginia, as well as Maryland, but distinguished and seperated afterwards from it by a Patent as Maryland was. There was indeed a Patent

[1] No private titles to land within the area of Maryland had been created by the old Virginia Company, the charter of which had been annulled.
[2] Than.

heretofore granted by King James in the 7. yeare of his reign[1] of a great part of that northern Continent of America, which was then called Virginia, to divers Lords and Gentlemen here in England, who were by that Patent erected into a Corporation, by the name of the Virginia Company, in which tract of land granted to the said Company, that Country which is now called Maryland, was included, but that Patent was Legally evicted by a *Quoranto* in the then Kings Bench, in 21. year of the sayd King James,[2] 8. or 9. years before the Patent of Maryland was granted to the L. Baltemore; which Company or Corporation the Inhabitants of Virginia desire not now to revive, by vertue of their Articles abovementioned, but abhor the memory of it, in regard of the great oppression and slavery they lived in under it, when it was on foot, so as they never having had any Patent, right, or possession of the sayd Province of Maryland, there could be no injury done to them by the Lord Baltemore's sayd Patent, after the eviction of the sayd Virginia Companies Patent thereof. For it was as free in the late Kings power to grant any part of that Continent not possessed before by any Legall grant then in force from the Crown of England (which Maryland was not, at the time of the Lord Baltemore's Patent thereof) as it was for King James to grant the aforesaid Country to the said Virginia Company.

2. *Object.* A pretended wrong done by the Lord Baltemore to the above mentioned Capt. Cleyborn, in dispossessing him of an Island in the sayd Province, called the Isle of Kent.[3]

2. *Answer.* It was a business above 14. years since, upon a full hearing of both parties, then present, decided by the then Lords Commissioners for Forraign Plantations, against the sayd Capt. Cleyborn and his Partners, Mr. Maurice Thomson and others, and the sayd Capt. Cleyborn hath himselfe, also by divers Letters of his to the Lord Baltemore, acknowledged the great wrong he did him therein; which Letters were proved at the Committee of the Navy, and are now remayning with that

---

[1] The second Virginia charter, of May 23, 1609.

[2] While the writ of *quo warranto* against the Virginia Company was issued out of the King's Bench on November 4, 1623, in 21 Jac. I., judgment was not finally rendered till May 24, 1624, in his twenty-second year.

[3] For an explanation of this claim see p. 50, *supra.*

Committee: wherefore the Lord Baltemore humbly conceives, that against the sayd Capt. Cleyborns owne acknowledgement, and a Determination so long since of that business, and above 14 years quiet possession in the Lord Baltemore of the said Island, the Parliament will not think fit upon a private Controversie of *meum* and *tuum*, between him and the said Cleyborne, to impeach his Patent of the said Province, or his right to the said Island, but leave both parties to their legall remedy.

3. *Object.* That the said Patent constitutes an hereditary Monarchy in Maryland, which is supposed, by some, to be inconsistent with this Common-wealth.

3. *Answ.* The Jurisdiction and stile which the Lord Baltemore useth in Maryland, is no other then what is warranted by his Patent (as may appeare by his answer at the Committee of the Navy to the Exceptions above mentioned, and by perusall of the said Patent) and that is onely in the nature of a County Palatine,[1] subordinate, and dependent on the Supreame Authority of England; for by the Patent, the soveraign Dominion, Allegiance, the fift part of all Gold and Silver Oare which shall happen to be found there, and severall other Duties are referred to the late King, his Heires, and Successors, who are now the Parliament of this Common-wealth: and although it be true, that a Monarchicall Government here which should have any power over this Common-wealth, would not be consistent with it, yet certainly any Monarchical Government in forraign parts which is subordinate to, and dependent on, this Commonwealth, may be consistent with it, aswell as divers Kings under that famous Common-wealth of the Romans heretofore were, insomuch as they thought it convenient and fit to constitute divers Kings under them. All Lords of Mannors or Liberties here in England may, in some kinde, be aswell accounted Monarches within their severall Mannors and Liberties as the Lord Baltemore in Maryland; for Writs issue, at this day, in their names out of their Courts[2] within their respective Mannors and Liberties, and not in the name of the Keepers of the Libertie of England; Oathes of Fealty are taken to them by their Tenants, and they have

---

[1] See charter of Maryland, pp. 103, 111, *supra.*

[2] Manorial courts, namely, courts lest, also called "view of frank pledge," and courts baron. *Cf.* charter of Maryland, p. 111, *supra.*

great Royalties and Jurisdictions, some more than others, and
some as great in proportion, within their said Mannors and
Liberties, as the Lord Baltemore hath in Maryland, except the
power of making Lawes touching life and Estate, power of
pardoning, and some few others of lesser concernment, which
although they may not be convenient for any one man to have in
England, yet they are necessary for any (whether one man or a
Company) that undertakes a Plantation, in so remote and
wild a place as Mariland, to have them there; especially with
such limitations as are in the Lord Baltemore's Patent; to wit,
that the Laws be made with the consent of the Freemen of the
said Province, or the major part of them, or their Deputies,
and that they be consonant to reason, and be not repugnant
or contrary; but, as neare as conveniently may bee, agreeable to the Laws of England; which limitations the Lord
Baltemore hath not exceeded, as may appeare by his Answer
to the Committee of the Navy to the Exceptions above mentioned: and although it be not fit that any one Person should
have a negative Voyce here in the making of Lawes, yet
certainly, as no Company, so no single man, that is well in
his wits, will be so indiscreet, as to undertake a Plantation at
so vast an expence as the Lord Baltemore hath, if after all his
charge, pains, and hazards, which are infinite in such a businesse, such necessitous factious people as usually new Plantations consist of, for the most part, and went thither at his
charge, or by contract or agreement with him, should have
power to make Lawes to dispose of him, and all his estate there,
without his consent, and he be left without remedy: for before
the Supream Authority here, upon any appeale to it, will probably be at leisure from business of greater consequence, or
perhaps have convenient means to relieve him, he may be
ruined and destroyed: such chargeable and hazardous things
as Plantations are, will not be undertaken by any, whether it be
a Company or a single man, without as great incouragements
of priviledges as are in the Lo. Baltemore's Patent of Maryland; and if it be not any prejudice, as certainly it is not, but
advantagious to the interest and honor of this Common-
wealth, that an Englishman (although a Recusant, for the
Lord Baltemore knows of no Lawes here against Recusants
which reach into America) should possess some part of that

great Continent of America with the priviledges and jurisdictions aforesaid dependent on, and subordinate to it, then
the Indian Kings or Forreigners (as the Dutch and Swedes afore
mentioned) who have no dependency on it, as certainly it is,
then he hopes the Parliament will not thinke it inconsistent
with this Common-wealth, but just, that he should injoy the
Rights and Priviledges of his Patent, upon confidence whereof,
he and his friends have adventured the greatest part of their
fortunes for the honour of this Nation, as well as their own
particular advantage; especially seeing no other person hath
any wrong done him therein, for none are compelled to go to
Maryland, or to stay there, but know beforehand upon what
termes they are to be in that place; and the English Inhabitants of that Province are so well pleased with the Government
constituted there by the said Patent, as that, by generall consent of the Protestants, aswell as Roman Catholiques, it is
established by a Law[1] there, aswell as freedome of Conscience
and exercise of Religion within that Province is, to all that
profess to believe in Jesus Christ, as appears by the Laws of
that Province now in the hands of the said Committee of the
Navy, which makes it evident that a Petition lately read at
that Committee, with ten unknown hands to it, in the name
of the Inhabitants of Maryland, against the Lord Baltemore's
sayd Patent, is eyther wholly fictitious, or else signed by some
few obscure factious fellows, which is easie to bee procured by
any ill affected person, against any Government whatsoever.

4. *Object*. That the Lord Baltemore gave his assent to
certaine Lawes for Maryland in 1650, in one of which Lawes the
late King Charles is stiled the late high and mighty Prince
Charles the first of that name K. of England, etc. And in
another of the said Lawes it is Enacted, That the L. Baltemore
shall have 10*s*. a hogs-head for all Tobacco's ship't from Maryland in any Dutch Vessell, and bound for any other Port then
his Majesties, whereby some would infer, that hee did acknowledge a Charles the second to be King, etc. for that the word
first, in one Law, inferred a second, and by the word Majesty,
in the other Law, the Lord Baltemore must mean the late
Kings eldest son, for the late King Charles was dead, when the
Lord Baltemore assented to that Law, to wit, in August 1650.

[1] See the Act concerning Religion, pp. 269–273, *infra*.

4. *Answ.* To this is answered, that although those Lawes were assented unto by the Lord Baltemore in August 1650, yet it appears by his said Declaration of assent, that some of them were enacted in Maryland by the Assembly there, in April 1649, whereof that Law was one, whereinthose words, to wit, any other Ports then his Majesties, are inserted (as was proved to the said Committee of the Navy) at which time, the people in Maryland could not know of the late Kings death, which was but in January then next before; for in February, March, and April, ships usually return from those parts, and in September, October, and November, goe thither; so as the Assembly in Maryland could mean no body by that word Majesty, but the late King, and the L. Baltemore could have no other meaning but what the Assembly had, for he did but assent to what they had done, and was before enacted, as aforesaid: as to the other law, wherein those other words are inserted, to wit, the late high and mighty Prince Charles, the first of that name, etc. it was one of those Laws which were passed by the Assembly in Maryland, in April 1650, when the people there knew of the late Kings death; to wit, a year after the other law above-mentioned, with divers others, which were enacted in April, 1649, as aforesaid, though in the ingrossement of them all here, (when the Lord Baltemore gave his assent to them altogether in August, 1650,) it is written before it, because they were transposed here in such order, as the Lord Baltemore thought fit, according to the nature, and more or lesse importance of them, placing the Act concerning Religion first, etc. And as to those words, the first of that name, etc. the word first, doth not necessarily imply a second, as some infer upon it, no more then when the first born of thy sonnes were commanded to be given to God, did imply a second, which was performed, though there were never a second; the word first, hath relation to the time past, and not to the time to come; King James is stiled in History, James the first of that name, King, etc. though there were never a second of that name King of England, etc. and it is usually written and said, that a King died in the first yeer of his Raign, when he lived not to enter into a second, the like whereof may be made out by many other instances; and as the L. Baltemore is confident the Assembly in Maryland had no intention by those words,

Charles the first, etc. to infer a second King of that name, no more had he, in his assent to that Law, any such thought or meaning; and the comportment of him and his Officers in Maryland above-mentioned, towards the Parliament, and their friends, doth sufficiently confirme it.

Among other priviledges granted to the L. Baltemore, and the Inhabitants of Maryland, by his said Patent, one is, (by an expresse clause therein inserted) that the said Province should not from thence forward be, or be reputed any part of Virginia,[1] or bee dependent or subject to their Government in any thing, (although the Government of Virginia was then immediately in the Kings hands) but was, by the said Patent, (in express words) seperated from it, and so it hath been ever since, which was one of the chiefest incouragements, upon confidence whereof, the L. Baltemore, and others, adventured so great a part of their estates thither as aforesaid, for it was the priviledges and immunities, and not the land only, granted by the said Patent, which did chiefly induce the Lord Baltemore to make so great an Adventure, without which he would not certainly, upon the conditions of a common Planter, have disbursed any thing upon a Plantation in America: Wherefore he hopes the Parliament will not think it just, or fit, to deprive him, and the Inhabitants of Maryland of so important a priviledge, (which is their inheritance, and dearly purchased by them) by putting them now under the Government of Virginia, upon colour of any Articles agreed on, when the Virginians were declared enemies of this Commonwealth, and the rather, because even in point of policy also, (as is humbly conceived) for certain Reasons of State heerunto annexed, it will be more advantageous to the honour and interest of this Commonwealth, to keep those two Governments still divided, and to preserve and protect the Lord Baltemore's rights and priviledges aforesaid in Maryland, then to destroy either of them.

[1] See the charter, p. 111, *supra.*

Reasons of State, concerning Maryland in America.

1. First, It is much better to keep that Government still divided from Virginia (as it hath beene for these twenty yeares last past,) then to unite them; for, by that meanes, this Common-wealth will have the more power over both, by making one an Instrument (as occasion shall require) to keep the other in its due obedience to this Common-wealth.

2. Secondly, in case any defection should happen in either Colony (as lately was in Virginia) the other may be a place of refuge for such as shall continue faithfull to this Common-wealth, as Maryland lately was, upon that occasion, which it could not have beene, in case the Government of that place had been, at that time, united unto, or had had any dependence on Virginia.

3. Thirdly, it will cause an emulation in both, which of them shall give the better account of their proceedings to the Supreme Authority of this Common-wealth, on which they both depend, and also which of them shall give better satisfaction to the Planters and Adventurers of both.

4. Fourthly, the Lord Baltemore having an estate, and his residence in England, this Commonwealth will have a better assurance of the due obedience of that Plantation, and the Planters and Adventurers thither, of having right done unto them, in case the Government thereof have still a dependence on him, and he upon this Commonwealth, (as he had before on the late King) then if the Government of that place at so remote a distance, should be disposed of into other hands who had little or nothing here to be responsible for it, and whose interest and residence were wholly there.

5. Fifthly, by the continuance of his Interest in the Government thereof, this Commonwealth and the people there, are eased of the charge of a Deputy Governour; which he, at his own charges, maintains, the Inhabitants there being yet so poor, (and so like to be for many years) as they are not able to contribute any thing towards it.

6. Sixthly, if the L. Baltemore should, by this Common-wealth, be prejudiced in any of the rights or priviledges of his Patent of that Province, it would be a great discouragement to

others in forraign Plantations, upon any exigency, to adhere
to the interest of this Commonwealth, because it is notoriously
known, that, by his expresse direction, his Officers and the
people there, did adhere to the interest of this Commonwealth,
when all other English Plantations (except New-England)
declared against the Parliament, and at that time received
their friends in time of distresse, for which he was like divers
times to be deprived of his Interest there, by the Colony of
Virginia, and others, who had Commission from the late Kings
eldest Sonne for that purpose, as appears by a Commission
granted by him to Sir William Davenant,[1] the Original whereof
remaines with the Councell of State, and a true Copy thereof
is hereunto annexed.

*A true Copy of a Commission, from the late Kings eldest
Sonne, to Mr. William Davenant, concerning Mary-
land, the Originall whereof remains with the Councel of
State.*

CHARLES R.

Charles, by the Grace of God, King of England, Scotland,
France, and Ireland, Defender of the Faith, etc. To Our
Trusty and Well-beloved Sir William Davenant, Knight, and
to all others, to whom these presents shall come, greeting:
Whereas the Lord Baltemore, Proprietary of the Province and
Plantations of Maryland in America, doth visibly adhere to
the Rebells of England, and admit all kinde of Schismaticks,
and Sectaries, and other ill-affected persons into the said Plantations of Maryland, so that We have cause to apprehend very
great prejudice to Our Service thereby, and very great danger
to Our Plantations in Virginia, who have carried themselves
with so much Loyalty and Fidelity, to the King Our Father, of
blessed memory, and to Us; Know yee therefore, That Wee,
reposing speciall trust and confidence in the courage, conduct, loyalty, and good affection to Us, of you Sir William
Davenant, and for prevention of the danger and inconveniences
above-mentioned, doe by these presents, nominate, consti-

[1] Sir William Davenant, the royalist poet (1605–1668), appointed poet-
laureate in 1637.

tute, and appoint you Our Lieutenant Governour of the said Province, or Plantations of Maryland, with all Forts, Castles, Plantations, Ports, and other Strengths thereunto belonging; to have, hold, exercise, and enjoy the said place and command of Our Lieutenant Governour of Maryland, during Our pleasure, with all Rights, Priviledges, Profits, and Allowances any wayes appertaining, or belonging to the same: And although Wee intend not hereby to prejudice the right of the Proprietary in the Soyle, but have for Our Security, thought fit to intrust you, during these troubles;[1] Wee notwithstanding give you full Power and Authority to doe all things in the said Plantations, which shall bee necessary for Our Service, and for securing them in their Loyalty, and Obedience to Us, and prevention of all dangers that may arise from thence to Our Loyall Plantations of Virginia: Further, requiring and commanding you to hold due correspondence with Our Trusty and Well-beloved Sir William Berkley, Knight, Our Governour of the said Plantations of Virginia, and to comply with him in all things necessary for Our Service, and the mutuall good of both Plantations, requiring and commanding hereby all Officers, and Ministers, and all other Our Subjects whatsoever of the said Plantations of Maryland, to admit and receive you Our said Lieutenant Governour, according to this Our Commission, and to obey and pursue your Order in all things, according to the Authority Wee have given you; and likewise requiring and commanding Our Governour and Counsell of Virginia, and likewise all other Our loving Subjects of Virginia, to bee aiding and assisting to you, not onely to the settling and establishing of your Authority, as our Lieutenant Governour of Maryland, but also in all such helps and assistances, as may be necessary for your preservation there, and for the mutuall good of both Plantations, as aforesaid.

Given at Our Court in Jersey, the 16. day of February, 16⁴⁹⁄₅₀ in the second Yeare of Our Reigne.

[1] "This clause includes Soyle and all". (Marginal note in the printed original.)

VIRGINIA AND MARYLAND, OR THE LORD
BALTAMORE'S PRINTED CASE UNCASED
AND ANSWERED, 1655

INTRODUCTION

THE following pamphlet, which was published in London in 1655, is in form of answer to the narrative next preceding in this publication, *The Lord Baltemore's Case*, which had been printed two years before. But as the letter was in fact a defence or plea to the attacks that had been made upon the authority and administration of the proprietary government in the province of Maryland by the commissioners of Parliament, this paper may be regarded rather as a rejoinder than an answer.

It is to be noted that the date of this pamphlet is subsequent to the termination of the Parliament by which the commissioners were appointed for the reduction of the plantations within the Chesapeake Bay, and the assumption of the supreme power in England by Cromwell as Lord Protector. While the commissioners were declaring their acts to be done in the name of the Lord Protector, there is no evidence that they had been re-commissioned by him. In fact they seem to have apprehended that their authority in Maryland was abrogated, for on September 26, 1655, Cromwell was moved to write in answer to inquiry from them an explanation of a former letter, referred to as dated January 12 preceding, which he declared was merely intended to forbid any violence between Virginia and Maryland on the subject of their respective boundaries.[1]

---

[1] Thurloe's *State Papers*, IV. 55. Bozman's *History of Maryland*, II. 688 (appendix, no. LXXXVI). The text of the letter dated January 12, 1654/5, is contained in the pamphlet *Hammond vs. Heamans*, reprinted in the *Maryland Historical Magazine*, IV. 248.

The events which led to the conflict or battle at the Severn near Annapolis on March 25, 1655, are as follows: Under circumstances already noted,[1] the Council of State of the English Parliament on September 26, 1651, appointed Captain Robert Denis, Mr. Richard Bennett, Mr. Thomas Stagge, and Captain Claiborne commissioners "to reduce all the plantations within the Bay of Chesapeake to their due obedience to the parliament of the Commonwealth of England." Captain Denis and Mr. Stagge sailed from England on the ship *John*, of which the former was commander, and perished in the wreck of that vessel. It was provided, however, in the commission, that in the event of the death of Captain Denis his place should be taken by Captain Edmund Curtis, commander of the frigate *Guinea*. Captain Curtis arrived safely in Virginia with a duplicate copy of the commission. There he was joined by the other two commissioners, Bennett and Claiborne, the former one of the Puritans from Virginia who had sought and obtained sanctuary in Maryland, and the other the persistent claimant of Kent Island. The government of Virginia was promptly reorganized, Bennett being declared governor, and Claiborne a member of the Council and secretary, "next in authority to the governor."

Attention was then given to Maryland. Governor Stone, a Protestant, was willing enough to take the engagement of submission to the Commonwealth of England, but declined to issue writs, etc., otherwise than in the name of the Lord Proprietary, declaring that to do so would be a violation of his oath already given to the latter. He was therefore summarily removed from office together with Mr. Thomas Hatton the secretary, and the other members of the Council, and a new Council of six persons appointed in their place. This action was taken by Bennett, Curtis, and Claiborne, commissioners, by an instrument dated at St. Mary's, March 29, 1652, and signed

[1] See p. 165, *supra*.

by all three. This is the last we hear of Captain Curtis upon this service. Probably his engagements as a seafarer took him away from the colonies.

But the remaining commissioners soon found that they had made a mistake, and in response to "the desire of the inhabitants" reinstated Governor Stone and Secretary Hatton to their places on the Council and their former offices, Governor Stone to act "according to his former power, reserving and saving to himself as also to the aforesaid Mr. Thomas Hatton, Robert Brooke esqr. and Captain John Price their oaths made to the Lord Baltimore, Lord Proprietor of this Province until the pleasure of the State of England be further known." [1]

This action was taken by the commissioners Bennett and Claiborne under date of June 28, 1652, just three months after Governor Stone had been removed from office. The latter accepted his reinstatement at the hands of the commissioners and continued to issue writs, etc., in the name of the Lord Proprietary, as he might reasonably have understood that he was authorized to do by the express reservation of the oath previously taken by him to the Proprietary.

For this and other alleged acts in recognition of the Lord Proprietary's authority, Governor Stone and Council were again summarily removed by commissioners Bennett and Claiborne, and ten commissioners, of whom Leonard Strong was one, were appointed in their stead "for the well ordering, directing and governing the affairs of Maryland." This was done by an instrument dated at Patuxent, July 22, 1654, and issued "in the name of his Highness the Lord Protector of England, Scotland, Ireland and all the Dominions thereto belonging." Of the former Council, but one, Mr. Richard Preston, was included among the new commissioners, of whom William Fuller, one of the refugees from Virginia, was made chief with William Durand as secretary. To the latter Secretary Hatton was required to deliver the records of the province.

[1] *Archives of Maryland*, III. 275.

Meanwhile, Cromwell had very effectively dissolved the Long Parliament by military intervention on April 20, 1653, and the Barebones Parliament on December 12, and had assumed the supreme authority under the title of Lord Protector, which was proclaimed by Stone in Maryland May 6, 1654. Lord Baltimore appears to have held that upon the dissolution of the Parliament the authority of the commissioners appointed by it ceased, and as the Lord Protector had taken no action against his charter, he was reinstated in the enjoyment of all his former rights simply by the termination of the power of those by whom he had been deprived. He therefore instructed Governor Stone to assert his authority, by force if necessary.[1]

The government of Maryland was finally peaceably surrendered into the hands of Lord Baltimore in 1658, under the terms of an agreement entered into in England between him and Richard Bennett, one of the commissioners. Josias Fendall was appointed Lieutenant Governor of Maryland by the Lord Proprietary, and acted as his representative in consummating the agreement, publishing its terms, and recovering from the committee of government the great seal and other evidences of authority.[2]

This pamphlet and the one preceding were written in advocacy respectively of the opposite sides of a controversy. The possession of Maryland was the real issue in the case. It has been sought to point out in foot-notes where the zeal of controversy has gone to the extent of coloring facts or of so presenting them as to cause misapprehension.

The text here given has been collated with a copy of the original edition in the Harvard College Library. The pamphlet was reprinted in 1838 by Peter Force, in *Historical Tracts*, vol. II., no. 9.

C. C. H.

[1] *Archives of Maryland*, III. 298, 300.
[2] *Archives of Maryland*, III. 332, etc.

VIRGINIA AND MARYLAND, OR THE LORD BALTAMORE'S PRINTED CASE UNCASED AND ANSWERED, 1655

Virginia and Maryland, or The Lord Baltamore's printed CASE, uncased and answered. Shewing, the illegality of his Patent, and Usurpation of Royal Jurisdiction and Dominion there.

With, The Injustice and Tyranny practised in the Government, against the Laws and Liberties of the English Nation, and the just Right and Interest of the Adventurers and Planters.

Also, A short Relation of the Papists late Rebellion against the Government of his Highness the Lord Protector, to which they were reduced by the Parliaments Commissioners ; but since revolting, and by Lord Baltamore's instructions caused to assault the Protestants there in their Plantations, were by a far lesser number repulsed, some slain, and all the rest taken Prisoners.

To which is added, A brief Account of the Commissioners proceedings in the reducing of Maryland, with the Grounds and Reason thereof ; the Commission and Instructions by which they acted ; the Report of the Committee of the Navy, concerning that Province ; and some other Papers and Passages relating thereunto : together with the Copy of a Writing under the Lord Baltamore's Hand and Seal, 1644, discovering his Practices, with the King at Oxford against the Parliament, concerning the Londoners and others trading in Virginia.

For the oppression of the poor, for the sighing of the needy, now will I arise, saith the Lord, I will set him in safety, from him that puffeth at him. Psal. 12. 5.

London, printed and are to be sold at the Crown in Popes-head-Ally, and in Westminster Hall. 1655.[1]

[1] The title-page of the original.

IN the yeer 1607, divers preceding discoveries having confirmed an Opinion, That the Country of Virginia was fit for Plantation; It pleased God to affect the mindes of very many worthily disposed Noblemen, Gentlemen, and others to conceive it as a matter of great Religion and Honour, to undertake the work of perfecting a Christian Plantation in those parts. Whereupon King James was pleased to become the first Founder of this noble work, and by his Letters Patents from time to time renewed and enlarged, granted all ample Privileges and Immunities, both to those that managed in England, and those that went to inhabit there: which gave so great an encouragement that fifty Earls and Barons, three hundred and fifty Knights, and six hundred Gentlemen, and Merchants of primest rank became incorporated, and were originally named in the Letters Patents by the name of the Company of Virginia, being a greater union of Nobles and Commons, then ever concurred to such an undertaking. But nevertheless, partly by the natural difficulties incident to all new Plantations; but chiefly, through the unnatural and faulty impediments arising by the cross agitations of two powerful factions in the Company, the work went heavily on for the first twelve yeers, appearing desperate in the several ill successes thereof. And though afterward somewhat advanced and prosperous, yet in the yeer 1621[1] by the fatal blow of a Massacre, it was almost shattered to pieces, and brought to a very low and calamitous condition; which occasion the contrary faction presently took hold of, insomuch that they exceedingly slighted the action, and cared [ceased?] not to cast aspersions on the Country, and on the whole management of that affair. And then further strongly possessed and advised the then King, against the form of the Companies Government, as consisting of an excessive number of Councellours, and a confused Popularity, as being a Nurse of Parliamentary spirits, and obnoxious to Monarchical Government. Thereupon Order was made upon the eighth day of October, 1623,[2] at the Council-Table, whereby the Company were moved to give in their assents for surrendering their Patent, and altering their form of Government, and a new one proposed,

[1] March 22, 1621/2.
[2] Its text is in Brock, *Virginia Company*, II. 229-230.

wherein the Interests and Rights of all men should be preserved: which Order the Company not submitting unto, A *Quo Warranto* was directed for the calling in of their Patent, and an advantage taken upon their mispleading. The Patent was condemned in Trinity-Term following; but for many yeers after, not vacated upon the Record in the Office of the Rolls, whereby some that sought the overthrow of the Lord Baltamore's Patent for Maryland, in the beginning of the Parliament, 1640, took out the Virginia Patent again under the broad Seal of England: therefore thought by primest Lawyers now to be unquestionably in force, at least to point of interest; and that Patent of Maryland unconsistent and void.

Thus in brief was the late Company dissolved, and a Commission given to divers Lords and others, for present directing and ordering the affairs of Virginia; and that they should advise touching a better form of Government for advancing and establishing the Colony. Then issued also severall Proclamations, and several Orders from the Council-Table, with great assurances under the Broad Seal and privy Seal, that all men, with the Adventurers and Planters, should be assured, that their Rights and Interests should be conserved and enlarged, onely alteration in point of Government. But both that Commission and renewing of the Companies Charter expired, and all those Proceedings were delayed, by reason of the death of King James, which then suddenly ensued. The principal scope of that Commission was, that they should finde a better form of Government for the Countryes advancement, and therein was especially promised the conservation of every man's right; intentions worthy the wisdom and justice of so great a Prince. But nothing was done by those Commissioners touching either of those ends, nor by those by whose prosecutions these things hapened, who having attained their private ends of spleen and profit upon the changes and revolutions of ensuing times deserted the interest of the Colony, and left her weltring in her blood, unsupplied with Ammunition and Arms in the heat of a difficult war with the Indians: the burthen and charge whereof was onely undergone by the remaining Planters, who thus forsaken by their former friends, were constrained both to work and fight for their lives and subsistance; and thereby preserved the Col-

ony from desertion, and at last restored it by the blessing of
God to peace and plenty.

And then, about the yeer 1633, Lord Baltamore pretending, though not truely, the greatest part of the Country was
unplanted, procured that the aforesaid judgement so long
delayed, was entred, and obtained a Patent, for that part
now called Maryland, which he hath since held with a few
people and small Adventurers, debarring of those to whom it
belonged from planting of it; destroying and ruinating those
formerly seated under Virginia, at the Isle of Kent; and inter-
dicting Trade with the Indians for Furs, discovered and begun
by the Virginians, by direction and commission from the
King; which since by this means is enjoyed by the Dutch and
Swedes, with the profit of many thousand pounds yeerly;
which Trade had been solely in the English Nations hands,
had not the Lord Baltamore interdicted it, and seized all Vessels, and displanted their Plantations.[1]   And those Swedes
and Dutch do trade for great quantities of Guns Powder and
Shot with our Indians, to the total endangering this Colony,
if not timely prevented.   Such a ground-Work, had the Patent
of Maryland upon the Rights and Labours of others; and as
unreasonable and unjust have been the whole proceedings
and management of their Colony and Interests, at their first
arrival surprising and confiscating many Vessels with the
Goods of divers that they found trading with the Natives
under the commissions of Virginia, which they had enjoyed
neer thirty yeers.   And professing an establishment of the
Romish Religion onely,[2] they suppressed the poor Protestants

---

[1] Maryland comprises, not the "greatest part," but a small area only of the
land embraced in the original grant to the Virginia Company, the charter of
which had been abrogated. No grants of land had been made within its area.
The contention of Claiborne in respect to Kent Island is briefly discussed in the
Introduction to the Letter of Thomas Yong (p. 50, *supra*).   Trade within Maryland by Virginians without licence from Lord Baltimore had been forbidden by
order of the Lords Commissioners for Plantations April 4, 1638, and by proclamation of the Governor of Virginia October 4, 1638; *Archives of Maryland*, III.
72, 79. There were neither Dutch nor Swedes within the limits of Maryland at
the date of the charter or of the settlement of the province.

[2] The missions in Maryland were in charge of the Jesuit Fathers, but there
was never any establishment of the Roman Catholic Church in the province.
See Lord Baltimore's Instructions, p. 16, *supra*, and the Act concerning Religion,
pp. 269-273, *infra*.

among them, and carried on the whold frame of their Government in the Lord Proprietaries name; all their Proceedings, Judicature, Tryals and Warrants, in his name, Power and Dignity, and from him onely:[1] not the least mention of the Soveraign Authority of England in all their Government; to that purpose, forceably imposing Oaths, (judged illegal in a Report made by Committee of the Council of State, 1652,) to maintain his royal Jurisdictions, Prerogatives, and Dominions, as absolute Lord and Proprietary, to protect chiefly the Roman Catholick Religion in the free exercise thereof; and all done by yeerly Instructions from him out of England, as if he had been absolute Prince and King. By all which it is easily evident, that the Patent of Maryland was grounded upon no good foundation.

The King being mis-informed; when in nothing more deeply and directly, could the Honour and Justice of his Throne be concerned, then[2] in confirming and conserving the Interest of so great a conjunction of Nobles, Knights, Gentlemen and Merchants, who so piously and worthyly adventured their Moneys, and expended their Estates and Labours; whose Rights and Interests, though their Patent were called in, for the time, in point of Government, yet had received the most solemn Declarations and Assurances, under the Broad Seal and Privy Signet, Orders of Councels, Letters to the Colony, and by general Proclamations there and here.

That it were impious to think that either the then King or King James being rightly enformed, would ever have granted such a Patent as this of Maryland, it being neer two third parts of the better Territory of Virginia;[3] and as no way consistent with Equity, and the Honor and publick Faith of the Kingdom: so was no way agreeable (in the absolute and regal power assumed and executed by him) to the late Monarchical Government, or to the present Authority of the Commonwealth of England, under his Highness the Lord Protector, and most injurious to the Rights and Interests of the noble Adventurers and the painful indefatigable Planters, who had so long under God, conserved the Country from total ruine.

[1] See charter, pp. 105, 106, *et seq.*, *supra.*

[2] Than.

[3] See preceding page, note 1.

A short and successive Narration of most of the aforesaid vublick Assurances, follows viz.

1. By an Order of the Councel the eighth of October, 1623, before the *Quo Warranto* brought, to Arm the mindes of the Adventurers and Planters against any mistaken fear and apprehension, as if their Estates should receive prejudice.

2. And whereas the Lords of the Councel were enformed, that the intended change of the Government, had begot a general discouragement amongst the Adventurers: notwithstanding sundry other Declarations made at the Board, *Viva Voce*, and that former Act of Councel, their Lordships were pleased by an Order of the twentieth of October, 1623,[1] to declare again, that there was no other intention, but onely and meerly in reforming and change of the present Government; and that no man should receive any prejudice, but have his Estate fully and wholly confirmed; and if in any thing defective, better to be secured; which Order was sent over by their Lordships command, and published in Virginia for encouragement of the Planter.

3. King James was also pleased to express the same in his Commission to sundry of his own privy Councel, and other Commissioners for the time being, for the affairs of Virginia, July 5, 1624,[2] that his intention was to alter the Letters Patents, as to the form of Government; but with the preservation of the Interest of every Adventurer and Planter.

4. The like Declaration of the King's intentions was exprest in the Commission[3] then sent to Sir Francis Wiat and the Councel then appointed by his Majesty, to direct the Affairs and People in Virginia; and the like hath been inserted in all King Charles his Commissions, and of all the Governours of Virginia, that have been since that time to this present.

5. The said King Charles by his Proclamation May 13, 1625,[4] declared, That his aim was only to reduce the Gov-

---

[1] Text in Brock, *Virginia Company*, II. 234–235.

[2] July 15. Text in Hazard's *Historical Collections*, I. 183, and Rymer's *Foedera*, XVII. 609–613.

[3] August 26, 1624. Hazard, I. 189–192; Rymer, XVIII. 618.

[4] Hazard, I. 203–205; Rymer, XVIII. 72.

ernment into such a right course, as might best agree with the form held in the rest of his Monarchy, and not intended to impeach the interest of any Adventurer or Planter in Virginia.

6. The Lords of the Councel by their Letter dated the 24 of October, 1625,[1] declare to the Colony, That the Kings pleasure was to preserve every man's particular right, and the Planters to enjoy their former priviledges; with addition of other requisite immunities; encouraging also the Planter to discoveries both by Sea and Land; and to perfect the Trade of Furs: which Letter, according to their Lordships command, was published in Virginia. But Captain Cleyborn, who was thereupon imployd by Commission from the Governour, under the King's Broad Seal, and the Seal of the Colony, and then discovered those parts of the Trade of Maryland, was thereby utterly undone, supplanted and expelled by the Lord Baltamore.

7. The King also, for the encouragement of the Planters, by his Royal Letters the 12 of September, 1628,[2] was pleased to promise thereby to renew and confirm unto the Colony under the great Seal of England, their Lands and Priviledges formerly granted to them.

8. And when the generall Assembly, consisting of the Governours, Councel, and Burgesses of the whole Colony complained to the Lords of the Councel, of the interruption of their Trade by the Lord Baltamore's Deputies their Lordships were pleased by their Letter July 22, 1634,[3] to signifie that the Plantation of Virginia should enjoy their Estates and Trade, with the same freedom and priviledge as they did before the recalling of their Patent.

By all which it appears, that howsoever the Government could not be reduced from that popular form of the Company in England, but by revocation of the Patent itself; yet in respect of both those Kings Declarations, and the Lords Orders, the Adventurers and Planters of Virginia, as to their Rights and Priviledges, according to the Rule of Equity, remain in the same condition, as if no such Judgement had been given.

[1] *Acts of the Privy Council, Colonial*, I. 92–95.
[2] *Virginia Magazine of History*, VII. 267.
[3] Printed in Chalmers, *Political Annals*, p. 131.

Object.[1] But they answer hereunto to this effect, though not truely neither, That the Lord Baltamore his Patent takes in no part, that the Virginians had then planted, and so the interests of all men is preserved; and, that Maryland is no other, then a particular Plantation, as the Company used to grant to divers Adventurers and Planters; and, that the King might do as much as the Company while they stood.

Answ. 1. We reply, That the Adventurers and Planters were encouraged to expend their Estates, in so vast a proportion, and to hazard their lives in all extremities, alwayes accompanying new designs and beginnings, in hope, that their shares upon the division of Lands, being four hundred Miles along the Seashore, and into the Land from Sea to Sea, would recompence them and their Heirs, as in Ireland, heretofore, and now is done. But this Interest by the Patent of the Lord Baltamore's comprehending neer two degrees, which is an hundred and twenty Miles, is wholly taken from them, and scarce is there any room for any Adventurers to take up any Land due unto them.

It is truely answered, that all the Adventurers of the Company were Tenants in common to all the Land, which was not actually divided and set out, and their claim cannot justly be thus nullified, and yet their interest said to be reserved.

3. It is granted, That the Lord Baltamore may have as large a proportion of Land, as ever was granted to any by the Company, though his adventures have never been proportionable to som mens. But we think it agreeing to reason, that he should people it, and either shew his right to it by the adventure of people sent over to plant it, which was by the Company appointed to be fifty Acres to every person transported thither; otherwise, how unreasonable is it, that he should possess two third parts of the Bay of Virginia, which may perhaps be said to be as big as the Kingdom of England and Scotland, and yet now in many years have not more men there, except such as have gone from Virginia, then can or do plant as much as is contained in a small corner thereof, and those chiefly employed in Tobacco; and the great name of Maryland is but in effect made a factory for Trade; Ammunition and Arms being as commonly sold to the Indians (though not altogether so

[1] *I. e.*, objection.

openly) as among the Swedes and Dutch: a Nursery for Jesuits, and a bar to keep off other Planters from the greatest part of the Country left void, and for the most part not known by him or his.

5. We say, that after we had discovered, and brought the Indians of those parts of Maryland to a Trade of Corn and Beaver, by virtue of the King's instructions under the Broad Seal of England, with the expence of our Bloods and Estates, and exercised annual intercourse with them above eight and twenty yeers: how can it be said, our Interests and Rights are preserved, when we are forbidden this Trade, our Men slain, Vessels and Goods seized, Persons imprisoned, and the whole Trade assumed onely to the Lord Baltamore's use, and he not able to manage it neither, but left it to the Swedes and Dutch?

6. And chiefly we answer, We claim Right by Possession, having planted the Isle of Kent almost three yeers before ever the name of Maryland was heard of, and Burgesses for that place sitting in the Assembly of Virginia; whereby it is evident, that the Lord Baltamore's suggestions to the King, mentioned in his Patent, that those parts were uncultivated and unplanted, unless by barbarous people not having the knowledge of God, was a mis-information; and by it, that Patent appears to be surreptitiously and illegally gotten:[1] and if the Lord Baltamore takes away those Lands from them, who have also purchased the Interest of the Natives (a Right not inconsiderable) and seize their Goods, and that in an hostile manner as he hath done; How can it be said, that those mens Interests and Rights are preserved, they being the first Discoverers of that Island, by vertue of the King's Commission, and planted there under the Government of Virginia, on the confidence they apprehended from the former assurances, and there began in great part the Trade of Furs.

How unjust an intrusion then will the Lord Baltamore's

[1] George, Lord Baltimore, visited Virginia in October, 1629, and upon his return to England shortly afterward applied to the king for the charter of Maryland. The region was correctly described as being uninhabited at that time, as Claiborne did not establish his post at Kent Island until 1631. The charter of Maryland was granted in June, 1632, to Cecilius Lord Baltimore, his father who was the applicant having died in April of that year.

Patent appear, which overthrows the Interests of so many and such Persons: for the Company of Virginia were of a nature diversified from other Companies; which if it had not been founded on so good Grounds, yet their zeal and pious endeavours to propagate the true Christian Religion, enlarge the English Dominions, and to encrease the Trade and Strength of shipping, and considerably the Customes, do deserve justice, with addition of reward for so honourable and good intentions.

In the next place, to prove the Lord Baltamore's usurpation of Royal Jurisdiction and Dominion in Maryland, as absolute Lord and Proprietary, there needs no more then his Commissions and Processes running in this stile, *viz.* We, Us, and, Given under our hand and greater Seal of Arms, in such a yeer of our Dominion, etc. The Oath also, that he tenders to all his Subjects and the Inhabitants, such being the very words thereof, as by the Oath itself, copied from his own hand, and herewith published, appears. This is surely incompatible to the English Nation, that there should be any such principality erected over them, whereas the books of Law teach us, that all Writs, Executions, and Commands ought to be done in the name of the Supream Authority onely, and is so appointed by the late Platform of Government, for all the Dominions of the Commonwealth, of which this is a part; and by a late Ordinance declaring Treason upon such penalty, that none ought to exercise any power, but in the Lord Protector's name; and these men acting so wilfully, cannot excuse themselves. By the ancient English Laws, all those Pleas that concern Life, and Member, and Pardons, cannot be done in the name of any inferior Person; and all Writs, Indictments, and Process as heretofore, so must now only be in the name of the Lord Protector, and not in the name of the Lord Baltamore's, as he hath assumed in Maryland. And whereas the Lord Baltamore pretends to the like priviledges as in the County-Palatine of Duresme,[1] even those priviledges of Duresme, and all the other County-Palatines of England,

---

[1] Durham. The palatine authority of the Bishop of Durham, although much curtailed in 1535 (27 Henry VIII. c. 25), was not finally abolished until 1836. Until that date courts were held and writs issued in the name of the Bishop, not of the Crown. The exercise by Lord Baltimore in Maryland of the powers mentioned in the text was in strict accordance with the express terms of his charter.

were, and are taken away as dishonorable, and incongruent to
the English Nation, by the Statute of the 27 Hen. 8. 25.   With
what strange confidence then doth the Lord Baltamore publish to the world, That these Royalties and Priviledges are
warranted by his Patent, when as they are contrary to Law,
and to the Government now established under his Highness,
and to a Clause in his Patent, wherein it is provided, That no
Construction be made thereof, whereby the Government in the
Common-wealth of England should suffer any prejudice or
diminution.

Whereby it appears there was as good Cause to reduce
Maryland as Virginia; the People and General Assembly
thereof also complaining of their Grievance, among many
other exorbitant Usurpations of Lord Baltamore over them,
as appears by their Complaint in Governor Green's time, made
and Recorded there by a Committee of that Assembly: But
'tis known that Governor Green was deposed by Lord Baltamore, for suffering that Committee, and not for proclaiming
the Kings Son,[1] as he aleadgeth, when no such thing appears
in *rerum natura*, nor no word in all his many Instructions, of
the Parliament, much less of his pretended affection to them,
or their friends, but clean contrary: And 'tis notoriously
known that all the Lord Baltamore's Governors usually took
the Kings part against the Parliament; and his Brother, Mr.
Leo. Calvert, his only Governor while he lived there, ever
declared himself against them: And to evince this irrefrage-
ably, and clearly to demonstrate the management and complexion of this business, both Lord Baltamore himself, and his
Brother, by long Solicitations at Oxford, procured and sent
over in Anno 1644 Commissions under the Kings Broad Seal,
to surprize the Parliaments and London-ships in Virginia; and

---

[1] On June 9, 1647, Governor Leonard Calvert on his death-bed commissioned
Thomas Greene, a member of the Council, as his successor.   On August 6, 1648,
Lord Baltimore, deeming it wise, in view of the situation of affairs in England,
that the governor of Maryland should be a Protestant, commissioned William
Stone to that office.   On September 20, 1649, Governor Stone, having occasion
to go to Virginia, appointed his predecessor Greene to act as his deputy during
his absence.   Greene seized upon the opportunity afforded by his brief authority
to proclaim Charles II. king.   This was on November 15, 1649.   Governor
Greene's temporary commission was shortly thereafter terminated by the return
of Governor Stone.   See p. 164, *supra*.

to impose Customs, raise Regiments, and Fortifie the Country against the Parliament; which appears by several Writings under the Lord Baltamore's Hand and Seal, (one of which is hereunto annexed.) They did with zeal proclaim the Kings Son, Charles the Second, at Maryland; and some that read it, and assisted therein, of the primest rank, are still continued Counsellors by him, and never a word of blame; whereas 'tis evident his own Interest is more than circumspectly watcht over, and contended for. How can he pretend that his Governor, Captain Stone, bare any affection to the Parliament, when without check from himself, in their Assemblies Laws, he used the name of King, and His Majesty; and of Charles the First, when the Second was Proclaimed there? And why did Lord Baltamore himself in England advisedly consent and approve those Laws *in terminis*, under his hand, 1650, if such had not been his own thoughts toward the Parliament?[1] The Commissioners that were imployed by the Parliament to Reduce Virginia, Anno 1652, were commanded to Reduce all the Plantations in the Bay of Chesapiak: and then, that all Writs should issue in the Names of the Keepers of the Libertie of England: They saw not how they could decline this service, well knowing how contrary to those Commands, and the Honor and Interest of the Parliament, the Government of Maryland was exercised; and think strange any should pretend assistance and supply of Victuals from Maryland to that Fleet, when no such thing ever was; that the Parliament Ships were entertained there in his Harbors, whenas never any of them came at Maryland, nor within near 100. miles thereof, save only the *Ginny*[2] Frigot, who went thither to Reduce that Province; they knew his Governor had alwayes bore affection to the Kings side, that Charles the Second (as hath been said) was proclaimed there, that the Councel were all Papists,[3] or indifferently affected, and that they refused to Govern the people by the Laws of England (another Clause in the Parliaments Commission) to which several of their actings, and even Lord Baltamore's Instructions were contrary, as in

---

[1] See *Lord Baltemore's Case*, pp. 175–177, *supra*.   [2] *Guinea.*

[3] At the time of the appointment of Governor Stone in August, 1648, Lord Baltimore changed the composition of the Council so that one-half the members were Protestants. Previous to that date they had all been Roman Catholics.

this particular, and many others, appears by the Reports of the Committee of the Navy, and the Councel of State, to whom the Parliament referred this Cause; a Copy of which Report is hereunto annexed: And they ruled in Maryland in such an absolute way and authority, as no Christian Prince or State in Europe exercises the like.

His Governor hath an absolute Negative Voice in all things, and in the Assembly of the Burgesses; calls into the Upper House (as he terms it)[1] whom he will, to over-vote the rest; places and dis-places whom he will in that Councel: and the Lord Baltamore himself, though in England, appoints all Officers, even to the meanest degree; and who flatter him most, are sure to have it: His Mandates are sent over to stop Justice, and the Judges imprisoned for proceeding according to Justice: Writs are given out under the Governors hand in his own Case, without any judgement of Court, to seize mens Goods into the Governors hands: His Governors are not suable for any just debts, and so they usually exercise their priviledges even to the oppression and discontent of the people: No Appeals allowed from their Courts, though consisting but of two men, and those perhaps of no great knowledg or skill in Government, no not to the general Representative Assemblies. It would be infinite to rake in this Dunghil; but all indifferent men that have lived and been there, know these things to be sad Truths; and surely not without cause, have the general Assemblies there, most of the Councel and the Freemen, been often contesting with the Lord Baltamore's Governors about these things, and yet could never obtain any redress from him; but have resolved to Petition the State of England.

Why therefore should Maryland, so ill Founded, and so ill Managed, be wrung from the right of Virginia, against all Law and Equity, as is before truely set forth? And be established to Lord Baltamore, a professed Recusant, as his publish'd Book intimates; who hath in effect made it a subject of his own domination and tyranny (being his main aim:) But to colour it, and the better to get friends, first made it a

---

[1] The Assembly was divided into two houses by its own act in April, 1650. The Upper House consisted of the members of the Council and was presided over by the Governor. *Archives of Maryland*, I. 272.

receptacle for Papists, and Priests, and Jesuites, in some extraordinary and zealous manner; but hath since discontented
them many times and many ways, though Intelligence with
Bulls, Letters, etc. from the Pope and Rome be ordinary for
his own Interests; and now admits all sorts of Religions, and
intended even 2000 Irish, and by his own Letters clears and
indemnifies one, that said, Those Irish would not leave a Bible
in Maryland. His Country, till he employed Captain Stone,
never had but Papist Governours and Counsellors, dedicated
to St. Ignatius, as they call him, and his Chappel and Holyday
kept solemnly: The Protestants for the most time miserably
disturbed in the exercise of their Religion,[1] by many wayes
plainly enforced, or by subtil practises, or hope of preferment,
to turn Papists, of which a very sad account may from time
to time be given, even from their first arrival, to this very day.

Virginia hath used all good Neighbourhood towards them,
without which assistance and supply, even of all things, they
could not have subsisted; for their numbers were inconsiderable, and their Adventures small and very little after the first
ship, in comparison of such a work. And though Lord Baltamore pretends great Adventures with his Friends thither;
yet none have appeared there to any considerable value from
him for many yeers, onely what Merchants, and some few
have done upon Returns of Tobacco and Beaver: so that in
Truth it will appear, and that by his own Letters too, Maryland hath been chiefly planted by Virginia from the first to
last, and by people from thence wanting seats in their narrow limits;[2] Maryland taking away above half the Country,
which (as hath been said before) was onely discovered by Virginia, with continual Trade and abode of people there for
above 20 yeers, by Commissions and Warrants in the King's
Name, and was planted by Colonel Claiborn under Virginia
Government, some yeers before ever the name of Maryland,
or Lord Baltamore was ever heard of there; which himself

[1] This statement, like many of the allegations in this pamphlet, is without
foundation in fact.

[2] The statement that settlers from Virginia moved to Maryland for lack of
space in the former colony is obviously incredible. The migration was in fact
that of Puritans, who, being harassed in Virginia, came to Maryland to enjoy the
religious liberty that was there extended to all. See p. 163, *supra*.

knew, though he mis-informed the King, and obtained his Patent upon pretence of Unplanted places onely.[1]

But the many illegal Executions and Murthers of several persons at the Isle of Kent by the Lord Baltamore's commands and his Officers; the Imprisonments, Confiscations of many mens Estates, and of Widows and Orphans, to the destruction of many Families there; especially his seizure of Captain Claiborn's Estate, though out of his Patent, because planted, to the value of 6000 pounds, with the great tyranny and wrong done there, although the then King Declared and Commanded the contrary, but was disobeyed by the Lord Baltamore's Agents, are too long to be inserted here.[2]

Many Inconveniences and Losses hath Virginia suffered by Maryland, of which the continual Invitation and Entertainment of run-away servants, and protecting fugitive persons and indebted, is not the least: But above all, it is easie to be made appear that the Lord Baltamore hath continually ever since their seating there, interposed in the matters of Government in Virginia by the potency of his friends in the late Kings Court, both by placing and displacing the Governnours, Counsellors, and Supream Officers, as they stood affected or were displeasing to him.

Mr. Bennet and Captain Claiborn being two of the Commissioners, that were imployed by the Parliament to reduce Virginia and Maryland, are strangely taxed by Lord Baltamore for being his declared enemies: indeed, it seems for their service to the Parliament, he is become implacable towards them, though Captain Curtis, another Commissioner now in England, and all Maryland can testifie how unwilling, and

---

[1] See p. 195, note 1, *supra*.

[2] A bill of attainder was unanimously found by the Assembly of Maryland on March 24, 1637/8, against Claiborne, on the charges of piracy and murder, and his estate declared forfeited to the Lord Proprietary. *Archives of Maryland*, I. 23. Three days later an order was issued to the sheriff of Kent Island to seize his goods and chattels, of which return was made June 20, 1638. *Ibid.*, III. 70, 76. On April 4 of the same year the Lords Commissioners of Plantations had denied Claiborne's title to Kent Island and confirmed that of Lord Baltimore as Proprietary. *Ibid.*, III. 71. The inhabitants of Kent Island had been reduced to obedience, and Thomas Smith, Claiborne's representative, taken prisoner by an armed force under Governor Leonard Calvert in February, 1637/8. See p. 152, *supra*.

how tenderly they did any thing there, and how much they
desired and endeavoured to have declined any alteration, if
either Captain Stone the Governour or the Councel, would have
issued out Writs in the name of the Keepers of the Liberty of
England, and have promised to govern according to the Laws
of England; both which they refused under their hands:[1]
and the Commissioners being sent to Maryland, is since owned
by the Report of the Committee of the Councel of State, and
the Lord Baltamore taxed and blamed for not issuing out Writs
as they required them; and therefore seems a bold aspersion
for the Lord Baltamore to publish, that Maryland being struck
out of their commission, was afterwards by some mistake put
into the Commission the second time: and as strange it seems,[2]
that now since the reduction of Maryland the Lord Baltamore
in opposition and contempt of the Supream Authority of
England, should cause his Governor and Councel most falsly
and rebelliously to revolt and recede from the same, and give
instructions under his own hand, as he had lately done, to
issue out all Writs and Proceedings in his own name onely:
which they have accordingly done, and not the least mention
of the Lord Protector's name in all their Government.[3]   This
the said Commissioners, though they received confirmation
of their Commission from the Parliament under the Seal (the
Original the first time miscarrying), yet bore with a long
time onely by Letters out of Virginia, admonished Captain
Stone and that Councel of their error, and protested against
their actings: but they continued obstinate.   The Commissioners were desirous still to expect and attend a settlement
and determination out of England, and to intermeddle as
little as they could.   But about a yeer since Lord Baltamore
sends over Instructions and Commands to Captain Stone and
his new made Councel, all or most Papists, or indifferent,
to seize the Lands and Estates of all such as would not take the
Oath of fidelity (as he stiles it) before specified.   But the
people of Maryland generally abhorred this Oath and justly as

[1] *Archives of Maryland*, III. 275, 300.

[2] See *Lord Baltemore's Case*, p. 169, *supra*.

[3] Parliament having been dissolved by Cromwell, it was claimed on behalf
of Lord Baltimore that the authority of the commissioners appointed by that
body had expired.

is conceived, especially those of Patuxent and Severn declined
to take it, as being against their Engagement, incompatible
with their subjection to the Commonwealth of England, and
incongruous to serve two absolute Superiours, whereupon
Captain Stone and his Counsel proclaim them seditious, and
rebels to Lord Baltamore, and forget not to include the two
Commissioners, though in Virginia under the same name,
with other opprobious terms: whereupon the people of Patuxent, Severn, and Kent often and earnestly apply themselves if possible to have relief from those Commissioners, yet
they still desirously forbore to intermeddle, hoping it would
be done out of England, until after many solicitations Mr.
Bennet and Captain Claiborn with onely two men in July
last went thither in a Boat, yet using all fair means: but how
ill they were treated for their moderation, and intended to be
surprised by night, and made Prisoners, and how they were
necessitated to prevent greater mischief and the present ruine
of hundreds of Families to interpose to have that Oath suspended, and the Government managed in the Lord Protector's
name; (which being denied to avoid bloodshed, they reassumed the Government out of those hands that so ill-man-
aged it, and placed it in others for the time being under his
Highness the Lord Protector, until he should please to signifie his further pleasure) will appear in a Declaration then
and herewith published, together with the peoples Petition,
the Commissioners answer thereunto, and an Order for setling
the Government in the hands of Captain William Fuller, and
others.

The Lord Baltamore also since gives particular Commission and Command to seize the persons of those Commissioners, under his Hand and Seal, dated in November last; and
for their service to the Lord Protector to proceed against them
as abettors in mutiny and sedition; chides, and upraids
Captain Stone for cowardise, provokes him to fighting and
bloodshed (a course too often acted in Maryland), appoints
another Governor in case he decline it, and yet sends no
revocation of the Commissioners reducement, though he ac-
knowledges he sought it earnestly of the Lord Protector but
could not obtain it; yet to blinde and delude Captain Stone
and his Counsel, there came over a Letter of Recommenda-

tion from his Highness of one Captain Barbar, and by what practise or mistake is not known, a subscription thereon to Captain Stone Governour of Maryland. And by this (together with a Copy of that Petition of the Merchants and others trading to Virginia, brought in by Mr. Eltonhead, and sent over by Lord Baltamore), Captain Stone and all Maryland fall to arms, and disarm and plunder those that would not accept the aforesaid Oath. A part of them at last stood upon their guard, onely sought to Captain Stone to shew his Commission, and they would submit; he caused to imprison their Messengers, and being of far greater number, assaulted them at their houses, threatens to have their blood, calls them Round-head Rogues and Dogs, brought whole bagfuls of chewed Bullets, rolled in powder, saying, The Devil take him that spares any; and so falls on upon the day dedicated to the Virgin Mary, with the word *Hey for St. Mary*: but the Protestants commanded their men not to shoot upon pain of death, until some being slain by a volly of shot from the Marylands, they defended themselves, and God confounded Capt. Stone and all his Company before them: there were near double the number in Prisoners to the Victors, twenty slain, many wounded, and all the place strewed with Papist beads where they fled; but the Proceedings thereof, and how the arm of the Lord was revealed, and his mighty power manifested even to admiration, together with the success, and the evils drawn upon themselves, appears by the relation thereof, at this time also published by a Messenger from thence.[1]

The Lord Baltamore pretends in print, his entertainment into Maryland of the Parliaments Friends thrust out of Virginia; but those very men whom he so stiles coming thither being promised by Captain Stone, that he would declare urging the Oath upon them, complain of it to the Parliament, are in answer thereunto vilified by Lord Baltamore, and publickly taxed for obscure factious fellows, and in his later Letters termed the basest of men, and unworthy of the least favour

---

[1] The accounts of the battle at the Severn, March 25, 1655, as narrated by those engaged on opposite sides, are conflicting. The two documents next following in this volume, *Babylon's Fall*, by Leonard Strong, and *The Refutation*, etc., by John Langford, give substantially the two versions.

or forbearance; such advantages doth he make on all sides, at such a distance, and in such incomposed times, that he confidently takes the liberty to aver such extream and contrary things which amaze other men that see them. The place as himself confesses, had been deserted, if not peopled from Virginia. He might with more reason scruple to supplant the Rights of the most considerable conjuncture of worthy men that ever undertook such an Adventure, as Plantation out of England; which hath been the beginner and parent of all the rest.

The late King James revoked the Virginia-Companies Patent for denying him to alter the Government, for which he had fundamentally provided to give Instructions from time to time, and was the same, which the last King did by his Commission to Sir William Davenant, of which the Lord Baltamore speaks so much,[1] and makes such inferences as serve his own ends. But the Truth is, all that can rightly and properly be collected from thence is onely this, (his right to the Soil being in express words reserved), if the King might dispose of the Government of Maryland, why not the Parliament, as they have done; and why not the Lord Protector as he also hath done? Another of those Fundamentals was, That no Papists should be tolerated to remain in Virginia, but sent away if they would not take the Oath of Allegiance, and was so practised: this the old Lord Baltamore refusing, stayed not in Virginia; and, *Hinc illa lachryma*, to all those that were of the Councel, who with their wives and children have not suffered a little for it; of which onely Colonel Matthews and Colonel Claiborn remain alive. His son this Lord Baltamore now publishes himself a Recusant, and avers contrarily that the Laws against Papists and Recusants extend not thither; yet his Patent says, No interpretation shall be admitted thereof, by which God's holy and truely Christian Religion, or the allegiance due to the Successors of the State of England,[2] should suffer any prejudice or diminution.

---

[1] The commission to Sir William Davenant was issued in February, 1649/50, by Charles II., then in exile, and not by the "last King" as stated in the text. See p. 180, *supra*.

[2] This expression, "the State of England," does not occur in the charter of Maryland.

By all which surely it's most evident, This County Palatine aimed and coveted by him, appears disagreeable to Law and to his own Patent: and as a Monster unlike the rest of the Dominions of the Commonwealth of England, and contrary to the late Platform of Government under his Highness the Lord Protector; yet hath he omitted no means to inforce his Dominion on those men that are most unwilling to submit to him as an absolute Prince and hereditary Monarch. Neither doth that instance of the Roman Commonwealth in his printed Pamphlet hold for him, who though they permitted and continued many Kingships over people that formerly had them, as is now done in Virginia among the Indians; yet he cannot shew, that ever they constituted King over the people of Rome to govern absolutely over them, as this case pleads for, to have a negative voice, yea, and a power *ad placitum*, in all things that is before specified, to the great regret of the Inhabitants, the oppression of many, and the obstruction of justice, of which Maryland hath afforded no mean examples and Complaints.

But although Virginia seeks the re-establishment of her bounds so often assured under the great Seal of England, and otherwise, yet to renew any such Authority as this of Maryland, or that of the Company over her, she desires it not; but to be from time to time under such Government as the State of England shall appoint.

Duplicate Instructions[1] *for Captain Robert Dennis, Mr. Rich. Bennet, Mr. Tho. [Stagge], and Capt. William Claiborn appointed Commissioners for the reducement of Virginia, and the Inhabitants thereof to their due obedience to the Commonwealth of England.*

Whereas the Parliament of England by an Act intituled, An Act prohibiting trade with Barbadoes, Virginia, Bermudas and Antego, hath committed to this Councel several powers therein expressed, for the setling, reducing, and governing the said Islands, printed copies of which Acts are herewith delivered you, In pursuance whereof, a Fleet is now set

---

[1] From the Council of State. the chief executive authority of England at this time.

forth victualled, armed, and manned under the command
and conduct of Captain Robert Dennis, to effect by the blessing of God the ends aforesaid; and for the management of
that service you are hereby joyntly nominated and appointed
Commissioners: and for your better directions and proceedings therein, you are to follow these Instructions following:

Such of you as are here to repair on board the ships, *John*
or the *Guinny*[1] Friggot of the States, which of them you shall
think fit, and winde and weather permitting to sail to Virginia, as Captain Robert Dennis shall direct and appoint.
And upon your arrival in Virginia, you, or any two or more
of you, (whereof Captain Robert Dennis to be one) shall use
your best endeavours to reduce all the Plantations within the
Bay of Chesepiak to their due obedience to the Parliament and
the Commonwealth of England.

For which purpose, you, or any two or more of you, (whereof Captain Robert Dennis to be one) have hereby power to
assure pardon and indemnity to all the Inhabitants of the said
Plantations that shall submit unto the present Government,
and Authority as it is established in this Commonwealth; in
which pardons you may make such limitations and exceptions,
as you or any two or more of you, whereof capt. Robert Dennis
to be one, shall think fit.

And in case they shal not submit by fair wayes and meanes,
you are to use all acts of hostility that lies in your power to
enforce them, and if you shal find people so to stand out as
that you can by no other wayes or means reduce them to their
due obedience, you or any two or more of you whereof capt.
Rob. Dennis to be one have power to appoint captains, and
other Officers, and to raise forces within every of the plantations aforesaid, for the furtherance and good of the service,
and such persons as shall come in unto you and serve as
soldiers, if their masters shal stand in opposition to the present Government of this Common-wealth, you or any two or
more of you whereof capt. Rob. Dennis to be one, have hereby power to discharge and set free from their masters all such
persons so serving as souldiers.

You shall cause and see all the several Acts of parlament
against Kingship, and the house of Lords to be received and

[1] *Guinea.*

published; as also the Acts for abolishing the Book of common prayer, and for subscribing the ingagement, and all of their Acts therewith delivered to you.

You or any two or more of you have ful power to administer an Oath to all the Inhabitants and planters there, to be true and faithful to the common-wealth of England as it is now established without a King or house of Lords: You or any two or more of you, whereof cap. Robert Dennis to be one, have power to give liberty to the inhabitants, and planters who shall have taken the engagement formerly mentioned to choose such Burgesses as they shall think fit, and send to the place you shal appoint for the better Regulating and governing affairs there; provided that nothing be acted contrary to the Government of the commonwealth of England, and the Laws established.

You shall cause all Writs, Warrants, and other processe whatsoever to be issued forth as occasion shall require, in the name of the Keepers of the Liberty of England, by authority of Parliament.

In case of Mortality, or absence of Cap. Rob. Dennis, you or any two, or more of you have power to put in execution these instructions. In case of Mortality or absence of Cap. Rob: Dennis, Edmund Curtis commander of the *Guinny* Frigot is hereby impowered to act as Commissioner with you, or any two or more of you, and he is also in the absence of Capt. Robert Dennis to take the charge of the Fleet so far as concerns the shipping, according to the power given to Cap. Rob: Dennis. And lastly as we doubt now but you will use your best dilligence, and care in carrying on of this affair of consequence with which you are intrusted, and that by your good endeavours it will have a good issue, so the Counsel wil take the same into consideration that respect may be had of your pains, and travel therein, and of a recompence agreeable to your service, when the same shall be compleated, and work upon which you are imployed shall be finished.

Signed in the name and by order of the Councel
of State appointed by authority of Parlam.

Whitehal 26   JOHN BRADSHAW *President.*
Sept: 1651.
Jo: Thurloe Cler: of the Counsel.

Committee Navy 31 December: 1652.

In pursuance of an order of Parlament of the 31 Aug. 1652, whereby the 4. and part of the 7. and 8. Articles agreed on at James City for the surrendring and setling of plantation of Virginia, with certain parchments concerning Mariland, and the petition of the Inhabitants of Virginia, are referred unto this Committee to consider what patent is fit to be granted to the said Inhabitants of Virginia, and to hear all parties, and to consider of their particular claims, and to report the same unto the Parlament,[1] This Committee upon examination of the matter of fact, and upon hearing both parties, and their Counsel, do find, and humbly certifie:

That by a Patent dated the 23 day of May, in the 7th year of King James,[2] there was granted to divers Adventurers and Planters by the name of the Virginia Company, all those Lands, Countries, and Territories scituate in that part of America called Virginia, from Cape or point comfort all along the sea coast to the Northward two hundred mile; and from the said Cape or point comfort all along the sea-coast to the Southward 200 miles; all that space of Land lying from the sea-coast of the precinct aforesaid up into the Lands throughout from sea to sea, West and Northwest, and all the Islands lying within 100 miles along the coast of both seas of the precincts aforesaid, with the soyls etc. thereunto belonging to hold to them and their heirs forever under the several reservations therein mentioned;

That the said patent was afterwards by a *Quo warranto* in the 21 of the said King repealed, and made void;

That in the 8th year of the late King, upon the humble petition of the Ld. Baltemore, that he might have and enjoy a collony or parcel of ground in America then uncultivated, and not inhabited by any save the Indians there was by patent dated 20 June 8 Car. granted to the said Lord Baltemore all that parcel of Land lying in the part of America, from the sea on the

---

[1] The original ha here a note: "See note, page 46." The reference is apparently to the parliamentary record mentioned, as there is no note on page 46 of the original edition of the pamphlet.

[2] The second Virginia patent, 1609.

East to the Bay of Chessaphia[1] on the West, extending from Watkins point to Delawar Bay, and from Delawar Bay to Potowmeek River, and so along to Watkins point, together with the Islands thereunto belonging, and by the said patent called the Province of Mariland, To hold the same in as ample manner as any Bishop of Durham, within the Bishoprick or County palatine of Durham in England, heretofore ever held or injoyed, and to hold the same in free and common soccadg, as of the Castle of Windsor, Reserving to the King, his Heirs, and successors faith, allegiance, and dominion, and two indian arrows yearly with the fifth part of all gold and silver Oar found in and upon the said province, and also liberty for any the people of England or Ireland to fish as well in those seas, as in any ports or Creeks of the said province, and to salt and cure their fish there, That in and by the said patent, power is granted to the Lord Baltemore and his heirs to make Laws by and with the Counsell assent, and approbation of the Freemen of the said Province, or the Major part of them, that shal concern life or Member as often as his Lordship shal think fit, etc. so as such Laws be consonant to reason, and not repugnant, nor contrary, but as neer as possible may be agreeable to the Laws of this Nation;

That by the said Patent the said Province is separated from Virginia, but by express provisoe declared to be subject, and depending upon the Crown of England, And in case any doubts arise about any claim in the said patent, the same were to be decided by the Courts of England.

It also appears by examinations taken by this Committee that Kentish Island was before the date of the said Patent part of Virginia, and planted and inhabited by Cap. Claiborn three years before the arrival of the Lord Baltemores Agents in Maryland, and that Burgesses sat in the Assembly at James Town in Virginia for the said Island, And that the Virginians had the sole possession of the Bay of Chesopiack, and a free Trade with the Indians;

That in the yeer 1633, upon the arrival of the Lord Baltemores Agents in Maryland, the Virginians were prohibited from trading with the Indians, in any part of Maryland, which formerly they had accustomed, whereupon severall

[1] Chesapeake.

differences arose between capt. Claiborns men and the L. B.[1] planters, and capt. Clayborn continuing his trade, a Vessell called the *Longtail* was seised upon by the Marilanders, and one Lieutenant Warren (with some others whom he sent to rescue the said Vessel) were killed by the Marilander in that attempt in Potomoke[2] River; That the goods of Mr. Harman and others were all seised by the Lord Baltemores Agents, and at length after three yeares suffering, Captaine Claiborn was forsibly disseisd and dispossest of his plantation in Kentish Island; and forced for safety of his life to fly into England, and ever since that L: B. hath had possession of the said Island, not suffering any of the Virginians to trade in the said Bay without ceisure and confiscation of their Goods.

It likewise appears unto this Committee upon perusal of the several parchments mentioned in the Order of Parlament, that the L: B. hath constituted forms of Oaths, and injoyned the taking thereof by all persons as wel Officers as others within the said province, and that not to the King, but to himself, and that he hath issued out Writs in his own name, all his Commissions and processe running in this stile (*viz.*) we, us, and given under our hand, and greater seal of arms in such a yeer of our Dominions over the said Province. That he hath likewise appointed an upper and lower house of Assembly and also a privie counsel of State, which is not mentioned in the said patent. And we further find that several of the Laws made by the said Lord Baltemore are not agreeable to the Laws, Statutes, and customs of England, as for instance:

That the Lands sold by the said Lord Baltemore are directed to be purchased and held of him, and his Heirs only in soccadg, as of the Mannor, etc.;

That the Oaths hereafter mentioned must be taken by all that shal bear Office, or shall inhabite, or come into the said province, upon pain of being banished, and if they return, and refuse, to be subject to such Fine as his Lordship shall think fit.

---

[1] Lord Baltimore's.   [2] Pocomoke.

The Oath of the Lieutenant or chief Governor of the Province of Maryland.[1]

I A. B. doe Sweare I will be true and faithfull to the Right Honourable Cecilius, Lord Baron of Baltemore, the true and absolute Lord and Proprietary of this Province of Maryland, and his Heires, and him and them, and his and their Rights, Royal Jurisdictions and Seignory, all and every of them into or over the said Province and Islands thereunto belonging, Will at all times Defend and Maintaine to the utmost of my power; and will never accept of, nor execute any Place, Office, or Employment within the said Province, any way concerning or relating to the Government of the said Province, from any Person or Authority, but by, from, or under the hand and Seale at Arms of his said Lordship, or his Heires or Assignes, Lords and Proprietaries of the said Province. I will faithfully serve his said Lordship as Lieutenant of the said Province, and in all other Offices committed to my Charge by his said Lordships Commission or Commissions to me, and will willingly yield up the said Commission and Commissions againe, and all Offices, Powers, and Authorities granted or to be granted by them or any of them, into the hands of his said Lordship, and his Heires and Assignes, or to such person or persons as he or they shall appoint, whensoever he or they shall appoint me so to doe, and shall signifie the same to me in writing under his or their hand and Seale at Armes. And will not presume to put in execution, or attempt to execute any Office, Power, or Authority granted unto me by any of the said Commissions, after that his Lordship, his Heires or Assignes, Lords and Proprietaries of the said Province shall repeale them or any of them respectively by any writing under his or their respective hand and Seale at Armes, and that the said Repeale be published in this Province. I will doe equall Right and Justice to the poore and to the rich, within the said Province, to my best skill, judgement, and power, according to the Lawes and Ordinances of the said province, and in default thereof according to my conscience, and best discretion, and the power granted and to be granted to me by his said Lordships Commission or Commissions; I will not for fear, favour, or affection,

---

[1] This was the form of oath prescribed for Governor Stone. It differs from the previous forms chiefly in the obligation to disturb no one on account of his religion, "and in particular no Roman Catholic." Thus Lord Baltimore sought to insure the continuance under the Protestant governor of the policy of religious liberty already established. The expressions, "Rights, Royal Jurisdictions, Seignory," etc., are in conformity with the terms of the charter.

or any other cause, let, hinder, or delay Justice to any, but shall truely execute the said Office and Offices respectively according to his said Lordships Commissions to me in that behalf, and to the true intent and meaning thereof, and not otherwise, to the best of my understanding and Judgment. I wil not know of any attempt against his said Lordships person, or his Rights or Dominion into, or over the said province, and the people therin, but I will prevent, resist, and oppose it with the utmost of my power, and make the same known with all convenient speed to his said lordship, and I will in all things from time to time as occasion shal serve faithfully counsel and advise his said Lordship according to my heart and conscience; And I do further swear I will not by my selfe, nor any other person directly, trouble, molest or discountenance any person whatsoever in the said province professing to beleeve in Jesus Christ, and in particular no Roman Catholick, for or in respect of his or her Religion, nor his or her free exercise thereof within the said province, so as they be not unfaithful to his said Lordship or molest or conspire against the civil Government established under him, nor will I make any difference of persons in conferring Offices, Rewards, or Favours proceeding from the Authority which his Lordship hath conferred on me as his Lietenant here, for or in respect to their said Religion respectively, but meerly as I shall find them faithful and wel-deserving of his said Lordship, and to the best of my understanding endowed with morall vertues and abilities fitting for such Offices, Rewards or Favours, wherein my prime aim and end shall be from time to time sincerely the advancement of his said Lordships service here, and the publick unity and good of the Province without partiallity to any, or any other sinister end, whatsoever. And if any other Officer or persons whatsoever shal during the time of my being his said Lordships Lieutenant here, without my consent or privity, molest or disturb any person within this province professing to beleeve in Jesus Christ meerly for or in respect of his or her Religion, or the free exercise thereof, upon notice or complaint thereof made unto him, I will apply my power and Authority to relieve any person so molested or troubled, whereby he may have Right done him for any damage which he shal suffer in that kind, and to the utmost of my power wil cause all and every such person or persons as shal molest or trouble any other person or persons in that manner to be punishment. I wil faithfully serve his lordship as his Chansellor and Keeper of his great Seal of this Province committed to my charge and custody by his said Lordships Commission to me, to the best of my skil, and understanding. I will cause the impression in Wax of the said Seal to be affixed to all such things as I have, or shal from time to time receive commission or Warrant for so doing from his said Lordship under his hand and Seal at arms; and that it shall not be affixed to any other Writing, or thing whatsoever, directly or indirectly with my privy consent, or knowledg. I wil do my best endeavour carefully to preserve the said Great Seal in my custody so long as it shall please his said Lordship to continue me in the charge and keeping thereof, to the end that it may not be lost, stollen, or unlawfully taken from me; And whereby any other Person may affix the impression thereof unto any Writing, or thing whatsoever without Authority for so doing lawfully derived, or to be derived from, by, or under a commission of Warrant under his said Lordships Hand and Seale at Arms, and that I will truly and faithfully deliver up againe the said great Seale into the hands of such Person or Persons as his said Lordship, or his Heirs shall appoint, when his, or their pleasure for that purpose shall be signified to me under his, or their hands and Seals at arms; so help me God, and by the contents of this Book.

The oath of fidelity to the Lord Proprietor

I A: B. Do faithfully and truly acknowledge the Right Honourable Cecilius Lord Baron of Baltemore to be the true and absolute Lord and Proprietary of this Province and Country of Maryland, and the Islands thereunto belonging; And I do swear that I will bear true faith unto his Lordship and his Heires as to the true and absolute Lords and proprietaries of the said Province and the Islands thereunto belonging, and will not at any time by words or actions in publick or private, wittingly or willingly to the best of my understanding any way derogate from; but will at all times as occasion shall require to the uttermost of my power defend and maintaine all such his said Lordships and his Heires Right, Title, Interest, Priveledges, Royal Jurisdiction, Prerogative,[1] propriety and Dominion over and in the said province of Maryland, and the Islands thereunto belonging, and over the people who are or shall be therein for the time being as are granted or mentioned to be granted to his said Lordship, and to his Heirs by the King of England in his said Lordships patent of the said province under the Great Seale of England. I do also swear that I will with all expedition discover to his said Lordship, or his Lieutenant or other chief Governor of the said province for the time being, and also use my best endeavours to prevent, any plot, conspiracy, or combination which I shall know or have cause to suspect is intended or shall be intended against the person of his said Lordship, or which shal tend any wayes to

---

[1] See p. 212, note 1.

the disinherison or deprivation of his said Lordships or his heirs
the Right, Title, Royal Jurisdiction or Dominion aforesaid, or any
part thereof, and I do swear that I will not either by myself or by
any other person, or persons directly, or indirectly, take, accept,
receive, purchase or posses any Lands, Tenements or Heredita[me]nts
within the said Province of Maryland, or the Islands thereunto belonging from any Indian or Indians to any other use or uses, but
to the use of his said Lordship and his heirs or knowingly from any
other person or persons not deriving a legall Title thereunto from
or under some Grant from his said Lordship, or his said Heirs legally passed or to be passed under his or their Great Seal of the
said province for the time being, so help me God and by the Contents of this Book.

The Oath of a Counsellor of State in Maryland.

I A: B. Do swear that I will be true and faithfull to the Right
Honorable Cecilius Lord Baron of Baltemore, the true, and absolute Lord and Proprietory of this Province of Maryland, and his
Heirs, and him and them and his and their Right, Royal Jurisdictions and signiory,[1] and every of them into and over the said Province and Islands hereunto belonging wil at all times defend and
maintaine to the utmost of my power, and will never accept of, nor
execute any Place, Office, or Imployment within the said Province,
any way concerning or relating to the Government from time to time,
but from his said Lordship, or his Heirs, Lords, and proprietaries
of the said Province, under his or their Hands and Seal at Arms.
The peace and welfare of the people of this Province I will ever
procure, as far as I can: I will aid and assist the administring and
execution of Justice in all things to my power: to none will I delay or
deny Right, for fear, favor, or affection; I will to my best skill, and
according to my heart and conscience, give good and faithful Counsel to the said Lord and Proprietary, and his Heirs, and to his, and
their Lieutenant and chief Governor of this Province for the time
being, when thereunto I shall be called; I will keep secret all matters committed or revealed unto me, or which shall be moved or
debated secretly in Councel, and faithfully declare my mind and
opinion therein, according to my heart and conscience: And if any
of the said Treaties and Councel shall touch any the Privy Counsellors of this Province, I will not reveal the same to him so touched
or concerned, but will keep the same secret until such time as by
the consent of the Lord Proprietary, or chief Governor here for the

[1] See p. 212, note 1, *supra*.

time being, publication shall be made thereof; I will as a Counsellor, as a Justice, and Commissioner, for conservation of the peace of this Province, do equal right unto the poor, and to the rich, to the best of my understanding and judgment, according to the Laws from time to time in force within this Province; and in default thereof, according to my best discretion, and generally in all things will do as a faithful Counsellor to the Lord Proprietary; And I do further Swear, I will not by myself, or any other person, directly or indirectly trouble, molest, or discountenance any person or persons in the said Province, professing to believe in Jesus Christ, and in particular, no Roman Catholick, for, or in respect of his or their Religion, nor in his or her free exercise thereof within the said Province, so as they be not unfaithful to his said Lordship, nor molest or conspire against the Civil Government established under him. So help me God, and the Contents of this Book.

That[1] whosoever shall call any one an Idolater, Papish Priest, Jesuite, Jesuited Papist, etc. to forfeit ten pounds; and that no Papist shall be troubled for exercise of his Religion, so as they be faithful to his Lordship.[2]

Whosoever shall be accessory to the running away of an Apprentice, shall suffer death; but the party himself, if apprehended, to serve his time double.

Whosoever shall counterfeit his Lordships Seal or Sign Manual, shall suffer the loss of his hand, imprisonment during life, or pains of death, or confiscation of Lands or Estate, or any one or more of them as the Governor, and Chancellor, and Councel, shall think fit.

[1] The text here returns to the enumeration of provincial statutes alleged to be repugnant to the laws of England.

[2] This prohibition against using epithets indicative of religious affiliations applied to all alike, but only if the terms were used in a reproachful manner. It was equally punishable so to call a person a Puritan, Presbyterian, Calvinist, or Lutheran. The penalty, however, was ten shillings, not ten pounds, as stated in the text. See the Act concerning Religion, p. 269, *infra*. *Archives of Maryland*, I. 244. At an Assembly held in Maryland in October, 1654, one year before the date of this pamphlet, during the sway of the commissioners appointed by Parliament, this act was repealed and a new one enacted, providing that liberty should not be extended to such as professed "popery or prelacy." *Ibid.*, I. 341, 351. In the writs issued for the election of this Assembly it was directed that no Roman Catholic should be eligible to membership or allowed to vote. See p. 228, *infra*. Upon the restoration of the authority of Lord Baltimore in 1658, this repeal was treated as a nullity and the old act providing for religious liberty revived. *Archives of Maryland*, II. 548.

His Lordship suffers Dutch, French, or Italian Descents to plant, and enjoy equal priviledges with the British and Irish Nations.[1]

And lastly, In one of his Laws he mentions the High and Mighty Prince Charles, the First of that name; and in another expresseth, That none shal transport any Tobacco's in any Dutch Vessel bound for any other Port than his Majesties.

Unto all which Exceptions, Answer having been made by the Lord Baltemore, which is hereunto annexed; the same is humbly submitted to the Judgment and further direction of this Honorable House.

It hath been confessed by the Lord Baltamore, That one Captain Green his Lieutenant-Governor of Maryland, did soon after the death of the late King, proclaim his Son Charles Stewart King of England, etc. for which his Lordship saith he did by a Writing under his hand and seal (which is one of the parchments remaining with this Committee) revoke the Commission granted to the said Captain Green, and appointed one Stone in his room: but there is no such cause mentioned in the said Writing.[2]

It likewise appears, That in March 1651 the Governor and Councel of Maryland, being required by the Commissioners that were sent thither, to issue forth Writs in the Name of The Keepers of the Libertie of England; they refused the same, saying, They could not do it without breach of their Trust and Oath.

---

[1] Acts of naturalization or *denization* as they were then called, were passed in favor of a number of persons natives of the continent of Europe, the first being in favor of Augustin Herrman, a distinguished Bohemian who became a valuable member of the province, and lord of Bohemia Manor in Cecil County, a name still preserved.

[2] See p. 197, note 1, *supra.*

To the Honourable, Richard Bennet, and Col. William Clai-bourn, Esquires, Commissioners of the Commonwealth of England, for Virginia and Maryland.

The Humble Petition of the Commissioners and Inhabitants of Severne, alias Ann Arundel County.

Sheweth,

That whereas we were invited and encouraged by Captain Stone, the Lord Baltamore's Governor of Maryland, to remove ourselves and Estates into this Province, with promise of enjoying the liberty of our Consciences in matter of Religion, and all other priviledges of English Subjects; And your Petitioners did upon this ground, with great cost, labor, and danger, remove ourselves; and have been at great charges in building and clearing: Now the Lord Baltamore imposeth an Oath upon us, by Proclamation, which he requireth his Lieutenant forthwith to publish; which if we do not take within three months after publication, all our Lands are to be seized for his Lordships use. This Oath we conceive not agreeable to the terms on which we came hither, nor to the liberty of our Consciences as Christians and free Subjects of the Common-wealth of England: Neither can we be perswaded in our Consciences by any light of God, or engagement upon us, to take such an Oath; but rather humbly conceive it to be a very real grievance, and such an oppression as we are not able to bear; neither do we see by what lawful power such an Oath, with such extream penalties can by his Lordship be exacted of us who are free Subjects of the Common-wealth of England, and have taken the Engagement to them. We have Complained of this grievance to the late honorable Councel of State in a Petition subscribed by us, which never received any answer, such as might clear the lawfulness of such his proceedings with us: but an aspersion cast upon us of being Factious fellows; neither have we received any Conviction of our error in not taking the said Oath, nor Order by that power, before whom our Petition is still depending, to take it hereafter; neither can we believe that the Common-wealth of England will ever expose us to such a manifest, and real bondage (who assert themselves, The maintainers of the lawful Liberties of the Subject) as to make us Swear absolute subjection to a Government, where the Ministers of State are bound by Oath to countenance and defend the Roman Popish Religion, which we apprehend to be contrary to the Fundamental Laws of England, the Covenant taken in the three Kingdoms, and the Consciences of true English Subjects: and doth carry on an arbitrary power, so as whatever is done by the people at great costs in Assemblies, for the good of the people, is liable to be made Null by the negative Voice of his Lordship; But affirmative Propositions and Commands are incessantly urged, and prest, and must not be denied.

In consideration whereof, we humbly tender our Condition and Distraction, upon this occasion falling upon the hearts of all the people, to your view and Consideration, intreating your honors to relieve us according to the Cause and the power wherewith you are intrusted by the Common-wealth of England: the rather, because upon such an exigent as this, we have none to flie to but your selves the honorable Commissioners of the Common-wealth of England; not doubting but God will direct you into what his mind and will is in this matter concerning us, and that you will faithfully apply your selves to our Redress in what is Just, and our lawful Liberty; which is the Prayer of your poor Petitioners.

Severn River, the 30. of January, 1653.[1]

Subscribed by EDW. LLOYD, and 77 persons of the House-keepers, and Freemen, Inhabitants.

To the Honorable Richard Bennet, and Colonel William Claibourn, Esquires, Commissioners for the Common-wealth of England, within the Bay of Chesopiak.

The humble Petition of the Inhabitants of the North-side of Patuxent River in the Province of Maryland.

Sheweth,

That we being reduced by your Honors from that Tyrannical power exercised over the people of this Province by the Lord Baltamore and his Agents, unto the Obedience of the Common-wealth of England, to which Government we have Subjected and Engaged, and have by your Honors been often

---

[1] *I. e.*, 1654, new style.

enjoyned reall conformity and obedience to the same, and not to own any other power or Authority as we will answer the contrary: In subjection whereunto, we have had peace and freedom hitherto, which with all thankfulness we cannot but acknowledg, and in our continued obedience, do expect from the Parliament next under God continued peace, liberty, and protection from the pride, rage, and insolency of their, and our adversaries: Now so it is, may it please your honors, that of late the Lord Baltamore doth by his Order and Agents seek to set over us the old form of Government formerly exercised by him in this Province, which we did conceive, by the blessing of God upon your honors endeavors, had been fully made Null and void; yet notwithstanding, by the Arbitrariness of his own will, he appoints Laws for us, and sets up Popish Officers over us, outing those Officers of Justice appointed by you; issuing forth Writs in his own name, contrary to your honors Order and appointment: And doth by Proclamation under his own Hand, and in his own Name, impose an Oath, which if refused by us, after three months, all our Lands and Plantations are to be seized upon to his Lordships use: And if taken by us, we shall be ingaged at his will to fight his battels, defend and maintain him in his Patent, as it was granted to him by the late King, etc. Which Oath, we humbly conceive, is contrary to the Liberty and freedom of our Consciences, as Christians, and contrary to the fundamental Laws of England; contrary to the Engagement we have taken in Subjection to the Common-wealth of England, and unsutable to Freemen, to own any other power than that to which we belong, and to whom we are, and have Engaged; and contrary to the Word of God, to fight for, and defend, and maintain Popery, and a Popish Antichristian Government; which we dare not do, unless we should be found Traytors to our Country, fighters against God, and Covenant-breakers.

The Premises Considered, we humbly spread our Condition before your view and Consideration, hoping that as you are Commissioners for the Common-wealth of England, and that power which God hath put into your hands, that you will up, and be doing, in the name and power of our God, that we be not left for our faithfulness as a prey to ungodly and unreasonable men, before we can make our Complaint and Griev-

ance known to the Supream Authority of England; which
with all readiness we shall endeavor to do by the first opportunity; and from whom we do hope, and shall expect, by
God's blessing, to have a gracious Answer, and sutable Redress; And your Petitioners hereunto Subscribed, shall pray,
etc.
Dated in Patuxent River, in the Province of
    Maryland, the first of March, 1653.[1]
       Subscribed, RICHARD PRESTON, and 60 more of the
       House-keepers, and Freemen.

*An Answer to the Petitions lately Received from the Inhabitants
of the Rivers of Severn and Patuxent.*

Gentlemen,
    We have lately Received from you a Petition and Com-
plaint against the Lord Baltamore his Governor and Officers
there, who upon pretence of some uncertain Papers and Relations to be sent out of England, but no way certified or au-
thenticated, have presumed to recede from their Obedience to
the Common-wealth of England, to which they were reduced by
the Parliaments Commissioners; to the contrary whereof, nothing hath been sent out of England, as far as is yet made appear
unto us; But Duplicates and Confirmation of the Commissioners Power and Actions were sent from the Parliament since
the Recution[2] of Virginia and Maryland. Now whereas you
Complain of real Grievances and Oppressions, as also of the
Imposition of an Oath upon you against the Liberty of your
Consciences, which you say you cannot take as Christians, or
as Free Subjects of the Common-wealth of England; We have
thought good to send you this Answer, That because we, nor
you, have not as yet received, or seen sufficient order, or directions from the Parliament and State of England, contrary to
the form to which you were Reduced and Established by the
Parliaments said Commissioners; Therefore we advise and
require you, that in no Case you depart from the same, but
that you continue in your due Obedience to the Common-
wealth of England, in such manner as you, and they, were

---

[1] 1654, N. S.   [2] Reduction.

then appointed and engaged; And not to be drawn aside from the same upon any pretence of such uncertain Relations, as we hear are divulged among you. To which we expect your real Conformity, as you will answer the contrary; notwithstanding any pretence of power from the Lord Baltamore's Agents, or any other whatsoever to the contrary.

Your very loving friends,

Virginia, March   RICHARD BENNET.
  the 12. 1653 [1654].   WILL. CLAIBOURN.

A Declaration published in Maryland.

It cannot be unknown to the Inhabitants of Maryland, that about two yeers since, this Province was Reduced and Settled under the Obedience of the Common-wealth of England, by the Parliaments Commissioners sent thither with special Commission and Instructions to that purpose: And that Captain William Stone, Mr. Tho. Hatton, and others, re-assuming the power and place of Governor and Councel here, undertook, and promised to continue in their said Obedience, and to issue out all Writs, Process, and proceedings in the Name of the Keepers of the Liberty of England, as was Commanded by the said Instructions, by which Maryland was reduced; which said Commission and Instructions have been since renewed, and the proceedings of the said Commissioners owned by the Committee of the Councel of State, as by their Order and Report drawn up for the Parliament may appear, wherein the Lord Baltamore's Agents are taxed for refusing to issue out Writs in the Name of the Keepers of the Liberty of England. Notwithstanding all which appearing so clear and evident, The said Captain Stone and Mr. Hatton, though they continued, and exercised the Government for some time, and for divers Courts, in the Name of the Keepers of the Liberty of England, yet have they since, upon no good ground, falsified their said trust and engagement, though acted publickly, and after long Advice and Consideration: And having rejected, and cast off their said Obedience to the Commonwealth of England, have further refused to Govern this Province according to the Laws of England, but declare and assume a power and practise contrary thereunto, and contrary to the late Platform of Government of the Commonwealth of England, Scotland, and Ireland, and the Dominions thereof; As namely, by the Governors Negative Voice in Assemblies, and his chusing and removing Counsellors at pleasure, and the like, is manifest. And whereas we have lately received Commands from his Highness the Lord Protector, to publish the said Platform of Government; and that all Writs and Proceedings should be issued in the Name of his Highness;[1] to which, though we desire this Government should be conformable, yet the said Captain Stone and Mr. Hatton, having lately Associated unto them divers Counsellors, all of the Romish Religion, and excluding others appointed by the Parliaments Commissioners, have, and do refuse to be obedient to the Constitutions thereof, and to the Lord Protector therein; And have in the name, and by special direction of the said Lord Baltamore, made Proclamation, and exacted an Oath of Fidelity from all the Inhabitants of the Province, contrary, and inconsistent to the said Platform of Government: which said Oath nevertheless, and the Law here commanding the same, and many other Laws, are likewise by the Report of the said Committee of the Councel of State, declared to be contrary to the Laws and Statutes of the English Nation; which is an express breach of his Patent, And whereas the said Oath, in many particulars, is distasted by all the Inhabitants of Maryland: and especially out of tenderness of Conscience by all Northern Plantations of Patuxent and Severne, who having lately engaged to the Parliament of England, do say, and declare, they cannot take the said Oath to the Lord Baltamore to be absolute Lord and Proprietary of Maryland, and to the utmost of their power, to defend and maintain all his Rights, and Royal Jurisdictions, Prerogatives, Dominion, etc., Upon which their refusal of the said Oath, the said Captain Stone, by the said Lord Baltamore's especial direction, hath set forth a Proclamation, declaring, That all such persons so refusing, shall be for ever debarred from any Right, or Claim to the Lands they now enjoy, and live on: And that the said Captain Stone, as his Lordships Governor, is thereby required to cause the said Lands to be entred, and seized upon, to his Lordships use;

[1] This assertion is not sustained by evidence.

By which strange, and exorbitant proceedings, many great Cruelties and Mischiefs are likely to be committed, and many hundreds, with their Wives and Families, are utterly ruined, as hath been formerly done here, and at Kent, though Planted before the Lord Baltamore's Claim to Maryland; with many Murders, and illegal Executions of men, Confiscations of Estates and Goods, and great miseries sustained by Women and Orphans: In Consideration and just fear whereof, the said Planters of Patuxent and Severne, have made their often Addresses to us, as some of the then Commissioners for the Reducement of Maryland, and most lamentably Complain of the great Danger they stand in of being utterly undone, and chiefly for engaging their Fidelitie to the Common-wealth and Parliament of England, now devolved to his Highness the Lord Protector; their Obedience and Faith to both, being plainly repugnant to each other, and inconsistent;

We therefore the Commissioners of the Parliament, having written and proposed to the said Captain Stone and that Councel, for a Meeting, to procure a right understanding in the matters aforesaid, and to prevent the great inconveniences likely to ensue: In Answer thereunto, though they acknowledge our Lines Peaceable, yet so exulcerated are their minds, that in the very next Line they add, *We in plain terms say, We suppose you to be Wolves in Sheeps clothing;* with many other following like uncivil, and uncomely words, and expressions;

In Contemplation therefore of all the Premises, we have thought fit for to make publication hereof, and to justifie and manifest our proceedings in these Affairs, lest many people may be ensnared by false and cunning suggestions and pretences, as lately hath been practised herein, the falsitie whereof time hath sufficiently demonstrated; And we are ready to give further satisfaction for the truth of any of the particulars before alleaged, if any shall desire it, or repair to us to that purpose, which they may securely do.

Wherefore we advise, and in the Name of his Highness the Lord Protector, Require all the Inhabitants of this Province, to take notice of the Premises, and to contain, and keep themselves in their due obedience under his Highness the Lord Protector of England, Scotland, and Ireland, and the Dominions thereto belonging, of which this is undoubtedly a part, and ought to be Governed accordingly; whereby they may assure themselves of the peaceable enjoyment of their Liberties, profession of their Religion, and their Estates, and that they shall be protected from wrong and violence in what kind soever.

Hereby also Protesting against the said Captain William Stone, Mr. Thomas Hatton, and all others any way Confederate, or Assistant with them in their unlawful practises, that they may be accomptable, and answerable to God and the State of England under his Highness the Lord Protector, for all the mischiefs, damages, losses, and disorders that may, or shall happen thereby.

Dated at Patuxent in Maryland the 15. of July 1654.

RICHARD BENNET
WILL. CLAIBORNE.

Captain William Stone's Resignation of the Government.

Whereas since the Orders or Directions of the Commissioners of the State of England for the Government of this Province of Maryland, of the 28 of June, 1652, I William Stone Esquire, Governor of the said Province, was Enjoyned by the Direction and Appointment of the Right Honorable, the Lord Baltamore, Lord Proprietary of the said Province, to issue out all Writs and Process, within this Province, in his the said Lord Proprietaries name, and to admit of those of the Councel which were appointed by his Lordship, and no other: And whereas upon my Compliance with his Lordships Commands therein, not any wayes contradictory, so far as I understand, to any Command from the Supream Authority in England, the said Commissioners, in pursuance of their Declarations lately here published, have threatened, and gone about by force of Arms to compel me to decline his, the said Lord Proprietaries, Directions and Commands before mentioned; which in regard of the trust reposed in me, by his said Lordship, as Governor here under him, I conceive I was engaged not to do; I have therefore thought fit, for prevention of the effusion of Blood, and ruine of the Country and Inhabitants, by an Hostile Contest upon this occasion, to lay down my Power as Governor of this Province under his Lordship; and do promise for the future, to submit to such Government as shall be set over us by the said Commissioners, in the Name, and under the Authority of his Highness the Lord Protector.

Witness my Hand the 20 of July, 1654.

WILLIAM STONE.

In presence of
    THOMAS GERRARD.
    THOMAS HATTON.
    EDM. SCARBURGH.

Order for settling the Government of Maryland.

Whereas by several Orders drawn up and Published at St. Marie's the 29 of March, and the 28 of June, 1652, Maryland was Reduced and settled under the Authority and Obedience of the Common-wealth of England, as to the Government thereof, by special Order and Command of the Councel of State by Commission from the Parliament, and was left in the hands of Captain William Stone, Mr. Hatton, and others; who were required, and promised to issue out Writs and other Process in the Name of the Keepers of the Liberty of England, according to the express words of the Commission and Instructions for Reducing, Settling, and Governing of all the Plantations in the Bay of Chesapiak to the Obedience of the Common-wealth of England, as in and by the aforesaid Orders and Proclamations may and doth appear: And whereas the aforesaid Captain Stone, by special Order and Directions from the Lord Baltamore as it appeareth, was perswaded and induced to go away from his Obligation and the Trust reposed in him, By issuing forth Writs and all other Process in the Name of the Lord Proprietary of this Province, placing and displacing those of the Councel, and imposing an Oath upon the Inhabitants, contrary unto and inconsistent with the said Engagement and Oath to the Common-wealth of England, upon the Penalty and Forfeiture of the Lands of all such as should Refuse to take the same within three Months after publication thereof, which were then to be Entred upon, and Seized to his Lordships use; thereby occasioning great discontent and disturbance among the Inhabitants, besides the Irregularity and Cruelty of the said proceedings, and the Opposition, Contempt, and Rebellion therein to the Common-wealth of England and his Highness the Lord Protector; And further, whereas by a late Proclamation, dated the 4th of this Month, published in this Province, both the Commissioners of State, and the people who adhered to their Engagement to the Common-wealth of England, and refused to own or acknowledge any other Name or Authority, as to Government, or take any other Oath but what they had already taken to that power, were charged, That they drew away the people, and led them into Faction, Sedition, and Rebellion against the Lord Baltamore; whereby not only the Lands and Plantations of many hundreds of people, but also their Estates and Lives were liable to be taken away at the pleasure of the aforesaid Lord Baltamore and his Officers: By all which unjust and unreasonable proceedings, the people were put upon a necessity of standing upon their own defence, for the Vindication of their just Rights and Liberties, and freeing themselves from those great Oppressions, whereby the whole Province was very much threatned, and apparently endangered; For the prevention whereof, as also for the Relief of those who were so deeply distressed, and for the Settlement of the Province in peace, and in their due Obedience under his Highness, The said Commissioners by Authority derived unto them from his Highness the Lord Protector, applyed themselves unto Captain William Stone the Governor, and the Councel of Maryland, according to a Declaration of the 15 of this Month, herewith published, who returning only opprobrious and uncivil language, presently mustered his whole power of men and Souldiers in Arms, intending to surprize the said Commissioners, and as could be imagined, to destroy all those that had refused the said unlawful Oath, and only kept themselves in their due obedience to the Common-wealth of England, under which they were Reduced and Settled by the Parliaments Authority and Commission as aforesaid; Then the said Commissioners in peaceable and quiet manner, with some of the people of Patuxent and Severne, went over the River of Patuxent, and there at length received a Message from Capt. Stone, That the next day they would meet and treat in the Woods; and thereupon being in some fear of a party to come from Virginia, he condescended to lay down his power lately assumed from the Lord Baltamore, and to submit (as he had once before done) to such Government as the Commissioners should appoint under his Highness the Lord Protector;

It is therefore Ordered and Declared by the said Commissioners, That for Conservation of the Peace and publick administration of Justice within the said Province of Maryland, Captain William Fuller, Mr. Richard Preston, Mr. William Durand, Mr. Edward Lloyd, Captain John Smith, Mr. Leonard Strong, Mr. Lawson, Mr. John Hatch, Mr. Richard Wells, and Mr. Richard Ewen, or any Four of them, whereof Captain William Fuller, Mr. Richard Preston, or Mr. William Durand to be always one, to be Commissioners for the well Ordering, Directing, and Governing the Affairs of Maryland, under his Highness the Lord Protector of England, Scotland, and Ireland, and the Dominions thereof, and in his Name only, and no other; and to proceed therein as they shall see cause, and as neer as may be, according to the Laws of England: To appoint and hold Courts for the due administration of Justice and Right in such places, and at such times as they shall think fit and necessary: And any of the Commissioners of the Quorum, to issue forth Writs, Warrants, Subpoena's, etc. As also that they Summon an Assembly to begin on the 20th day of October next; For which Assembly all such shall be disabled to give any Vote, or to be Elected Members thereof, as have born Arms in War against the Parliament, or do profess the Roman Catholick Religion. And the said Mr. William Durand is hereby appointed to be Secretary to the said Commissioners, and to receive the Records from Mr. Thomas Hatton; And Captain John Smith, to be Sheriff for this ensuing yeer.

Dated at Patuxent, in the Province
of Maryland, the 22 of July   RICHARD BENNET.
1654.   WILLIAM CLAIBORNE.

Cecilius, Lord Baltamore, To all to whom these Presents shall come, Greeting. Whereas our Sovereign Lord the King, by His Highness Commission under the Great Seal of England, bearing date at Oxford the 28 day of February now last past, Hath authorized Leonard Calvert Esquire, Brother of me the said Lord Baltamore, to Treat, Conclude, and Agree at,

and with the General Assembly of the Colony of Virginia, for
and concerning the Ascertaining and Establishing by Act of
General Assembly there, of Customs and Duties to be paid to
His Majesty, His Heirs, and Successors in Virginia, upon
Exportation of Tobacco, and other Goods and Merchandizes
from thence, and upon all other Goods and Merchandizes
brought in and imported there, other then for necessary supply for Cloathing imported, as by the said Commission more
at large appeareth: And whereas by a Contract or Agreement in Writing, bearing date the day of the date of the said
Commission, made between our Sovereign Lord the King, of
the one party; and me, the said Lord Baltamore, on the other
party, Reciting the said Commission herein before recited;
our said Sovereign Lord the King, for the considerations in the
said Contract or Agreement expressed, Is pleased, and hath
agreed with me the said Lord Baltamore, that in case a certainty of Customs and Duties shall be Established by Act of
General Assembly of the said Colony of Virginia, according
to the tenor of the said Commission, That then His said Majesty will make a Lease or Grant to me, and such others as I
shall desire to be joyned with me, of the same Customs and
Duties which shall be established as aforesaid, for such term,
and under such Rents and Covenants as in the same Contract
or Agreement, are expressed; And that immediately after
the Establishing of the said Customs and Duties as aforesaid,
and until such Lease or Grant shall be made as aforesaid, I
the said Lord Baltamore, and such as I shall appoint, shall
be the Receiver or Receivers, Collector or Collectors of all such
Customs and Duties as shall be established as aforesaid, to the
proper use of me the said Lord Baltamore, my Executors,
Administrators, and Assigns, without accompt; paying certain Rents, Salaries, and Entertainments in the said Contract
or Agreement expressed and mentioned; And his Majesty
hath by the same Contract or Agreement, Constituted and
Ordained me, the said Lord Baltamore, and my Deputy or
Deputies, to be appointed by me, to be his Collector and Receiver of all Customs and Duties which shall become due and
payable to His Majesty, as aforesaid, as by that part of the said
Contract or Agreement which is remaining with me the said
Lord Baltamore, being under the Great Seal of England, more

at large appeareth: Know ye now, That I the said Lord Baltamore, for divers good Causes and Considerations me thereunto moving, Have substituted, ordained, made, and appointed; And by these Presents do Substitute, Ordain, Make, and Appoint   to be my Deputy in this behalf, and do by force and vertue of the same Contract or Agreement, Authorize and put the said in my place and stead, and to the use of me, my Heirs, Executors, Administrators, and Assigns, to Receive, Collect, and Gather all such Customs and Duties whatsoever, as in pursuance of the before recited Commission, and Contract, or Agreement shall be established to be paid to his Majesty, his Heirs and Successors in Virginia aforesaid, by Act of General Assembly of the said Colony, and out of the same to pay, and discharge all such Rents, Salaries, and Entertainments, as by the said Contract or Agreement are mentioned to be by me paid and discharged; rendring to me, my Executors, Administrators, and Assigns, the Overplus or Remainder of the same Customs and Duties: Giving, and hereby Granting unto the said   as full Power and Authority to recover, and receive the said Customs and Duties to be Established as aforesaid, to the use aforesaid, when the same shall grow due; and to give Acquittances and Receipts for the same, and to Substitute and Appoint one or more Person or Persons under him in this behalf, and the same to revoke at his will and pleasure, and to pay and discharge the said Salaries and Entertainments, as I my self have, or may, or might claim to have by force and vertue of the said Contract or Agreement; And further, to do, execute, and finish all and every such further, and other Acts and things which shall be expedient and necessary to be done by the said touching the Premises by reason of his being my Deputy as aforesaid, as effectually as I might do the same being personally present: Ratifying, Confirming, and Allowing all, and whatsoever the said shall do, or cause to be done in the Premises in pursuance hereof. In witness whereof I the said Lord Baltamore have hereunto put my Hand and Seal at Arms, the tenth day of April, 1644, Annoq; Regis Caroli Angl. etc. vicessimo.

C. Baltamore.

BABYLON'S FALL, BY LEONARD STRONG, 1655

INTRODUCTION

LEONARD STRONG, the author of this pamphlet published in London in 1655, who is described on the title-page as Agent for the people of Providence in Maryland, was one of the Puritan settlers at that place. On July 22, 1654, Governor Stone having been ousted by Richard Bennett and William Claiborne, the commissioners of Parliament, Strong was named by them as one of the ten commissioners appointed "for the conservation of peace and the administration of Justice in the Said Province of Maryland." [1]

This pamphlet, *Babylon's Fall*, and the one which immediately follows in this volume, the *Refutation of Babylon's Fall*, by John Langford, give very contradictory accounts of the same events. For their better understanding the two papers should be read in conjunction, so that each may cast light upon the other.

In respect to the battle at the Severn between the forces under Governor Stone, representing the Lord Proprietary, and those under William Fuller, representing the government at Providence, established by the commissioners appointed by the Parliament of England, it is to be observed that in these conflicting reports each side is charged by the other with responsibility for the strife and with having begun hostilities. Discrepancies like these, and as to the number engaged on each side and the number slain, are not unusual in accounts of military events written respectively from the viewpoint of the victors and the vanquished, in respect to matters

[1] See p. 228, *supra*.

conducted on a larger scale than those which are here recorded.

The words "royal jurisdictions" complained of in this pamphlet as contained in the oath prescribed by Lord Baltimore in the form of oath for the Governor and Councillors, has already been noted as expressing merely acknowledgment and recognition of the "royalties, royal rights and temporal franchises" such as belonged to the Bishop of Durham, within the county palatine of Durham, and which were conferred upon Lord Baltimore in Maryland by the terms of his charter.

The Governor was not required by his oath to uphold the Roman Catholic religion, but merely not to molest or discriminate against those that professed it.

In respect to the Assembly convened by the commissioners which is described as "a full and lawful representative of the whole Province" it is to be noted that in the writs for the election it was expressly directed that no Roman Catholic should be eligible for election, or permitted to vote.

In this pamphlet it is charged that Governor Stone had issued "several Commissions to Papists and other desperate and bloody fellows." This grouping of descriptive terms well illustrates the animus of the writer.

The text here printed is taken from an example of the original edition in the library of the Boston Athenæum. The pamphlet was reprinted in the *Maryland Historical Magazine*, III. 228, from a transcript made from a copy in the British Museum.

C. C. H.

BABYLON'S FALL

Babylon's Fall in Maryland: a Fair Warning to Lord Baltamore; or a Relation of an Assault made by divers Papists, and Popish Officers of the Lord Baltamore's against the Protestants in Maryland; to whom God gave a great Victory against a greater force of Souldiers and armed Men, who came to destroy them.
Published by Leonard Strong, Agent for the people of Providence in Maryland. Printed for the Author, 1655.[1]

In the yeer 1649, many, both of the congregated Church, and other well-affected people in Virginia, being debarred from the free exercise of Religion under the Government of Sir William Barkely,[2] removed themselves, Families and Estates into the Province of Maryland, being thereunto invited by Captain William Stone, then Governor for Lord Baltamore, with promise of Liberty in Religion and Priviledges of English Subjects.

An Oath to the Lord Baltamore was urged upon this people soon after their coming up, which if they did not take, they must have no Land, nor abiding in the Province. This Oath was very scrupulously looked upon: first, In regard it bindes to acknowledge and be subject to a Royal Jurisdiction and absolute Dominion of the Lord Baltamore, and to defend it and him against all power whatsoever. This was thought far too high for him, being a Subject, to exact upon such terms as it was exacted and too much unsutable to the present liberty which God had given the English Subjects from Arbitrary and Popish Government as the Lord Baltamore's Government doth plainly appear to be. Secondly, It was exceedingly scrupled on another account *viz.*: That they must swear to uphold that Government and those Officers who are sworn to

[1] Title-page of the original.   [2] Berkeley.

countenance and uphold Antichrist, in plain words exprest in the Officers Oath, the Roman Catholick Religion.[1] And for these people to own such by an Oath, whom in their hearts they could by no means close with; what could it be accounted but Collusion?

Yet nevertheless the people that were then come up to Providence, considering Lord Baltamore to be Lord of the soil, and willing to acknowledge him, and pay him his due Rents and Services; upon that account took an Oath which was much qualified and moderated from its former rigour: but this, though it was accepted by Captain Stone, the Lord Baltamore's Lieutenant, yet utterly rejected by his Lordship, who gave order, That the Oath absolutely should be urged; and gave special instructions and charge to his Lieutenant to proclaim, That all that would not take the Oath within three Months after publication, and pay Rents, and sue out Patents, should be expulsed the Province, and the Land seized to his Lordships use; who required his Officers to see the contents of the Proclamation executed.

Now the people having been formerly sensible of such yokes, imposed contrary to what was promised them before they came into the Province, complained by their Agent in England.

First, to the Lord Baltamore, desiring his Lordship, That such burthens as the Oath and other great inconveniences mentioned in our instructions, might be removed. But the Lord Baltamore rejected the motion. Our Agent presented a Petition to the Council of State, where it hath been depending neer four yeers, without any hearing, Answer or Relief; which hath brought unspeakable troubles upon this Province, and now at last occasioned the Shedding of much English blood, yea, of the Saints in Maryland. God grant that Right and Justice may have a more open course to flow into all the Dominions of England, without obstructions, and that innocent blood be not shed any more for want thereof.

In the yeer 1652 Richard Bennet Esq., Colonel William Cleyborne, and Captain Edmund Curtis, Commissioners from the supream Authority of the Commonwealth of England, arrived in Maryland, in the *Guiny*[2] Friggot, to reduce that

---

[1] See p. 212, *supra*, and note 1, there.   [2] *Guinea.*

Province into the obedience of the Commonwealth of England, according to their Commission; which was effected by them, first, in their taking away the Commissions and Powers of the Lord Baltamore, in the hands of Captain William Stone his Governour, and Thomas Hatton his Secretary, and the rest of the Lord Baltamores Councel; as they had very good cause so to do; for none of the English Dominions had more need of being reduced; and caused them to take the Engagement to the Commonwealth of England, as it was then without King or House of Lords. And so they might have continued in their places still, onely to the Commonwealth of England; but they would not yield to issue out Writs in any other name, then Lord Baltamore's because of their Oath to him.

In the yeer 1654, upon some Instructions and Relations from the Lord Baltamore out of England, Captain William Stone and Mr. Thomas Hatton, and the Popish Councellors, rose up against the Reducement, displacing those whom the States Commissioners had placed, and introducing the old Popish Councel; calling that which was done by commission from the Councel of State in England, Rebellion against the Lord Baltamore; and those that were Actors in it, Factious and Seditious Persons: which was done by a Proclamation full of railing terms, published at Providence in the Church-meeting.

The Commissioners for the Commonwealth of England, hearing that new Orders and Instructions were come to Maryland from Lord Baltamore, and that one Scarborough, a mischievous instrument of the Lord Baltamore, was gone up [to] Maryland, resolved to come and see in what condition their affairs stood. And finding a direct contradiction to, and receding from that obedience to the Commonwealth of England which was promised but not performed by the Lord Baltamore's Officers, applied themselves in a peaceable and loving way to perswade them into their due and promised obedience, yet because the said Commissioners were given to understand, That there was a mischievous design by Lord Baltamore's Officers and their Complices to apprehend their persons, and to raise Forces against the lawful Power of the Commonwealth of England;

The said Commissioners desired some to come down from Providence, and some from Putuxent to guard their Persons, and defend themselves and people from that power of men in Arms which by this time Captain Stone had pressed in Lord Baltamore's name, upon pain of death to assist him against the said Commissioners, and gathered together in a formidable manner. But the said Commissioners being greatly desirous of peace, and willing to avoid the shedding of blood, applyed themselves to the said Captain Stone to bring him to a parley and conference; where after some arguing, the said Captain Stone resigned up the Government which he took up in the Lord Baltamore's name, into the hand of the Commissioners of England; promising to be obedient to that Government, which by their Authority should be set over them, under his Highness the Lord Protector.

The ordering and governing the affairs of Maryland, was then committed to Captain Will. Fuller, Mr. Rich. Preston, Mr. Richard Durand, Mr. Edward Lloyd, and others mentioned in the Commission, who were required to attend the Engagement of the Commonwealth of England, to keep Courts, and to summon an Assembly in October following. At this Assembly there was a full and lawful Representative of the whole Province,[1] where the Act of Reducement of this Province by Commission from the Councel of State in England to Richard Bennet Esq., Col. William Cleyborne, Edmund Curtis, was freely and fully acknowledged by the whole Assembly; the Burgesse of every respective County and Limit confirming the same and submitting thereunto. And did pass and record an Act, That whosoever did publish any Writ or Summons, Declaration or Proclamation, either in the Lord Baltamore's or any other name, then the Government so settled as aforesaid had and received should be accounted a Delinquent against the Commonwealth of England, and dealt with accordingly.

The same Assembly did make Protestation against a Declaration sent over by his Lordship and recorded by his Secretary; wherein the said Lord did declare the people at Providence, by him called Annardundel,[2] to be Rebels; and strictly

---

[1] This was the session from which Roman Catholics were excluded and prohibited from voting at the election of members.   [2] Ann Arundell.

charged his Officers efficaciously to deal with them accordingly: but no ground or reason thereof could be found, But their not compliance with his Arbitrary and Popish Government, and the adhering to the Engagement and the Reducement aforesaid, and Government setled by the aforesaid Commissioners.

After this Assembly, the Province was quiet, and so continued until the later end of January; about which time the Ship *Golden Fortune*, whereof Captain Tilman was Commander, arrived in Maryland.

Then the Lord Baltamore's Officers, and the Popish party began to divulge abroad, and boast much of power which came in that ship from his Highness the Lord Protector to confirm the Lord Baltamore's Patent to him, and to re-establish his Officers in their former places under him: which pretended power they assumed to themselves; Captain Stone and the rest giving out threatning speeches, That now the Rebels at Putuxent and Severne, should know that he was Governour again; giving Order, That neither Act of the said Assembly should be observed, nor Writ from the power established by the Commissioners aforesaid obeyed, but what should issue forth in the name of the Lord Proprietory, *viz.* Lord Baltamore. And further, the said Captain Stone gave several Commissions to the Papists and other desperate and bloody fellows, to muster and raise men in arms to be ready upon all occasions, giving out that he would go to Putuxent and seize the Records of the Province at the place where they were appointed to be kept by an Act of the Assembly, and to apprehend Mr. Richard Preston also, at whose house they were; which shortly after was effected by Vertue of a Warrant in Captain Stone's name, without Proclaiming, or shewing any power by which he acted such high Robberies. But in threatning speeches declared, That they would have the Government; and for the terror of others, would hang some of the Commissioners, which were entrusted with the Government by the Commissioners of the Commonwealth of England, under his Highness the Lord Protector, namely Captain William Fuller, Mr. Richard Preston, and Mr. William Durand.

About this time Captain William Fuller, Mr. William Durand, Mr. Leonard Strong and Mr. Richard Ewen, to whom among others the Government was committed, sent two Messengers of quality and trust with Letters to Captain Stone in a way of peace and love; desiring him to make it known by what power he surprised the Records; and desiring him, the said Captain Stone, to give an Answer, as by the Letter, relation thereunto being had, more at large appeareth: But the said Captain Stone, instead of giving a satisfactory Answer, imprisoned the Messengers, and in much wrath and fury said he would show no power: at last he affirmed, that he acted by a power from Lord Baltamore; and that the Lord Protector had confirmed the Lord Baltamore's power. If so, Sir, said one of the Messengers, if it be confirmed, let that appear and it will satisfie. Confirmed, said Captain Stone, I'll confirm it; and so sent them home. After this the said Captain Stone and his Officers proceeded in their wicked design; yet to colour it over, the said Captain Stone published a Proclamation to deceive the amazed and distracted people at Putuxent; wherein he called God to witness, that he intended not to use any hostile way to them or the people at Providence. Which Protestation, how false and feigned it was, the following proceedings of himself and Officers will clearly evidence to all the World: for notwithstanding this Proclamation and Protestation, the said Captain Stone sent up to Putuxent one William Eltonhead and Josias Fendall, and with them twenty men in Arms, who did beset and entred the house of Mr. Richard Preston, with intent to surprise him; but not finding him at home, took away in Guns, Swords and Ammunition to the value of 30 *l.* sterling; ransacked every place in and about the house, to seek for the said Richard Preston; and as some of the Company then said with purpose to hang him for his rebellion against the Lord Baltamore. At the same time they surprised John Sutton, who was appointed by the Assembly and Secretary to attend the Records for any that should have occasion to use them either for search or Copy; and carried him away Prisoner with such Guns and Ammunition he had, and kept him about twenty dayes; even so they dealt with Lieutenant Peter Johnson; several other houses at Putuxent, they served in the like kinde. And when they were desired to shew by what power or Commission they so acted, they would in a proud bravado clap their hands on their swords, and say, Here is a Commission. This was no sooner effected at Putuxent, but presently they mustered in Arms two hundred or two hundred and fifty men at the house of the aforesaid Eltonhead, which Eltonhead and Fendall sent up by night several Boats with armed men, and forced many of Putuxen whether they would or not to go with them upon their warlike Expedition to Providence; taking all the Guns, Powder, Shot, and Provision, they could anywhere finde. And when they had done what they pleased at Putuxent, they bent all their forces towards Providence, the chief place of the residence of most of the Commissioners, and people that were forced out of Virginia by Sir William Barkely for conscience sake, Some of the said Company marching by Land, others by Water; they that marched by Land, did much spoil and robbery in all the Houses and Plantations where they came, breaking open Doors, Trunks and Chests. In this barbarous manner, they carried it for about forty miles.

Now again the Commissioners at Providence sent other Messengers with a Letter to Capt. Stone, still complaining his proceedings and seeking the knowledge of his power; and that some better accomodation might be attended to prevent the ruine and desolation of the whole Province, which this course was very likely to bring to pass. If he were resolved to come to no Parley or Treaty they protested in the said writing, that by the help of God, they were resolved to commit themselves into the hand of God, and rather die like men, than live like slaves. This was also rejected by the said Captain Stone and his Complices, the Messengers apprehended, their Boat seized, and onely three of six escaped to bring the report of their desperate and bloody design, and that they were upon their march in a hostile way.

Capt. Stone and his Company still drew neerer to Providence, into a place called Herring-Creek, where they apprehended one of the Commissioners, and forced another man of quality to flie for his life, having threatned to hang him up at his own door; and not finding the man, affrighted his wife, and plundered the house of Ammunition and Provision, threatning still what they would do to the people at Providence, and that they would force the rebellious factious Roundheads to submit; and then they would show their power.

Having now left the Country behinde them bare of men, save only such as fled into the Woods from their cruelty and rapine, as also of Arms and Ammunition; the poor women urging this to them, What should they do if the Indians should come upon them, being thus strip'd of men and Arms to defend them; and in what a sad and sorrowful condition they were left: These merciless men answered scoffingly, It matters not, your sorrow is our joy.

And indeed, it is too apparent, that the Indians waited upon their motions, and by examination it was found at Providence, that the Indians were resolved in themselves, or set on by the Popish faction, or rather both together to fall upon us: as indeed after the fight they did, besetting houses, killing one man, and taking another prisoner.

Now the people at Providence perceiving such a tempest ready to fall upon them, and all messages rejected, prepared for their coming, looking up and crying to the Lord of Hosts and King of Sion, for counsel, strength and courage, being resolved in the strength of God to stand on their Guard, and demand an account of these proceedings; seeing no other remedy, for so great a mischief, could be found.

About this time Captain Stone sent two men to publish a Proclamation quite against the Law established by the Commissioners of the Commonwealth of England, and against an Act of a lawful Assembly; which being read, and having no other Treaty to offer, they were quietly dismissed to their own Company, to whom they might have gone if they would.

That night Captain Stone and his Army appeared in the River of Severne at Providence, with eleven or twelve Vessels, greater and lesser, some of which had plundred by the way, in which their whole Army were wafted.

Capt. Fuller and the Councel of War appointed at Providence Mr. Wil. Durand, Secretary, to go aboard the *Golden Lion*, which then lay at Anchor in the River, and to fix a Proclamation in the main mast, directed to Captain Heamans, Commander of the said Ship, wherein he was required in the name of the Lord Protector, and Commonwealth of England, and for the maintenance of the just Libertyes, Lives and Estates of the free Subjects thereof against an unjust power to be aiding and assisting in this service.

The said Captain Heamans at first was unwilling; but afterwards seeing the equity of the Cause, and the groundless proceedings of the Enemy, he offered himself, Ship, and Men for that service, to be directed by the said William Durand.

The enemy was come within the command of the Ship at the shutting in of the evening: the Captain of the Ship was required to command them aboard by a piece of Ordnance. The enemy with a great noise rejected the warning. Then another Piece was levelled where they heard the Boats rowing; the Shot whereof lighting something neer, but doing no hurt; A Messenger came aboard; but had nothing of any message to deliver, save onely that Captain Stone thought the Captain of the Ship had been satisfied. To which the Captain answered, Satisfied, with what? I never saw any power Captain Stone had, to do as he hath done; but the Superscription of a Letter.[1] I must, and will, appear for these in a good Cause.

That night the Enemy run into the Creek, where they landed out of reach of the Ship.

But in the morning; all their Vessels were block'd up by a small Barque with two pieces of Ordinance, which was commanded to lie in the mouth of the Creek, and so kept from coming out.

The same day, being the first day of the week, and the 25 of March, the Enemy appeared in a body upon a narrow neck of the Land, neer their Vessels, and with Drums and shoutings said, *Come ye Rogues, come ye Rogues, Roundheaded Dogs;* which caused the Captain of the Ship to give fire at them, and forced them to march further off, into the neck of Land.

In the meantime Capt. Will. Fuller with his Company came up the River with shoutings and couragious rejoycings, and landed with a hundred and twenty men, six mile distant from the Enemy: and immediately sent away all their Sloaps and Boats, committing themselves into the hand of God: he marched directly where the Enemy lay waiting for him. The Enemies Sentry shot; immediately they appeared in order. Captain Fuller still expecting that then at last possibly they might give a reason of their coming, commanded his men upon pain of death not to shoot a Gun, or give the first onset; setting

[1] See p. 204.

up the Standard of the Commonwealth of England: against which the Enemy shot five or six Guns, and killed one man in the front before a shot was made by the other. Then the word was given *In the name of God fall on; God is our Strength*, that was the word for Providence; the Marylanders Word was *Hey for Saint Maries*. The Charge was fierce and sharp for the time; but through the glorious presence of the Lord of Hosts manifested in and towards his poor oppressed people, the Enemy could not endure, but gave back; and were so effectually charged home, that they were all routed, turned their backs, threw down their Arms, and begged mercy. After the first Volley of shot, a small Company of the Enemy, from behinde a great tree fallen, galled us, and wounded divers of our men, but were soon beaten off. Of the whole Company of the Marylanders there escaped onely four or five, who run away out of the Army to carry news to their Confederates. Captain Stone, Colonel Price, Captain Gerrard, Captain Lewis, Captain Hendall, Captain Guither, Major Chandler, and all the rest of the Councellors, Officers and Souldiers of the Lord Baltamore among whom, both Commanders and Souldiers, a great number being Papists, were taken, and so were all their Vessels, Arms, Ammunition, provisions; about fifty men slain and wounded. We lost onely two in the field; but two died since of their wounds. God did appear wonderful in the field, and in the hearts of the people; all confessing him to be the onely Worker of this victory and deliverance.

Examinatur per me,

WILLIAM DURAND,
Secretary of Maryland.

The Postscript.

Thus God our Strength appeared for us; and the blood which they thirsted after in others, was given to themselves to drink; the miseries which they threatned to the innocent, fell upon the guilty; the pit which they digged for others, themselves fell into; the cords which they brought to binde us, bound themselves. This is the Lord's doing, it may well be marvellous in our eyes.

What hath been written, is but a very abstract of those

great and various providences of God toward his people, and
against Antichrist; a great Volume would not contain the
wonders which the Lord himself hath wrought and manifested
to the hearts of his people in this dispensation. The sum is,
Satan and his seed, rising up against the seed of the woman,
bruises the heel of Christ, but destroyes himself utterly. The
further evil men proceed in their own way, the neerer to destruction: so it is with all flesh, it works itself into ruine,
through the adored depths of the wisdom of God.

Those who are acquainted with the clear and familiar appearances of God to his people in times of distress, can understand and rejoyce in what may be now a little further hinted.

First, the Lord confounded the Language of Babel in the
hearts, projects, and consultations of his people, when they
were devising to defend themselves from this danger, till they
came to that condition of Jehosaphat, we know not what to
do, but our eyes are towards thee; wilt thou judge them? for
we have no strength against this multitude.[1]

Secondly, Now the Lord gives testimony from himself in
the Spirits of many of his Saints in a wonderful, plain, yet
glorious manner; (for the secret of the Lord is with them that
fear him) so that as well women as men spake, or rather God
spake in them an express testimony what should be the issue
of this conflict, that is, glory to God in the highest, delivrance
to his people, destruction to Babylon, Songs unto Sion; which
was revealed so powerfully, evidently, and certainly, that it
ravish'd the hearts of some, astonish'd others, and encouraged
the heart both of General, Captains, and Souldiers, as well as
others that could not fight, to a Triumph before the Engagement, and the enjoyment of a victory by the assurance of faith,
before one stroke of the battle.

The bow of the Lord was made quite bare, to be seen of all
that had an eye to see, and his arrows were seen to be sharp in
the heart of the Kings enemies before they fell under him.
God made the feeble to be as David, and David as God: they
were carried out in the strength of the Lord, who gave this
testimony to one of the Captains, just as the Enemy came up,
The Victory is yours: but God shall be seen, and not man in
it. After the battle, what acknowledgement of God in it was

[1] II Chronicles xx. 12.

in every mean Souldiers mouth, as well as the Commanders, what praising of God, is beyond expression. They run through all the Company, Give God the glory, Blessed be the name of the Lord.

REFUTATION OF BABYLON'S FALL, BY JOHN LANGFORD, 1655

INTRODUCTION

THIS pamphlet, as its title indicates, was prepared in reply to the document next preceding in this volume. Its author, John Langford, is described on the title-page as "Gentleman, servant to the Lord Baltimore," and in the first paragraph he declares that he had been employed by his Lordship in his affairs relating to the province for above twenty years.

The original receipt for the first delivery of two Indian arrows, the yearly tribute reserved under the charter of Maryland, at Windsor Castle, Tuesday, April 23, 1633 (this paper is in the possession of the Maryland Historical Society), recites that they were delivered at the Castle by John Langford. This was six months before the sailing of the first colonists. Langford was among the early settlers of Maryland, where he became surveyor general and a member of the Council.

A brief summary of the events which led up to the conditions mentioned in this and the two preceding papers, and to the battle at the Severn, is given in the introduction to *Virginia and Maryland,* pp. 184–186, *supra.*

It is to be noted that in this conflict Captain Fuller had the support of Captain Heamans, commanding the ship *Golden Lion,* an armed merchantman trading from England, and then lying at anchor in the river. The motives which induced Captain Heamans to take sides in the conflict are differently represented by the narrators of this and the preceding account, the one claiming his sympathy with the cause, the other that his services were bought and paid for. It is evident, however, that Captain Fuller did formally demand the support of Heamans in the name of his Highness the Lord Protector. Fuller also secured the service of a small bark trading out of New England, equipped with two pieces of ordnance, which he caused to blockade the mouth of the creek where the boats were lying which had brought the greater part of Governor Stone's men to the scene. This was done during the night preceding the engagement, and thus cut off in advance their means of retreat.

The letters of Mr.[1] Luke Barber and Mrs. Virlinda Stone, wife of the Governor, contain valuable accounts from persons who had the best possible means of information. The killing of certain of the prisoners after they had surrendered upon promise of quarter, mentioned in these letters, is an undisputed fact.

Following the letters is the text[2] of the oath of fidelity required of grantees of land, with an explanatory note pointing out the differences between this oath and that required of the Governor and the members of Council; a copy of the Act concerning Religion enacted in 1649; and of a declaration signed by the Governor and numbers of other Protestant inhabitants of the province dated April 17, 1650, and certifying to the completeness of religious liberty enjoyed by them under the proprietary government.

The Act concerning Religion has been the subject of much controversy and consequent misapprehension. By many it has been supposed that the establishment of religious freedom in Maryland dates from this enactment in 1649. But it is clear from the instructions given by Lord Baltimore, under date of November 13, 1633, to the first colonists,[3] that this was the fixed policy of Lord Baltimore from the beginning. That it was prescribed by proclamation of the Lord Proprietary ap-

---

[1] Also referred to as Dr. Barber. He was a member of the Council and for a short time Deputy Governor. *Archives of Maryland*, III. 323, 331.

[2] This text differs somewhat from that of the oath of fidelity prescribed in 1648 (*Archives of Maryland*, III. 196), chiefly in omitting the word "royal" before the word "jurisdiction." See p. 214, *supra*.

[3] See pp. 13, 16, *supra*.

pears from the record of the trial of William Lewis in 1638. Lewis, a Roman Catholic, had forbidden certain Protestants, servants quartered with him, to read certain books in his house. He seems to have had sufficient cause of provocation, but being tried before a court composed of three Roman Catholics, Governor Calvert, Secretary Lewger, and Captain Cornwaleys, he was convicted and fined for having interfered with those persons in the exercise of their religion "contrary to his Lordship's proclamation." Another case arose in 1642, in which the traverser was also punished by fine.

The credit for the enactment of 1649 has been claimed both for Roman Catholic and Protestant influence in the Assembly; and to substantiate such claims, the rival disputants have each asserted a majority in the Assembly for the religious faith which they championed. The facts upon this point are hardly now susceptible of conclusive proof, but even if established, nothing as to the controlling influence by which this legislation was enacted would be proved; for it would have to be further shown that the measure was carried by the solid, or at least majority, vote of members adhering to one or the other of these two religious factions. And this is impossible, for no record of the proceedings of the Assembly of 1649 exists beyond the record of the laws enacted and of the adoption of an address to the Lord Proprietary, remonstrating against the transmission of laws prepared in advance for the assent of the Assembly. There is no record as to how the vote stood on any question.

In view of its record in other countries, notably in Spain and the Netherlands, it can hardly be claimed that the establishment of religious liberty was in accordance with the general policy of the Church of Rome; and that it was not in accordance with the views of the Puritans in Maryland is shown with emphasis by the fact that as soon as the controlling hand of the Proprietary was removed, at the first Assembly held under their sway, and from which Roman Catholics were excluded, this Act concerning Religion was repealed, and one substituted by which "this liberty" was denied to *popery* and *prelacy*. Members of the Churches of Rome and of England were alike excluded from the benefits of toleration.[1]

The facts seem to be easily reducible to the following conclusion:

Lord Baltimore, himself a Roman Catholic, perceived that in order to secure religious freedom for those of his own communion whom he invited to settle in Maryland, it would be necessary to accord it impartially to all who professed Christianity. He therefore in a broad-minded spirit of liberality and fairness adopted from the beginning the principle of religious liberty as the fixed policy of his government. This is in accordance with the explanation of his course given by his son and successor, Charles, in a letter to the Lords of the Council of Trade and Plantations, dated in March, 1678.[2]

When, after the overthrow of the royal power in England, Lord Baltimore recognized the necessity of committing the government of Maryland into the hands of Protestants, which he did by the appointment of William Stone as governor, together with that of Protestant members of the Council, he sought to preserve the continuance of his policy by securing the passage of a law upon the subject by which the people would become committed by their own act to the principle of religious liberty. With this view he sent to the Governor for submission to the Assembly a body of sixteen laws, apparently a sort of code, of which an act for religious liberty was one. The Assembly did not accept these laws in the form transmitted, enacted only a portion of them, and made alterations in those. Among those so passed was the "Act concerning Religion." The latter part of this act, in which the object is

---

[1] *Archives of Maryland*, I. 340.
[2] *Archives of Maryland*, V. 267, 268.

declared to be "the promotion of love and amity among the inhabitants," contains some language identical with that used in the oath prescribed for the Governor and may therefore be reasonably concluded to have been adopted from the original draft sent over by Lord Baltimore.

It is instructive to note that upon the restoration to Lord Baltimore in 1658 of his authority in the province, the laws enacted by the assemblies held under the authority of the commissioners of Parliament being deemed without legal force and void, the commissioners demanded and obtained from Lord Baltimore his promise that he would never consent to the repeal of that law which they had themselves attempted to repeal at the Assembly held by them in 1654, as above noted. (*Archives of Maryland,* III. 334.)

The original copy of the Act concerning Religion, engrossed on sheepskin and bearing the signature "C. Baltemore," is in the possession of the Maryland Historical Society, being among the large collection of Calvert Papers acquired by that society from England in 1888. How an act relating solely to Maryland should have been among them is explained by the endorsement upon it:—"Brought from Maryland in the troublesome times." (*Calvert Papers,* I. 75, *Fund Publication* no. 28.)

The text of the following pamphlet has been collated with a copy of the original edition in the library of the Boston Athenæum. It was reprinted in the *Maryland Historical Magazine,* IV. 42, from a transcript made from an original copy in the Bodleian Library, Oxford.

C. C. H.

REFUTATION OF BABYLON'S FALL

A Just and Cleere Refutation of a False and Scandalous Pamphlet Entituled Babylons Fall in Maryland &c and A true Discovery of certaine strange and inhumane proceedings of some ungratefull people in Maryland, towards those who formerly preserved them in time of their greatest distresse.
To which is added a law in Maryland concerning Religion, and a Declaration concerning the same.
By John Langford, Gentleman, servant to the Lord Baltemore.
Hee that is first in his owne cause seemeth just, but his neighbour commeth and searcheth him. Prov. 18. 17.
Whose hatred is covered by deceit, his wickednesse shall be shewed before the whole Congregation. Prov. 26, 26.
London, Printed for the Author, 1655.[1]

HAVING lately met with a Pamphlet, entituled, *Babylons Fall in Maryland* etc. which layes many false and scandalous aspersions upon the Lord Baltemore, his Government and Officers in Maryland, put forth by one Leonard Strong and attested by William Durand pretending to be Secretary of that Province, It was thought fit, in regard I have beene acquainted with and imployed by my Lord Baltemore in his affairs relating to that Province, both heere and there, for above twenty years last past, That I should publish this brief Refutation thereof, to undeceive such as may be deluded by it.

Captaine Stone (who is well known to be a Zealous and well affected Protestant) being Governour of Maryland under the Lord Baltemore did receive and protect in Maryland those people and their families mentioned by Mr. Strong when they were distressed in Virginia under Sir William Berkley, among whom it is to be noted that Mr. Richard Bennet (afterwards Governour of Virginia) was one, and thereupon a Commission was granted by Charles Stuart the eldest son of the late King

[1] Title-page of the original.

to Sir William Davenant, constituting him Governor of the said Province, alleadging therein the reasons to be, because the Lord Baltemore did visibly adhere to the Rebels in England (as he terms them in that Commission) and admitted all kind of Sectaries and Schismaticks, and ill affected persons into that Plantation.

These people seated themselves at a place by them called Providence, but by an Act of a Generall Assembly there called Anne-Arundell in Mariland and there was nothing promised by my Lord or Capt. Stone to them, but what was performed. They were first acquainted by Capt. Stone before they came there, with that Oath of Fidelity, which was to be taken by those who would have any Land there from his Lordship, and the Oath which was required of them to take before they could have any Patent for Land there, was ratifyed by an Act of a Generall Assembly of that Province, wherin those very men had their Burgesses, there being an expresse Clause in it, That it should not bee understood to infringe or prejudice Liberty of Conscience in point of Religion, as will appeare by the Oath it selfe, nor had they any regrett to the Oath till they were as much refreshed with their intertainment there, as the Snake in the Fable was with the Country-mans breast, for which some of them are equally thankfull.

But it is now, it seems, thought by some of those people too much below them to take an Oath to the Lord Proprietary of that Province, though many Protestants of much better quality have taken it and (which is more then can be hoped for from some of these men) kept it.

As to the Government there, they knew it very well before they came thither, and if they had not liked it they might have forborne comming or staying there, for they were never forced to either. The chiefe Officers under my Lord there are Protestants. The Jurisdiction exercised there by them is no other then what is warranted by his Lordships Patent of that Province, which gives him the power and priviledges of a Count Palatine there, depending on the Supream Authority of England, with power to make Lawes with the Peoples consent, and of Martiall Law in cases of Mutiny, Rebellion, or Sedition, without which powers and priviledges, his Lordship would not have undertaken that Plantation, and have beene at so great a charge, and run so many hazards as he hath done for it.

There are none there sworn to uphold Antichrist, as Mr. Strong falsly suggests, nor doeth the Oath of Fidelity bind any man to maintain any other Jurisdiction, or Dominion of my Lords, than what is granted by his Patent; for by expresse words it relates to such only as are therein contained, whatsoever Mr. Strong sayes to the contrary.

Though some of those people (it seemes) thinke it unfit that my Lord should have such a jurisdiction and dominion there, (unto which he hath as good a right as Mr. Strong or any of those people can claime to any thing they have) yet they it seemes by their arrogant and insolent proceedings thinke it fit for them to exercise farre more absolute Jurisdictions and Dominion there then my Lord ever did, such as in truth are Arbitrary and Barbarous without any lawfull right or Authority at all, nor are they contented with freedome for themselves of Conscience, Person and Estate, (all of which are establisht to them by Law there and injoyed by them in as ample manner as ever any people did in any place of the world) unlesse they may have the liberty to debarr others from the like freedome, and that they may domineere, and doe what they please.

As to the pretended Commission mentioned by Mr. Strong from the supreame Authority of England in 1652, for reducing of Maryland, there was no such thing; but the ground of that pretence was this. In September 1651, when the Councell of State sent Commissioners from hence, that is to say, Capt. Dennis, Capt. Steg, and Capt. Curtis, to reduce Virginia to the obedience of the Parliament, the said Councell appointed a Committee of themselves for the carrying on of the Affaires of the Admirallty, to give instructions to the said Commissioners for that business, and Colonell George Thomson being then in the Chaire of that Committee, Maryland was at first inserted in their instructions to bee reduced as well as Virginia, but the Committee being afterwards satisfied by all the Merchants that traded thither (who were engaged to assist with their ships in the reducement of Virginia) that Maryland was not in opposition to the Parliament, that Captaine Stone the Lord Baltemores Lieutenant there, was generally knowne to have beene alwayes zealously affected to the Parliament, and that divers of the Parliaments friends were by the Lord Balte- mores especiall directions received into Maryland, and well treated there, when they were faine to leave Virginia for their good affections to the Parliament; then the said Committee thought it not fit at all to disturbe that Plantation and there- fore in the presence of many of the said Merchants, caused Maryland to bee struck out of the said instructions, and the Councell of State did thereupon give Licence to many Ships to trade at that time to Maryland, but would not permit any to goe to Virginia, till that Colony were reduced to obedience; all which will bee testified by divers Merchants and others to be true.

In this expedition to Virginia Captaine Dennis and Cap- taine Steg the two chiefe Commissioners (who were present when Maryland was struck out of the said Instructions) were cast away outward bound, in the Admirall of that Fleet which was sent from hence upon that service, and with them the Originall Commission for that service was lost.

But Capt. Curtes having a Coppy of the said Commission and Instructions with him in another ship, arrived safe in Vir- ginia, and there being also nominated in the sayd Commission two other persons resident in Virginia, that is, Mr. Richard Bennett before mentioned, and Capt. Cleyborne (known and declared Enemies of the Lord Baltemores) they together with Capt. Curtes proceeded to the reducement of Virginia, which was effected accordingly; and Captaine Stone being then the Lord Baltemores Lieutenant of Maryland, did actually assist them therein. After all which, the sayd Mr. Bennett and Capt. Cleyburne went notwithstanding to Maryland, and upon pre- tence of a certaine Clause in their Instructions, That they should reduce all the Plantations in the Bay of Cheseapeacke, to the obedience of the Parliament, because some part of Maryland, where the Lord Baltemores chiefe Colony there is seated, is within that Bay, as well as all the Plantations of Virginia are, they required Capt. Stone and the rest of the Lord Baltemores Officers there, first to take the Engagement, which they all readily subscribed, and declared, that they did in all humility submit themselves to the Government of the Common-wealth of England, in chiefe under God: then the

said Commissioners required them to issue out Writs and Processe out of the Lord Baltemores Courts there, in the name of
the Keepers of the Liberty of England, and not in the name
of the Lord Proprietary as they were wont to doe; wherein
they desired to bee excused, because they did conceive the
Parliament intended not to devest the Lord Baltemore of his
right there; and that they understood out of England that
the Councell of State intended not that any alteration should
be made in Maryland, that the Kings name was never used
heertofore in the said Writs, but that they had alwayes beene
in the name of the Lord Proprietary according to the Priviledges of his Patent, ever since the beginning of that Plantation. That the Act in England for changing of the formes
of Writs declared onely, that in such Writs and Processe wherein the Kings name was formerly used, the Keepers of the
Liberty of England should for the future be put in stead thereof.
That the continuing of the Writs in the Lord Proprietaries
name was essentiall to his interest there, and therefore they
could not without breach of trust concur to any such alteration:
Whereupon the said Commissioners demanded of Captaine
Stone the Lord Baltemore's Commission to him, which hee
shewed them, and then without any other cause at all they
detained it and remooved him, and his Lordships other Officers
out of their employment there under him, and appointed others
to mannage the Government of that Plantation independent
of his Lordship.

By which it appears Mr. Bennet and Capt. Cleyborne took
upon them an Authority much contrary to the intention of the
Councell of State, and indeed contrary to common sense and
reason; for certainly if the Councell had had any excuse to
have altered their mind in that particular of Maryland, after
they had strucke it out of the sayd Instructions, they would
have caused it to have been put in againe by the same name,
whereby their Intention might have beene cleerely understood; much lesse could they have any Intention of reducing
any place that was not in opposition against them, but in due
obedience; so as if Maryland had been by any mistake put in
by name to be reduced, upon a supposition in the Councell
that it had been in opposition, yet they could not in reason
intend that in case their Commissioners had found when they

came upon the place (as they did) that it was not in opposition, that they should reduce it or prejudice any mans right upon that accompt: so that whatsoever was done in Maryland by the sayd Mr. Bennet, then Governour of Virginia, and the other persons Mr. Strong mentioneth as Commissioners from England for reducing of Maryland, or their subordinate Officers, having no firmer foundation from hence, was done without Authority, which makes all those proceedings mentioned by Mr. Strong of his friends and their pretended assembly there, illegall, mutinous, and usurp'd, and the Lord Baltemore and his Officers had just reason to rectifie the same by all lawfull means, other then which they used none, when they reassumed the Government; for by his Lordships Patent he and his Substitutes have power to make use of what force they can, to compell such as shall unlawfully oppose his Government there, and by a Law made with the consent of a generall Assembly of that Province, wherein the sayd people above mentioned had also their Burgesses, it was enacted that such as should by force of Armes oppose the Government there under the Lord Proprietary, or attempt the disinherison or dispossessing him (as those people did before Capt. Stone attempted any force upon them) of his rights or Jurisdiction there, according to his Patent, should be punished with Death and confiscation of their Estates, as is usuall and necessary in the like cases to be done in all such Governments whatsoever; though no such severity is ever put in execution there, but when all fair and gentle means, being first tried to reduce such people to obedience will not prevail.

Moreover that pretended authority of the said Commissioners for reducing of Maryland was urged heere in England by Colonell Matthews,[1] Agent for the said Mr. Bennet, and the Colonie of Virginia, when his Petition was debated before the Committee of Petitions of the late Parliament which began in July 1653, and was by that Committee dismissed, and yet notwithstanding, after the sayd dismission and Dissolution of that Parliament, the sayd Mr. Bennet and Capt. Cleyborne did again in July 1654, come into Maryland, and with the as-

---

[1] See Yong's letter, p. 59, *supra*, as to Samuel Matthews. He acted more than once as agent in London on behalf of Bennett and Claiborne, commissioners of Parliament in Virginia and Maryland.

sistance of some of the people above mentioned, by force of
Armes turned out Capt. Stone and the Lord Baltemore's other
Officers, and put others in their roomes, by what Authority no
man knowes; for although they had had, as they pretended,
an Authority (which in truth they had not) from the Parliament which was dissolved in April 1653, to do what they did
in Maryland in 1652, according to Mr. Strong's relation, yet
after the Dissolution of that Parliament the Authority from
it ceased, so as all proceedings in prosecution thereof afterwards was unwarrantable, unless that Authority which they
pretended had been given them by an Act or Ordinance of
Parliament for a certain time then not expired, or confirmed
by the succeeding supream Authority heer which it was not.

And although Mr. Strong shelter most of the bloudy
actions done by those who imploy him hither, under pretence that the Governement the Counsellors and Officers in
Maryland were Popish, and therefore there must needs be
some designe to extirpate those of another Judgement, yet he
doth not (because indeed he cannot) make appeare any disturbance given by Lord Baltemores Government to any person there for matter of Religion, but contrariwise it is well
known that no Nation affords better Lawes to prevent any
difference arising upon that Accompt, nor more freedome of
Conscience then that Government doth, as the most considerable Protestants in that Province have attested by an Instrument under their hands, unto which the sayd Mr. Durand
(attestor of the aforesayd Pamphlet) hath also subscribed his
name, wherein they doe also acknowledge that the sayd freedome is provided for not only by the sayd Lawes there, with
his Lordships assent unto them, but by severall other strict
Injunctions and Declarations of his Lordships for that purpose.

There are as well affected Councellors and Officers to his
Highnesse and this Government imployed and intrusted by
the Lord Baltemore in Maryland as any that oppose his Lordship there. And his Highnesse was by Capt. Stone caused to
be publikely and in a solemn manner proclaymed there as
Soveraign Lord of that place.[1]

As for the late unhappy contests there which (as Mr. Strong
saith) were desired by those people above mentioned to be

[1] *Archives of Maryland*, III. 304.

composed in an amicable way, how doth that agree with their
turning Captaine Stone out of his Governement in July 1654,
by force of Armes, and ferrying their men over the River
towards Capt. Stone in the last conflict, and the shooting of
Ordnance from Capt. Hemans Ship at Capt. Stone, and the
blocking up of Capt. Stones Boats by a Barque with two
peeces of Ordnance (as Mr. Strong confesseth they did before
any hostile attempt made by Captain Stone upon them) which
forced Capt. Stone to engage with them in his own defence.
As to Capt. Stones taking away the Records and Arms from
those of Patuxent, if he did so, it was but what every discreet
man ought to have done in the like case, they having been
Actors in displacing him as formerly; and lest in his absence
they should attempt upon the Colony behind him; but Mr.
Strong, I suppose, is the more impudent in alleadging untruths,
and indeavouring to smother under them the barbarous and
bloudy actions of those people, because he knows that they
have taken order to hinder what they can, all persons and
Letters which may come from thence hither, and have imposed
Oaths upon all those of concernment whom they had in their
custody, that they neither should endeavour to com over into
England, nor write any Letters or Petitions into England, to
manifest to his Highness the truth of their proceedings in
Maryland, which will reflect upon Mr. Strong as much as any
one else; nevertheless providence, notwithstanding all their
diligence to the contrary, hath brought some Letters and
Persons lately over from thence, which much contradict Mr.
Strongs Relation of the last contests there, viz. a Letter from
Mr. Luke Barber to his Highness the Lord Protector, which
the sayd Mr. Barber wrote when he thought he should not have
been able to have got away from thence, the people above
mentioned having detained him as well as others, but afterwards finding means to come hither himself in the same ship
wherein hee intended to have sent that Letter, hee thought fit
instead thereof to declare by word of mouth to his Highness
what was therein contayned, a Copy of which Letter subscribed by the said Mr. Barber is heerunto annexed, and he will
affirm the contents thereof upon Oath to be true. Another
is a Letter from Captain Stones wife (hee being a Prisoner,
and not suffered to write himselfe) to my Lord Baltemore, a

Copy whereof is also heereunto annexed: by both which it appears cleerly that Mr. Strong hath omitted to mention the putting to death of fowr of Captain Stones party by the people above mentioned in cold bloud, severall dayes after the fight, and hath very falsly related Capt. Stones and the Lord Baltemores other Officers proceedings in that last contest as well in relation to his Highness, as to those people above mentioned; wherfore for the present I shall refer the Reader to the said Letters for satisfaction therin, till further proofe bee made thereof in such a way as his Highness shall please to direct; whereupon my Lord Baltemore doubts not but his Highness will be pleased to do him and his Officers in Maryland right, and to call those to a strict accompt who were actors in the horrid murthers aforesaid: for certainly that pretence of theirs of acting what they did (as Mr. Strong sayes) in his Highness name will not excuse them; no man I conceive doubting but that whosoever shall presume to put any man to death in his Highness name, without any lawfull Authority from him, doth put a great dishonour upon his Highnesse, and not mitigate but aggravate the crime of murther in so doing.

And lastly, though it be a good thing to sing prayses and give thankes to God as Mr. Strong doth at the end of his Pamphlet, so tis a good thing to know God is not mocked, but will render unto every man according to his actions, and vindicate the innocent.

The Coppy of a Letter intended for his Highnesse.

May it please your Highnesse:
Having formerly had the honour to relate to your Highnes not only in your Army, but also as a domestick servant, I humbly thought it my duty to give to your Highness a true relation of the late disaster of this Countrey, which although it bee not a place any way considerable or worth your Highness trouble, yet when I consider the great care and pains your Highness hath formerly taken both below your selfe, and almost incredible to those that have not been eye-witnesses of them, for the true setling of Government, and avoyding the needless shedding of bloud, it gives encouragement to my pen, and assures me that the score upon which I write, will obtain

a pardon of your Highness for my presumption, it being
humbly and in the name of that great God (whom I know had
not your Highness feared would never have so palpably helpt
your Highness in your greatest necessity, and fought your
Battels) to beg a boon which will, I doubt not, absolutely end
the needless shedding of bloud, in this part of the World, in
regard now both parties pretend to fight for your Highness:
My Lord, my humble Petition to your Highness is, that your
Highness would be pleased graciously to condescend so low
as to settle the Country, so as we may heere understand the
absolute pleasure and determinate will of your Highness therein, the disobeyers of which cannot after your Highnesse known
pleasure but in a moment perish, and the rest live secure and
happie. My Lord I am an absolute stranger heere, as yet
having not been a month in the Countrie, in which time this
unfortunate action fell out, so much the sadder, in regard of
the common enemie the Indian who ever takes advantage by
our intestine troubles being both cruel and potent, and therfore I hope will be a motive to further the charitable conde-
sending of your Highnesse for setling the Country. My Lord
having had a very tedious passage being necessitated to stay
above two months in Bermudas and above one month in Virginia, so that I was above halfe a yeare from the time that I
came out of England to my arrivall in Maryland, at which
arival I found the Country in a great disturbance, the Governour Captain Stone being ready to march with his Army
(which heere is considerable if it consist of 200 men) against a
partie of men at a place called Anne-Arundell who the yeer
before (pretending a power from your Highnesse as also that
your Highnesse had taken the Lord Baltemores Country from
him) bred a great disturbance in the Countrey and withall
tooke away the Governours Commission from him, which
Governour being since informed by a Gentleman by name
Mr. Elkonhead[1] (one that came out of England 2 or 3
months after me) that the Lord Baltemore kept his Patent,
and that your Highnesse had neither taken the Lord Baltemores Patent from him nor his Land, hee thought hee might
act by the contents of his former Commission from the Lord
Baltemore and accordingly went up to reduce those people

[1] Eltonhead.

to the Lord Baltemores Governement, but still under your Highness command, as formerly under the Kings, having heer in the Country before I came first solemnly proclaymed your Highness, as also in all Proclamations and publick Edicts ending with *God preserve the Lord Protector and the Lord Proprietary.* Now going up to reduce these people, if possible by fair meanes, a Declaration to which purpose the Governour desiring me to bear him company [upon] the march, I got leave to carry to them, in the end of which the Governour did protest, as in the presence of Almighty God, that he came not in a hostile way to do them any hurt, but sought all meanes possible to reclaime them by faire means; and to my knowledge at the sending out of Parties (as occasion served) he gave strict command, that if they met any of the Anne-Arundell men they should not fire the first Gun, nor upon paine of death plunder any: these were his actings to my knowledge upon the march; but comming neerer to them, there was a Ship a Merchant man called the *Golden Lion,* one Hemans Commander, and as appeares hired by them, having since received his reward of them, who seeing the Governour land his men under the command of his ship, shot at them as they landed over night, and the next morning, continuing his course (as I am credibly informed) kild one of the Governours men, and so began the war which after fell out, for the Anne-Arundell men comming suddenly upon them on the one side, and the *Golden Lyon* being on the other side, they being in a neck of Land invironed round with water, except one little place by which the Anne-Arundel men came in upon them, where after a skirmish the Governour upon quarter given him and all his company in the field, yielded to be taken Prisoners. But two or three dayes after the Victors condemnd ten to death, and executed fowre, and had executed all had not the incessant Petitioning and begging of some good women sav'd some, and the souldiers others; the Governour himselfe being condemn'd by them and since begd by the Souldiers, some being sav'd just as they were leading out to execution, and since fall a sequestring their Estates, and taking away what they have as if they were meere Malignants, and had fought directly against your Highnesse, in which I cannot but speake my conscience knowing that at their first setting out the generall cry was that they went to reduce the Country and bring it under the obedience of your Highnesse and the Lord Proprietary, as also the Governour who protested to mee before he went out, that had he not been very credibly informed that your Highnesse had not taken away the Lord Baltemores Patent, nor his Land as the Anne-Arundel men pretended, he would not stirre in the business. My Lord, the reason why I take upon mee to give your Highnesse an account of this action is nothing but out of my duty to your Highnesse to give a true and impartiall account of the proceedings heere, in regard they still keepe the Governour and most of the Councell Prisoners, as also all the chiefe Officers till all the shipping is already gone out of the Country except one, and till that is gone I heare for certain none of them shall be releast, by which meanes, they are not onely debard from comming for England (as some desired to answer for what they had done before your Highnesse, and were denied it) but are likewise hindered from writing their grievances, as not being suffered to write to their own Wives, but their Letters are broke open, so that I cannot but thinke my selfe bound in conscience to declare the truth, as also to remaine so long as I possesse a being in this world,

> My Lord
> Your Highnesse most obedient and ever
> Loyall Subject
> L. BARBER.

Maryland this 13. of Aprill, 1655.

For the Right Honourable the Lord Baltemore, these present.
   Right Honourable:
I am sorry at present for to let your Honour understand of our sad condition in your Province. So it is, that my Husband, with the rest of your Councell went about a month agone with a party of men up to Anne-Arundell County, to bring those factious people to obedience under your Government. My Husband sent Dr. Barber with one Mr. Coursey with a Message to them, but they never returned againe before the fight began. Also he sent one Mr Packer the day after, with a Message, and he likewise never returned, as I heard: but so it is, that upon Sunday the 25. of March they did ingage with the people of Anne-Arundell, and lost the field, and not above

five of our men escaped; which I did conceive ranne away
before the fight was ended; the rest all taken, some killed and
wounded; my Husband hath received a wound in his shoulder,
but I heare it is upon the mending. My Husband, I am confident, did not thinke that they would have engaged, but it
did proove too true to all our great damages; They as I heare,
being better provided then my Husband did expect; for they
hired the Captain of the *Golden Lion,* a great ship of burden,
the Captains name is Roger Hemans a yong man, and his
Brother, who have beene great sticklers in the businesse, as I
hear. Captaine Heman was one of their Councell of War,
and by his consent would have had all the Prisoners hanged;
but after Quarter given, they tried all your Councellors by a
Councell of Warre, and Sentence was passed upon my Husband to be shot to death, but was after saved by the Enemies
owne Souldiers, and so the rest of the Councellors were saved
by the Petitions of the Women, with some other friends which
they found there; onely Master William Eltonhead was shot
to death, whose death I much lament, being shot in cold bloud;
and also Lieutenant William Lewis, with one Mr Leggat and a
Germane, which did live with Mr. Eltonhead, which by all
Relations that ever I did heare of, the like barbarous act was
never done amongst Christians. They have Sequestred my
Husbands Estate, only they say they will allow a maintenance
for me and my Children, which I doe beleeve will bee but small.
They keep my Husband, with the rest of the Councell, and all
other Officers, still Prisoners; I am very suddenly, God willing, bound up to see my Husband. They will not so much
as suffer him to write a Letter unto mee, but they will have
the perusall of what hee writes. Captaine Tylman and his
Mate Master Cook are very honest men, and doe stand up
much for your Honour; they will informe you of more passages then I can remember at the present; and I hope my
Brother will be downe before Captain Tylman goes away, and
will write to you more at large; for he is bound up this day
for to see his Brother, if they doe not detain him there as well
as the rest; the occasion I conceive of their detainment there
is, because they should not goe home, to informe your Honour
of the truth of the businesse before they make their owne tale
in England, which let them doe their worst, which I do not

question but you will vindicate my Husbands honour which hath ventured Life and Estate to keep your due heere, which by force he hath lost. And they give out words, that they have won the Country by the sword, and by it they will keepe the same, let my Lord Protector send in what Writing hee pleaseth. The Gunners Mate of Hemans, since his comming down from Anne-Arundell to Patuxent, hath boasted that he shot the first man that was shot of our Party. All this I write is very true, which I thought goode to informe your Lordship, because they will not suffer my Husband for to write himselfe: I hope your Honour will be pleased for to looke upon my Sonne, and for to wish him for to be of good comfort, and not for to take our afflictions to heart. And nothing else at present, I rest

Your Honours most
humble Servant
VIRLINDA STONE.

Post-script.

I hope your Honour will favour me so much, that if my Sonne wants twenty or thirty pounds you will let him have it, and it shall be payd your Honour againe.

Hemans the Master of the *Golden Lion* is a very Knave, and that will be made plainly for to appeare to your Lordship for he hath abused my Husband most grosly.

A True Copy of the Oath of Fidelity to the Lord Proprietary of the Province of Maryland.[1]

I A. B. Doe sweare that I will be true and faithfull (so long as I shall be a member of this Province) to the Right Hon. Cæcilius, Lord Baron of Baltemore, Lord and Proprietary of this Province of Maryland, and the Islands therunto belonging, and to his Heyres Lords and Proprietaries of the same, and to his Lieutenant or Chiefe Governour heer for the time being: And will not at any time by words or actions in publique or in private, wittingly or willingly, to the best of my understanding, any way derogate from, but will at all times, as occasion shall require, to the utmost of my power, defend

---

[1] This form of oath differs in some particulars from that prescribed in 1648, printed in *Archives of Maryland*, I. 196, and at p. 214, *supra*, with which it is to be compared. The changes are apparently due to the changed political conditions in England.

and maintain all such his sayd Lordships and his Heyres just and lawfull Right, Title, Interest, Privileges, Jurisdictions, Prerogative, Propriety and Dominion, over and in the sayd Province and Islands thereunto belonging, and over the people who are or shall be therein for the time being, as are granted to his sayd Lordship and his Heyres by the late King of England in his sayd Lordships Patent of the sayd Province under the Great Seale of England, not any wise understood to infringe or prejudice Liberty of Conscience, in point of Religion; And I doe also sweare that I will with all expedition discover to his Lordship or to his Lieutenant or other Chiefe Governour of the sayd Province for the time being, and also use my best endeavour to prevent any Plot, Conspiracy, or Combination, which I shall know, or have just cause to suspect, is or shall be intended against the person of his sayd Lordship, or which shall tend any way to the disinherison or deprivation of his sayd Lordship or his Heyres their Right, Title, Jurisdiction, and Dominion aforesayd, or any part thereof; And I doe swear that I will not either by myself or by any other person or persons, directly or indirectly take, accept, receive, purchase or possesse any Lands, Tenements, or Hereditaments within the sayd Province of Maryland, or the Islands thereunto belonging from any Indian or Indians to any other use or uses but to the use of his sayd Lordship, and his Heires Lords and Proprietaries of this Province, or knowingly from any other person or persons not deriving a legall Title thereunto, by, from, or under some grant from his said Lordship or his Heires Lords and Proprietaries of this Province, legally passed or to be passed under his or their great Seale of the said Province for the time being.

So help me God, etc.

This Oath was appointed by my Lord to bee taken by everyone who had any Land granted to him in Maryland from his Lordship before any Patent thereof should passe the Seale to him; and it was also appointed to be taken by a Law made in Maryland in An. 1649, with the consent of the Protestants as wel as the Roman Catholiks there, by every inhabitant above the age of sixteene yeeres, upon paine of Banishment in case of refusal, and of fine in case of return and a second refusall; but it was never yet imposed upon any, nor any ever yet banished or fined for refusall of it, onely they could have no land granted them from his Lordship, unlesse they tooke it; nor was there any other Oath appointed to bee taken upon any penalty whatsoever. But there was another

Oath appointed for the Governour and Councell onely in Maryland to take, which have these clauses among others in them (*viz.*) That they shall not accept or execute any Place, Office, or Imployment in Maryland relating to the Government thereof from any Person or Authority but from the Lord Baltemore or his Heires: and another Clause (*viz.*) that they shall not directly or indirectly, trouble, molest, or discountenance, any person whatsoever in the said Province, professing to believe in Jesus Christ, and in particular no Roman Catholick, for or in respect of his or her Religion, nor in his or her free exercise thereof within the said Province. But this Oath was never imposed upon any body, nor any penalty appointed for the refusall thereof; for it was free for any man, if he did not like the Oath not to accept of the place of Governour, or one of the Councel there; and this last mentioned Oath of the Governour and Councel was appointed in the life time of the late King. The Lord Baltemore conceiving it lawfull and justifiable by his Patent to require such an Oath from such as hee should employ in Offices of so great trust in so remote a place; for although by his Patent the sovereign Dominion of that Province bee reserved to the late King, his Heirs, and Successors, yet the immediate and subordinate authority of the Government thereof is granted to his Lordship and his Heyres, so as no man ought to act therein but by authority derived from him. And hee appointed this Oath to be taken by the aforesayd Officers when he made Capt. Stone Governour and Mr. Tho. Hatton Secretary, and others of his Councell there who being of different Judgement in Religion from himselfe, his Lordship thought it but reasonable and fit that as he did oblige them by Oath not to disturbe any there who professed to beleeve in Jesus Christ, so to expresse the Roman Catholickes in particular, who were of his own judgement in matter of Religion.

A true Copy of a Law made in Maryland entituled, An Act concerning Religion.

Forasmuch as in a well Governed and Christian Commonwealth, matters concerning Religion and the Honour of God ought in the first place to bee taken into serious consideration and indevoured to be setled. Bee it therefore ordayned and Enacted by the Right Honourable Cæcilius Lord Baron of Baltemore,[1] absolute Lord and Proprietary of this Province, with the Advice and Consent of the Upper and Lower House[2] of this Generall Assembly, that whatsoever Person or Persons within this Province and the Islands thereunto belonging, shall from henceforth Blaspheame GOD, that is curse him, or shall deny our Saviour JESUS CHRIST to bee the Son of God, or shall deny the Holy Trinity, the Father, Son, and Holy Ghost, or the Godhead of any of the sayd Three Persons of the Trinity, or the Unity of the Godhead, or shall use or utter any reproachfull speeches, words, or language, concerning the Holy Trinity, or any of the sayd three Persons thereof, shal be punished with death, and confiscation or forfeiture of all his or her Land and Goods to the Lord Proprietary and his Heires. And bee it also Enacted by the Authority and with the advice and assent aforesaid, That whatsoever Person or Persons shall from henceforth use or utter any reproachfull words or speeches concerning the blessed Virgin Mary, the Mother of our Saviour, or the holy Apostles or Evangelists, or any of them, shall in such case for the first Offence forfeit to the sayd Lord Proprietary and his heires Lords and Proprietaries of this Province, the sum of 5 *l.* sterling, or the value thereof, to bee levied on the goods and chattells of every such person so offending; but in case such offender or offenders shall not then have goods and chattels sufficient for the satisfying of such forfeiture, or that the same be not otherwise speedily satisfied, that then such offender or offenders shall be publikely whipt, and bee imprisoned during the pleasure of the Lord Proprietary, or the Lieutenant or Chiefe Governour of this Province for the time being; and that every such offender and offenders for every second offence shall forfeit 10 *l.* sterling or the value thereof to be levied as afore-

---

[1] "This title is given his Lordship in his Patent of Maryland." (Marginal note in the original pamphlet.) The reference is to the words "absolute Lord." The title Baron of Baltimore was conferred on his father by James I.

[2] These words, " of the Upper and Lower House," are interlined in the engrossed copy of the act. They are not in the record, *Archives of Maryland*, I. 244. The assembly was divided into two houses in April, 1650 (*ibid.*, 272), subsequent to the passage of the act, but prior to its approval by the Lord Proprietary.

sayd, or in case such offender or offenders shall not then have goods and chattels within this Province sufficient for that purpose, then to be publikely and severely whipt and imprisoned as before is expressed. And that every person or persons before mentioned, offending heerin the third time, shall for such third offence, forfeit all his lands and goods and be forever banisht and expelled out of this Province. And be it also further Enacted by the same authority, advice and assent, that whatsoever person or persons shall from henceforth upon any occasion of offence or otherwise in a reproachfull maner or way, declare, call or denominate, any person or persons whatsoever, inhabiting, residing, trafficking, trading, or commercing, within this Province, or within any the Ports, Harbors, Creeks or Havens to the same belonging, an Heretick, Schismatick, Idolater, Puritan, Presbyterian, Independent, Popish Priest, Jesuit, Jesuited Papist, Lutheran, Calvinist, Anabaptist, Brownist, Antinomian, Barrowist, Roundhead, Separatist, or other name or terme in a reproachfull maner relating to matter of Religion, shall for every such offence forfet and lose the sum of 10 s. sterling, or the value therof to be levied on the goods and Chattels of every such offender and offenders, the one halfe thereof to be forfeted and payd unto the person and persons of whom such reproachfull words are or shall bee spoken or uttered, and the other halfe thereof to the Lord Proprietary and his Heirs, Lords and Proprietaries of this Province; But if such person or persons who shall at any time utter or speak any such reproachfull words or language, shall not have goods or chattells sufficient and overt within this Province to bee taken to satisfie the penalty aforesayd, or that the same bee not otherwise speedily satisfied, that then the person and persons so offending shal be publikely whipt, and shall suffer imprisonment without Bayle or Mainprise until he, she, or they, respectively shall satisfie the party offended or grieved by such reproachfull language by asking him or her respectively forgivenes publikely for such his offence before the Magistrate or Chiefe Officer or Officers of the Towne or Place where such offence shall bee given. And be it further likewise Enacted by the Authority and consent aforesayd, that every person and persons within this Province, that shall at any time heereafter prophane the Sabaoth or Lords day called Sunday, by frequent swearing, drunkennesse, or by any uncivill or disorderly Recreation, or by working on that day, when absolute nécessity doth not require, shall for every such first offence forfet 2s. 6d. sterling or the value thereof; and for the second offence 5s. sterling or the value thereof; and for the third offence and for every time he shall offend in like manner afterwards 10s. sterling or the value thereof; and in case such offender or offenders shall not have sufficient goods or chattells within this Province to satisfie any of the aforesayd penalties respectively heereby imposed for prophaning the Sabaoth or Lords day called Sunday as aforesaid, then in every such Case the party so offending shall for the first and second offence in that kind be imprisoned till hee or she shall publikely in open Court before the cheif Commander, Judge, or Magistrate of that County, Towne, or Precinct wherein such offence shall be committed, acknowledge the scandall and offence hee hath in that respect given, against God, and the good and civill Government of this Province: And for the third offence and for every time after shall also be publikely whipt. And wheras the inforcing of the Conscience in matter of Religion hath frequently fallen out to bee of dangerous Consequence in those Commonwealths where it hath beene practised, and for the more quiet and peaceable Government of this Province, and the better to preserve mutuall love and unity[1] amongst the Inhabitants here, Bee it therefore also by the Lord Proprietary with the advice and assent of this Assembly, Ordained and Enacted, except as in this present Act is before declared and set forth, that no person or persons whatsoever within this Province or the Islands, Ports, Harbors, Creeks, or Havens thereunto belonging, professing to beleeve in Jesus Christ shall from henceforth be any waies troubled, molested or discountenanced, for or in respect of his or her Religion, nor in the free Exercise thereof within this Province or the Islands thereunto belonging, nor any way compelled to the beleefe or exercise of any other Religion against his or her consent, so as they be not unfaithful to the Lord Proprietary, or molest or conspire against the civill Government, established or to be established in this

---

[1] "Amyty" in the original act (engrossed copy). See *Archives of Maryland*, I. 246. There are a few other verbal differences which do not affect the sense.

Province under him and his Heyres. And that all and every person and persons that shall presume contrary to this Act and the true intent and meaning thereof, directly or indirectly, eyther in person or estate, wilfully to wrong, disturbe, or trouble, or molest any person or persons whatsoever within this Province professing to beleeve in Jesus Christ, for or in respect of his or her Religion, or the free Exercise therof within this Province, otherwise then is provided for in this Act, That such person or persons so offending shall be compelled to pay treble damages to the party so wronged or molested, and for every such offence shall also forfet 20 *s.* sterling in Money or the value thereof, half thereof for the use of the Lord Proprietary and his Heires Lords and Proprietaries of this Province, and the other halfe thereof for the use of the partie so wronged or molested as aforesayd; or if the party so offending as aforesayd, shall refuse or bee unable to recompence the party so wronged or to satisfie such fine or forfeiture, then such offender shall be severely punished by publike whipping and imprisonment during the pleasure of the Lord Proprietary or his Lieutenant or chiefe Governour of this Province for the time being, without Bayle or Mainprise. And be it further also Enacted by the authority and consent aforesayd, that the Sheriffe or other Officer or Officers from time to time to be appointed and authorised for that purpose of the County, Town, or Precinct where every particular offence in this present Act contained, shall happen at any time to be committed, and whereupon there is heerby a forfeiture, fine, or penalty imposed, shall from time to time distrain, and seise the goods and estate of every such person so offending as aforesayd, against this present Act or any part therof, and sell the same or any part therof, for the full satisfaction of such forfeiture, fine, or penalty as aforesayd, restoring to the Party so offending, the Remainder or overplus of the sayd goods, or estate, after such satisfaction so made as aforesayd.

This act was passed by a Generall Assembly in Maryland in April 1649, and assented unto by the Lord Baltemore in 1650, and the intent of it being to prevent any disgusts between those of different judgements in Religion there, it was thought necessary to insert that clause in it concerning the

Virgin Mary, of whom some, otherwise might perhaps speake reproachfully, to the offence of others. And in the time of the Long Parliament when the differences between the Lord Baltemore and Colonell Samuel Matthews, as Agent for the Colony of Virginia were depending before a Committee of that Parliament for the Navy, that Clause in the sayd Law concerning the Virgin Mary was at that Committee objected as an exception against his Lordship, wherupon a worthy Member of the sayd Committee stood up and sayd, that he wondered that any such exception should be taken against his Lordship; for (sayes hee) doth not the Scripture[1] say, that all Generations shall call her blessed? and the Committee insisted no more on that exception.

The Declaration and Certificate of William Stone Esquire, Lieutenant of the Province of Maryland, by Commission from the Right Honourable the Lord Baltemore, Lord Proprietary thereof, and of Captaine John Price, Mr. Thomas Hatton, and Captain Robert Vaughan of his sayd Lordships Councell there, and of divers of the Burgesses now met in an Assembly there, and other Protestant Inhabitants of the sayd Province, made the 17. day of April, Anno Dom. one thousand six hundred and fifty.

We the said Lieutenant, Councell, Burgesses, and other Protestant Inhabitants above mentioned, whose names are heerunto subscribed, doe declare and certifie to all persons whom it may concerne, That according to an Act of Assembly heer, and severall other strict Injunctions and Declarations by his sayd Lordship for that purpose made and provided, wee doe heere enjoy all fitting and convenient freedome and liberty in the exercise of our Religion under his sayd Lordships Government and Interest; And that none of us are any wayes troubled or molested, for or by reason thereof within this his Lordships sayd Province.

> William Stone Governour
> Jo. Price ⎱
> Robert Vaughan ⎰ Councell
> Tho. Hatton

[1] "Lu. i. 48." (Marginal note in the original pamphlet.)

James Cox
Tho. Steerman
John Hatche
George Puddington

Burgesses.

Note that
James Cox and
George Puddington
were then Burgesses

Robert Robines
Walter Bain
William Brough
Francis Poesy

for the people at Anne-
Arundell

*William Durand
Anthony Rawlins
Thomas Maydwell
Marke Blomefield
Thomas Bushell
William Hungerford
William Stumpson
Thomas Dinyard
John Grinsdith
William Edwin
Richard Browne
Stanhop Roberts
William Browne
John Halfehead
William Hardwich
Elias Beech
Raph Beane
John Slingsby
James Morphen
Francis Martin
John Walker
William Hawley
William Smoot
John Sturman
John Nichols

*Note that this is
the same man who
attests Mr. Strongs
pamphlet before
mentioned.

George Sawyer
William Edis
John Gage
Robert Ward
William Marshall
Richard Smith
Arthur Turner
William Pell
William Warren
Edward Williams
Hugh Crage
George Whitacre
Daniel Clocker
John Perin
Patrick Forrest
George Beckwith
Thomas Warr
Walter Waterling

LEAH AND RACHEL, OR, THE TWO FRUITFULL
SISTERS VIRGINIA AND MARY–LAND, BY
JOHN HAMMOND, 1656

INTRODUCTION

JOHN HAMMOND, the author of this pamphlet, which was published in London in 1656, represents himself as having been twenty-one years in the American plantations, resident for nineteen years in Virginia, and for the last two years in Maryland, whence he escaped after sentence of death had been passed upon him for the part he took in support of Governor Stone and the Lord Proprietary.

The first portion, which relates to Leah "the elder sister," as he calls Virginia, has much of the character of a prospectus put forth by a promotor of emigration. He paints in glowing colors the charm of life in the New World as contrasted with the struggling and painful existence which many were compelled to lead in the crowded cities of the Old, and gives, moreover, very practical advice to those proposing to migrate, either as independent adventurers or as servants, laborers, etc., whose only means of paying their passage over would be by binding themselves to work it out in service during a prescribed term.

The misrule which is described as prevailing during the earlier years of the Virginia colony is what led to the annulment of the charter of the old Virginia Company.

In the portion of the pamphlet devoted to Rachel, or Maryland, the latter is described as the younger sister, of whose beauty the writer became enamored as the patriarch Jacob was of his younger wife. The greater part of the account of Maryland is, however, given to the battle of the Severn and the events which preceded it,[1] and is written with

---

[1] For other accounts, see the three documents or narratives next preceding.

the partisan zeal which might not unreasonably be expected from one who, as told in the postscript, had been condemned to death by the one party to the contest as a punishment for his loyalty to the other side.

The protestation of the author that he wrote this pamphlet without reward may perhaps be regarded with doubt, unless it be assumed that, having been condemned to death once, he deemed that he was under obligations to those through whose agency he had escaped execution, and whose protection or assistance he might yet need.

The following text is taken from a copy of the original edition, now very rare, in the Harvard College Library. The pamphlet was reprinted in 1844, by Peter Force, *Historical Tracts*, vol. III., no. 14.

C. C. H.

LEAH AND RACHEL, OR, THE TWO FRUITFULL SISTERS VIRGINIA AND MARY-LAND, BY JOHN HAMMOND, 1656

Leah and Rachel, or, the Two Fruitfull Sisters Virginia and Mary-land: Their Present Condition, Impartially stated and related.

With A Removall of such Imputations as are scandalously cast on those Countries, whereby many deceived Souls, chose rather to Beg, Steal, rot in Prison, and come to shamefull deaths, then to better their being by going thither, wherein is plenty of all things necessary for Humane subsistance.

By John Hammond.

Eccles. 22. v. 8. If children live honestly and have wherewith, they shall put away the shame of their Parents.

London, Printed By T. Mabb, and are to be sold by Nich. Bourn, neer the Royall Exchange, 1656.[1]

TO

His Honoured and Worthy Friends the Worshipfull William Stone Esquire, Governour and Leiut. General of the Province of Mary-land, and Mr. James Williamson of Rapahanock in Virginia Gentlemen.

Gentlemen,

As yee both are Eminent in your Places, and are as well beloved where ye live, and that your loves to each other are such, as I wish the Union between Virginia and Mary-land to be, my Subject being concerning both places: I know none more fit then your selves to Dedicate it to, (not so much for your kindnesses, which I have often tasted of) as that the truth hereof under your Patronage may obtain belief and

[1] From the title-page of the original.

credit: I crave your Pardons, for intruding this unknown to
you, and using your names to so mean a piece; I have certified you wherefore I did it; to which I add, that I am desirous the whole country may note your affections to each
other; And that I dare in England own and Entitle him my
Governour, that in Mary-land I fled for submitting to. I
shall no further enlarg here more, then to let you know, that
I am to those Countries and Your selves, an

Humble Servant, and Well-wisher
whilest I am

JO. HAMMOND.

TO

*Those two worthy Commanders and Marriners, Capt. John
    Whittie, Commander of the good Ship, the* Freeman, *now
    bound for Virginia; And Capt. Sam. Tilghman, Commander
    of the* Golden Fortune, *now bound for the Province of
    Mary-Land.*

Sirs,

As I have made choice of two Honourable Gentlemen, the
one belonging to Virginia, the other to Mary-land; So I
thought it not impertinent equally with them to Dedicate
this to you two living in England, and using the Trade of
Virginia and Mary-land, that your selves may judge and
testifie, who well know the Country, that I have not added
to their worths, but rather been sparing of what is justly their
dues: For it is a received errour amongst the many slanders
cast on these places, that we are sworn neither to Speak nor
Write but glossingly of them; If we are so sworn, they cannot
believe yee are; and therefore will credite your Affirmations.
Both places speak worthily of you, both for affable usage of
your Passengers, and noble deportments towards the inhabitants in those Countries; and so are yee both noted, that I
wish yee were as well known to all strangers desirous to ship
themselves thither, as to us that have lived there: They then
would as much covet to be your Passengers, as we that by
experience have felt and known your goodnesse; many other
Gentlemen of good repute uses the Trade: but this I dare
affirm, that though they may be had in equall esteem, yet

men more generally beloved and applauded I have not known, using that Course than your selves: You know I flatter not; therefore I crave no excuse, unlesse for my presumption in this attempt; but seeing unknown to your selves, I have published your names here in Print, pray call me not to account for it: This Book I confess is not worthy of it, nor I of your angers; but how ever ye see it is past, and *litera scripta manet;*[1] yee must either buy up and burn all, or ye will be found here, and I hope not blemisht in it, nor in owning the truth of,

Your reall Servant,
JOHN HAMMOND.

Leah and Rachell, or the two fruitfull Sisters of Virginia and Mary-land; their present condition impartially stated and related.

It is the glory of every Nation to enlarge themselves, to encourage their own forraign attempts, and to be able to have of their own, within their own territories, as many several commodities as they can attain to, that so others may rather be beholding to them, then they to others; and to this purpose have Encouragements, Priviledges and Emunities been given to any Discoveries or Adventurers into remote Colonies, by all politique Common Wealths in the world.

But alas, we Englishmen (in all things else famous, and to other Countries terrible) do not onely faile in this, but vilifie, scandalize and cry down such parts of the unknown world, as have been found out, setled and made flourishing, by the charge, hazzard and diligence of their own brethren, as if because removed from us, we either account them people of another world or enemies.

This is too truly made good in the odiums and cruell slanders cast on those two famous Countries of Virginia and Mary-land, whereby those Countries, not onely are many times at a stand, but are in danger to moulder away, and come in time to nothing; nor is there any thing but the fertility and natural gratefulnesse of them, left a remedy to prevent it.

---

[1] The written word abides.

To let our own Nation (whose common good I covet, and whose Common-wealths servant I am, as born to no other use) be made sensible of these injuries: I have undertaken in this Book to give the true state of those places, according to the condition they are now in; and to declare either to distressed or discontented, that they need not doubt because of any rumour detracting from their goodnesses, to remove and cast themselves and Fortunes upon those Countries, in which if I should deviate from the truth, I have at this present carping enemies in London enough, to contradict and cry down me and this, for Impostours.   It is not long since I came from thence (God knows sore against my will) having lived there upward of one and twenty years; nor do I intend (by Gods assistance) to be long out of it again: and therefore can by experience, not hearsay (as Bullock[1] and other lying Writters have done, who at randome or for their own private lucre have rendred their Books rediculous and themselves infamous lyars, nor will I like them, over extoll the places, as if they were rather Para-dices than earthly habitations; but truly let ye know, what they are, and how the people there live.)   Which when im-partially viewed, will undoubtedly clear up those Foggy Mists, that hath to their own ruine blinded and kept off many from going thither, whose miseries and misfortunes by staying in England are much to be lamented, and much to be pittied.

In respect these two Sister Countries (though distinct Governments) are much of one nature, both for produce and manner of living; I shall only at present, Treat of the elder Sister Virginia, and in speaking of that include both: And ere I leave off, shall in particular rehearse the unnaturall usuage Maryland the younger Sister, hath had, not by Vir-ginia; but by those Vipers she hath received and harboured with much kindnesse and hospitalitie.

The Country is reported to be an unhealthy place, a nest of Rogues, whores, desolute and rooking[2] persons; a place of intolerable labour, bad usage and hard Diet, etc.

To Answer these several calumnies, I shall first shew what it was? next, what it is?

---

[1] *Virginia Impartially Examined*, by William Bullock, Gent. (London, 1649), a pamphlet in which the government of Virginia is denounced, and its condition described as wretched.   [2] Cheating.

At the first settling and many years after, it deserved most of those aspersions (nor were they then aspersions but truths) it was not settled at the publique charge; but when found out, challenged, and maintained by Adventurers, whose avarice and inhumanity, brought in these inconveniences, which to this day brands Virginia,

Then were Jayls emptied, youth seduced, infamous women drilled in, the provisions all brought out of England, and that embezzlled by the Trustees (for they durst neither hunt, fowl, nor Fish, for fear of the Indian, which they stood in aw of), their labour was almost perpetuall, their allowance of victual small, few or no cattle, no use of horses nor oxen to draw or carry, (which labours men supplyed themselves) all which caused a mortality; no civil courts of justice but under a Marshall law, no redresse of grievances, complaints were repaied with stripes, moneys with scoffes, tortures made delights, and in a word all and the worst that tyrany could inflict or act, which when complained of in England, (but so were they kept under that it was long ere they would suffer complaints to come home); the bondage was taken of, the people set free, and had lands a signed to each of them to live of themselves, and enjoy the benefit of their own industry; men then began to call what they laboured for their own, they fell to making themselves convenient housing to dwell in, to plant corne for their food, to range the wood for flesh, the rivers for fowle and fish, to finde out somwhat staple for supplie of cloathing, to continue a commerce, to purchase and breed cattle, etc. but the bud of this growing happinesse was again nipt by a cruell Massacre committed by the Natives,[1] which again pull'd them back and kept them under, enforcing them to get into Forts (such as the infancy of those times afforded): they were taken off from planting; their provisions destroyed, their Cattle, Hogs, Horses, etc. kill'd up, and brought to such want and penury, that diseases grew rife, mortality exceeded; but receiving a supply of men, amunition and victuals out of England, they again gathered heart, pursued their enemies, and so often worsted them, that the Indians were glad to sue for peace, and they desirous of a cessation, consented to it.

They again began to bud forth, to spread further, to gather

[1] *Narratives of Early Virginia*, p. 357.

wealth, which they rather profusely spent (as gotten with ease) then providently husbanded, or aimed at any publique good; or to make a Country for posterity; but from hand to mouth, and for a present being; neglecting discoveries, planting of Orchards, providing for the Winter preservation of their stocks, or thinking of any thing staple or firm; and whilest Tobacco, the onely Commodity they had to subsist on, bore a price, they wholy and eagerly followed that, neglecting their very planting of Corn, and much relyed on England for the chiefest part of their provisions; so that being not alwayes amply supplied, they were often in such want, that their case and condition being related in England, it hindred and kept off many from going thither, who rather cast their eyes on the Barren and freezing soyle of New England, than to joyn with such an indigent and sottish people, as were reported to be in Virginia.

Yet was not Virginia all this while without divers honest and vertuous inhabitants, who observing the general neglect and licensiousnesses there, caused Assemblies to be call'd and Laws to be made tending to the glory of God, the severe suppression of vices, and the compelling them not to neglect (upon strickt punishments) planting and tending such quantities of Corn, as would not onely serve themselves, their Cattel and Hogs plentifully, but to be enabled to supply New England (then in want) with such proportions, as were extream reliefs, to them in their necessities.

From this industry of theirs and great plenty of Corn, (the main staffe of life) proceeded that great plenty of Cattel and Hogs (now innumerable) and out of which not only New England hath been stocked and relieved, but all other parts of the Indies inhabited by Englishmen.

The inhabitants now finding the benefit of their industries, began to look with delight on their increasing stocks (as nothing more pleasurable then profit), to take pride in their plentifully furnished Tables, to grow not onely civil, but great observers of the Sabbath, to stand upon their reputations, and to be ashamed of that notorious manner of life they had formerly lived and wallowed in.

They then began to provide and send home for Gospel Ministers, and largely contributed for their maintenance;

But Virginia savouring not handsomely in England, very few of good conversation would adventure thither, (as thinking it a place wherein surely the fear of God was not), yet many came, such as wore Black Coats, and could babble in a Pulpet, roare in a Tavern, exact from their Parishoners, and rather by their dissolutenesse destroy than feed their Flocks.

Loath was the Country to be wholly without Teachers, and therefore rather retain these then to be destitute; yet still endeavours for better in their places, which were obtained, and these Wolves in sheeps cloathing, by their Assemblies questioned, silenced, and some forced to depart the Country.

Then began the Gospel to flourish, civil, honourable, and men of great estates flocked in: famous buildings went forward, Orchards innumerable were planted and preserved; Tradesmen set on work and encouraged, staple Commodities, as Silk, Flax, Pot-ashes, etc. of which I shall speak further hereafter, attempted on, and with good successe brought to perfection; so that this Country which had a mean beginning, many back friends, two ruinous and bloody Massacres, hath by Gods grace out-grown all, and is become a place of pleasure and plenty.

And having briefly laid down the former state of Virginia, in its Infancy, and filth, and the occasion of its scandalous aspersions: I come to my main subject, its present Condition and Hapinesse (if any thing can be justly called happy in this transatory life otherwise then as blessings which in the well using whereof, a future happinesse may be expected.)

I affirme the Country to be wholesome, healthy and fruitfull; and a modell on which industry may as much improve itself in, as in any habitable part of the World; yet not such a Lubberland as the Fiction of the land of Ease is reported to be, nor such a Utopian as Sr. Thomas Moore hath related to be found out.

In the Countries minority, and before they had well cleared the ground to let in ayre (which now is otherwise) many imputed the stifling of the wood to be the cause of such sicknesse; but I rather think the contrary; for divers new Rivers lately settled, were at their first comming upon them as woody as James Rivers, the first place they setled in, and yet those Rivers are as healthy as any former setled place in Virginia or

England it self: I believe (and that not without reason) it was only want of such diet as best agreed with our English natures, good drinks and wholesome lodgings were the cause of so much sicknesses, as were formerly frequent, which we have now amended; and therefore enjoy better healths; to which I add, and that by experience since my comming into England, (and many if not all Virginians can do the like,) that change of ayre does much alter the state of our bodies: by which many travellers thither may expect some sickness, yet little danger of mortality.

A Geographicall description of the Country I shall not attempt (as having little skill in the Mathematicks) enough of that hath been formerly Written; nor is it a place now to learn to discover. I shall abhor to spirit[1] over any; but go along with such as are voluntarily desirous to go thither, and lead them with my blunt relation (for truth knows little of eloquence) aboard the Ships thither bound, and carrying you into the Country, shew you the courtesie of the place, the disposition of the Inhabitants, the commodities, and give all sorts of people advice how and where to set down for their present benefit and future accommodation.

If any are minded to repair thither, if they are not in a capacity to defray their own charges (if they are I wish they might and so be at their own disposing) let them not be seduced by those mercinary spirits that know little of the place, nor aime at any good of theirs, but onely by foysting and flattering them to gain a reward of those they procure them for; beware them, for it is not only hab nab[2] whether ye go to a good service or a bad, but scandalous to your selves to be so seduced, and it were good and very just that such vagabond people were severely punished, as great betrayers of their own Nation, for ye cannot imagine but there are as well bad services as good; but I shall shew ye if any happen into the hands of such crooked dispositions, how to order them and ease your selves, when I come to treat of the justice of the Country, which many being ignorant of suffer inconveniences, which by this they may prevent.

[1] Carry any over against their will; kidnappers were in the seventeenth century called "spirits."

[2] Haphazard.

Let such as are so minded not rashly throw themselves upon the voyage, but observe the nature, and enquire the qualities of the persons with whom they ingage to transport themselves, or if (as not acquainted with such as inhabit there, but go with Merchants and Mariners, who transport them to others), let their covenant be such, that after their arrival they have a fortnights time assigned them to enquire of their Master, and make choyce of such as they intend to expire their time with, nor let that brand of selling of servants, be any discouragement to deter any from going, for if a time must be served, it is all one with whom it be served, provided they be people of honest repute, with which the Country is well replenished.

And be sure to have your contract in writing and under hand and seal, for if ye go over upon promise made to do this or that, or to be free or your own men, it signifies nothing, for by a law of the Country (waving all promises) any one coming in, and not paying their own passages, must serve if men or women four years, if younger according to their years, but where an Indenture is, that is binding and observing.

The usual allowance for servants is (besides their charge of passage defrayed) at their expiration, a years provision of corne, dubble apparrell, tooles necessary, and land according to the custome of the Country, which is an old delusion, for there is no land accustomary due to the servant, but to the Master, and therefore that servant is unwise that will not dash out that custom in his covenant, and make that due of land absolutely his own, which although at the present not of so great consequence, yet in few years will be of much worth, as I shall hereafter make manifest.

When ye go aboard, expect the Ship somewhat troubled and in a hurliburly, untill ye cleer the lands end, and that the Ship is rummaged, and things put to rights, which many times discourages the Passengers, and makes them wish the Voyage unattempted: but this is but for a short season, and washes off when at Sea, where the time is pleasantly passed away, though not with such choise plenty as the shore affords.

But when ye arrive and are settled, ye will find a strange alteration, an abused Country giving the lye in your own approbations to those that have calumniated it, and these infalable arguments may convince all incredible and obstinate opinions, concerning the goodnesse and delightfulnesse of the Country, that never any servants of late times have gone thither, but in their Letters to their Friends commend and approve of the place, and rather invite than disswade their acquaintance from comming thither. An other is this, that seldom (if ever) any that hath continued in Virginia any time, will or do desire to live in England, but post back with what expedition they can; although many are landed men in England, and have good Estates here, and divers wayes of preferments propounded to them, to entice and perswade their continuance.

The Country is as I said of a temperate nature, the dayes, in summer not so long as in England, in winter longer; it is somewhat hotter in June, July and August then here, but that heat sweetly allayed by a continual breaze of winde, which never failes to cool and refresh the labourer and travller; the cold seldom approaches sencibly untill about Christmas, (although the last winter was hard and the worst I or any living there knew) and when winter comes, (which is such and no worse then is in England), it continues two monthes, seldom longer, often not so long and in that time although here seldom hard-weather keep men from labour, yet there no work is done all winter except dressing their own victuals and making of fires.

The labour servants are put to, is not so hard nor of such continuance as Husbandmen, nor Handecraftmen are kept at in England, as I said little or nothing is done in winter time, none ever work before sun rising nor after sun set, in the summer they rest, sleep or exercise themselves five houres in the heat of the day, Saturdayes afternoon is alwayes their own, the old Holidayes are observed and the Sabboath spent in good exercises.

The Women are not (as is reported) put into the ground to worke, but occupie such domestique imployments and houswifery as in England, that is dressing victuals, righting up the house, milking, imployed about dayries, washing, sowing, etc. and both men and women have times of recreations, as much or more than in any part of the world besides, yet som wenches that are nasty, beastly and not fit to be so imployed are put into the ground, for reason tells us, they must not at charge be transported and then mantained for nothing, but those that prove so aukward are rather burthensome then servants desirable or usefull.

The Country is fruitfull, apt for all and more then England can or does produce. The usuall diet is such as in England, for the rivers afford innumerable sortes of choyce fish, (if they will take the paines to make wyers or hier the Natives, who for a small matter will undertake it), winter and summer, and that in many places sufficient to serve the use of man, and to fatten hoggs. Water-fowle of all sortes are (with admiration to be spoken of) plentifull and easie to be killed, yet by many degrees more plentifull in some places then in othersome. Deare all over the Country, and in many places so many that venison is accounted a tiresom meat; wilde Turkeys are frequent, and so large that I have seen some weigh neer threescore pounds; other beasts there are whose flesh is wholsom and savourie, such are unknowne to us; and therefore I will not stuffe my book with superfluous relation of their names; huge Oysters and store[1] in all parts where the salt-water comes.

The Country is exceedingly replenished with Neat cattle, Hoggs, Goats and Tame-fowle, but not many sheep; so that mutton is somwhat scarce, but that defect is supplied with store of Venison, other flesh and fowle. The Country is full of gallant Orchards, and the fruit generally more luscious and delightfull then here, witnesse the Peach and Quince, the latter may be eaten raw savourily, the former differs and as much exceeds ours as the best relished apple we have doth the crabb, and of both most excellent and comfortable drinks are made. Grapes in infinite manners grow wilde, so do Walnuts, Smalnuts, Chesnuts and abundance of excellent fruits, Plums and Berries, not growing or known in England; graine we have, both English and Indian for bread and Bear, and Pease besides English of ten several sorts, all exceeding ours in England; the gallant root of Potatoes are common, and so are all sorts of rootes, herbes and Garden stuffe.

It must needs follow then that diet cannot be scarce,

---

[1] Huge oysters, and plenty of them.

since both rivers and woods affords it, and that such plenty of Cattle and Hogs are every where, which yeeld beef, veal, milk, butter, cheese and other made dishes, porke, bacon, and pigs, and that as sweet and savoury meat as the world affords; these with the help of Orchards and Gardens, Oysters, Fish, Fowle and Venison, certainly cannot but be sufficient for a good diet and wholsom accommodation, considering how plentifully they are, and how easie with industry to be had.

Beare is indeed in some place constantly drunken, in other some, nothing but Water or Milk and Water or Beverige;[1] and that is where the goodwives (if I may so call them) are negligent and idle; for it is not for want of Corn to make Malt with (for the Country affords enough) but because they are sloathfull and carelesse: but I hope this Item will shame them out of those humours, that they will be adjudged by their drink, what kinde of Housewives they are.

Those Servants that will be industrious may in their time of service gain a competent estate before their Freedomes, which is usually done by many, and they gaine esteeme and assistance that appear so industrious. There is no Master almost but will allow his Servant a parcell of clear ground to plant some Tobacco in for himself, which he may husband at those many idle times he hath allowed him and not prejudice, but rejoyce his Master to see it, which in time of Shipping he may lay out for commodities, and in Summer sell them again with advantage, and get a Sow-Pig or two, which any body almost will give him, and his Master suffer him to keep them with his own, which will be no charge to his Master, and with one years increase of them may purchase a Cow Calf or two, and by that time he is for himself, he may have Cattel, Hogs and Tobacco of his own, and come to live gallantly; but this must be gained (as I said) by Industry and affability, not by sloth nor churlish behaviour.

And whereas it is rumoured that Servants have no lodging other then on boards, or by the Fire side, it is contrary to reason to believe it: First, as we are Christians; next as people living under a law, which compels as well the Master as the Servant to perform his duty; nor can true labour be either

[1] A name then given to various refreshing drinks, e. g., grape juice, or cider and water.

expected or exacted without sufficient cloathing, diet, and lodging; all which both their Indentures (which must inviolably be observed) and the Justice of the Country requires.

But if any go thither, not in a condition of a Servant, but pay his or her passage, which is some six pounds: Let them not doubt but it is money well layd out; yet however let them not fail, although they carry little else, to take a Bed along with them, and then few Houses but will give them entertainment, either out of curtesie, or on reasonable tearms; and I think it better for any that goes over free, and but in a mean condition, to hire himself for reasonable wages of Tobacco and Provision, the first year, provided he happen in an honest house, and where the Mistresse is noted for a good Housewife, of which there are very many (notwithstanding the cry to the contrary) for by that means he will live free of disbursment, have something to help him the next year, and be carefully looked to in his sicknesse (if he chance to fall sick) and let him so covenant that exceptions may be made, that he work not much in the hot weather, a course we alwayes take with our new hands (as they call them) the first year they come in.

If they are women that go after this manner, that is paying their own passages, I advise them to sojourn in a house of honest repute, for by their good carriage, they may advance themselves in marriage, by their ill, overthrow their fortunes; and although loose persons seldome live long unmarried if free, yet they match with as desolate as themselves, and never live handsomly or are ever respected.

For any that come over free, and are minded to dyet and quarter in another mans house, it matters not whether they know on what term or conditions they are there; for by an excellent Decree, made by Sir William Berkly, when Governour, (as indeed he was the Author of many good Laws:) It was ordered, that if any inhabitant received any stranger Merchant, or border into their houses, and did not condition in Writing with him or them so entertained on what tearms he received them, it should be supposed an invitation, an[d] no satisfaction should be allowed or recovered in any Court of Justice; thereby giving notice that no stranger coming into the Country should be drilled in, or made a purchase of under colour of friendship: but that the Inhabitants at first coming shall let them know how they mean to deal with them, that if they like not the terms they may remove themselves at pleasure; a Law so good and commendable, that it is never like to be revoked or altered.

Now for those that carry over Families and estates with a determination to inhabit, my advice is that they neither sojourn, for that will be chargeable; nor on the sudden purchase, for that may prove unfortunate; but that they for the first year hire a house (for seats are alwayes to be hired) and by that means, they will not onely finde content and live at a cheap rate, but be acquainted in the Country and learn the worth and goodnesse of the Plantation they mean to purchase; and so not rashly intangle themselves in an ill bargain, or finde where a convenient parcell of Land is for their turns to be taken up.

Yet are the Inhabitants generally affable, courteous and very assistant to strangers (for what but plenty makes hospitality and good neighbourhood) and no sooner are they settled, but they will be visiting, presenting and advicing the stranger how to improve what they have, how to better their way of livelihood.

Justice is there duly and daily administred; hardly can any travaile two miles together, but they will finde a Justice, which hath power of himself to hear and determine mean differences, to secure and bind over notorious offenders, of which very few are in the Country.

In every County are Courts kept, every two moneths, and oftener if occasion require, in which Courts all things are determined without exceptions; and if any dislike the proceedings of those Courts, they have liberty to appeal to the Quarter Court, which is four times a year; and from thence to the Assembly, which is once or oftner every year: So that I am confident, more speedy Justice and with smaller charge is not in any place to be found.

Theft is seldome punished, as being seldome or never committed; for as the Proverb is, where there are no receivers, there are no thieves; and although Doores are nightly left open (especially in the Summer time), Hedges hanging full of Cloathes, Plate frequently used amongst all comers and goers (and there is good store of Plate in many houses) yet I never heard of any losse ever received either in Plate, Linnen, or any thing else out of their Houses all the time I inhabited there.

Indeed I have known some suffer for stealing of Hogs, (but not since they have been plentifull) and whereas Hogstealing was once punished with death, it is now made penal, and restitution given very amply to the owner thereof.

Cases of Murther are punished as in England, and Juries allowed, as well in Criminal causes, as in all other differences between party and party, if they desire it.

Servants complaints are freely harkened to, and (if not causlesly made) there Masters are compelled either speedily to amend, or they are removed upon second complaint to another service; and often times not onely set free, (if the abuse merit it) but ordered to give reparation and damage to their servant.

The Country is very full of sober, modest persons, both men and women, and many that truly fear God and follow that perfect rule of our blessed Saviour, to do as they would be done by; and of such a happy inclination is the Country, that many who in England have been lewd and idle, there in emulation or imitation (for example moves more than precept) of the industry of those they finde there, not onely grow ashamed of their former courses, but abhor to hear of them, and in small time wipe off those stains they have formerly been tainted with; yet I cannot but confesse, there are people wicked enough (as what Country is free) for we know some natures will never be reformed, but these must follow the Fryers rule, *Si non caste, tamen caute;*[1] for if any be known, either to prophane the Lords day or his Name, be found drunk, commit whoredome, scandalize or disturb his neighbour, or give offence to the world by living suspiciously in any bad courses; there are for each of these, severe and wholsome laws and remedies made, provided and duly put in execution. I can confidently affirm, that since my being in England, which is not yet four moneths, I have been an eye and ear witnesse of more deceits and villanies (and such as modesty forbids me to utter) then I either ever saw or heard mention made of in Virginia, in my one and twenty years aboad in those parts.

---

[1] If not chastely, then at any rate, cautiously.

And therefore those that shall blemish Virginia any more, do but like the Dog bark against the Moon, untill they be blind and weary; and Virginia is now in that secure growing condition, that like the Moon so barked at, she will passe on her course, maugre all detractors, and a few years will bring it to that glorious happinesse, that many of her calumniators will intercede to procure admittance thither, when it will be hard to be attained to; for in smal time, little land will be to be taken up; and after a while none at all; and as the Mulberry Trees grows up, which are by every one planted, Tobacco will be laid by, and we shall wholy fall to making of Silk (a Sample of 400*l.* hath already been sent for England, and approved of) which will require little labour; and therefore shall have little use of Servants; besides, Children increase and thrive so well there, that they themselves will sufficiently supply the defect of Servants: And in small time become a Nation of themselves sufficient to people the Country: And this good policy is there used; As the Children there born grow to maturity, and capable (as they are generally very capable and apt) they are still preferred and put into authority, and carry themselves therein civilly and discretly; and few there are but are able to give some Portions with their daughters, more or lesse, according to their abilities; so that many comming out of England have raised themselves good fortunes there meerly by matching with Maidens born in the Country.

And therefore I cannot but admire, and indeed much pitty the dull stupidity of people necessitated in England, who rather then they will remove themselves, live here a base, slavish, penurious life; as if there were a necessity to live and to live so, choosing rather then they will forsake England to stuff New-Gate, Bridewell, and other Jayles with their carkessies, nay cleave to tyburne[1] it selfe, and so bring confusion to their souls, horror and infamie to their kindred or posteritie, others itch out their wearisom lives in reliance of other mens charities, an uncertaine and unmanly expectation; some more abhorring such courses betake themselve to almost perpetuall and restlesse toyle and druggeries out of which (whilst their strength lasteth) they (observing hard diets, earlie and late houres) make hard shift to subsist from hand to mouth, untill

---

[1] The famous place of execution.

age or sicknesse takes them off from labour and directs them
the way to beggerie, and such indeed are to be pittied, relieved
and provided for.

I have seriously considered when I have (passing the
streets) heard the several Cryes, and noting the commodities, and the worth of them they have carried and cryed up
and down, how possibly a livelihood could be exacted out of
them, as to cry Matches, Smal-coal, Blacking, Pen and Ink,
Thred-laces, and a hundred more such kinde of trifling merchandizes; then looking on the nastinesse of their linnen
habits and bodies, I conclude if gain sufficient could be raised
out of them for subsistance, yet their manner of living was
degenerate and base, and their condition to be far below the
meanest servant in Virginia.

The other day, I saw a man heavily loaden with a burden
of Faggots on his back, crying, Dry Faggots, Dry Faggots;
he travailed much ground, bawled frequently, and sweat with
his burthen: but I saw none buy any, neer three houres I
followed him, in which time he rested, I entered into discourse
with him, offered him drink, which he thankfully accepted of,
(as desirous to learn the mistery of his trade) I enquired what
he got by each burden when sold? he answered me three
pence: I further asked him what he usually got a day? he
replyed, some dayes nothing some dayes six pence; some
time more, but seldome; me thought it was a pittifull life,
and I admired how he could live on it; And yet it were dangerous to advise these wretches to better their conditions by
travaile, for fear of the cry of, a spirit, a spirit.[1]

The Country is not only plentifull but pleasant and profitable, pleasant in regard of the brightnesse of the weather, the
many delightfull rivers, on which the inhabitants are settled
(every man almost living in sight of a lovely river) the abundance of game, the extraordinary good neighbourhood and
loving conversation they have one with the other.

Pleasant in their building, which although for most part
they are but one story besides the loft, and built of wood, yet
contrived so delightfull, that your ordinary houses in England are not so handsome, for usually the rooms are large,
daubed and whitelimed, glazed and flowered, and if not

[1] A kidnapper.

glazed windows, shutters which are made very pritty and convenient.

Pleasant in observing their stocks and flockes of Cattle, Hoggs, and Poultry, grazing, whisking and skipping in their sights, pleasant in having all things of their own, growing or breeding without drawing the peny to send for this and that, without which, in England they cannot be supplyed.

The manner of living and trading there is thus; each man almost lives a free-holder, nothing but the value of 12 *d.* a year to be paid as rent, for every 50. Acrees of land; firing cost nothing, every man plants his own corne and neede take no care for bread: if any thing be bought, it is for commodity,[1] exchanged presently, or for a day; payment is usuall made but once a year, and for that Bill taken (for accounts are not pleadable.)

In summer when fresh meat will not keep, seeing every man kils of his own, and quantities are inconvenient, they lend from one to another, such portions of flesh as they can spare, which is repaied again when the borrower kils his.

If any fall sick, and cannot compasse to follow his crope which if not followed, will soon be lost, the adjoyning neighbours will either voluntarily or upon a request joyn together, and work in it by spels, untill the honour[2] recovers, and that gratis, so that no man by sicknesse loose any part of his years worke.

Let any travell, it is without charge, and at every house is entertainment as in a hostery, and with it hearty welcome are stranger entertained.

In a word, Virginia wants not good victual, wants not good dispositions, and as God hath freely bestowed it, they as freely impart with it, yet are there aswel bad natures as good.

The profit of the country is either by their labour, their stockes, or their trades.

By their labours is produced corne and Tobacco, and all other growing provisions, and this Tobacco however now low-rated, yet a good maintenance may be had out of it, (for they have nothing of necessity but cloathing to purchasse), or can this mean price of Tobacco long hold, for these reasons,

---

[1] Convenience.   [2] Owner.

First that in England it is prohibited, next that they have attained of late those sorts equall with the best Spanish, Thirdly that the sicknesse in Holland is decreasing, which hath been a great obstruction to the sail of Tobacco.

And lastly, that as the mulbery tree grows up, tobacco will be neglected and silke, flax, two staple commodities generally fallen upon.

Of the increase of cattle and hoggs, much advantage is made, by selling biefe, porke, and bacon, and butter etc. either to shipping, or to send to the Barbadoes, and other Islands, and he is a very poor man that hath not sometimes provision to put off.

By trading with Indians for Skins, Beaver, Furres and other commodities oftentimes good profits are raised; The Indians are in absolute subjection to the English, so that they both pay tribute to them and receive all their severall king from them, and as one dies they repaire to the English for a successor, so that none neede doubt it a place of securitie.

Several ways of advancement there are and imployments both for the learned and laborer, recreation for the gentry, traffique for the adventurer, congregations for the ministrie (and oh that God would stir up the hearts of more to go over, such as would teach good doctrine, and not paddle in faction, or state matters; they could not want maintenance, they would find an assisting, an imbracing, a conforming people.)

It is knowne (such preferment hath this Country rewarded the industrious with) that some from being wool-hoppers and of as mean and meaner imployment in England have there grown great merchants, and attained to the most eminent advancements the Country afforded. If men cannot gaine (by diligence) states in those parts (I speake not only mine own opinion, but divers others, and something by experience) it will hardly be done, unlesse by meere lucke as gamsters thrive, and other accidentals in any other part whatsoever.

Now having briefly set down the present state of Virginia not in fiction, but in realitie, I wish the juditious reader to consider what dislike can be had of the Country, or upon what grounds it is so infamously injured. I only therein covet to stop those blackmouthed babblers, that not only have and do abuse so noble a plantation, but abuse Gods great blessing in adding to England so flourishing a branch, in perswading many souls, rather to follow desparate and miserable courses in England, then to ingage in so honourable an undertaking as to travile and inhabite there; but to those I shall (if admonition will not worke on their recreant spirits) only say, Let him that is filthie be filthie still.

Mary-lands Additions.

Having for 19 yeare served Virginia the elder sister, I casting my eye on Mary-land the younger, grew in amoured on her beauty, resolving like Jacob when he had first served for Leah, to begin a fresh service for Rachell.

Two year and upward have I enjoyed her company with delight and profit, but was enforced by reason of her unnatural disturbances to leave her weeping for her children and would not be comforted, because they were not; yet will I never totally forsake or be beaten off from her.

Twice[1] hath she been deflowred by her own Inhabitants, stript, shorne and made deformed; yet such a naturall fertility and comelinesse doth she retain that she cannot but be loved, but be pittied; and although she would ever have vailed to Virginia as her elder, yet had not these two fatall mischiefs hapened, she would erelong have spread her self as largly, and produced as much in every respect as Virginia does or could doe.

Mary-land is a province not commonly knowne in England, because the name of Virginia includes or clouds it, it is a Country wholy belonging to that honorable Gentleman the Lord of Baltamore, granted him by Pattent under the broad Seal of England long since, and at his charge settled, granted for many reasons, and this for one; that Virginia having more land then they could manure or look after in convenient time, first the Duch came and tooke from the English much land which they still hold, next the Swead, who intrenched neerer and had not this Pattent came and prevented it, Dutch, Swead, French and other strangers had pend up our Nation

---

[1] The reference is to Ingle's rebellion, 1645, and the intervention of the commissioners of Parliament, 1651.

with in the bounds of Virginia, whereas now they have now all
Mary-land, as it were their own, it being only granted for the
use of Brittaines and Irish.

It is (not an Island as is reported, but) part of that maine
adjoyning to Virginia, only separated or parted from Virginia, by a river of ten miles broad, called Patomack river;
the commodities and manner of living as in Virginia, the soyle
somewhat more temporate (as being more Northerly). Many
stately and navigable rivers are contained in it, plentifully
stored with wholsome springs, a rich and pleasant soile, and
so that its extraordinary goodnes hath made it rather desired
then envied, which hath been fatall to her (as beauty is often
times to those that are endued with it) and that the reader
may thoroughly be informed how she hath suffered, I shall in
brief relate, and conclude.

It is to be understood that in the time of the late King,
Virginia being whol for monarchy, and the last Country
belonging to England that submitted to obdience of the Commonwealth of England, And there was in Virginia a certaine
people congregated into a Church, calling themselves Inde-
pendents, which daily encreasing, severall consultations were
had by the state of that Coloney, how to suppresse and ex-
tinguish them, which was daily put in execution, as first their
Pastor was banished, next their other Teachers, then many
by informations clapt up in prison, then generally disarmed
(wch was very harsh in such a country where the heathen live
round about them) by one Colonel Samuel Mathews[1] then a
Counsellor in Virginia and since Agent for Virginia to the then
parliament, and lastly in a condition of banishment, so that
they knew not in those streights how to dispose of themselves.

Mary-land (my present subject) was courted by them as
a refuge, the Lord Proprietor and his Governor solicited to,
and severall addresses and treaties made for their admittance
and entertainment into that province, their conditions were
pittied, their propositions were harkened to and agree on,
which was that they should have convenient portions of land
assigned them, libertie of conscience and priviledge to choose

[1] See letter of Thomas Yong, p. 59, *supra;* also Winthrop's *Journal,* II. 167,
168.

their owne officers, and hold courts within themselves. All
was granted them, they had a whole County of the richest
land in the province asigned them, and such as themselves
made choyce of, the conditions of plantations (such as were
common to all adventurers) were shewed and propounded to
them, which they extreamly approved of, and nothing was in
those conditions exacted from them, but appeales to the
Provincial court, quit-rents, and an oath of fidelitie to the
Proprietor: An assembly was called throughout the whole
Country after their comming over (consisting aswell of themselves as the rest) and because there were some few papists
that first inhabited these themselves, and others being of
different judgments, an act passed that all professing in Jesus
Christ should have equall justice, priviledges and benefits in
that province, and that none on penaltie (mentioned) should
disturb each other in their several professions, nor give the
urging termes, either of Roundheads, sectarie, Independent,
Jesuit, Papist, etc., Intending an absolute peace and union;
the Oath of Fidelitie (although none other then such as every
Lord of a manner¹ requires from his tenant) was over hauled,
and this clause added to it (provided it infring not the libertie
of the conscience.)

They sat downe joyfully, followed their vocations chear-
fully, trad increased in their province, and divers others were
by this incouraged and invited over from Virginia.

But these people finding themselves in a capacitie not
only to capitulate, but to oversway, those that had so received and relieved them,

Began to pick quarrells, first with the Papists, next with
the oath, and lastly declared their aversness to all conformali-
tie, wholy ayming (as themselves since confessed) to deprive
the Lord proprietor of all his interest in that country, and
make it their own: with [what] unworthiness? What ingratitude? with [what] unparalled inhumanitie was in these
practices made obvious.

Amongst others that became tenants in this aforesaid
distress was one Richard Bennett Merchant, who seated and
settled amongst them, and so (not only owed obedience to
that government, but) was obliged as a man received in his

¹ Manor.

pretended distresse, to be a gratfull benefactor. Upon the
setting forth of a fleet intended for the reducement of Virginia,
the said Bennet and one Claiborne, a pestilent enemie to the
wel-faire of that province and the Lord Proprietor, although he
had formerly submissively acknowledged he owed his forfeited life to the said proprietor, for dealing so favorably with
him for his misdemeanors, as by his treacherous letters under
his hand (now in print) is manifest, and many other acts of
grace conferred on him, having a commission directed to
them and others (who miscarried by sea) to reduce Virginia
(not Mary-land, for they were in obedience to the Common-
wealth of England, and great assistance to the said fleet)
although they knew Mary-land to be excluded and dasht out of
their Commission, yet because the commission mentioned the
Bay of Chesapeack, in which Mary-land was (as well as Virginia) yet they were resolved to wreth and stretch their commission to the prejudice of Mary-land and becomming ab-
betters and confederats with those serpents that have been
so taken in, presumed to alter the government and take
away the governours Commission, putting in others in their
place, *viz.* a Papist in cheife, and one more, who misgoverning
the Country, they were excluded, and the former governor
restored with an addition of Commissioners of their owne
creatures, and as taking power from them, untill further
knowledge from England, driving herein at their own interest.

The governour (so restored) being truly informed that their
proceedings were illegal, held Courts and proceeds as if no
such alteration had been made, issues out Writs (according to order) In the name of the Lord proprietor, but they
require and command them to do it in the name of the Keepers of the Liberties of England, according to act of Parliament, to which answer sufficient was given, that they never
were in opposition to the present power, they had taken the
Engagement, and for the tenure or form of writs, they were not
compelled by vertue of that act to make them otherwise then
they always had done, for by Patent from the late K. they had
power to issue out in the Proprietors name, and never had
used the Kings name at all, therefore that act requiring all
Writs formerly issuing out in the late Kings name, now to re-
volve to the Keepers of the Liberties of England, was no

way binding to them, who had never used the kings name at all.

But it was not religion, it was not punctilios they stood upon, it was that sweete, that rich, that large Country they aimed at; and therefore agrees amongst themselves to frame petitions, complaints, and subscriptions from those bandetoes to themselves (the said Bennet and Claiborne) to ease them of their pretended sufferings, and then come with arms, and againe make the Province their own, exalting themselves in all places of trust and command, totally expulsing the Governer, and all the hospitable Proprietors, Officers out of their places.

But when his Highnesse (not acquainted with these matchinations) had owned and under his hand and signet acknowledged Cap. Will. Stone (the former governor) Governor for the Lord Baltamore of his Province of Mary-land, he again endeavored to reasume the government, and fetched away the records from those usurpers, proclaimed peace to all not obstinate, and favorably received many submissives, who with seeming joy returned, bewailing their unworthy ingratitude and inhumanitie, blaming the unbridled ambition and base averice of those that had misled them.[1]

The Province consists of foure Counties already inhabited, viz. St. Maries, Calverton, An Arundal and Kent. St. Maries and Calverton submitted, An Arundall and part of Kent opposed.

The Governor desirous to reclaim those opposing, takes a partie about 130 persons with him, and sailes into those parts, one Roger Heamans who had a great ship under him, and who had promised to be instrumentall to the governor, to wind up those differences (being Judas-like, hired to joyn with those opposing Countries) and having the Governour and his vessells within reach of his Ordnance, perfidiously and contrary to his undertaking and ingagments, fires at them and enforces them to the first shore to prevent that mischief.

The next morning he sends messengers to those of An Arundall to treat, and messengers aboard that Shittlecock Heamans, but all were detained; and on the 25 of March last (being the next day and the Lords day) about 170 and odd

[1] See *Archives of Maryland*, III. 275; and *supra*, pp. 203, 239, 260, *et seq.*, for other accounts of the occurrences above narrated.

of Kent and Anne Arundall came marching against them. Heaman fires a pace at them, and a small vessel of New-England under the command of one John Cutts comes neere the shore and seazes the boats, provision and amunition belonging to the Governour and his partie, and so in a nick, in a streight were they fallen upon.

The Governour being shot in many places yeilds on quarter, which was granted; but being in hold, was threatned (notwithstanding that quarter given) to be imediatly executed, unlesse he would writ to the rest to take quarter, which upon his request they did, twentie odd were killed in this skirmish, and all the rest prisoners on quarter, who were disarmed and taken into custodie.

But these formerly distressed supplicants for admittance, being now become High and Mighty States, and supposing their Conquest unquestionable, consult with themselves (notwithstanding their quarter given) to make their Conquest more absolute, by cutting off the heads of the Province, *viz.* the Governor, the Counsel and Commanders thereof: And so make themselves a Counsel of War, and condemn them to death: Foure were presently executed, *scilicet*, Mr. William Eltonhead, one of the Councel; Capt. William Lewis, Mr. John Legate Gentleman, and John Pedro; the rest at the importunity of some women, and resolution of some of their souldiers (who would not suffer their designe to take thorough effect, as being pricked in Conscience for their ingratitudes) were saved, but were Amerced, Fined and Plundred at their pleasures:[1] And although this was prophetiquely foreseen by diverse eminent Merchants of London, who Petitioned his Highnesse for prevention, and that his Highnesse sent a gracious command to Bennet, and all others, not to disturb the Lord Baltamores Officers, nor People in Mary-land, but recalled all Power or pretence of Power from them; yet they still hold, and possesse (in defiance of so sacred a mandate) the said Province of Maryland, and sent an impious Agent home to Parlie whilest they plundred; but he hath long since given up his account to the great avenger of all injuries: Although sticklers (somewhat more powerfull, but by many

---

[1] For other accounts of this conflict see *Babylon's Fall*, and *Refutation of Babylon's Fall*, *supra*.

degrees more brazen fac't then his spirit could bare him forth
to appear) Now labour to justifie these inhumanities, disorders, contempts, and rebellions; so that I may say with the
Prophet Jeremiah;[1] How doth the Citty sit solitary that was
full of people? How is she become as a widdow? She that
was great amongst the Nations, and Princesse amongst the
Provinces? How is she become tributary? Thus have they
brought to desolation, one of the happiest Plantations that
ever Englishmen set foot in, and such a Country (that if it
were again made formall) might harbor in peace and plenty
all such as England shall have occasion to disburthen, or desire to forsake England.

A pious consideration of these distractions is by his Highnesse taking notice of, and these controversies are by him
referred to the Hearing, and Report of those two Honourable
and judicious Gentlemen the Lords Whitlock and Widdrington,[2] whose Pains and Moderation in Hearing, and mildly disputing indifferently the condition of these uproars, gives not
onely hopes of relief, but have added to their renowns, by all
those that (as observed) have been present at the severall
Hearings, an account whereof will ere long be published in
print.[3]

Upon determination whereof, it must be concluded that a
settlement will follow, and then many families will flock over
to inhabit these ruines, the fertility of the Province will (in
short time) make good (excepting the blood spilt which can
never be recalled nor satisfied for.)

Let this be no discouragement to any to goe over, for it
will now be more firmly settled then ever, and so throughly
setled that neither envy nor deceipt can again ever shake it.

And being so setled, I know no country (although I have
travelled many) that I more affect, more esteem; that which
profits delights, and here is both absolute profit, reall delight;
I shall forget my undertaking in the beginning of my booke,

---

[1] Lamentations i. 1.

[2] Bulstrode Whitelocke and Sir Thomas Widdrington, commissioners of the
Great Seal, called lords as members of Cromwell's upper house.

[3] *Archives of Maryland*, III. 320, 330, 331. The matter was finally adjusted
and Lord Baltimore's authority restored by agreement between him and the
commissioners. *Ibid.*, 332.

which was not to over extall the Country: for should I indeed give it its due commendations, I should seem to be suborn'd; but in few words, it is that Country in which I desire to spend the remnant of my dayes, in which I covert to make my grave.

This I have not written for profit, for it is known I have given away the copy, and therefore am the less to be mistrusted for a deluder, for popular applause I did it not, for in this pregnant age, my lines appear so harsh and disordered, that I would not have affixed my name to it, but in obedience to those commands that so require it, and to prevent the imputation of a libeller. The maine drift and scope I have herein aimed at, is to discover Virginia and Mary-land, and stand up in their just defences when calumniated, to let many that pine in England know, they are to their ruines deluded, that are frighted from going thither, if their wayes of livelihood be not certaine in England.

POST-SCRIPT.

A Word to the Governour and Counsell in Virginia.

Gentlemen,

As I have done your Country of Virginia justice in standing up in its defence, so I expect and entreat the like from you: I know ye are honest and understand your selves; I cannot except nor speake against any of ye, but Will. Claiborne, whom ye all know to be a Villaine, but it is no more blemish to your degree, to have him of your societie, then it was to the Apostles to have Judas of theirs. I have had injury by him by palpable cousinages done me, as I shal one day demonstrate. But for the decree of your court against one Captaine Thomas Thoroughgood, late Commander of the shipp *Cressent*, I desire you to consider of it again and reverse it for these reasons following.

I was an inhabitant of Mary-land of two years standing, proscribe to die by the rebells of the Bay. I fled disguised to Virginia, came a bord his Ship by an unknowne name, made my condition, not my person, known to him, and he charitably brought me for England, otherewise I had causelesly been put to death. For which letters certifies us in England,

that ye have amersed him in deep penalties, by an acte of
Assembly made against masters or Commanders of ships that
shall carrie away any of the inhabitants of your colonie without a pass.

First, know I was no inhabitant of Virginia, but Maryland, a government ye have nothing to doe with.

Next I came with my Governours consent, Captaine William Stone who in England justifies Captaine Thoroughgoods
bringing me home: and here I must and will abide such cen-
sure or vindication as the supreame power of England shall
find me to have merited; and therfore I humbly request ye to
peruse and reverse that order against him for bringing me for
England.

I shall hereafter give such an account to Virginia of my
actions from time to time, that they shall be fully satisfied;
I never deserved the least injurie either from any Government, nor any private person, since I first inhabited there.
But that shall be a subject particular: and a peece not usefull in England, but only to scatter in Virginia amongst my
friends, whos good opinion I covet, and that they may know in
many odiums I have been wronged, and that I am the man
that have seene affliction.

JOURNAL OF THE DUTCH EMBASSY TO MARY LAND, BY AUGUSTINE HERRMAN, 1659

INTRODUCTION

AUGUSTINE HERRMAN, the author of the following journal, was a prominent figure in Maryland's history. A Bohemian by birth, he was first a member of the Dutch colony of New Netherland. The high esteem in which he was there held is sufficiently proved by his selection by Governor Stuyvesant as one of the two envoys sent on a mission to Maryland, the account of which is here presented. Herrman was so much impressed by what he saw there that he subsequently removed to Maryland and became a large landholder, lord of a manor, which he called Bohemia in remembrance of the land of his birth, and an influential and valuable member of the community. In 1661 he was naturalized by special order of the Proprietary[1] and was the first person not a subject of the English Crown to enjoy the rights of a freeman in Maryland.

The circumstances which led to the mission to Maryland are briefly as follows:

Soon after the settlement of Dutch colonists, under the auspices of the Dutch West India Company, upon the island of Manhattan in 1624, several attempts were made by them to effect a settlement upon the west bank of the Delaware River. None of these became permanent, however, and in 1631 the inhabitants at a place they called Swanendael on the Lewes River were all massacred by the Indians.

The charter of Maryland was granted by Charles I. to Lord Baltimore in 1632; the first colonists set sail in November,

---

[1] *Archives of Maryland*, III. 398. This order is dated January 14, 1660/1. See also petition for naturalization in *Archives of Maryland*, II. 144. The inclusion of Herrman's name in the petition seems to have been unnecessary.

1633, and landed at St. Mary's in March, 1634. At that time there were no Europeans settled upon the west bank of the Delaware, which by the terms of his charter was included in Lord Baltimore's grant.

In 1638, a party of adventurers from Sweden sailed into Delaware Bay and effected a settlement at what is now the site of Wilmington, and there erected a fort which in honor of their queen they called Fort Christina. This colony grew in strength, and the Dutch, becoming concerned at this, built in 1651 a fort to which they gave the name of Nieuw Amstel,[1] where Newcastle now is; but this was soon captured by the Swedes and renamed Fort Casimir. The Dutch in turn captured both forts in 1655, and reduced the Swedish settlement to their obedience.

All this strife had been conducted within the territory granted to Lord Baltimore, and in order to prevent these settlers from claiming title by adverse possession the Governor and Council of Maryland in 1659 despatched Colonel Nathaniel Utie, a settler near the head of the Chesapeake Bay and a member of the Council, to proceed to the Delaware and notify the Deputy Governor, Alrichs, that the settlement was within the limits of Maryland, and that the settlers must submit to the authority of the Lord Proprietary's government. Colonel Utie appears to have exceeded the letter of his instructions by adding certain direful threats as to what would follow in the event of noncompliance on their part. The Dutch were not prepared to submit, and were not prepared for the war which they understood would be immediately thrust upon them. Therefore, while making preparations for the latter contingency, they despatched Augustine Herrman and Resolved Waldron as envoys to the Governor and Council of Maryland to negotiate for a settlement of the matters in dispute.

In the preamble of the charter of Maryland the territory

---

[1] New Amstel.

granted to Lord Baltimore is described as *hactenus inculta* (rendered in the translation printed in this volume[1] as "not yet cultivated and planted") and inhabited only by savages. This expression *hactenus inculta* is the basis of the claim on the part of the Dutch that the territory along the Delaware was not included in Lord Baltimore's grant for the reason that there *had been* Dutch settlements there prior to 1631. It has already been noted that there was no settlement there either at the date of Lord Baltimore's charter or at the date of the landing of the colonists in Maryland.

In response to the contention of the Marylanders that the English claimed the continent of North America by right of discovery, the envoys boldly carried the claim of title for the Dutch to the time of Columbus, asserting that the benefit of his discoveries inured to them as assignees of the Spanish Crown to which they formerly were subject. A map of Maryland was made by Herrman in 1670[2] which was engraved by W. Faithorne in London in 1673. It is remarkably accurate so far as the tide-water portion of the state is concerned, but largely conjectural as to the western, mountainous, and then unexplored portion.

The Dutch original of this journal is in the archives of the state of New York at Albany, where it is designated as "New York Colonial Manuscripts, vol. 18, p. 96." A translation was printed in *Documents Relating to the Colonial History of the State of New York*, II. 88 *et seq.* In the text which follows, the translation has been carefully revised, and certain corrections made, by Dr. A. J. F. van Laer, archivist of the state of New York.

C. C. H.

[1] See *A Relation of Maryland*, p. 101, *supra.*

[2] In conferring naturalization upon Herrman ten years before, Lord Baltimore mentions such a map as having been already drawn by him.

JOURNAL OF THE DUTCH EMBASSY TO MARYLAND, BY AUGUSTINE HERRMAN, 1659

Journal kept by Augustine Herrman during his Embassy from the Right Honorable the Director-General, Petrus Stuyvesant and the Supreme Council of New Netherland, to the Honble Governor-General and Council of Maryland, touching the pretensions set up by Colonel Nathaniel Utie to the South river.

Journal kept during the Journey to Virginia.

September 30, *Tuesday.* Set out on our journey from New Amstel about noon, accompanied by Resolved Waldron and our attached soldiers and guides, and, after travelling about an hour, arrived at a small creek which comes from Jagersland. Our course, as we computed, was west-northwest. About an hour and a half further came to a little creek or run of water, which we suppose flows also from Jagersland. Our course was westerly, and, having travelled about an hour[1] further, came to another run of water flowing southwards, where we must encamp for the night, as the Indians would not proceed any farther. Nothing occurred on the way except hearing a shot fired to the north of us, which the Indians doubted not was by an Englishman. Whereupon we fired three shots, to see if we should be answered, but heard nothing.

October 1, *Wednesday.* In the morning, before sunrise, proceeded on our course a little south of west by south, crossed two other little runs of water, branches, as we surmised, of the South River, and some dry thickets. The country afterwards rose somewhat, and again descended; about nine o'clock, came to the first stream that, the Indians said, flowed into the

---

[1] The "hour" by which distances are indicated in the manuscript equals three nautical miles.

Bay of Virginia, where we breakfasted; we computed it to be about five leagues from New Amstel. This stream, the Indians stated, is called, in their tongue, *Cimamus*, which signifies Hare Creek,[1] because the whole of this point is so named.

From this stream we proceeded southwest and west-southwest straight through the woods, without a path, and about one league or somewhat more, struck, as we presumed, the same creek; following it along to where the tide comes up, we found the boat which the Indians had mentioned, hauled on shore, and entirely dried out.

We embarked and dismissed our four guides, but Sander Poeyer, with his Indian, accompanied us; shortly after we pushed off, the boat became almost half full of water, whereupon we were obliged to land and turn the boat upside down; we caulked the seams somewhat with old linen, our people having left behind them the tow which had been given them for that purpose, and thus made it a little tighter, but one was obliged to sit continually and bail out the water. In that way, we came with the same tide a good league and a half down Elk River, and found ourselves at its east branch, where we built a fire in the woods, and proceeded with the night ebb on our journey with great labor, as the boat was very leaky, and we had neither rudder nor oar, but merely paddles.

October 2, Thursday. Having paddled down Elk River almost the whole of the night, came about 8 o'clock to Sassafracx River, where we stopped during that tide at   ,[2] on the plantation of one Mr. Jan Turner. Here we found Abraham the Finn, a soldier who had run away from Christina, and also a Dutch woman, whom he, the Jaeger,[3] brought hither. We offered them the General's pardon, in case they would return to New Amstel within six months, and should they then be unwilling to stay there, they would be at liberty to go to the Manhattans. The woman accepted these conditions, having three months more to serve, when she would return. But the soldier raised many objections. We prevailed, however, so far on him, that he made us a pair of new

---

[1] This stream, a tributary of the Elk River, appears from the description to be what is now known as Big Elk Creek.

[2] Blank in original.

[3] Hunter. *Cf.* Jagersland, above.

oars. We set Sander Poyer on shore here to obtain information, but we could not learn anything, as the only residents there were some Swedes and Finns, who had run away in the time of Governor Prins.[1] Having thus had a little rest, and the tide being favorable, we prosecuted our journey; but after we had pushed off from the shore, the aforesaid Abraham with one Marcus, a Finn, came to our side in a canoe, and would not let us pass, as they claimed the boat, and, notwithstanding we assured them that they should have the boat on our return, they forcibly held on to us, and this Marcus drew a pocket-pistol and threatened to fire if we would not stop. They had, besides, two snaphances; we finally got rid of them with a great deal ado. On leaving the river, we heard heavy volley firing on Colonel Utie's island, otherwise called ,[2] which we presumed must have proceeded from fifty or sixty men; it was mingled with music. This lasted until night, so that we conjectured they were making ready to go to the South River. On looking around for information, we accidentally found a newly begun plantation on our road, where people had come and were busy cutting down timber for a house, but the carpenter, who was one of my acquaintances, knew not what the firing meant, unless it might possibly be some feasting or frolic. He invited us, it being late, to remain with him through the night, as there was not another house on the way between this and Kent Island, but we proceeded on our journey and got two leagues farther. We would have gladly dispatched an Indian, could we have got one, to carry intelligence to New Amstel and to return to the Swedes with the boat, but we feared to be detained, so that we had no doubt but under the circumstances Sander Poeyer would do his duty.

This Sassafrax River runs close to our creek, which empties near Reedy Island. There is only a high hill between the two, whence both streams are visible at the same time. From that place the woman said she came down with the Jaeger. I understood that ships could sail up as far as this river, but no farther, because it is then shallow and navigable only for sloops, especially Elk River, which is quite shallow.

---

[1] Johan Printz, governor of New Sweden from 1642 to 1653.

[2] Manuscript defective; the island is called Spesutia (Utie's Hope).

October 3, *Friday.* We rowed forward during the tide of that night and day until opposite Pools Island,[1] which we estimate to be   miles from Sassafracx River. It lies near the west shore, and we passed with our leaky boat along the east shore, observing nothing on the way except that there was no fresh water to be found along here as far as Kent Island. We arrived, towards evening, at the north end of Kent Island, where, meeting a strong flood tide against us, and being fatigued, we took up our quarters with Captain [2] Wikx, who resides on the point and is one of the three magistrates of that island. Getting into discourse with him, we could learn nothing of any general design that the English might have, up to this time, of invading the South River, but he had understood that it belonged to Maryland, and they were bound, by agreement, to aid in maintaining my Lord Balthamoor's patent, or right and title. We replied on the contrary and said, we should be able to prove that the river belonged to us of old and to no one else, and whoever should wish to have it, must, by force of arms, wrest it from us; but that we, in the meantime, were prepared, and that 100 soldiers had already arrived and that in case of need fully 100 more might be expected, to defend the river to the last man. But we hoped that the English, with whom we had lived so long in neighborly friendship, would not try to get another man's land and rights, and thereby commence an open war, etc. From this conversation, he turned to certain news he had heard from Mr. Bateman, which Mr. Wright, the Indian interpreter, had brought down to Accomacq, from above the Bay, that in regard to the war which the Indians and the English are at present waging against one another, the former acknowledged that they were incited by the Dutch of the Hoerekill to murder the English, and that it happened in the following manner. A certain Indian came to a Dutchman in the Hoerekill and told him that he intended to kill a Dutchman because his father had been formerly slain by one. To which the Dutchman answered, that his father had been killed by the English and not by the Dutch, and therefore that he should revenge himself on one of the former. Thereupon the

[1] Poole's Island.
[2] Blank in original. Joseph Wicks; *Archives of Maryland*, I. 382.

Indian went off and slew an Englishman, and in this way the war commenced. It was suspected that the Dutch had not only secretly fomented it, but had furnished the Indians with powder and ball and guns, with which they were most abundantly supplied, a circumstance that the English took very ill. At first denying, then extenuating the case, I inquired the name of the Dutchman who had given the Indian such counsel; but he answered, he did not know; in such matters no witnesses were called, but things were done in secret, so that he could not be persuaded to the contrary.

We further inquired for a boat to convey us thence to the Governor and back, as our little skiff could not be used any longer, and was, also, too small. He offered us his own, but inquired what security he should have that he would get the boat back or be paid for it, as he had frequently before been deceived in that manner. To which we stated, that we could not give him any other security than our words and credentials, and that we should draw for security and payment on Mr. Brouwne, who, we presumed, was arrived with his ketch at Seavorn. And so we agreed at 20 *lbs.* of tobacco per day for the boat, and 20 *lbs.* tobacco for one man to accompany us, which was the lowest terms we could agree on. Otherwise, we should have been greatly perplexed, as we could not learn of any other opportunity here. We found here   's[1] wife, who said she had come away with her husband's consent, as he intended to follow her; but when we offered her pardon if she were willing to return with us, Captain Wikx complained that she was so lazy that she did not earn her salt; whereupon we observed, that it was easy to infer from this, that she had run away from the South River through laziness and unwillingness to work.

October 4. We sailed or rowed over to Seavorne to see if Mr. Brown had arrived there and would accept the draft, but he had not come. Captain Wicx wished to lodge us that night at Colonel Utie's, who, we understood, was at his plantation at Seavorn, but we declined, saying that we believed he was above on his island, as there had been so much firing, and so we took up our quarters, it being dark, at the house of Mr.   ,[1] father-in-law of Godtfried Harmer, the Indian

---

[1] Blanks in original.

trader, who, only a few days before, had gone up to his plantation; but his wife and child were at home. We gave the former to understand that our nation attributed great blame to Godtfried for enticing and transporting our fugitives from New Amstel, and that he would, therefore, do well to get the runaways back again there. Whereupon his father-in-law and mother-in-law excused him, saying that they had come, from time to time, to him, and had eaten him so bare that he would scarce have food enough for himself for the winter, and that he could not get the people to return nor could he refuse them a night's lodging, with many other excuses and complaints that the majority of the people they had seen, and even a poor, old man, with his wife and child, whom they had received in the greatest misery, were utterly idle and lazy, and not worth their food; nay, that they were too lazy to wash their own spoons and the plates which they ate off. We again took occasion to answer, that it was evident enough from this, that the people had not run away on account of the badness of the place, nor on account of ill-treatment, but because they had neglected, at the time, to do anything for a living and had come to Virginia to gain the bread of idleness. But it was replied, with all that, many had died of hunger, and the people had been refused bread for money, etc. To this we again replied, that this could not be supposed to be true. Nevertheless, even had they suffered any wrong, they must complain to the General and Council of New Netherland and not run to a strange nation. To which they made answer, that the Director in the South River[1] had refused and prevented their passage; with many other debates, too long to be here stated, the substance whereof was finally as follows: That the General and Council of New Netherland should publish a general pardon so that each may re-establish himself, and that the condition of the colony be redressed, and that those who will not remain there but wish to go to the Manhattans, be conveyed thither. The old man, who is a farmer and husbandman, promised to accompany us back to the Manhattans, but not to remain in the colony, which was allowed him. We understood, also, that there were many in

[1] Alrichs.

Seavorne who hired themselves and their children as servants. We requested that they be notified to return.

October 5: (7ᵇᵉʳ 25.)[1] *Sunday.* Rising early in the morning, gave a draft on Mr. Brouwne to pay Captain Josiae Wiks, on account of General Stuyvesant, in New Netherland, so much of his goods for the hire or use of the boat, to the value of 20 *lbs.* of tobacco, and for one man to accompany us, also 20 *lbs.* of tobacco, the amount whereof should be stated on our return, and reimbursed in beavers or other articles at the Manhattans. But this was not sufficient for Captain Wicks; he made us sign an obligation that we should deliver his boat safe at his house, or pay therefor 1500 *lbs.* of tobacco, at Seavorne or Kent, or make it good in brandy at the Manhattans. Being thus agreed, we received intelligence that Colonel Utie was at home at his plantation, and Captain Wicks importuned us to pay him a visit. But we answered that we dare not lose the opportunity of wind and weather, and that our message to the Governor required dispatch, and therefore Colonel Utie must excuse us from visiting him. As it was Sunday, he would probably entertain us too elaborately and detain us, for which we could not answer, and thus, with such like excuses, we set forth on our journey, with a fair breeze and fine weather, which brought us towards evening to May Billingsly's plantation at the Cliffs, estimated to be   miles from Seavorn. We did not observe any public preparations against the South River.

October 6: (*September* 26). *Monday.* Reached Potucxen river towards evening, where our people requested a night's lodging at Mr. Coerse's.[2] He welcomed us politely, being one of the Council with whom we had divers friendly conversations, and observed that Colonel Utie had been authorized to state at the colony of New Amstel that it was seated within their limits, and should therefore submit to them, but not to go to work with such menaces; and he was not well pleased

---

[1] The double notation of dates at this point and subsequently marks the period of divergence between the Julian calendar and the Gregorian—September 25 O. S., October 5 N. S. The Dutch at this time used the new style, the English and Swedes the old.

[2] Henry Coursey.

that, on that account, 100 soldiers, as we stated, had gone thither, for whose sakes we urged the more to hasten our journey. We also learned here that my Lord Balthamoer's patent dated only from about the year 1634,[1] to which we answered that our patent was issued nearly forty years ago. Whereupon they claimed to derive theirs originally from Sir Walther Ralegh since the year 1584, and we, on the other hand, take our origin, as vassals and subjects, from the King of Spain, then the first finder and founder of all America. Thus we finally concluded our conversation, with the hope, which we mutually expressed, that this matter might be settled and adjusted without bloodshed, and thereupon parted.

October 7: (*September* 27). *Tuesday.* Left our boat there and marched a-foot overland nine English miles, to the secretary's, Mr. Philip Calvert,[2] and Mr. Coersy conducted us full three English miles on the right road. Reaching Mr. Calvert's plantation early in the afternoon, we sent two of our people in advance to announce our approach and that we could not forbear paying him our respects, requesting passage across his creek to Mr. Ooverzee's [Overzee's], with whom we proposed to lodge, whereupon he invited us in, and after salutation we informed him that we had been sent by the Governor-General and Council of New Netherland to the Governor and Council of Maryland on weighty affairs, requesting him, therefore, with all speed, to be pleased to send intelligence thereof to the Governor, who lived   English miles farther up, and to recommend that we have an early audience and dispatch. We then took our leave, crossed the creek and arrived at Mr. Symon Overzee's, to whom we were very welcome guests.

October 8: (*September* 28). *Wednesday.* Mr. Overzee having invited the secretary, Mr. Philip Calvert, to dine, he came, being the next neighbor, early in the forenoon to visit us, whom we again requested, in Mr. Overzee's presence, to inform Governor Fendall,[3] as early as possible, of our coming, so that we may have an audience and be dismissed without delay, as

---

[1] The patent or charter of Maryland was dated June 20, 1632. The colonists sailed in November, 1633, and the settlement in Maryland was begun March 25, 1634.

[2] A younger half-brother of Cecil Lord Baltimore.

[3] Josias Fendall, governor 1656–1660.

the business was of great consequence, and caused daily great
expenses not only as regards ourselves individually, who had,
in addition, at our cost, a boat with a man at 40 *lbs.* of tobacco per day, but principally in regard to the military and
other preparations and expenses, which were expressly await-
ing our return with over 100 soldiers who had come from the
Manhattans. Thereupon he promised to do his utmost, but
that nothing could be effected before the next court, which
was to meet on   of October. We then conversed about New
Netherland and Virginia, and the conveniences of both being
considered, he wished Maryland may be so fortunate as to have
cities and villages like the Manhattans. And hereabouts, we
gave him to understand that Manhattans signified the entire
country, having preserved the ancient name of the Indian nation among whom the Dutch had first settled. And in this way
proceeded to the boundaries, when he said that the Maryland
patent extended along the sea from 38 to 40 degrees, wherein
Delowar bay was also included, and so across to Pamans[1] Island
and thence to the source of Potomock River. To which we
observed, that the 38th to the 40th degree must be understood
[to apply] only to the upper part of Cheseapeak Bay, and
that then the colony of Virginia extended from the lower part
of the said bay to the sea. To this he replied: Not so; and
that it was expressly stipulated that they should extend unto
New England, whereupon we inquired: If they wish to touch
New England, where would New Netherland be in that case?
He answered: He knew not. And we said, that therefore we,
both of us, well knew that such was a mistake; that our people
were in possession of New Netherland and had settled on that
place several years before Lord Balthamoer had obtained his
patent; further alleging, among other things, that Sir Edm.
Ployten[2] had, in former times, set up a claim to Delowar Bay,
and that, therefore, one claim must be as good as the other.

---

[1] Palmer's Island, now generally called Watson's Island, lies within the mouth
of the Susquehanna River, but south of the fortieth degree of north latitude.

[2] Plowden. In 1634 Sir Edmund Plowden received a patent under the great
seal of Ireland for a palatine province called New Albion, embracing the present
New Jersey, Long Island, eastern Pennsylvania, and parts of Delaware and
Maryland. Little came of the grant; for its history, see Winsor, *Narrative
and Critical History of America*, III. 457–468.

Whereunto he replied that Ploythen had had no commission, and lay in jail in England on account of his debts, relating that he had solicited a patent for *Nova Albium* from the King, but it was refused him, and he thereupon applied to the Viceroy of Ireland, from whom he had obtained a patent, but that it was of no value. Hereupon we confounded him by his own words, and said, that it was not certain whether my Lord Balthamoer's claim to Delowar Bay, should he have any, was not obtained by falsehood and misrepresentation, since it was very probable that the King of England would not have done anything against us, as he once had knowledge of, and consented to, the Dutch plantation of New Netherland, and had most expressly ordered and commanded those of Virginia and New England, as we should prove by their own English authorities, not to approach within one hundred leagues[1] of each other. It was, therefore, clear and evident, if their patent set forth that they could go as far as New England, that it was fraudulently obtained and of no value whatsoever.

October 9: (*September* 29). *Thursday.* Nothing occurred, except drawing up our proposals, which we thought best to do in English, in order to bring matters sooner to a speedy conclusion.

October 10: (*September* 30). *Friday.* Again, nothing has occurred, except that we heard the secretary has communicated our arrival to the Governor by a letter forwarded from constable to constable. He invited us to dinner on Sunday.

October 1/11, *Saturday.* Again, nothing special has occurred. We are impatiently waiting for the Governor's answer.

October 1/2, *Sunday.* Accompanied Mr. Overzee to Secretary Calvert's to dinner, where Mr. Doughty, the minister,[2] accidentally called. After dinner talked about his charts or maps of the country, of which he laid on the table two that

---

[1] One hundred *miles*. (Virginia patent of 1606.)

[2] Francis Doughty, one of the first Presbyterian ministers in America, founded Mespath near Newtown on Long Island in 1642, and preached there, but in 1655 removed to Maryland, his daughter, the widow of Adriaen van der Donck, having married a Maryland settler. See *Narratives of New Netherland*, pp. 334, 366, 401.

were engraved and one in manuscript. One was printed at Amsterdam, by direction of Captain Smith, the first discoverer of the great bay of Chesapeack, or Virginia; the second appeared also to be printed at Amsterdam, at the time of Lord Balthamoer's patent; we knew not by whom or where the manuscript one was drawn. All differed, one from the other. He wished to prove from them the extent of Lord Balthamoer's boundaries, but we, on the contrary, showed and maintained that if Chesapeak Bay ran, above, so crooked towards the northeast, they would come so far within our line. To this, he asked how could that be, for the English first discovered and possessed all these parts. Thereunto, we answered that the Dutch came but three years later in our parts than they in theirs. To which he replied, that they took their beginning from Sir Walder Ralegh; and we said, then we derive our origin from the King of Spain. But, he retorted, you were then not yet a free and independent nation. Whereupon he was told that the King of Spain was, at the time of the discovery of America, our king, and we were as much his vassals and subjects as they were the subjects of their king or republic of England, but afterwards, when we were obliged to take up arms, and achieved our liberty, the King of Spain conveyed over and to us, in full propriety, by lawful right and title, all his own and other conquered lands in Europe and America.[1] To this, he said that the King of Spain was, indeed, in the West Indies, but not so far to the north, and that the English were the first discoverers. And we again observed that the contrary could be proved from Spanish journals and chronicles, and also that even the French had, in the year 1524,[2] been before them in these parts. Lastly, being half angry, he demanded whether the English had not been the first in Delowar bay, for it obtained its name from them. And we answered, No; that the Dutch had been the first in the river, long before Lord Delowar ever came to Virginia,[3] and we again asked: What right had the Kings of Spain, France or England, more than the Hollanders or the Dutch,

---

[1] By the treaty of Münster, in 1648, Spain confirmed to the Dutch the possession of their colonies in regions formerly claimed by Spain.

[2] The allusion is to the voyage of Verrazano.

[3] There is no evidence in support of this statement.

to the New World—America? But these and such like discourses, running higher and higher, were left off; he said he
had invited us as a welcome to the country, and thencefor-
ward we conversed on other subjects, and parted from one
another with expressions of friendship.

October $\frac{13}{3}$, *Monday.* Nothing occurred.

October $\frac{14}{4}$, *Tuesday.* This being court day at Potuxen,
and Mr. Overzee going thither, we deemed it advisable to
have a brief request presented to [the court] for audience and
a place of reception, copy whereof is hereunto annexed.

October $\frac{15}{5}$, *Wednesday.* In the evening, about sunset, we
received in answer an invitation written by Philip Calvert,
in the name and on the behalf of the Governor and Council, that we should have an audience at the house of Mr.
Bateman, sending, with this view, two horses to convey us
there.

October $\frac{16}{6}$, *Thursday.* We took our departure in the morning from Mr. Overzee's for Mr. Bateman's, at Potucxen, being
about eighteen or twenty English miles, and about between
three and four o'clock in the afternoon, arrived Governor
Josiah Fendall with the secretary Philip Calvert and the
councillors William Stone, Thomas Gerrard, Nathaniel Utye,
Edward Loyd, Luke Barber, Baker Broukx,[1] who, after having welcomed us, and, after we had complimented them on
the part of our Director General and Council of New Netherland, thanked us cordially; and dinner being ready, the Governor said he would give us an audience after we had dined.
And, sitting down to table, they placed me beside the Governor
on his left hand; on his right sat Philip Calvert, the secretary,
next to him Resolved Waldron, and so on the other members
of the Council around the table. During the dinner a varied
conversation was held.

The cloth having been removed, we were invited to the
audience, and after we had again presented the friendly,
neighborly respects and compliments of the Honorable Director
General and Council of New Netherland, we delivered, in the
first place, our letters of credence, which the Governor, opening and seeing that they were written in Dutch, had Mr.
Overzee called to translate them. Meanwhile, their sub-

[1] Brooks.

stance being stated, we proceeded to deliver our speech[1] in English, by way of declaration and manifest, which, for this purpose, we had previously committed to paper. In order that no mistake may be hereafter pleaded in the one or the other, we gave the secretary the original, with the request that he would be pleased to collate it with us, and we distinctly and clearly read the duplicate, which we moreover delivered under the seal of our commission, with the statement, at the end of the certificate, that that was all we had to say and to propose at that time, on the part and in the name of the Director General and Council, subscribing the same with our own hand, in the presence of all; and we exchanged the duplicate for the original, and the original again for the copy, which we kept for ourselves, and left them the other.

We perceived a great change, for some of the Council, as it seems, had no correct knowledge of what passed; and the Governor, in answer, inquired whether his letter, which he had sent with or by Colonel Utie, had not been shown to the Governor General of the Manhattans? We replied, No: his Honor had not seen any formal letter, but that we had, indeed, understood, at the South River, that Mr. Allericks[2] had received a private letter in answer to his, but without day or date, or place where written, whereof the Director General and Council did not take any notice. Whereupon the Governor made answer, that he had nothing to do with the government of the Manhattans, but with the governor and people who had lately seated themselves within his limits in Delowar Bay, to whom they had sent Colonel Uty; not that he should have communicated his instruction which had been given him for his guidance and vindication only, as we were not obliged to deliver our instruction to them. To this we replied, that the governor and people in the South River were not a separate, but subaltern and dependent government, and simply deputy governor and members of New Netherland, so that whatever was presented and given to them in

[1] An English translation of the letter of Governor Stuyvesant, together with the speech of the envoys and the reply of the Governor and Council, is printed in full in *Archives of Maryland*, III. 366–378.

[2] Jacob Alrichs was director of the Dutch colony of New Amstel, possessed at this time by the city of Amsterdam, yet deemed a part of New Netherland.

the matter of high jurisdiction, etc., did not affect them but the General and Council, and consequently, the whole state of New Netherland, and the lords proprietors thereof; yea, the sovereignty of Their High Mightinesses. Whereunto he again rejoined, that they did not know nor understand any better than that the governor in Delowar derived his commission from the city of Amsterdam, and had come with his people to settle there as a separate government. To which we again answered, No; but that the city of Amsterdam owned the place as a colony and particular district of New Netherland, which was similar, in manner and style, to their counties in Virginia or Maryland, and we had more such colonies planted in New Netherland, so that whatever injury was done to the colony of New Amstel, was, I say, inflicted on the entire state of New Netherland. Meanwhile, Colonel Nathaniel Utie began to bluster and to say, that they ought not to take any notice at all of this matter; his acts had been directed against a people that had intruded into my Lord Balthamore's province, and if the Governor and Council will again command him, he will again act as he had done. We rejoined thereto, If he returned and comported himself as he had done, he would lose the name of ambassador and be dealt by as a disturber of the public peace, because a deputy or ambassador could not attempt anything except to notify the magistracy and regents of the place in a courteous manner of his embassy; but to summon a place by fire and sword was the style of avowed enmity, war and hostility. To this he replied, that he had done nothing in contradiction to his commission and instructions. To which we rejoined, that they had only to look at the answer he had brought back, which would clearly show how he had acted. And he, thereupon, further said, that he heard they had threatened to send him to Holland; he only wished they had done so. We replied, that should he return and act as he had done, probably he would not fare any better. Whereupon he inquired, how, then, should he behave? He had certainly sent two men before him to announce his approach; afterwards put up at the public tavern, and was he, then, not to walk out and see the place and converse with the people who requested to have some discourse with him? To which we again remonstrated, that he was at liberty to see the place and converse with the people, but not to excite them to revolt and rebellion against their magistrates, and threaten them with being plundered and driven off in case they would not willingly surrender. So that these criminations and recriminations being bandied somewhat sharply and angrily, especially by the colonel, the Governor was pleased to put a stop to him, and we were at liberty to express our meaning without any interruption, whereupon we referred entirely to our manifest and declaration, and to the answer which Colonel Uty himself had brought from New Amstel. We requested that such might be taken into consideration and that no frivolous discourses be allowed.

The Governor submitted to the Council, among other things, that we had come without asking proper permission, which Colonel Uty ought to have given and signified. To which we answered that we were not acquainted with the state and form of their government, but that we should in future regulate ourselves according to such custom as may be pleasing to them to establish in such cases. Hereupon, Colonel Utie began again to exclaim, saying that we ought to have first recognized him and gone to his island, and inquired if we should be permitted to proceed farther, adding in so many words that, had he met us, or had he known of our coming, he would have detained us there, and not allowed us to go on. But one of the Council softened that expression by saying that we should have been furnished with a better boat and accommodation, for we had stated that we had come down in a small, leaky boat, and dared not venture from the shore. But we readily discovered that, had we not done our best to avoid Colonel Utie on the way, he would have at once endeavored to prevent our design.

At length, after some debate, we were invited to withdraw, and, after a short deliberation, were recalled and informed that they had acted by special order and command of Lord Balthamoore, whose right and jurisdiction they are sworn to maintain, and that they would exhibit Lord Balthamoer's patent on the morrow, until when they should defer any further public business, and pass the remainder of the evening over a glass of wine, promising, on our request, to dismiss us by next Saturday.

Meanwhile, we proceeded now and then to engage one and another of them in private conversation, in the first place to dispose them to a friendly course, and to have the claim they set up to our limits, and we to theirs, decided by commissioners, in order to avoid further mischief and bloodshed; and in the second place, to agree to an intimate correspondence and confederation for reciprocal trade and intercourse. We found the majority of them favorably inclined to this view, but yet, they gave it to be understood that it was not in their power, and that they had no other commission than to defend Lord Balthamoor's lawful patent. This they were disposed to do, however, with all possible and justifiable prudence.

I had also a private conversation on that point with the Governor, who declared that he would prefer to continue in peace and quietness than to live in hostility and war.

October ¹⁷/₇, Friday morning. After breakfast, the Governor and Council laid before us Lord Balthamoore's patent, and read to us the article respecting his jurisdiction. We requested a copy thereof, when we should answer it. We were then allowed to make an extract of it ourselves. Meanwhile, the Governor and Council went to hold their court at the next plantation, whilst we, in the meantime, had time to read and reread the above mentioned patent, and to extract the point respecting the boundary, to which we drew up on paper a written refutation. For we found that it was set forth in the preamble that Lord Balthamoer had applied to and petitioned His Majesty for a tract of country in America, which was neither cultivated nor planted, but only inhabited as yet by barbarous Indians. In answer whereunto, we maintained that our South River, called of old Nassaw River, had been long before occupied, appropriated and purchased by us in virtue of a commission and grant of Their High Mightinesses the Lords States General of the United Netherlands, and therefore that it was His Royal Majesty's intention and justice not to have given away and granted that part of a country which had been previously taken possession of and settled by the subjects of Their High Mightinesses the Lords States General, as already declared and demonstrated, and that Lord Balthamor's patent was invalid where it makes mention of Delowar Bay, or any part thereof, as well as in various other respects and particulars. We requested a note might be made of this. The Governor and Council returning in the afternoon, and supper being over, we delivered the above mentioned answer in writing, having read the same aloud. Whereupon we perceived another change, and the Governor made his defence: That, on the contrary, our assertion and action were invalid, for the aforesaid patent was granted by the King, with full knowledge and understanding of the case, that Delowar Bay should remain and belong to the English, and demanded a view of our patent to New Netherland or Delowar Bay. We answered that at that time we did not have to show it, much less had we come for that purpose, but only to prepare a way for a future meeting of deputies on both sides, then to dispose chiefly of that point, agreeably to our advice contained in our declaration. The Governor thereupon made answer that they then need not have exhibited their patent either, from which we concluded that they regretted having discovered and exposed themselves so far, saying if that part of the patent was invalid, or if they yielded it, the entire patent might then become void. We replied that we drew no inferences on that subject except so far as it concerned us, and they set up a claim to our limits. Whereupon the Governor rejoined: That Col. Clabborne[1] had heretofore set up the same exception against Lord Balthamoer in regard to the Island of Kent, of which said Col. Clabbort held that he had taken actual possession before the aforesaid patent had been granted, but that it did not avail, and fared badly with him, so that he was obliged to beg his life from Lord Balthemor. To this we answered that this was a different case; that we were not subjects of England, but a free, sovereign people belonging to the Dutch nation, who, as we had already declared, had as much right to take possession of any lands in America as any other nation. And with this and such like debates, was the meeting adjourned for the night.

October ⅛, *Saturday*. The Governor and Council [being met in order to our][2] dismissal, they again demanded the exhibition of the patent we had to the South River. We gave them for answer as before, that we had not brought it with us, but referred that point to future comissioners on both

---

[1] Claiborne.   [2] Manuscript destroyed.

sides, and we again withdrew. They drew up their answer, which they read to us who were called in for that purpose.

Hereupon we asked their Honors whether this writing contained all they had to dispatch by us. To this they declared, they had nothing else; but that they persisted therein. We then again inquired, how we were to act in the matter of our military; whether all further hostility and encroachment should cease, and we might safely send back our garrisons and soldiers, or whether we must let them continue there. To this they answered, that we must please ourselves in that matter, and they would act as they thought best. Whereunto we replied, that we should in that case remain on our defensive, as we had declared and protested, and that we hoped nevertheless that they would not be guilty of any clandestine and sudden attack, as is usual in public and open war, but according to the custom in neighborly and public peace and alliance between nations, first give notice and warning that friendship is at an end. To which they rejoined: that they should act therein as would be most advisable. We further inquired, what was to be the understanding on the subject of our fugitives, and received for answer that they should, by law, oblige such as were in debt to pay, but they did not mean to send them back, inasmuch as they considered the people in Delowar Bay to be under their jurisdiction, and consequently were not fugitives from the General and Council of the Manhattans. Whereupon we replied, that we too would adhere to the *lex talionis*, in order to act in like manner towards their fugitives. And thus terminated our meeting and business.

The Governor also asked what Dutch Swedes meant—why we named them so in our declaration? And we answered, because the greatest number of them were partners of Dutchmen and formerly resorted under the Honble Company's jurisdiction, and had been heretofore winked at and tolerated, until they began to be so insolent in the river as not to hesitate forcibly to seize, in a treacherous manner, on Fort New Amstel, previously Casimier, whereby the General and Council of New Netherland were compelled and obliged to clear and purge the river, once for all, of such dishonest and hypocritical friends.

October $\frac{19}{9}$, *Sunday morning*. Again, having breakfasted, their Honors' answer, fairly written out by the secretary, was placed in our hands, and so took a most friendly leave, as we could not but perceive, that were it in their power they would willingly incline to a friendly agreement, but that they must first have authority to that effect from Lord Balthamoer, or otherwise wait for such order as he may send respecting it this summer; for I so understood, in private conversation, from the secretary, Philip Calvert, who is Lord Balthamoer's half-brother, that they expected something to this purpose, though they knew not what; for Lord Balthamoer had, last year, ordered them to inform him what they had done with the people of Delowar Bay, to which they had answered, that they could not yet write anything as to the effect, but that they intended to do so and so.

We had likewise some private conversation on the subject of establishing mutual trade and commerce, overland, between Maryland and Delowar Bay, which, I assured him, could easily be carried on, as soon as this question was terminated and the limits on both sides adjusted. I recommended him to notify his brother thereof, in order to engage him therein in all reasonableness, for not only his province in general, but himself in particular, would be most highly benefited by such trade, so that an effort might then be made to establish an easy passage by land for mutual intercourse.

He also particularly inquired about the hill, which we had proposed in our declaration for a neutral meeting, where the Sassafrax River, in Virginia, and the creek which enters the South River behind Reedy Island, seem to take their rise; and we are to institute and make further inquiry respecting that hill at the earliest opportunity.

Finally, we returned together from Patuxen river to St. Mary's, to our quarters at Master Simon Overzee's.

October $\frac{20}{10}$, *Monday*. Nothing particular occurred, except preparing to dispatch things with Resolved Waldron to the South River and the Manhattans.

October $\frac{21}{11}$, *Tuesday*. Sent off the said Resolved Waldron on his return overland, with the reports, papers and documents respecting our negotiations, and I set out for Virginia to ascertain the opinions of the Governor and others there concerning this matter, and thus to create some diversion between them both; also to clear ourselves, at the same time, of the slander which some people seek to attach to us, that we had excited the Indians to massacre the English at Accomacq.

God grant that the whole may redound to the glory of His name and the general advantage and safety of us all, and that we may be directed by His Divine Majesty.   Amen.

In haste,

AUGUSTINE HERRM[AN].[1]

To the honorable, worshipful, wise and very prudent Mr. Cornelis van Ruyven, to be delivered to the Hon. Director General and Council of New Netherland.

[1] Manuscript imperfect.

A CHARACTER OF THE PROVINCE OF MARY-
LAND, BY GEORGE ALSOP, 1666

INTRODUCTION

Of George Alsop little is known beyond what is disclosed by his own statements. He appears to have been born in London of parents in moderate or humble circumstances, and was apprenticed to some manual trade or handicraft. From his brief period of service, two years, it may be suspected that he did not complete his term of indenture. He admits in the dedication to Lord Baltimore that he was "wilde and confused," and the letters purporting to have been written to his father and brother aboard ship, just before sailing, indicate that he had embarked for Maryland in the capacity of an indentured servant. Persons who embarked for Maryland without being able to pay passage money, which at this time amounted to about £6, entered into an agreement or indenture to work out their passage by service in the province. The usual term for which they became thus bound was four years. These persons were known as indentured, or more generally as indented servants. At a later date they were called redemptioners.[1]

This author had in some way acquired a quantity of ill-assorted information, and also an extensive vocabulary, but was without sufficient education to enable him to make proper use of either. His style is therefore extravagant, inflated and grandiloquent. It is also coarse and vulgar, even for the seventeenth century. Certain passages which add nothing to the narrative, but were apparently inserted merely for the sake of their impropriety, have been omitted from the following text.

[1] For the terms of employment of indented servants see *A Relation of Maryland,* p. 99, *supra.*

337

Alsop served according to the customary indenture or agreement for four years upon the plantation of Mr. Thomas Stockett, in Baltimore County, who was evidently a most humane and generous master; and he describes in this narrative the lot of an indented servant in Maryland as being both easy and alluring, especially in contrast with the struggle for life among the poorer classes in London. It is not unlikely that Alsop was able to practise some mechanical trade, and this fact alone would have secured for him consideration and good treatment in a colony where skilled artisans were few. His story no doubt describes his own personal experiences rather than general conditions throughout the province. The situation of laborers in the tobacco fields of southern Maryland was probably not so fortunate, but of this he would be likely to know little. At the period at which Alsop wrote the need of laborers to till the land was great in Maryland, and servants of all grades and capacities were in demand and valued. A century later a very different picture of the condition of the indented servants is presented in the letters of William Eddis (*Letters from America*, p. 63); but during that interval negro slaves from Africa had been introduced in large numbers, and there had been also the transportation from England of convicts who were sold into penal servitude. These conditions had completely revolutionized and lowered the condition of servants in the province.

It may reasonably be assumed that Alsop was encouraged and probably rewarded by Lord Baltimore for the preparation of this pamphlet, to be used as an inducement for persons to ship for Maryland in the capacity of servants. His statements are often exaggerated, but the truth of many of them is borne out by other authorities. Those which relate to facts within the range of his personal knowledge, may be regarded as reasonably trustworthy. Many of his opinions, such as, for instance, that the Indians were naturally white, and that their brown complexion was due to the use of dyes, are manifestly without foundation.

This book was printed in London in 1666 and reprinted in New York among "Shea's Tracts" in 1869; and in 1880 by the Maryland Historical Society, *Fund Publication* no. 15. A limited *édition de luxe* was published in Cleveland in 1902 under the editorship of Dr. N. D. Mereness.

C. C. H.

A CHARACTER OF THE PROVINCE OF MARY-LAND, BY GEORGE ALSOP, 1666

A Character of the Province of Mary-land, wherein is Described in four distinct Parts, (Viz.)

    I.   The Scituation, and plenty of the Province.

    II. The Laws, Customs, and natural Demeanor of the Inhabitant.

    III. The worst and best Usage of a Mary-Land Servant, opened in view.

    IV. The Traffique, and vendable Commodities of the Countrey.

Also, A small Treatise on the wilde and naked Indians (or Susquehanokes) of Mary-Land, their Customs, Manners, Absurdities, and Religion. Together with a Collection of Historical Letters By George Alsop.

London, Printed by T. J. for Peter Dring, at the sign of the Sun in the Poultrey: 1666.[1]

To the Right Honorable Cæcilius Lord Baltemore, Absolute Lord and Proprietary of the Provinces of Mary-Land and Avalon in America.

My Lord,

I HAVE adventured on your Lordships acceptance by guess; if presumption has led me into an Error that deserves correction, I heartily beg Indempnity, and resolve to repent soundly for it, and do so no more. What I present I know to be true, *Experientia docet;*[2] It being an infallible Maxim, That there is no Globe like the occular and experimental view of a Countrey. And had not Fate by a necessary imploy-ment, confin'd me within the narrow walks of a four years

---

[1] Title-page of the original.   [2] Experience teaches.

Servitude, and by degrees led me through the most intricate and dubious paths of this Countrey, by a commanding and undeniable Enjoynment, I could not, nor should I ever have undertaken to have written a line of this nature.

If I have wrote or composed any thing that's wilde and confused, it is because I am so my self, and the world, as far as I can perceive, is not much out of the same trim; therefore I resolve, if I am brought to the Bar of Common Law for any thing I have done here, to plead *Non compos mentis*, to save my Bacon.

There is an old Saying in English, He must rise betimes that would please every one. And I am afraid I have lain so long a bed, that I think I shall please no body; if it must be so, I cannot help it. But as Feltham in his *Resolves*[1] says, In things that must be, 'tis good to be resolute; And therefore what Destiny has ordained, I am resolved to wink, and stand to it. So leaving your Honour to more serious meditations, I subscribe my self,

My Lord,
Your Lordship most
Humble Servant,
GEORGE ALSOP.

To all the Merchant Adventurers for Mary-Land, together with those Commanders of Ships that saile into that Province.

Sirs,

You are both Adventurers, the one of Estate, the other of Life: I could tell you I am an Adventurer too, if I durst presume to come into your Company. I have ventured to come abroad in Print, and if I should be laughed at for my good meaning, it would so break the credit of my Understanding, that I should never dare to shew my face upon the Exchange of (conceited) Wits again.

This dish of Discourse was intended for you at first, but it was manners to let my Lord have the first cut, the Pye being his own. I beseech you accept of the matter as 'tis drest, only to stay your stomachs, and I'le promise you the next shall be better done. 'Tis all as I can serve you in at present,

[1] Owen Felltham, *Resolves, Divine, Moral, and Political* (London, 1628, etc.).

and it may be questionable whether I have served you in this or no. Here I present you with *A Character of Mary-Land*, it may be you will say 'tis weakly done, if you do I cannot help it, 'tis as well as I could do it, considering the several Obstacles that like blocks were thrown in my way to hinder my proceeding: The major part thereof was written in the intermitting time of my sickness, therefore I hope the afflicting weakness of my Microcosm may plead a just excuse for some imperfections of my pen. I protest what I have writ is from an experimental knowledge of the Country, and not from any imaginary supposition. If I am blamed for what I have done too much, it is the first, and I will irrevocably promise it shall be the last. There's a Maxim upon Tryals at Assizes, That if a thief be taken upon the first fault, if it be not to hainous, they only burn him in the hand and let him go: So I desire you to do by me, if you find any thing that bears a criminal absurdity in it, only burn me for my first fact and let me go. But I am affraid I have kept you too long in the Entry, I shall desire you therefore to come in and sit down.

G. ALSOP.

The Preface to the Reader.

THE Reason why I appear in this place is, lest the general Reader should conclude I have nothing to say for my self; and truly he's in the right on't, for I have but little to say (for my self) at this time: For I have had so large a Journey, and so heavy a Burden to bring Mary-Land into England, that I am almost out of breath: I'le promise you after I am come to my self, you shall hear more of me. Good Reader, because you see me make a brief Apologetical excuse for my self, don't judge me; for I am so self-conceited of my own merits, that I almost think I want none. *De Lege non judicandum ex solâ linea*, saith the Civilian; We must not pass judgement upon a Law by one line: And because we see but a small Bush at a Tavern door, conclude there is no Canary. For as in our vulgar Resolves 'tis said, A good face needs no Band, and an ill one deserves none: So the French Proverb sayes, *Bon Vien il n'a faut point de Ensigne*, Good Wine needs no Bush. I suppose by this time some of my speculative observers have judged me vainglorious; but if they did but rightly consider me, they would not be so censorious. For I dwell so far from Neighbors, that if I do not praise my self, no body else will: And since I am left alone, I am resolved to summon the *Magna Charta* of Fowles to the Bar for my excuse, and by their irrevocable Statutes plead my discharge, For its an ill Bird will befoule her own Nest: Besides, I have a thousand Billingsgate[1] Collegians that will give in their testimony, That they never knew a Fish-woman cry stinking Fish. Thus leaving the Nostrils of the Citizens Wives to demonstrate what they please as to that, and thee (Good Reader) to say what thou wilt, I bid thee Farewel.

GEO. ALSOP.

A CHARACTER OF THE PROVINCE OF MARY-LAND.

CHAP. I.

Of the situation and plenty of the Province of Mary-Land.

Mary-Land is a Province situated upon the large extending bowels of America, under the Government of the Lord Baltemore, adjacent Northwardly upon the Confines of New-England, and neighbouring Southwardly upon Virginia, dwelling pleasantly upon the Bay of Chæsapike, between the Degrees of 36 and 38,[2] in the Zone temperate, and by Mathematical computation is eleven hundred and odd Leagues in Longitude from England, being within her own imbraces extraordinary pleasant and fertile. Pleasant, in respect of the multitude of Navigable Rivers and Creeks that conveniently and most profitably lodge within the armes of her green, spreading, and delightful Woods; whose natural womb (by her plenty) maintains and preserves the several diversities of Animals that rangingly inhabit her Woods; as she doth otherwise generously fructifie this piece of Earth with almost all sorts of Vegetables, as well Flowers with their varieties of colours and smells, as

---

[1] Billingsgate, the great London fish-market. After this preface, six pages of verses are omitted.

[2] Should be 38 and 40.

Herbes and Roots with their several effects and operative
virtues, that offer their benefits daily to supply the want of
the Inhabitant whene're their necessities shall *Sub-pœna* them
to wait on their commands. So that he, who out of curiosity
desires to see the Landskip of the Creation drawn to the life,
or to read Natures universal Herbal without book, may with
the Opticks of a discreet discerning, view Mary-Land drest
in her green and fragrant Mantle of the Spring. Neither do I
think there is any place under the Heavenly altitude, or that
has footing or room upon the circular Globe of this world, that
can parallel this fertile and pleasant piece of ground in its
multiplicity, or rather Natures extravagancy of a superabounding plenty.[1] For so much doth this Country increase
in a swelling Spring-tide of rich variety and diversities of all
things, not only common provisions that supply the reaching
stomach of man with a satisfactory plenty, but also extends
with its liberality and free convenient benefits to each sensi-
tive faculty, according to their several desiring Appetites.
So that had Nature made it her business, on purpose to have
found out a situation for the Soul of profitable Ingenuity, she
could not have fitted herself better in the traverse of the whole
Universe, nor in convenienter terms have told man, Dwell
here, live plentifully and be rich.

The Trees, Plants, Fruits, Flowers, and Roots that grow
here in Mary-Land, are the only Emblems or Hieroglyphicks
of our Adamitical or Primitive situation, as well for their
variety as odoriferous smells, together with their vertues,
according to their several effects, kinds and properties, which
still bear the Effigies of Innocency according to their original
Grafts; which by their dumb vegetable Oratory, each hour
speaks to the Inhabitant in silent acts, That they need not
look for any other Terrestrial Paradice, to suspend or tyre their
curiosity upon, while she is extant. For within her doth
dwell so much of variety, so much of natural plenty, that
there is not any thing that is or may be rare, but it inhabits
within this plentious soyle: So that those parts of the Creation
that have borne the Bell away (for many ages) for a vegetable
plentiousness, must now in silence strike and vayle all, and

---

[1] Compare *A Briefe Relation of the Voyage unto Maryland*, p. 45, and *A Relation of Maryland*, p. 79, *supra*.

whisper softly in the auditual parts of Mary-Land, that None but she in this dwells singular; and that as well for that she doth exceed in those Fruits, Plants, Trees and Roots, that dwell and grow in their several Clymes or habitable parts of the Earth besides, as the rareness and super-excellency of her own glory, which she flourishly abounds in, by the abundancy of reserved Rarities, such as the remainder of the World (with all its speculative art) never bore any occular testimony of as yet. I shall forbear to particularize those several sorts of vegetables that flourishingly grows here, by reason of the vast tediousness that will attend upon the description, which therefore makes them much more fit for an Herbal, than a small Manuscript or History.

As for the wilde Animals of this Country, which loosely inhabits the Woods in multitudes, it is impossible to give you an exact description of them all, considering the multiplicity as well as the diversity of so numerous an extent of Creatures: But such as has fallen within the compass or prospect of my knowledge, those you shall know of; *videlicet*, the Deer, because they are oftner seen, and more participated of by the Inhabitants of the Land, whose acquaintance by a customary familiarity becomes much more common than the rest of Beasts that inhabit the Woods by using themselves in Herds about the Christian Plantations. Their flesh, which in some places of this Province is the common provision the Inhabitants feed on, and which through the extreme glut and plenty of it, being daily killed by the Indians, and brought in to the English, as well as that which is killed by the Christian Inhabitant, that doth it more for recreation, than for the benefit they reap by it. I say, the flesh of Venison becomes (as to food) rather denyed, than any way esteemed or desired. And this I speak from an experimental knowledge; For when I was under a Command, and debarr'd of a four years ranging Liberty in the Province of Mary-Land, the Gentleman whom I served my conditional and prefixed time withall, had at one time in his house fourscore Venisons, besides plenty of other provisions to serve his Family nine months, they being but seven in number; so that before this Venison was brought to a period by eating, it so nauseated our appetites and stomachs, that plain bread was rather courted and desired than it.

The Deer here neither in shape nor action differ from our Deer in England: The Park they traverse their ranging and unmeasured walks in, is bounded and impanell'd in with no other pales then the rough and billowed Ocean: They are also mighty numerous in the Woods, and are little or not at all affrighted at the face of a man, but (like the Does of Whetstons Park)[1] though their hydes are not altogether so gaudy to extract an admiration from the beholder, yet they will stand (all most) till they be scratcht.

As for the Wolves, Bears, and Panthers of this Country, they inhabit commonly in great multitudes up in the remotest parts of the Continent; yet at some certain time they come down near the Plantations, but do little hurt or injury worth noting, and that which they do is of so degenerate and low a nature, (as in reference to the fierceness and heroick vigour that dwell in the same kind of Beasts in other Countries), that they are hardly worth mentioning: For the highest of their designs and circumventing reaches is but cowardly and base, only to steal a poor Pigg, or kill a lost and half starved Calf. The Effigies of a man terrifies them dreadfully, for they no sooner espy him but their hearts are at their mouths, and their spurs upon their heels, they (having no more manners than Beasts) gallop away, and never bid them farewell that are behind them.

The Elke, the Cat of the Mountain, the Rackoon, the Fox, the Beaver, the Otter, the Possum, the Hare, the Squirril, the Monack,[2] the Musk-Rat, and several others (whom I'le omit for brevity sake) inhabit here in Mary-Land in several droves and troops, ranging the Woods at their pleasure.

The meat of most of these Creatures is good for eating, yet of no value nor esteem here, by reason of the great plenty of other provisions, and are only kill'd by the Indians of the Country for their Hydes and Furrs, which become very profitable to those that have the right way of traffiquing for them, as well as it redounds to the Indians that take the pains to catch them, and to flay and dress their several Hydes, selling

[1] Whetstone Park is the name of a street in London between Lincoln's Inn Fields and High Holborn. The reference is evidently to frail females by whom in Alsop's time it was frequented.

[2] Probably this is a name for the woodchuck, or the chipmunk.

and disposing them for such Commodities as their Heathenish fancy delights in.

As for those Beasts that were carried over at the first seating of the Country, to stock and increase the situation, as Cows, Horses, Sheep and Hogs, they are generally tame, and use near home, especially the Cows, Sheep and Horses. The Hogs, whose increase is innumerable in the Woods, do disfrequent home more than the rest of Creatures that are look'd upon as tame, yet with little trouble and pains they are slain and made provision of. Now they that will with a right Historical Survey, view the Woods of Mary-Land in this particular, as in reference to Swine, must upon necessity judge this Land lineally descended from the Gadarean Territories.[1]

Mary-Land (I must confess) cannot boast of her plenty of Sheep here, as other Countries; not but that they will thrive and increase here, as well as in any place of the World besides, but few desire them, because they commonly draw down the Wolves among the Plantations, as well by the sweetness of their flesh, as by the humility of their nature, in not making a defensive resistance against the rough dealing of a ravenous Enemy. They who for curiosity will keep Sheep, may expect that after the Wolves have breathed themselves all day in the Woods to sharpen their stomachs, they will come without fail and sup with them at night, though many times they surfeit themselves with the sawce that's dish'd out of the muzzle of a Gun, and so in the midst of their banquet (poor Animals) they often sleep with their Ancestors.

Fowls of all sorts and varieties dwell at their several times and seasons here in Mary-Land: The Turkey, the Woodcock, the Pheasant, the Partrich, the Pigeon, and others, especially the Turkey, whom I have seen in whole hundreds in flights in the Woods of Mary-Land, being an extraordinary fat Fowl, whose flesh is very pleasant and sweet. These Fowls that I have named are intayled from generation to generation to the Woods. The Swans, the Geese and Ducks (with other Water-Fowl) derogate in this point of setled residence; for they arrive in millionous multitudes in Mary-Land about the middle of September, and take their winged farewell about the midst of March: But while they do remain, and beleague the borders of the shoar with their winged Dragoons, several of them are summoned by a Writ of *Fieri facias*, to answer their presumptuous contempt upon a Spit.

As for Fish, which dwell in the watry tenements of the deep, and by a providential greatness of power, is kept for the relief of several Countries in the world (which would else sink under the rigid enemy of want), here in Mary-Land is a large sufficiency, and plenty of almost all sorts of Fishes, which live and inhabit within her several Rivers and Creeks, far beyond the apprehending or crediting of those that never saw the same, which with very much ease is catched, to the great refreshment of the Inhabitants of the Province.

All sorts of Grain, as Wheat, Rye, Barley, Oates, Pease, besides several others that have their original and birth from the fertile womb of this Land (and no where else), they all grow, increase, and thrive here in Mary-Land, without the chargable and laborious manuring of the Land with Dung; increasing in such a measure and plenty, by the natural richness of the Earth, with the common, beneficial and convenient showers of rain that usually wait upon the several Fields of Grain (by a natural instinct), so that Famine (the dreadful Ghost of penury and want) is never known with his pale visage to haunt the Dominions of Mary-Land.

> Could'st thou (O Earth) live thus obscure, and now
> Within an Age, shew forth thy plentious brow
> Of rich variety, gilded with fruitful Fame,
> That (Trumpet-like) doth Heraldize thy Name,
> And tells the World there is a Land now found,
> That all Earth's Globe can't parallel its Ground?
> Dwell, and be prosperous, and with thy plenty feed
> The craving Carkesses of those Souls that need.

CHAP. II.

Of the Government and Natural disposition of the People.

Mary-Land, not from the remoteness of her situation, but from the regularity of her well ordered Government, may (without sin, I think) be called Singular: And though she is not supported with such large Revenues as some of her Neighbours are, yet such is her wisdom in a reserved silence, and not in pomp, to shew her well-conditioned Estate, in relieving at a distance the proud poverty of those that wont be seen they want, as well as those which by undeniable necessities are drove upon the Rocks of pinching wants: Yet such a loathsome creature is a common and folding-handed Beggar, that upon the penalty of almost a perpetual working in Imprisonment, they are not to appear, nor lurk near our vigilant and laborious dwellings. The Country hath received a general spleen and antipathy against the very name and nature of it; and though there were no Law provided (as there is) to suppress it, I am certainly confident, there is none within the Province that would lower themselves so much below the dignity of men to beg, as long as limbs and life keep house together; so much is a vigilant industrious care esteem'd.

He that desires to see the real Platform of a quiet and sober Government extant, Superiority with a meek and yet commanding power sitting at the Helme, steering the actions of State quietly, through the multitude and diversity of Opinionous waves that diversely meet, let him look on MaryLand with eyes admiring, and he'le then judge her, The Miracle of this Age.

Here the Roman Catholick, and the Protestant Episcopal, (whom the world would perswade have proclaimed open Wars irrevocably against each other) contrarywise concur in an unanimous parallel of friendship, and inseparable love intayled unto one another:[1] All Inquisitions, Martyrdom, and Banishments are not so much as named, but unexpressably abhorr'd by each other.

The several Opinions and Sects that lodge within this Government, meet not together in mutinous contempts to disquiet the power that bears Rule, but with a reverend quietness obeys the legal commands of Authority. Here's never seen Five Monarchies[2] in a Zealous Rebellion, opposing the Rights

[1] Religious liberty and freedom of conscience were secured by law under the proprietary government. That there were religious animosities, however, was manifest during the sway of the commissioners of Parliament, 1652-1658.

[2] The sect known as "Fifth Monarchy Men" who made an uprising in London in 1661.

and Liberties of a true setled Government, or Monarchical Authority: Nor did I ever see (here in Mary-Land) any of those dancing Adamitical Sisters, that plead a primitive Innocency for their base obscenity, and naked deportment; but I conceive if some of them were there at some certain time of the year, between the Months of January and February, when the winds blow from the North-West quarter of the world, that it would both cool, and (I believe) convert the hottest of these Zealots from their burning and fiercest Concupiscence.

The Government of this Province doth continually, by all lawful means, strive to purge her Dominions from such base corroding humors, that would predominate upon the least smile of Liberty, did not the Laws check and bridle in those unwarranted and tumultuous Opinions. And truly, where a Kingdom, State or Government, keeps or cuts down the weeds of destructive Opinions, there must certainly be a blessed Harmony of quietness. And I really believe this Land or Government of Mary-Land may boast, that she enjoys as much quietness from the disturbance of Rebellious Opinions, as most States or Kingdoms do in the world: For here every man lives quietly, and follows his labour and imployment desiredly; and by the protection of the Laws, they are supported from those molestious troubles that ever attend upon the Commons of other States and Kingdoms, as well as from the Aquafortial operation of great and eating Taxes. Here's nothing to be levyed out of the Granaries of Corn; but contrarywise, by a Law every Domestick Governor of a Family is enjoyned to make or cause to be made so much Corn by a just limitation, as shall be sufficient for him and his Family: So that by this wise and Janus-like providence, the thin-jawed Skeliton with his starv'd Carkess is never seen walking the Woods of Mary-Land to affrighten Children.

Once every year within this Province is an Assembly called, and out of every respective County (by the consent of the people) there is chosen a number of men, and to them is deliver'd up the Grievances of the Country; and they maturely debate the matters, and according to their Consciences make Laws for the general good of the people; and where any former Law that was made, seems and is prejudicial to the good or quietness of the Land, it is repeal'd. These men that determine on these matters for the Republique, are called Burgesses, and they commonly sit in Junto about six weeks, being for the most part good ordinary Householders of the several Counties, which do more by a plain and honest Conscience, than by artificial Syllogisms drest up in gilded Orations.

Here Suits and Tryals in Law seldome hold dispute two Terms or Courts, but according as the Equity of the Cause appears is brought to a period. The Temples and Grays-Inne are clear out of fashion here: Marriot[1] would sooner get a paunch-devouring meal for nothing, then for his invading Counsil. Here if the Lawyer had nothing else to maintain him but his bawling, he might button up his Chops, and burn his Buckrom Bag, or else hang it upon a pin untill its Antiquity had eaten it up with durt and dust: Then with a Spade, like his Grandsire Adam, turn up the face of the Creation, purchasing his bread by the sweat of his brows, that before was got by the motionated Water-works of his jaws. So contrary to the Genius of the people, if not to the quiet Government of the Province, that the turbulent Spirit of continued and vexatious Law, with all its querks and evasions, is openly and most eagerly opposed, that might make matters either dubious, tedious, or troublesom. All other matters that would be ranging in contrary and improper Spheres, (in short) are here by the Power moderated, lower'd and subdued. All villanous Outrages that are committed in other States, are not so much as known here: A man may walk in the open Woods as secure from being externally dissected, as in his own house or dwelling. So hateful is a Robber, that if but once imagin'd to be so, he's kept at a distance, and shun'd as the Pestilential noysomness.

It is generally and very remarkably observed, That those whose Lives and Conversations have had no other gloss nor glory stampt on them in their own Country, but the stigmatization of baseness, were here (by the common civilities and deportments of the Inhabitants of this Province) brought to detest and loath their former actions. Here the Constable hath no need of a train of Holberteers,[2] that carry more

---

[1] John Marriott, a lawyer of Gray's Inn, noted for his large appetite.

[2] Halberdiers.

Armour about them, then heart to guard him: Nor is he ever troubled to leave his Feathered Nest to some friendly successor, while he is placing of his Lanthern-horn Guard at the end of some suspicious Street, to catch some Night-walker, or Batchelor of Leachery, that has taken his Degree three story high in a Bawdy-house. Here's no Newgates for pilfering Felons, nor Ludgates for Debtors, nor any Bridewels to lash the soul of Concupiscence into a chast Repentance. For as there is none of these Prisons in Mary-Land, so the merits of the Country deserves none, but if any be foully vitious, he is so reserv'd in it, that he seldom or never becomes popular. Common Alehouses, (whose dwellings are the only Receptacles of debauchery and baseness, and those Schools that trains up Youth, as well as Age, to ruine) in this Province there are none;[1] neither hath Youth his swing or range in such a profuse and unbridled liberty as in other Countries; for from an antient Custom at the primitive seating of the place, the Son works as well as the Servant (an excellent cure for untam'd Youth), so that before they eat their bread, they are commonly taught how to earn it; which makes them by that time Age speaks them capable of receiving that which their Parents indulgency is ready to give them, and which partly is by their own laborious industry purchased, they manage it with such a serious, grave and watching care, as if they had been Masters of Families, trained up in that domestick and governing power from their Cradles. These Christian Natives of the Land, especially those of the Masculine Sex, are generally conveniently confident, reservedly subtle, quick in apprehending, but slow in resolving; and where they spy profit sailing towards them with the wings of a prosperous gale, there they become much familiar. The Women differ something in this point, though not much: They are extreme bashful at the first view, but after a continuance of time hath brought them acquainted, there they become discreetly familiar, and are much more talkative then men. All Complemental Courtships, drest up in critical Rarities, are meer strangers to them, plain wit comes nearest their Genius; so that he that intends to Court a Mary-

---

[1] This was probably true of Baltimore County where Alsop lived and where the population was sparse. There was a tavern at St. Mary's which at a later date (1686) was ordered suppressed on account of disorders occurring there.

Land Girle, must have something more than the Tautologies of a long-winded speech to carry on his design, or else he may (for ought I know) fall under the contempt of her frown, and his own windy Oration.

One great part of the Inhabitants of this Province are desiredly Zealous, great pretenders to Holiness; and where any thing appears that carries on the Frontispiece of its Effigies the stamp of Religion, though fundamentally never so imperfect, they are suddenly taken with it, and out of an eager desire to any thing that's new, not weighing the sure matter in the Ballance of Reason, are very apt to be catcht. Quakerism is the only Opinion that bears the Bell away: The Anabaptists have little to say here, as well as in other places, since the Ghost of John of Leyden[1] haunts their Conventicles. The Adamite, Ranter, and Fift-Monarchy men, Mary-Land cannot, nay will not digest within her liberal stomach such corroding morsels: So that this Province is an utter Enemy to blasphemous[2] and zealous Imprecations, drain'd from the Lymbeck[3] of hellish and damnable Spirits, as well as profuse prophaness, that issues from the prodigality of none but cract-brain Sots.

> 'Tis said the Gods lower down that Chain above,
> That tyes both Prince and Subject up in Love;
> And if this Fiction of the Gods be true,
> Few, Mary-Land, in this can boast but you:
> Live ever blest, and let those Clouds that do
> Eclipse most States, be alwayes Lights to you;
> And dwelling so, you may for ever be
> The only Emblem of Tranquility.

[1] Leader of the Anabaptists of Münster in 1534–1535.

[2] Blasphemy was a punishable offence. See act concerning religion, p. 270, supra.

[3] Alembic.

CHAP. III.

The necessariness of Servitude proved, with the common usage
of Servants in Mary-Land, together with their Priviledges.

As there can be no Monarchy without the Supremacy of a
King and Crown, nor no King without Subjects, nor any
Parents without it be by the fruitful off-spring of Children;
neither can there be any Masters, unless it be by the inferior
Servitude of those that dwell under them, by a commanding
enjoynment: And since it is ordained from the original and
superabounding wisdom of all things, That there should be
Degrees and Diversities amongst the Sons of men, in acknowl-
edging of a Superiority from Inferiors to Superiors; the Servant with a reverent and befitting Obedience is as liable to
this duty in a measurable performance to him whom he serves,
as the loyalest of Subjects to his Prince.   Then since it is a
common and ordained Fate, that there must be Servants as
well as Masters, and that good Servitudes are those Colledges of
Sobriety that checks in the giddy and wild-headed youth from
his profuse and uneven course of life, by a limited constrain-
ment, as well as it otherwise agrees with the moderate and
discreet Servant: Why should there be such an exclusive
Obstacle in the minds and unreasonable dispositions of many
people, against the limited time of convenient and necessary
Servitude, when it is a thing so requisite, that the best of
Kingdoms would be unhing'd from their quiet and well setled
Government without it. Which levelling doctrine we here of
England in this latter age (whose womb was truss'd out with
nothing but confused Rebellion) have too much experienced,
and was daily rung into the ears of the tumultuous Vulgar
by the Bell-weather Sectaries of the Times: But (blessed be
God) those Clouds are blown over, and the Government of the
Kingdom coucht under a more stable form.

There is no truer Emblem of Confusion either in Monarchy
or Domestick Governments, then when either the Subject, or
the Servant, strives for the upper hand of his Prince, or Master,
and to be equal with him, from whom he receives his present
subsistance: Why then, if Servitude be so necessary that no

place can be governed in order, nor people live without it, this may serve to tell those which prick up their ears and bray against it, That they are none but Asses, and deserve the Bridle of a strict commanding power to reine them in: For I'me certainly confident, that there are several Thousands in most Kingdoms of Christendom, that could not at all live and subsist, unless they had served some prefixed time, to learn either some Trade, Art, or Science, and by either of them to extract their present livelihood.

Then methinks this may stop the mouths of those that will undiscreetly compassionate them that dwell under necessary Servitudes; for let but Parents of an indifferent capacity in Estates, when their Childrens age by computation speak them seventeen or eighteen years old, turn them loose to the wide world, without a seven years working Apprenticeship (being just brought up to the bare formality of a little reading and writing) and you shall immediately see how weak and shiftless they'le be towards the maintaining and supporting of themselves; and (without either stealing or begging) their bodies like a Sentinel must continually wait to see when their Souls will be frighted away by the pale Ghost of a starving want.

Then let such, where Providence hath ordained to live as Servants, either in England or beyond Sea, endure the prefixed yoak of their limited time with patience, and then in a small computation of years, by an industrious endeavour, they may become Masters and Mistresses of Families themselves. And let this be spoke to the deserved praise of Mary-Land, That the four years I served there were not to me so slavish, as a two years Servitude of a Handicraft Apprenticeship was here in London; *Volenti enim nil difficile:*[1] Not that I write this to seduce or delude any, or to draw them from their native soyle, but out of a love to my Countrymen, whom in the general I wish well to, and that the lowest of them may live in such a capacity of Estate, as that the bare interest of their Livelihoods might not altogether depend upon persons of the greatest extendments.

Now those whose abilities here in England are capable of maintaining themselves in any reasonable and handsom manner, they had best so to remain, lest the roughness of the

[1] Nothing is difficult to the willing.

Ocean, together with the staring visages of the wilde Animals, which they may see after their arrival into the Country, may alter the natural dispositions of their bodies, that the stay'd and solid part that kept its motion by Doctor Trigs purgationary operation, may run beyond the byas of the wheel in a violent and laxative confusion.

Now contrarywise, they who are low, and make bare shifts to buoy themselves up above the shabby center of beggarly and incident casualties, I heartily could wish the removal of some of them into Mary-Land, which would make much better for them that stay'd behind, as well as it would advantage those that went.

They whose abilities cannot extend to purchase their own transportation over into Mary-Land, (and surely he that cannot command so small a sum for so great a matter, his life must needs be mighty low and dejected) I say they may for the debarment of a four years sordid liberty, go over into this Province and there live plentiously well. And what's a four years Servitude to advantage a man all the remainder of his dayes, making his predecessors happy in his sufficient abilities, which he attained to partly by the restrainment of so small a time?

Now those that commit themselves unto the care of the Merchant to carry them over, they need not trouble themselves with any inquisitive search touching their Voyage; for there is such an honest care and provision made for them all the time they remain aboard the Ship, and are sailing over, that they want for nothing that is necessary and convenient.

The Merchant commonly before they go aboard the Ship, or set themselves in any forwardness for their Voyage, has Conditions of Agreements[1] drawn between him and those that by a voluntary consent become his Servants, to serve him, his Heirs or Assigns, according as they in their primitive acquaintance have made their bargain, some two, some three, some four years; and whatever the Master or Servant tyes himself up to here in England by Condition, the Laws of the Province will force a performance of when they come there: Yet here is this Priviledge in it when they arrive, If they dwell

---

[1] For form of indenture see p. 99, *supra.*

not with the Merchant they made their first agreement withall, they may choose whom they will serve their prefixed time with; and after their curiosity has pitcht on one whom they think fit for their turn, and that they may live well withall, the Merchant makes an Assignment of the Indenture over to him whom they of their free will have chosen to be their Master, in the same nature as we here in England (and no otherwise) turn over Covenant Servants or Apprentices from one Master to another. Then let those whose chaps are always breathing forth those filthy dregs of abusive exclamations, which are Lymbeckt from their sottish and preposterous brains, against this Country of Mary-Land, saying, That those which are transported over thither, are sold in open Market for Slaves, and draw in Carts like Horses; which is so damnable an untruth, that if they should search to the very Center of Hell, and enquire for a Lye of the most antient and damned stamp, I confidently believe they could not find one to parallel this: For know, That the Servants here in Mary-Land of all Colonies, distant or remote Plantations, have the least cause to complain, either for strictness of Servitude, want of Provisions, or need of Apparel: Five dayes a.·d a half in the Summer weeks is the alotted time that they work in; and for two months, when the Sun predominates in the highest pitch of his heat, they claim an antient and customary Priviledge, to repose themselves three hours in the day within the house, and this is undeniably granted to them that work in the Fields.

In the Winter time, which lasteth three months (*viz.*) December, January, and February, they do little or no work or imployment, save cutting of wood to make good fires to sit by, unless their Ingenuity will prompt them to hunt the Deer, or Bear, or recreate themselves in Fowling, to slaughter the Swans, Geese, and Turkeys (which this Country affords in a most plentiful manner:) For every Servant has a Gun, Powder and Shot allowed him, to sport him withall on all Holidayes and leasurable times, if he be capable of using it, or be willing to learn.

Now those Servants which come over into this Province, being Artificers, they never (during their Servitude) work in the Fields, or do any other imployment save that which their Handicraft and Mechanick endeavours are capable of putting them upon, and are esteem'd as well by their Masters, as those that imploy them, above measure. He that's a Tradesman here in Mary-Land (though a Servant), lives as well as most common Handicrafts do in London, though they may want something of that Liberty which Freemen have, to go and come at their pleasure; yet if it were rightly understood and considered, what most of the Liberties of the several poor Tradesmen are taken up about, and what a care and trouble attends that thing they call Liberty, which according to the common translation is but Idleness, and (if weighed in the Ballance of a just Reason) will be found to be much heavier and cloggy then the four years restrainment of a Mary-Land Servitude. He that lives in the nature of a Servant in this Province, must serve but four years by the Custom of the Country; and when the expiration of his time speaks him a Freeman, there's a Law in the Province, that enjoyns his Master whom he hath served to give him Fifty Acres of Land, Corn to serve him a whole year, three Sutes of Apparel, with things necessary to them, and Tools to work withall; so that they are no sooner free, but they are ready to set up for themselves, and when once entred, they live passingly well.

The Women that go over into this Province as Servants, have the best luck here as in any place of the world besides; for they are no sooner on shoar, but they are courted into a Copulative Matrimony, which some of them (for aught I know) had they not come to such a Market with their Virginity, might have kept it by them untill it had been mouldy, unless they had let it out by a yearly rent to some of the Inhabitants of Lewknors-lane,[1] or made a Deed of Gift of it to Mother Coney, having only a poor stipend out of it, untill the Gallows or Hospital called them away. Men have not altogether so good luck as Women in this kind, or natural preferment, without they be good Rhetoricians, and well vers'd in the Art of perswasion, then (probably) they may ryvet themselves in the time of their Servitude into the private and reserved favour of their Mistress, if Age speak their Master deficient.

In short, touching the Servants of this Province, they live well in the time of their Service, and by their restrainment in

---

[1] A disreputable neighborhood in London.

that time, they are made capable of living much better when they come to be free; which in several other parts of the world I have observed, That after some servants have brought their indented and limited time to a just and legal period by Servitude, they have been much more incapable of supporting themselves from sinking into the Gulf of a slavish, poor, fettered, and intangled life, then all the fastness of their prefixed time did involve them in before.

Now the main and principal Reason of those incident casualties, that wait continually upon the residencies of most poor Artificers, is (I gather) from the multiplicity or innumerableness of those several Companies of Tradesmen, that dwell so closely and stiflingly together in one and the same place, that like the chafing Gum in Watered-Tabby,[1] they eat into the folds of one anothers Estates. And this might easily be remedied, would but some of them remove and disperse distantly where want and necessity calls for them; their dwellings (I am confident) would be much larger, and their conditions much better, as well in reference to their Estates, as to the satisfactoriness of their minds, having a continual imployment, and from that imployment a continual benefit, without either begging, seducing, or flattering for it, encroaching that one month from one of the same profession, that they are heaved out themselves the next. For I have observed on the other side of Mary-Land, that the whole course of most Mechanical endeavours, is to catch, snatch, and undervalue one another, to get a little work, or a Customer; which when they have attained by their lowbuilt and sneaking circumventings, it stands upon so flashy, mutable, and transitory a foundation, that the best of his hopes is commonly extinguisht before the poor undervalued Tradesman is warm in the enjoyment of his Customer.

Then did not a cloud of low and base Cowardize eclipse the Spirits of these men, these things might easily be diverted; but they had as live take a Bear by the tooth, as think of leaving their own Country, though they live among their own National people, and are governed by the same Laws they have here, yet all this wont do with them; and all the Reason they can render to the contrary is, There's a great Sea betwixt

---

[1] Presumably, gum arabic used in making watered silk.

them and Mary-Land, and in that Sea there are Fishes, and not only Fishes but great Fishes, and then should a Ship meet with such an inconsiderable encounter as a Whale, one blow with his tayle, and then *Lord have Mercy upon us*: Yet meet with these men in their common Exchange, which is one story high in the bottom of a Celler, disputing over a Blackpot, it would be monstrously dreadful here to insert the particulars, one swearing that he was the first that scaled the Walls of Dundee, when the Bullets flew about their ears as thick as Hail-stones usually fall from the Sky; which if it were but rightly examined, the most dangerous Engagement that ever he was in, was but at one of the flashy battels at Finsbury, where commonly there's more Custard greedily devoured, then men prejudiced by the rigour of the War. Others of this Company relating their several dreadful exploits, and when they are just entring into the particulars, let but one step in and interrupt their discourse, by telling them of a Sea Voyage, and the violency of storms that attends it, and that there are no back-doors to run out at, which they call, a handsom Retreat and Charge again; the apprehensive danger of this is so powerful and penetrating on them, that a damp sweat immediately involves their Microcosm, so that Margery the old Matron of the Celler, is fain to run for a half-peny-worth of Angelica to rub their nostrils; . . .

Now I know that some will be apt to judge, that I have written this last part out of derision to some of my poor Mechanick Country-men: Truly I must needs tell those to their face that think so of me, that they prejudice me extremely, by censuring me as guilty of any such crime: What I have written is only to display the sordidness of their dispositions, who rather than they will remove to another Country to live plentiously well, and give their Neighbors more Elbow-room and space to breath in, they will crowd and throng upon one another, with the pressure of a beggarly and unnecessary weight.

That which I have to say more in this business, is a hearty and desirous wish, that the several poor Tradesmen here in London that I know, and have borne an occular testimony of their want, might live so free from care as I did when I dwelt in the bonds of a four years Servitude in Mary-Land.

Be just (Domestick Monarchs) unto them
That dwell as Household Subjects to each Realm;
Let not your Power make you be too severe,
Where there's small faults reign[1] in your sharp Career:
So that the Worlds base yelping Crew
May'nt bark what I have wrote is writ untrue,
So use your Servants, if there come no more,
They may serve Eight, instead of serving Four.

CHAP. IV.

*Upon Trafique, and what Merchandizing Commodities this
Province affords, also how Tobacco is planted and made fit
for Commerce.*

Trafique, Commerce, and Trade, are those great wheeles
that by their circular and continued motion, turn into most
Kingdoms of the Earth the plenty of abundant Riches that
they are commonly fed withall: For Trafique in his right description, is the very soul of a Kingdom; and should but Fate
ordain a removal of it for some years, from the richest and
most populous Monarchy that dwells in the most fertile clyme
of the whole Universe, he would soon find by a woful experi-
ment, the miss and loss of so reviving a supporter. And I am
certainly confident, that England would as soon feel her
feebleness by withdrawment of so great an upholder; as well
in reference to the internal and healthful preservative of her
Inhabitants, for want of those Medicinal Drugs that are landed
upon her Coast every year, as the external profits, Glory and
beneficial Graces that accrue by her.

Paracelsus might knock down his Forge, if Trafique and
Commerce should once cease, and grynde the hilt of his Sword
into Powder, and take some of the Infusion to make him so
valorous, that he might cut his own Throat in the honor of
Mercury: Galen might then burn his Herbal, and like Joseph
of Arimathea, build him a Tomb in his Garden, and so rest
from his labours: Our Physical Collegians of London would
have no cause then to thunder Fire-balls at Nich. Culpeppers

---

[1] Rein.

Dispensatory:[1] All Herbs, Roots, and Medicines would bear their original christening, that the ignorant might understand them: *Album grecum* would not be *Album grecum* then, but a Dogs turd would be a Dogs turd in plain terms, in spight of their teeth.

If Trade should once cease, the Custom-house would soon miss her hundreds and thousands Hogs-heads of Tobacco, that use to be throng in her every year, as well as the Grocers would in their Ware-houses and Boxes, the Gentry and Commonalty in their Pipes, the Physician in his Drugs and Medicinal Compositions: The (leering) Waiters[2] for want of imployment, might (like so many Diogenes) intomb themselves in their empty casks, and rouling themselves off the Key into the Thames, there wander up and down from tide to tide in contemplation of Aristotles unresolved curiosity, until the rottenness of their circular habitation give them a *Quietus est,* and fairly surrender them up into the custody of those who both for the profession, disposition and nature, lay as near claim to them, as if they both tumbled in one belly, and for name they jump alike, being according to the original translation both Sharkes.

Silks and Cambricks, and Lawns to make sleeves, would be as soon miss'd at Court, as Gold and Silver would be in the Mint and Pockets: The Low-Country Soldier would be at a cold stand for Outlandish Furrs to make him Muffs, to keep his ten similitudes warm in the Winter, as well as the Furrier for want of Skins to uphold his Trade.

Should Commerce once cease, there is no Country in the habitable world but would undoubtedly miss that flourishing, splendid and rich gallantry of Equipage, that Trafique maintained and drest her up in, before she received that fatal Eclipse: England, France, Germany and Spain, together with all the Kingdoms——

But stop (good Muse) lest I should, like the Parson of Pancras, run so far from my Text in half an hour, that a two hours trot back again would hardly fetch it up: I had best while I am alive in my Doctrine, to think again of Mary-Land,

---

[1] The allusion is to a contemporary controversy over the unauthorized publication of an English translation of the *Pharmacopoeia.*

[2] Tide-waiters. A term formerly applied to customs inspectors.

lest the business of other Countries take up so much room in my brain, that I forget and bury her in oblivion.

The three main Commodities this Country affords for Trafique, are Tobacco, Furrs, and Flesh. Furrs and Skins, as Beavers, Otters, Musk-Rats, Rackoons, Wild-Cats, and Elke or Buffeloe, with divers others, which were first made vendible by the Indians of the Country, and sold to the Inhabitant, and by them to the Merchant, and so transported into England and other places where it becomes most commodious.

Tobacco is the only solid Staple Commodity of this Province: The use of it was first found out by the Indians many Ages agoe, and transferr'd into Christendom by that great Discoverer of America Columbus. It's generally made by all the Inhabitants of this Province, and between the months of March and April they sow the seed (which is much smaller than Mustard-seed) in small beds and patches digg'd up and made so by art, and about May the Plants commonly appear green in those beds: In June they are transplanted from their beds, and set in little hillocks in distant rowes, dug up for the same purpose; some twice or thrice they are weeded, and succoured from their illegitimate Leaves that would be peeping out from the body of the Stalk. They top the several Plants as they find occasion in their predominating rankness: About the middle of September they cut the Tobacco down, and carry it into houses, (made for that purpose) to bring it to its purity: And after it has attained, by a convenient attendance upon time, to its perfection, it is then tyed up in bundles, and packt into Hogs-heads, and then laid by for the Trade.

Between November and January there arrives in this Province Shipping to the number of twenty sail and upwards, all Merchant-men loaden with Commodities to Trafique and dispose of, trucking with the Planter for Silks, Hollands, Serges, and Broad-clothes, with other necessary Goods, priz'd at such and such rates as shall be judg'd on is fair and legal, for Tobacco at so much the pound, and advantage on both sides considered; the Planter for his work, and the Merchant for adventuring himself and his Commodity into so far a Country: Thus is the Trade on both sides drove on with a fair and honest Decorum.

The Inhabitants of this Province are seldom or never put
to the affrightment of being robb'd of their money, nor to
dirty their Fingers by telling of vast sums: They have more
bags to carry Corn, then Coyn; and though they want, but why
should I call that a want which is only a necessary miss? the
very effects of the dirt of this Province affords as great a profit
to the general Inhabitant, as the Gold of Peru doth to the
straight-breecht Commonalty of the Spaniard.

Our Shops and Exchanges of Mary-Land, are the Merchants
Store-houses, where with few words and protestations Goods
are bought and delivered; not like those Shop-keepers Boys
in London, that continually cry, What do ye lack Sir? What
d'ye buy? yelping with so wide a mouth, as if some Apothe-
cary had hired their mouths to stand open to catch Gnats and
Vagabond Flyes in.

Tobacco is the currant Coyn of Mary-Land, and will
sooner purchase Commodities from the Merchant, then money.
I must confess the New-England men that trade into this
Province, had rather have fat Pork for their Goods, then Tobacco or Furrs, which I conceive is, because their bodies being
fast bound up with the cords of restringent Zeal, they are fain
to make use of the lineaments of this Non-Canaanite creature physically to loosen them; for a bit of a pound upon a
two-peny Rye loaf, according to the original Receipt, will
bring the costiv'st red-ear'd Zealot in some three hours time
to a fine stool, if methodically observed.

Medera-Wines, Sugars, Salt, Wickar-Chairs, and Tin Candle-
sticks, is the most of the Commodities they bring in: They
arrive in Mary-Land about September, being most of them
Ketches and Barkes, and such small Vessels, and those dis-
persing themselves into several small Creeks of this Province,
to sell and dispose of their Commodities, where they know the
Market is most fit for their small Adventures.

Barbadoes, together with the several adjacent Islands, has
much Provision yearly from this Province: And though these
Sun-burnt Phaetons think to outvye Mary-Land in their
Silks and Puffs, daily speaking against her whom their necessities makes them beholding to, and like so many Don Diegos
that becackt Pauls, cock their Felts and look big upon't; yet if
a man could go down into their infernals, and see how it fares

with them there, I believe he would hardly find any other
Spirit to buoy them up, then the ill-visaged Ghost of want,
that continually wanders from gut to gut to feed upon the
undigested rynes of Potatoes.

Trafique is Earth's great Atlas, that supports
The pay of Armies, and the height of Courts,
And makes Mechanicks live, that else would die
Meer starving Martyrs to their penury:
None but the Merchant of this thing can boast,
He, like the Bee, comes loaden from each Coast,
And to all Kingdoms, as within a Hive,
Stows up those Riches that doth make them thrive:
Be thrifty, Mary-Land, keep what thou hast in store,
And each years Trafique to thy self get more.

*A Relation of the Customs, Manners, Absurdities, and Religion
of the Susquehanock Indians in and near Mary-Land.*

As the diversities of Languages (since Babels confusion)
has made the distinction between people and people, in this
Christendompart of the world; so are they distinguished Nation from Nation, by the diversities and confusion of their
Speech and Languages here in America: And as every Nation
differs in their Laws, Manners and Customs, in Europe, Asia and
Africa, so do they the very same here; That it would be a most
intricate and laborious trouble, to run (with a description)
through the several Nations of Indians here in America, considering the innumerableness and diversities of them that dwell
on this vast and unmeasured Continent: But rather then I'le
be altogether silent, I shall do like the Painter in the Comedy,
who being to limne out the Pourtraiture of the Furies, as they
severally appeared, set himself behind a Pillar, and between
fright and amazement, drew them by guess. Those Indians
that I have convers'd withall here in this Province of Mary-
Land, and have had any occular experimental view of either
of their Customs, Manners, Religions, and Absurdities, are
called by the name of Susquehanocks, being a people lookt
upon by the Christian Inhabitants, as the most Noble and
Heroick Nation of Indians that dwell upon the confines of
America; also are so allowed and lookt upon by the rest of

the Indians, by a submissive and tributary acknowledgement; being a people cast into the mould of a most large and Warlike deportment, the men being for the most part seven foot high in latitude,[1] and in magnitude and bulk suitable to so high a pitch; their voyce large and hollow, as ascending out of a Cave, their gate and behavior strait, stately and majestick, treading on the Earth with as much pride, contempt, and disdain to so sordid a Center, as can be imagined from a creature derived from the same mould and Earth.

Their bodies are cloth'd with no other Armour to defend them from the nipping frosts of a benumbing Winter, or the penetrating and scorching influence of the Sun in a hot Summer, then what Nature gave them when they parted with the dark receptacle of their mothers womb. They go Men, Women and Children, all naked,[2] only where shame leads them by a natural instinct to be reservedly modest, there they become cover'd. The formality of Jezabels artificial Glory is much courted and followed by these Indians, only in matter of colours (I conceive) they differ.

The Indians paint upon their faces one stroke of red, another of green, another of white, and another of black, so that when they have accomplished the Equipage of their Countenance in this trim, they are the only Hieroglyphicks and Representatives of the Furies. Their skins are naturally white, but altered from their originals by the several dyings of Roots and Barks, that they prepare and make useful to metamorphize their hydes into a dark Cinamon brown. The hair of their head is black, long and harsh, but where Nature hath appointed the situation of it any where else, they divert it (by an antient custom) from its growth, by pulling it up hair by hair by the root in its primitive appearance. Several of them wear divers impressions on their breasts and armes, as the picture of the Devil, Bears, Tigers, and Panthers, which are imprinted on their several lineaments with much difficulty and pain, with an irrevocable determination of its abiding there: And this they count a badge of Heroick Valour, and the only Ornament due to their Heroes.

[1] Altitude. The Susquehannah Indians were a large and warlike people; but the stature here ascribed to them is an obvious exaggeration.

[2] Compare the description of the dress of the Pascataway Indians, p. 43, *supra.*

These Susquehanock Indians are for the most part great Warriours, and seldom sleep one Summer in the quiet armes of a peaceable Rest, but keep (by their present Power, as well as by their former Conquest) the several Nations of Indians round about them, in a forceable obedience and subjection.

Their Government is wrapt up in so various and intricate a Laborynth, that the speculativ'st Artist in the whole World, with his artificial and natural Opticks, cannot see into the rule or sway of these Indians, to distinguish what name of Government to call them by; though Purchas in his Peregrination between London and Essex, (which he calls the whole World) will undertake (forsooth) to make a Monarchy[1] of them, but if he had said Anarchy, his word would have pass'd with a better belief. All that ever I could observe in them as to this matter is, that he that is most cruelly Valorous, is accounted the most Noble: Here is very seldom any creeping from a Country Farm, into a Courtly Gallantry, by a sum of money; nor feeing the Heralds to put Daggers and Pistols into their Armes, to make the ignorant believe that they are lineally descended from the house of the Wars and Conquests; he that fights bests carries it here.

When they determine to go upon some Design that will and doth require a Consideration, some six of them get into a corner, and sit in Juncto; and if thought fit, their business is made popular, and immediately put into action; if not, they make a full stop to it, and are silently reserv'd.

The Warlike Equipage they put themselves in when they prepare for Belona's March, is with their faces, armes, and breasts confusedly painted, their hair greazed with Bears oyl, and stuck thick with Swans Feathers, with a wreath or Diadem of black and white Beads upon their heads, a small Hatchet, instead of a Cymetre, stuck in their girts behind them, and either with Guns, or Bows and Arrows. In this posture and dress they march out from their Fort, or dwelling, to the number of Forty in a Troop, singing (or rather howling out) the Decades or Warlike exploits of their Ancestors, ranging the wide Woods untill their fury has met with an Enemy

---

[1] See *A Relation of Maryland*, p. 84, *supra*. The contemptuous reference above is to Purchas's *Pilgrimes* (1625), that great storehouse of narratives of voyages.

worthy of their Revenge. What Prisoners fall into their
hands by the destiny of War, they treat them very civilly
while they remain with them abroad, but when they once
return homewards, they then begin to dress them in the habit
for death, putting on their heads and armes wreaths of Beads,
greazing their hair with fat, some going before, and the
rest behind, at equal distance from their Prisoners, bellow-
ing in a strange and confused manner, which is a true presage and fore-runner of destruction to their then conquered
Enemy.

In this manner of march they continue till they have
brought them to their Barken City, where they deliver them
up to those that in cruelty will execute them, without either
the legal Judgement of a Council of War, or the benefit of
their Clergy at the Common Law. The common and usual
deaths they put their Prisoners to, is to bind them to stakes,
making a fire some distance from them; then one or other of
them, whose Genius delights in the art of Paganish dissection,
with a sharp knife or flint cuts the Cutis or outermost skin of
the brow so deep, untill their nails, or rather Talons, can fasten
themselves firm and secure in, then (with a most rigid jerk)
disrobeth the head of skin and hair at one pull, leaving the skull
almost as bare as those Monumental Skelitons at Chyrurgions-
Hall; but for fear they should get cold by leaving so warm
and customary a Cap off, they immediately apply to the skull
a Cataplasm of hot Embers to keep their Pericranium warm.
While they are thus acting this cruelty on their heads, several
others are preparing pieces of Iron, and barrels of old Guns,
which they make red hot, to sear each part and lineament of
their bodies, which they perform and act in a most cruel and
barbarous manner: And while they are thus in the midst of
their torments and execrable usage, some tearing their skin
and hair of their head off by violence, others searing their
bodies with hot irons, some are cutting their flesh off, and
eating it before their eyes raw while they are alive; yet all this
and much more never makes them lower the Top-gallant sail
of their Heroick courage, to beg with a submissive Repentance
any indulgent favour from their persecuting Enemies; but
with an undaunted contempt to their cruelty, eye it with so
slight and mean a respect, as if it were below them to value

what they did, they courageously (while breath doth libertize them) sing the summary of their Warlike Atchievements.

Now after this cruelty has brought their tormented lives to a period, they immediately fall to butchering of them into parts, distributing the several pieces amongst the Sons of War, to intomb the ruines of their deceased Conquest in no other Sepulchre then their unsanctified maws; which they with more appetite and desire do eat and digest, then if the best of foods should court their stomachs to participate of the most restorative Banquet. Yet though they now and then feed upon the Carkesses of their Enemies, this is not a common dyet, but only a particular dish for the better sort; for there is not a Beast that runs in the Woods of America, but if they can by any means come at him, without any scruple of Conscience they'le fall too (without saying Grace) with a devouring greediness.

As for their Religion, together with their Rites and Ceremonies, they are so absurd and ridiculous, that its almost a sin to name them. They own no other Deity than the Devil, (solid or profound) but with a kind of wilde imaginary conjecture, they suppose from their groundless conceits, that the World had a Maker, but where he is that made it, or whether he be living to this day, they know not. The Devil, as I said before, is all the God they own or worship; and that more out of a slavish fear then any real Reverence to his Infernal or Diabolical greatness, he forcing them to their Obedience by his rough and rigid dealing with them, often appearing visibly among them to their terrour, bastinadoing them (with cruel menaces) even unto death, and burning their Fields of Corn and houses, that the relation thereof makes them tremble themselves when they tell it.

Once in four years they Sacrifice a Childe to him, in an acknowledgement of their firm obedience to all his Devillish powers, and Hellish commands. The Priests to whom they apply themselves in matters of importance and greatest distress, are like those that attended upon the Oracle at Delphos, who by their Magic-spells could command a *pro* or *con* from the Devil when they pleas'd. These Indians oft-times raise great Tempests when they have any weighty matter or design in hand, and by blustering storms inquire of their Infernal

God (the Devil) How matters shall go with them either in publick or private.

When any among them depart this life, they give him no other intombment, then to set him upright upon his breech in a hole dug in the Earth some five foot long, and three foot deep, covered over with the Bark of Trees Arch-wise, with his face Du-West, only leaving a hole half a foot square open. They dress him in the same Equipage and Gallantry that he used to be trim'd in when he was alive, and so bury him (if a Soldier) with his Bows, Arrows, and Target, together with all the rest of his implements and weapons of War, with a Kettle of Broth, and Corn standing before him, lest he should meet with bad quarters in his way. His Kinred and Relations follow him to the Grave, sheath'd in Bear skins for close mourning, with the tayl droyling on the ground, in imitation of our English Solemners, that think there's nothing like a tayl a Degree in length, to follow the dead Corpse to the Grave with. Here if that snuffling Prolocutor, that waits upon the dead Monuments of the Tombs at Westminster, with his white Rod were there, he might walk from Tomb to Tomb with his, Here lies the Duke of Ferrara and his Dutchess, and never find any decaying vacation, unless it were in the moldering Consumption of his own Lungs. They bury all within the wall or Pallisado'd impalement of their City, or *Connadago* as they call it. Their houses are low and long, built with the Bark of Trees Arch-wise, standing thick and confusedly together. They are situated a hundred and odd miles distant from the Christian Plantations of Mary-Land, at the head of a River that runs into the Bay of Chæsapike, called by their own name The Susquehanock River, where they remain and inhabit most part of the Summer time, and seldom remove far from it, unless it be to subdue any Forreign Rebellion.

About November the best Hunters draw off to several remote places of the Woods, where they know the Deer, Bear, and Elke useth; there they build them several Cottages, which they call their Winter-quarter, where they remain for the space of three months, untill they have killed up a sufficiency of Provisions to supply their Families with in the Summer.

The Women are the Butchers, Cooks, and Tillers of the ground, the Men think it below the honour of a Masculine, to stoop to any thing but that which their Gun, or Bow and Arrows can command. The Men kill the several Beasts which they meet withall in the Woods, and the Women are the Pack horses to fetch it in upon their backs, fleying and dressing the hydes, (as well as the flesh for provision) to make them fit for Trading, and which are brought down to the English at several seasons in the year, to truck and dispose of them for course Blankets, Guns, Powder, and Lead, Beads, small Looking-glasses, Knives, and Razors.

I never observed all the while I was amongst these naked Indians, that ever the Women wore the Breeches, or dared either in look or action predominate over the Men. They are very constant to their Wives; and let this be spoken to their Heathenish praise, that did they not alter their bodies by their dyings, paintings, and cutting themselves, marring those Excellencies that Nature bestowed upon them in their original conceptions and birth, there would be as amiable beauties amongst them, as any Alexandria could afford, when Mark Anthony and Cleopatra dwelt there together. Their Marriages are short and authentique; for after 'tis resolv'd upon by both parties, the Woman sends her intended Husband a Kettle of boyl'd Venison, or Bear; and he returns in lieu thereof Beaver or Otters Skins, and so their Nuptial Rites are concluded without other Ceremony.

.   .   .   .

A Collection of some Letters that were written by the same Author, most of them in the time of his Servitude.

To my much Honored Friend Mr. T. B.

Sir,

I have lived with sorrow to see the Anointed of the Lord tore from his Throne by the hands of Paricides, and in contempt haled, in the view of God, Angels and Men, upon a public Theatre, and there murthered.[1] I have seen the sacred Temple of the Almighty, in scorn by Schismaticks made the Receptacle of Theeves and Robbers; and those Religious Prayers, that in devotion Evening and Morning were offered up as a Sacrifice to our God, rent by Sacrilegious hands, and

[1] An allusion to the execution of Charles I. in 1649.

made no other use of, then sold to Brothel-houses to light Tobacco with.

Who then can stay, or will, to see things of so great weight steer'd by such barbarous Hounds as these: First, were there an Egypt to go down to, I would involve my Liberty to them, upon condition ne'er more to see my Country. What? live in silence under the sway of such base actions, is to give consent; and though the lowness of my present Estate and Condition, with the hazard I put my future dayes upon, might plead a just excuse for me to stay at home; but Heavens forbid: I'le rather serve in Chains, and draw the Plough with Animals, till death shall stop and say, It is enough. Sir, if you stay behind, I wish you well: I am bound for Mary-Land, this day I have made some entrance into my intended voyage, and when I have done more, you shall know of it. I have here inclosed what you of me desired, but truly trouble, discontent and business, have so amazed my senses, that what to write, or where to write, I conceive my self almost as uncapable as he that never did write. What you'le find will be *Ex tempore*, without the use of premeditation; and though there may want something of a flourishing stile to dress them forth, yet I'm certain there wants nothing of truth, will, and desire.

Heavens bright Lamp, shine forth some of thy Light,
But just so long to paint this dismal Night;
Then draw thy beams, and hide thy glorious face,
From the dark sable actions of this place;
Leaving these lustful Sodomites groping still,
To satisfie each dark unsatiate will,
Untill at length the crimes that they commit,
May sink them down to Hells Infernal pit.
Base and degenerate Earth, how dost thou lye,
That all that pass hiss, at thy Treachery?
Thou which couldst boast once of thy King and Crown,
By base Mechanicks now art tumbled down,
Brewers and Coblers, that have scarce an Eye,
Walk hand in hand in thy Supremacy;
And all those Courts where Majesty did Throne,
Are now the Seats for Oliver and Joan:
Persons of Honour, which did before inherit
Their glorious Titles from deserved merit,
Are all grown silent, and with wonder gaze,

To view such Slaves drest in their Courtly rayes;
To see a Drayman that knows nought but Yeast,
Set in a Throne like Babylons red Beast,
While heaps of Parasites do idolize
This red-nos'd Bell, with fawning Sacrifice.
What can we say? our King they've Murthered,
And those well born, are basely buried:
Nobles are slain, and Royalists in each street
Are scorn'd, and kick'd by most men that they meet:
Religion's banisht, and Heresie survives,
And none but Conventicks in this Age thrives.
Oh could those Romans from their Ashes rise,
That liv'd in Nero's time: Oh how their cries
Would our perfidious Island shake, nay rend,
With clamorous screaks unto the Heaven send:
Oh how they'd blush to see our Crimson crimes,
And know the Subjects Authors of these times:
When as the Peasant he shall take his King,
And without cause shall fall a murthering him;
And when that's done, with Pride assume the Chair,
And Nimrod-like, himself to heaven rear;
Command the People, make the Land Obey
His baser will, and swear to what he'l say.
Sure, sure our God has not these evils sent
To please himself, but for mans punishment:
And when he shall from our dark sable Skies
Withdraw these Clouds, and let our Sun arise,
Our dayes will surely then in Glory shine,
Both in our Temporal, and our State divine:
May this come quickly, though I may never see
This glorious day, yet I would sympathie,
And feel a joy run through each vain of blood,
Though Vassalled on t'other side the Floud.
Heavens protect his Sacred Majesty,
From secret Plots, and treacherous Villany.
And that those Slaves that now predominate,
Hang'd and destroy'd may be their best of Fate;
And though great Charles be distant from his own,
Heaven I hope will seat him on his Throne.

Vale.

Yours what I may,

G. A.

From the Chimney-corner upon a
low Cricket, where I writ this in
the noise of some six Women,
Aug. 19. Anno

To my Honoured Father, at his House.

Sir,

Before I dare bid Adieu to the old World, or shake hands
with my native Soyl for ever, I have a Conscience inwards
tells me, that I must offer up the remains of that Obedience of
mine, that lyes close centered within the cave of my Soul,
at the Alter, of your paternal Love: And though this Sacrifice
of mine may shew something low and thread-bare, (at this
time) yet know, That in the Zenith of all actions, Obedience is
that great wheel that moves the lesser in their circular motion.

I am now entring for some time to dwell under the Government of Neptune, a Monarchy that I was never manured
to live under, nor to converse with in his dreadful Aspect,
neither do I know how I shall bear with his rough demands;
but that God has carried me through those many gusts a shoar,
which I have met withall in the several voyages of my life, I
hope will Pilot me safely to my desired Port, through the worst
of Stormes I shall meet withall at Sea.

We have strange, and yet good news aboard, that he whose
vast mind could not be contented with spacious Territories
to stretch his insatiate desires on, is (by an Almighty power)
banished from his usurped Throne to dwell among the dead.
I no sooner heard of it, but my melancholly Muse forced me
upon this ensuing Distich.

> Poor vaunting Earth, gloss'd with uncertain Pride,
> That liv'd in Pomp, yet worse than others dy'd:
> Who shall blow forth a Trumpet to thy praise?
> Or call thy sable Actions shining Rayes?
> Such Lights as those blaze forth the vertues dead,
> And make them live, though they are buried.
> Thou'rt gone, and to thy memory let be said,
> There lies that Oliver which of old betray'd
> His King and Master, and after did assume,
> With swelling Pride, to govern in his room.
> Here I'le rest satisfied, Scriptures expound to me,
> Tophet was made for such Supremacy.

The death of this great Rebel (I hope) will prove an Omen
to presage destruction on the rest. The World's in a heap
of troubles and confusion, and while they are in the midst of

their changes and amazes, the best way to give them the bag, is to go out of the World and leave them. I am now bound for Mary-Land, and I am told that's a New World, but if it prove no better than this, I shall not get much by my change; but before I'le revoke my Resolution, I am resolv'd to put it to adventure, for I think it can hardly be worse then this is: Thus committing you into the hands of that God that made you, I rest

Your Obedient Son,

From aboard a Ship at Graves-
end, Sept. 7th. Anno [1658]

G. A.

To my Brother.

I Leave you very near in the same condition as I am in my self, only here lies the difference, you were bound at Joyners Hall in London Apprentice-wise, and I conditionally at Navi-gators Hall, that now rides at an Anchor at Gravesend; I hope you will allow me to live in the largest Mayordom, by reason I am the eldest: None but the main Continent of America will serve me for a Corporation to inhabit in now, though I am affraid for all that, that the reins of my Liberty will be something shorter then yours will be in London: But as to that, what Destiny has ordered I am resolved with an adventerous Resolution to subscribe to, and with a contented imbracement enjoy it. I would fain have seen you once more in this Old World, before I go into the New, I know you have a chain about your Leg, as well as I have a clog about my Neck: If you can't come, send a line or two, if not, wish me well at least: I have one thing to charge home upon you, and I hope you will take my counsel, That you have alwayes an obedi-ent Respect and Reverence to your aged Parents, that while they live they may have comfort of you, and when that God shall sound a retreat to their lives, that there they may with their gray hairs in joy go down to their Graves.

Thus concluding, wishing you a comfortable Servitude, a prosperous Life, and the assurance of a happy departure in the immutable love of him that made you, *Vale.*

Your Brother,

G. A.

From Gravesend, Sept. 7. Anno

To My much Honored Friend Mr. T. B. at his House.

I Am got ashoar with much ado, and it is very well as it is, for if I had stayed a little longer, I had certainly been a Creature of the Water, for I had hardly flesh enough to carry me to Land, not that I wanted for any thing that the Ship could afford me in reason: But oh the great bowls of Pease-porridge that appeared in sight every day about the hour twelve, ingulfed the senses of my Appetite so, with the restringent quality of the Salt Beef, upon the internal Inhabitants of my belly, that a Galenist for some dayes after my arrival, with his Bag-pipes of Physical operations, could hardly make my Puddings dance in any methodical order.

But to set by these things that happened unto me at Sea, I am now upon Land, and there I'le keep my self if I can, and for four years I am pretty sure of my restraint; and had I known my yoak would have been so easie, (as I conceive it will) I would have been here long before now, rather then to have dwelt under the pressure of a Rebellious and Trayterous Government so long as I did.   I dwell now by providence in the Province of Mary-Land, (under the quiet Government of the Lord Baltemore) which Country abounds in a most glorious prosperity and plenty of all things.   And though the Infancy of her situation might plead an excuse to those several imperfections, (if she were guilty of any of them) which by scandalous and imaginary conjectures are falsly laid to her charge, and which she values with so little notice or perceivance of discontent, that she hardly alters her visage with a frown, to let them know she is angry with such a Rascality of people, that loves nothing better then their own sottish and abusive acclamations of baseness: To be short, the Country (so far forth as I have seen into it) is incomparable.

Here is a sort of naked Inhabitants, or wilde people, that have for many ages I believe lived here in the Woods of Mary-Land, as well as in other parts of the Continent, before e'er it was by the Christian Discoverers found out; being a people strange to behold, as well in their looks, which by confused paintings makes them seem dreadful, as in their sterne and heroick gate and deportments; the Men are mighty tall and big limbed, the Women not altogether so large; they are most of them very well featured, did not their wilde and ridiculous dresses alter their original excellencies: The men are great Warriours and Hunters, the Women ingenious and laborious Housewives.

As to matter of their Worship, they own no other Deity then the Devil, and him more out of a slavish fear, then any real devotion, or willing acknowledgement to his Hellish power. They live in little small Bark-Cottages, in the remote parts of the Woods, killing and slaying the several Animals that they meet withall to make provision of, dressing their several Hydes and Skins to Trafique withall, when a conveniency of Trade presents. I would go on further, but like Doctor Case, when he had not a word more to speak for himself, I am affraid my beloved I have kept you too long. Now he that made you save you, Amen.

Yours to command,
G. A.

From Mary-Land, Febr. 6. Anno

And not to forget Tom Forge I beseech you, tell him that my Love's the same towards him still, and as firm as it was about the overgrown Tryal, when Judgements upon Judgements, had not I stept in, would have pursued him untill the day of Judgement, etc.

To my Father at his House.
   Sir,
After my Obedience (at so great and vast a distance) has humbly saluted you and my good Mother, with the cordialest of my prayers, wishes, and desires to wait upon you, with the very best of their effectual devotion, wishing from the very Center of my Soul your flourishing and well-being here upon Earth, and your glorious and everlasting happiness in the World to come.

These lines (my dear Parents) come from that Son which by an irregular Fate was removed from his Native home, and after a five months dangerous passage, was landed on the remote Continent of America, in the Province of Mary-Land, where now by providence I reside. To give you the particulars of the several accidents that happened in our Voyage by Sea, it would swell a Journal of some sheets, and therefore too

large and tedious for a Letter: I think it therefore necessary
to bind up the relation in Octavo, and give it you in short.

We had a blowing and dangerous passage of it, and for
some dayes after I arrived, I was an absolute Copernicus, it
being one main point of my moral Creed, to believe the World
had a pair of long legs, and walked with the burthen of the
Creation upon her back. For to tell you the very truth of it,
for some dayes upon Land, after so long and tossing a passage,
I was so giddy that I could hardly tread an even step; so that
all things both above and below (that was in view) appeared
to me like the Kentish Britains to William the Conqueror, in a
moving posture.

Those few number of weeks since my arrival, has given me
but little experience to write any thing large of the Country;
only thus much I can say, and that not from any imaginary
conjectures, but from an occular observation, That this
Country of Mary-Land abounds in a flourishing variety of
delightful Woods, pleasant Groves, lovely Springs, together
with spacious Navigable Rivers and Creeks, it being a most
healthful and pleasant situation, so far as my knowledge has
yet had any view in it.

Herds of Deer are as numerous in this Province of Mary-
Land, as Cuckolds can be in London, only their horns are not
so well drest and tipt with silver as theirs are.

Here if the Devil had such a Vagary in his head as he had
once among the Gadareans, he might drown a thousand head
of Hogs and they'd ne're be miss'd, for the very Woods of this
Province swarms with them.

The Christian Inhabitant of this Province, as to the general, lives wonderful well and contented: The Government
of this Province is by the loyalness of the people, and loving
demeanor of the Proprietor and Governor of the same, kept in a
continued peace and unity.

The Servant of this Province, which are stigmatiz'd for
Slaves by the clappermouth jaws of the vulgar in England,
live more like Freemen then the most Mechanick Apprentices
in London, wanting for nothing that is convenient and necessary, and according to their several capacities, are extraordinary well used and respected. So leaving things here as
I found them, and lest I should commit Sacriledge upon your

more serious meditations, with the Tautologies of a long-winded Letter, I'le subscribe with a heavenly Ejaculation to the God of Mercy to preserve you now and for evermore, Amen.

Your Obedient Son,

G. A.

From Mary-Land, Jan. 17. Anno

To my much Honored Friend Mr. M. F.
  Sir,
You writ to me when I was at Gravesend, (but I had no conveniency to send you an answer till now) enjoyning me, if possible, to give you a just Information by my diligent observance, what thing were best and most profitable to send into this Country for a commodious Trafique.

Sir, The enclosed will demonstrate unto you both particularly and at large, to the full satisfaction of your desire, it being an Invoyce drawn as exact to the business you imployed me upon, as my weak capacity could extend to.

Sir, If you send any Adventure to this Province, let me beg to give you this advice in it; That the Factor whom you imploy be a man of a Brain, otherwise the Planter will go near to make a Skimming-dish of his Skull: I know your Genius can interpret my meaning. The people of this place (whether the saltness of the Ocean gave them any alteration when they went over first, or their continual dwelling under the remote Clyme where they now inhabit, I know not) are a more acute people in general, in matters of Trade and Commerce, then in any other place of the World; and by their crafty and sure bargaining, do often over-reach the raw and unexperienced Merchant. To be short, he that undertakes Merchants imployment for Mary-Land, must have more of Knave in him then Fool; he must not be a windling piece of Formality, that will lose his Imployers Goods for Conscience sake; nor a flashy piece of Prodigality, that will give his Merchants fine Hollands, Laces, and Silks, to purchase the benevolence of a Female: But he must be a man of solid confidence, carrying alwayes in his looks the Effigies of an Execution upon Command, if he supposes a baffle or denyal of payment, where a debt for his Imployer is legally due.

Sir, I had like almost to forgot to tell you in what part
of the World I am: I dwell by providence Servant to Mr.
Thomas Stocket, in the County of Baltemore, within the
Province of Mary-Land, under the Government of the Lord
Baltemore, being a Country abounding with the variety and
diversity of all that is or may be rare. But lest I should
Tantalize you with a relation of that which is very unlikely
of your enjoying, by reason of that strong Antipathy you have
ever had 'gainst Travel, as to your own particular: I'le only,
tell you, that Mary-Land is seated within the large extending
armes of America, between the Degrees of 36 and 38,[1] being in
Longitude from England eleven hundred and odd Leagues.

Vale.

G. A.

From Mary-Land, Jan. 17.   Anno

To my Honored Friend Mr. T. B. at his House.
Sir,
Yours received, wherein I find my self much obliged
to you for your good opinion of me, I return you millions
of thanks.

Sir, you wish me well, and I pray God as well that those
wishes may light upon me, and then I question not but all
will do well. Those Pictures you sent sewed up in a Past-
board, with a Letter tacked on the outside, you make no
mention at all what should be done with them: If they are
Saints, unless I knew their names, I could make no use of
them. Pray in your next let me know what they are, for my
fingers itch to be doing with them one way or another. Our
Government here hath had a small fit of a Rebellious Quotid-
ian,[2] but five Grains of the powder of Subvertment has qualified it. Pray be larger in your next how things stand in
England: I understand His Majesty is return'd with Honour,
and seated in the hereditary Throne of his Father; God bless
him from Traytors, and the Church from Sacrilegious Schisms,
and you as a loyal Subject to the one, and a true Member

---

[1] Should be 38 and 40.

[2] The reference is to the treachery of Governor Fendall, who after accepting
appointment from the Proprietary sought to cast off his authority, and accepted a new appointment as governor from the Assembly (1660).

to the other; while you so continue, the God of order, peace and tranquility, bless and preserve you, Amen.

Vale.

Your real Friend,

G. A.

From Mary-Land, Febr. 20.   Anno [1661].

To my Honored Father at his House.

Sir,

With a twofold unmeasurable joy I received your Letter: First, in the consideration of Gods great Mercy to you in particular, (though weak and aged) yet to give you dayes among the living.   Next, that his now most Excellent Majesty Charles the Second, is by the omnipotent Providence of God, seated in the Throne of his Father.   I hope that God that has placed him there, will give him a heart to praise and magnifie his name for ever, and a hand of just Revenge, to punish the murthering and rebellious Outrages of those Sons of shame and Apostacy, that Usurped the Throne of his Sacred Honour. Near about the time I received your Letter, (or a little before) here sprang up in this Province of Mary-Land a kind of pigmie Rebellion: A company of weak-witted men, which thought to have traced the steps of Oliver in Rebellion.   They began to be mighty stiff and hidebound in their proceedings, clothing themselves with the flashy pretences of future and imaginary honour, and (had they not been suddenly quell'd) they might have done so much mischief (for aught I know) that nothing but utter ruine could have ransomed their headlong follies.

His Majesty appearing in England, he quickly (by the splendor of his Rayes) thawed the stiffness of their frozen and slippery intentions.   All things (blessed be God for it) are at peace and unity here now: And as Luther being asked once, What he thought of some small Opinions that started up in his time? answered, That he thought them to be good honest people, exempting their error: So I judge of these men, That their thoughts were not so bad at first, as their actions would have led them into in process of time.

I have here enclosed sent you something written in haste upon the Kings coming to the enjoyment of his Throne, with a reflection upon the former sad and bad times; I have done

them as well as I could, considering all things: If they are not
so well as they should be, all I can do is to wish them better for
your sakes. My Obedience to you and my Mother alwayes
devoted.

Your Son

G. A.

From Mary-Land, Febr. 9.   Anno

To my Cosen Mrs. Ellinor Evins.[1]

E' re I forget the Zenith of your Love,
L et me be banisht from the Thrones above;
L ight let me never see, when I grow rude,
I ntomb your Love in base Ingratitude:
N or may I prosper, but the state
O f gaping Tantalus be my fate;
R ather then I should thus preposterous grow,

E arth would condemn me to her vaults below.
V ertuous and Noble, could my Genius raise
I mmortal Anthems to your Vestal praise,
N one should be more laborious then I,
S aint-like to Canonize you to the Sky.

The Antimonial Cup (dear Cosen) you sent me, I had; and
as soon as I received it, I went to work with the Infirmities
and Diseases of my body.   At the first draught, it made such
havock among the several humors that had stoln into my body,
that like a Conjurer in a room among a company of little
Devils, they no sooner hear him begin to speak high words,
but away they pack, and happy is he that can get out first,
some up the Chimney, and the rest down stairs, till they are
all disperst.   So those malignant humors of my body, feeling
the operative power, and medicinal virtue of this Cup, were
so amazed at their sudden surprizal, (being alwayes before
battered only by the weak assaults of some few Emporicks)
they stood not long to dispute, but with joynt consent made
their retreat, some running through the sink of the Skullery, the
rest climbing up my ribs, took my mouth for a Garret-window,
and so leapt out.

---

[1] An acrostic.

Cosen, For this great kindness of yours, in sending me this medicinal vertue, I return you my thanks: It came in a very good time, when I was dangerously sick, and by the assistance of God it hath perfectly recovered me.

I have sent you here a few Furrs, they were all I could get at present, I humbly beg your acceptance of them, as a pledge of my love and thankfulness unto you; I subscribe,

Your loving Cosen,
G. A.

From Mary-Land, Dec. 9. **Anno**

To my Brother P. A.
  Brother,
I have made a shift to unloose my self from my Collar now as well as you, but I see at present either small pleasure or profit in it: What the futurality of my dayes will bring forth, I know not; For while I was linckt with the Chain of a restraining Servitude, I had all things cared for, and now I have all things to care for my self, which makes me almost wish my self in for the other four years.

Liberty without money, is like a man opprest with the Gout, every step he puts forward puts him to pain; when on the other side, he that has Coyn with his Liberty, is like the swift Post-Messenger of the Gods, that wears wings at his heels, his motion being swift or slow, as he pleaseth.

I received this year two Caps, the one white, of an honest plain countenance, the other purple, which I conceive to be some antient Monumental Relique; which of them you sent I know not, and it was a wonder how I should, for there was no mention in the Letter, more then, that my Brother had sent me a Cap: They were delivered me in the company of some Gentlemen that ingaged me to write a few lines upon the purple one, and because they were my Friends I could not deny them; and here I present them to you as they were written.

> Haile from the dead, or from Eternity,
> Thou Velvit Relique of Antiquity;
> Thou which appear'st here in thy purple hew,
> Tell's how the dead within their Tombs do doe;
> How those Ghosts fare within each Marble Cell,

Where amongst them for Ages thou didst dwell.
What Brain didst cover there? tell us that we
Upon our knees vayle Hats to honour thee:
And if no honour's due, tell us whose pate
Thou basely coveredst, and we'l joyntly hate:
Let's know his name, that we may shew neglect;
If otherwise, we'l kiss thee with respect.
Say, didst thou cover Noll's[1] old brazen head,
Which on the top of Westminster high Lead
Stands on a Pole, erected to the sky,
As a grand Trophy to his memory.
From his perfidious skull didst thou fall down,
In a disdain to honour such a crown
With three-pile Velvet? tell me, hadst thou thy **fall**
From the high top of that Cathedral?
None of the Heroes of the Roman stem,
Wore ever such a fashion'd Diadem,
Didst thou speak Turkish in thy unknown dress,
Thou'dst cover Great Mogull, and no man less;
But in thy make methinks thou'rt too too scant,
To be so great a Monarch's Turberant.
The Jews by Moses swear, they never knew
E're such a Cap drest up in Hebrew:
Nor the strict Order of the Romish See,
Wears any Cap that looks so base as thee;
His Holiness hates thy Lowness, and instead,
Wears Peters spired Steeple on his head:
The Cardinals descent is much more flat,
For want of name, baptized is A Hat;
Through each strict Order has my fancy ran,
Both Ambrose, Austin, and the Franciscan,
Where I beheld rich Images of the dead,
Yet scarce had one a Cap upon his head:
Episcopacy wears Caps, but not like thee,
Though several shap'd, with much diversity:
'Twere best I think I presently should gang
To Edenburghs strict Presbyterian;
But Caps they've none, their ears being made so large,
Serves them to turn it like a Garnesey Barge;
Those keep their skulls warm against North-west gusts,
When they in Pulpit do poor Calvin curse.
Thou art not Fortunatus, for I daily see,

---

[1] Oliver Cromwell's.

That which I wish is farthest off from me:
Thy low-built state none ever did advance,
To christen thee the Cap of Maintenance;
Then till I know from whence thou didst derive
Thou shalt be call'd, the Cap of Fugitive.

You writ to me this year to send you some Smoak; at that instant it made me wonder that a man of a rational Soul, having both his eyes (blessed be God) should make so unreasonable a demand, when he that has but one eye, nay he which has never a one, and is fain to make use of an Animal conductive for his optick guidance, cannot endure the prejudice that Smoak brings with it: But since you are resolv'd upon it, I'le dispute it no further.

I have sent you that which will make Smoak, (namely Tobacco) though the Funk it self is so slippery that I could not send it, yet I have sent you the Substance from whence the Smoak derives: What use you imploy it to I know not, nor will I be too importunate to know; yet let me tell you this, That if you burn it in a room to affright the Devil from the house, you need not fear but it will work the same effect, as Tobyes galls did upon the leacherous Fiend.[1] No more at present.

Vale.
Your Brother,

From Mary-Land, Dec. 11.   Anno   G. A.

To my Honored Friend Mr. T. B.
   Sir,
This is the entrance upon my fifth year, and I fear 'twill prove the worst: I have been very much troubled with a throng of unruly Distempers, that have (contrary to my expectation) crouded into the Main-guard of my body, when the drowsie Sentinels of my brain were a sleep. Where they got in I know not, but to my grief and terror I find them predominant: Yet as Doctor Dunne, sometimes Dean of St. Pauls, said, That the bodies diseases do but mellow a man for Heaven, and so ferments him in this World, as he shall need no long concoction in the Grave, but hasten to the Resurrection. And if this were weighed seriously in the Ballance of Religious

[1] Tobit viii. 2, 3.

Reason, the World we dwell in would not seem so inticing and bewitching as it doth.

We are only sent by God of an Errand into this World, and the time that's allotted us for to stay, is only for an Answer. When God my great Master shall in good earnest call me home, which these warnings tell me I have not long to stay, I hope then I shall be able to give him a good account of my Message.

Sir, My weakness gives a stop to my writing, my hand being so shakingly feeble, that I can hardly hold my pen any further then to tell you, I am yours while I live, which I believe will be but some few minutes.

If this Letter come to you before I'me dead, pray for me, but if I am gone, pray howsoever, for they can do me no harm if they come after me.

Vale.
Your real Friend,

From Mary-Land, Dec. 13.   Anno   G. A.

To my Parents.

From the Grave or Receptacle of Death am I raised, and by an omnipotent power made capable of offering once more my Obedience (that lies close cabbined in the inwardmost apartment of my Soul) at the feet of your immutable Loves.

My good Parents, God hath done marvellous things for me, far beyond my deserts, which at best were preposterously sinful, and unsuitable to the sacred will of an Almighty: But he is merciful, and his mercy endures for ever. When sinful man has by his Evils and Iniquities pull'd some penetrating Judgment upon his head, and finding himself immediately not able to stand under so great a burthen as Gods smallest stroke of Justice, lowers the Top-gallant sayle of his Pride, and with an humble submissiveness prostrates himself before the Throne of his sacred Mercy, and like those three Lepars that sate at the Gate of Samaria, resolved, If we go into the City we shall perish, and if we stay here we shall perish also: Therefore we will throw our selves into the hands of the Assyrians and if we perish,[1] we perish: This was just my condition as to eternal state; my Soul was at a stand in this black storm of

[1] II Kings vii. 3, 4, 5.

affliction: I view'd the World, and all that's pleasure in her, and found her altogether flashy, aiery, and full of notional pretensions, and not one firm place where a distressed Soul could hang his trust on. Next I viewed my self, and there I found, instead of good Works, lively Faith, and Charity, a most horrid neast of condemned Evils, bearing a supreme Prerogative over my internal faculties. You'l say here was little hope of rest in this extreme Eclipse, being in a desperate amaze to see my estate so deplorable: My better Angel urged me to deliver up my aggrievances to the Bench of Gods Mercy, the sure support of all distressed Souls: His Heavenly warning, and inward whispers of the good Spirit I was resolv'd to entertain, and not quench, and throw my self into the armes of a loving God, If I perish, I perish. 'Tis beyond wonder to think of the love of God extended to sinful man, that in the deepest distresses or agonies of Affliction, when all other things prove rather hinderances then advantages, even at that time God is ready and steps forth to the supportment of his drooping Spirit. Truly, about a fortnight before I wrote this Letter, two of our ablest Physicians rendered me up into the hands of God, the universal Doctor of the whole World, and subscribed with a silent acknowledgement, That all their Arts, screw'd up to the very Zenith of Scholastique perfection, were not capable of keeping me from the Grave at that time: But God, the great preserver of Soul and Body, said contrary to the expectation of humane reason, Arise, take up thy bed and walk.

I am now (through the help of my Maker) creeping up to my former strength and vigour, and every day I live, I hope I shall, through the assistance of divine Grace, climbe nearer and nearer to my eternal home.

I have received this year three Letters from you, one by Capt. Conway Commander of the *Wheat-Sheaf*, the others by a Bristol Ship. Having no more at present to trouble you with, but expecting your promise, I remain as ever,

Your dutiful Son,

Mary-Land, Apr. 9. Anno

G. A.

I desire my hearty love may be remembered to my Brother, and the rest of my Kinred.

FROM THE JOURNAL OF GEORGE FOX.

1672, 1673

INTRODUCTION

PRIOR to the grant, by Charles II. to William Penn, in 1681, of the charter of Pennsylvania, many members of the Society of Friends, or Quakers, had availed themselves of the religious liberty established in Maryland to settle in that province, especially in that portion on the eastern shore of the Chesapeake Bay. These people had received scant hospitality in other colonies. In Massachusetts a law was passed banishing Quakers, with severe and cruel punishment for returning: for the first offense flogging and imprisonment at hard labor; for the second offense the ears were to be cut off; and for the third the tongue was to be bored with a hot iron. At length, in 1658, capital punishment was decreed, and in October, 1659, members of that Society were actually hanged on Boston Common.[1] It is true that at one time in Maryland there was an order of Council which bore hardly upon the Quakers, but it had no reference to their religious beliefs. It was required by general law that every settler should take the oath of fidelity to the Lord Proprietary, and that every man capable of bearing arms should be enrolled in the militia and provided with arms and ammunition. The punishment prescribed in the order of Council above referred to for refusal to comply with these requirements was banishment from the province, and for returning after such banishment, the offender was to be whipped from constable to constable until he was again out of the province.[2]

[1] Fiske, *The Beginnings of New England*, p. 189.
[2] *Archives of Maryland*, III. 362.

The Quakers refused compliance, and they were accused of dissuading others from military service, of refusing to be sworn as witnesses or to serve as jurors; but it does not appear that the penalty was ever imposed upon any one. This order of Council was never a law of the province, and it continued in effect for little more than one year. It was during Governor Fendall's brief and inglorious administration.

Under these conditions, the number of Quakers in Maryland had become so large that in 1661 stated meetings were established.

In 1672, George Fox, the founder of the Society, visited its members in America. The following extracts from his journal contain the portions relating to Maryland.

The first extract tells of two general meetings held, one at West River and the other in Talbot County, shortly after Fox's arrival in Maryland from Jamaica and before his departure for New England. The second and third extracts tell of the meetings held in Maryland after his return from New England and before sailing for the Old World.

The following text is taken from the original publication made in London by Thomas Northcott in 1694. There have been many subsequent editions of the *Journal* published.

C. C. H.

FROM THE JOURNAL OF GEORGE FOX,
1672, 1673

HERE[1] we found John Burneyate, intending shortly to Sail for Old England: but upon our Arrival he altered his purpose; and joined with us in the Lord's Service, which we were upon. He had appointed a General Meeting for all the Friends in the Province of Maryland, that he might see them together, and take his Leave of them, before he departed out of the Country: And it was so ordered by the good Providence of God, that we landed just time enough, to reach that Meeting; by which means we had a very seasonable Opportunity of taking the Friends of the Province together. A very large Meeting this was, and held Four Days; to which (besides Friends) came many of the World's People, divers of which were of considerable Quality in the World's Account: For there were amongst them five or six Justices of the Peace, a Speaker of their Parliament or Assembly, One of the Council, and divers others of Note; who seemed well satisfied with the Meeting. After the Publick Meetings were over, the Mens and Womens Meetings began; wherein I opened to Friends the Service thereof, to their great Satisfaction.[2] After this we went to another Place, called the Cliffs, where another General Meeting was appointed: We went some part of the way by Land, and the rest by Water; and a Storm arising, our

---

[1] That is, in Maryland. John Burnyeat, like William Edmundson mentioned below, was a famous travelling Friend. Their narratives of their travels were also printed, the former's under the name *The Truth Exalted* (London, 1691), those of the latter as *Journal of the Life, Travels,* etc., *of William Edmundson* (Dublin, 1715). Another account of Maryland, or at least of the northeastern part of it, by two other sectaries, writing a few years later, 1679–1680, may be found in the *Journal of Dankers and Sluyter*, which it is intended to publish later in this series.

[2] This "meeting for discipline" was the origin of Baltimore Yearly Meeting, still one of the chief organizations of American Friends.

Boat was run on ground, in danger to be beaten to pieces: and the Water came in upon us. I was in a great Sweat, having come very hot out of a Meeting before; and now was Wet with the Water beside: yet having Faith in the Power of the Lord, I was preserved from taking hurt, blessed be the Lord. To this Meeting also many of the World's People came, and did receive the Truth with Reverence. We had also a Mens-Meeting, and a Womens-Meeting, at which most of the Backsliders came in again; and several of those Meetings were established for taking Care of the Affairs of the Church.

After these Two General Meetings were over, we parted Company, dividing our selves into several Coasts, for the Service of Truth. James Lancaster and John Cartwright went by Sea for New-England; William Edmundson, and three Friends more with him, sailed for Virginia, where things were much out of Order: John Burneyate, Robert Widders, George Pattison and I, with several Friends of the Province, went over by Boat to the Eastern Shore,[1] and had a Meeting there on the First Day; where many People received the Truth with Gladness, and Friends were greatly refreshed. A very large and Heavenly Meeting it was, and several Persons of Quality in that Country were at it; two of which were Justices of the Peace. And it was upon me from the Lord, to send to the Indian Emperor and his Kings, to come to that Meeting: The Emperor came, and was at the Meeting; but his Kings, lying further off, could not reach thither time enough: Yet they came after with their Cockarooses.[2] I had in the Evening (for they staid all Night) two good Opportunities with them; and they heard the Word of the Lord willingly, and did confess to it. What I spake to them, I desired them to speak to their People; and let them know, That God was setting up his Tabernacle of Witness in their Wilderness-Country, and was setting up his Standard, and glorious Ensign of Righteousness. They carried themselves very courteously and lovingly, and inquired, Where the next Meeting would be, and they would come to it: Yet they said, They had had a great Debate with their Council about their Coming, before they came now.

[1] The part of Maryland east of Chesapeake Bay.
[2] See p. 84, note 1.

The next Day we began our Journey by Land to New-England, a tedious Journey through the Woods and Wilderness, over Boggs and great Rivers. We took Horse at the Head of Tredaven-Creek,[1] and travelled through the Woods, till we came a little above the Head of Miles-River; by which we passed, and rode on to the Head of Wye-River: and so got to the Head of Chester-River; where making a Fire, we took up our Lodging in the Woods. Next Morning setting forward again, we travelled through the Woods, till we came to Saxifrax-River, which we went over in Canoos (which are Indian-Boats;) causing our Horses to swim by. Then we rode on to Bohemia-River; where in like manner swimming our Horses, we our selves went over in Canoos. We rested a little at a Plantation by the Way, but could not stay long, for we had Thirty Miles to ride that Afternoon, if we would reach a Town; which we were willing to do, and therefore rid hard for it. And I with some others, whose Horses were stronger, got to the Town that Night, exceedingly tired; and withal wet to the Skin: But George Pattison and Robert Widders, being weakerhorsed, were fain to fall short, and lie in the Woods that Night also; making themselves a Fire. The Town we went to, was a Dutch Town, called New-Castle;[2] whither Robert Widders and George Pattison came to us next Morning. . . .

On the Sixteenth of the Seventh Month[3] we set forward again from hence,[4] and travelled (as near as we could compute) about Fifty Miles that Day, through the Woods, and over the Boggs, heading Bohemia-River and Saxifrax River. At Night we made us a Fire (as we used to do) in the Woods, and lay there all Night: and it being rainy Weather, we got under some thick Trees for Shelter; and afterwards dried our selves

[1] Tred Avon Creek, a tributary of the Choptank River, in Talbot County. Miles or St. Michael's River is in the same county. The Wye forms in part the border between that and Queen Anne's County. The heads of Chester and Sassafras Rivers lie on the border between Kent County and Delaware; that of Bohemia River on the boundary between Cecil County and that state.

[2] Newcastle, Delaware.

[3] The narrative is resumed at the point where the return of the writer from New England is recorded. The date intended is September 16, 1672, Fox beginning his years with March.

[4] From Newcastle.

again by the Fire. Next Day we waded through Chester-River, a very broad Water, and afterwards passing through many bad Boggs, lay that Night also in the Woods by a Fire; not having gone (by reason of Hindrances in the River and Boggs) above Thirty Miles that day. But on the day following we travelled hard: and though we had some troublesom Boggs in our way, we rode about Fifty Miles; and got safe that Night, but very weary, to a Friend's House, one Robert Harwood, at Miles-River in Mary-land. This was the Eighteenth Day of the Seventh Month: and though we were very weary, and much dirtied with getting through the Boggs in our Journey; yet hearing of a Meeting next day, we went to it, and from it to John Edmundson's: from whence we went three or four Miles by Water to a Meeting on the First-Day following. At this Meeting there was a Judge's Wife, who had never been at any of our Meetings before; and she was reached, and said after the Meeting: She had rather hear us once, than the Priests a thousand times. Many others also of the World's People, that were there, were very well satisfied; For the Power of the Lord was eminently with and amongst us: blessed for ever be his holy Name! We passed from thence about twenty two Miles, and had a Meeting upon the Kentish Shore, to which one of the Judges came; and a good Meeting it was. Then, after we had had another good Meeting hard by there, at one Henry Wilcock's House, where also we had good Service for the Lord; we went by Water about twenty Miles, to a very large Meeting, where were some Hundreds of the World's People, and divers of the Chief Rank, both English and Indians: For there were four Justices of the Peace, and the High-Sheriff of Delaware, and some others from thence: and there was an Indian Emperor, or Governour, and two others of the Chief Men among the Indians. With these Indians I had a good Opportunity the Night before the Meeting; and I spake to' them by an Interpreter: and they heard the Truth attentively, and were very loving. A blessed Meeting this was, and of great Service, both for Convincing, and Establishing in the Truth them, that were convinced of it; blessed be the Lord, who causeth his blessed Truth to spread. After the Meeting a Woman came to me, (whose Husband was one of the Judges of that part of the Country, and a Member of the Parliament or Assembly there) and told me, Her Husband was sick, not like to live; and desired me to go home with her to see him. It was three Miles to her House; and I being just come hot out of the Meeting, it was hard for me then to go: Yet considering the Service, I got an Horse, and went with her, and visited her Husband; and spake, what the Lord gave me to him: And the Man was much refreshed, and finely raised up by the Power of the Lord; and he afterwards came to our Meetings. I went back again to the Friends that Night; and next day we departed thence, and went about nineteen or twenty Miles to Tredhaven-Creek, to John Edmundson's again: from whence, on the Third of the Eighth Month, we went to the General Meeting for all Maryland-Friends.

This Meeting held five Days together: the first three Days we had Meetings for Publick Worship, to which People of all sorts came; the other two days were spent in the Mens and Womens Meetings. To those Publick Meetings came many of the World, both Protestants of divers sorts, and some Papists; and amongst these were several Magistrates, and their Wives, and other Persons of chief Account in the Country: and of the common People there were so many, besides Friends, that they thought, there were sometimes a Thousand People at one of those Meetings. So that, although they had not long before enlarged their Meeting-place, and made it as big again, as it was before; yet it could not contain the People. I went by Boat every Day four or five Miles to the Meeting, and there were so many Boats at that time passing upon the River, that it was almost like the Thames; and People said, There were never so many Boats seen there together before. And as the Concourse of People was very great (so that one of the Justices, who was there, said, He never saw so many People together in that Country before;) so it was a very Heavenly Meeting, wherein the Presence of the Lord was gloriously manifested, and Friends were thereby sweetly refreshed, and the People generally satisfied, and many convinced: for the blessed Power of the Lord was over all; everlasting Praises to his Holy Name for ever. After the Publick Meetings were over, the Mens and Womens-Meetings began, and were held the other two Days: for I had something to

impart to them, which concerned the Glory of God, and the
Order of the Gospel, and the Government of Christ Jesus.
So when these Meetings were all over, we took our Leaves
of Friends in those parts; whom we left well established in
the Truth (which is of good Report amongst the People there,
and great Enquirings there are after it, amongst all sorts of
People.)   And upon the Tenth Day of the Eighth Month we
went from thence about Thirty Miles by Water, passing by
Cranes-Island, and Swan-Island, and Kent-Island in very
foul Weather and much Rain; whereby (our Boat being
open) we were not only very much wetted, but in great danger of being overset: Insomuch that some of the World
thought, we could not have escaped casting away, till they
saw us come to Shore next morning.   But blessed be God,
we were very well.   And having got a little House, and dried
our Cloths by the Fire, and refreshed our selves a little, we
betook us to our Boat again; and put off from Land, sometimes Sailing, and sometimes Rowing: but having very foul
Weather that day too, we could not get above twelve Miles
forward that Day.   At Night we got to Land, and made us
a Fire, and some lay by that; and some lay by a Fire at an
House a little way off.   Then, next Morning pursuing our
Journey, we passed over the great Bay, and sailed about
Forty Miles that day; and making to Shore at Night, we lay
there, some in the Boat, and some at an Ale-house by.   Next
morning (it being the First-Day of the Week) we went Six
or Seven Miles to a Friend's House, who was a Justice of the
Peace; where we had a Meeting that Day: and this was a
little above the Head of the Great Bay.   So we were almost
four Days upon the Water, weary with Rowing; yet all was
very well, blessed and praised be the Lord.   We went next
Day to another Friend's House, near the Head of Hatton's-
Island, where we had good Service amongst Friends and
others: as we had also the Day following at Geo. Wilson's, a
Friend, that lived about three Miles further; where we had
a very precious Meeting, there being a great Tenderness
amongst the People.

After this Meeting we sailed thence about Ten Miles to James
Frizby's (who was a Justice of the Peace) and there, on the
Sixteenth of the Eighth Month, we had a very large Meeting;

at which, besides Friends, were some Hundreds of People, as it was supposed, and amongst them were several Justices of the Peace, and Captains, and the Sheriff, with other Persons of Note in the World's Account. A blessed, heavenly Meeting this was, and a powerful, thundering Testimony for Truth was born therein; and a great Sense there was upon the People, and a great Brokenness and Tenderness was amongst them. We stay'd after Meeting, till about the Eleventh Hour in the Night, that the Tide turned, and was with us: and then taking Boat again, we passed that Night and the next Day about Fifty Miles, to another Friend's House. The two next days we made short Journies, visiting Friends: and on the Twentieth we had a great Meeting at a place called Severn,[1] where there was a Meeting-Place, but not large enough to hold the People by many; for the People of those parts came generally to it. Divers of the Chief Magistrates were at it, and many other considerable People; and it gave them generally great Satisfaction. Two days after we had a Meeting with some, that walked disorderly; and we had good Service in it. Then spending a day or two in visiting Friends thereabouts, we passed to the Western-Shore;[2] and on the Twenty fifth Day had a large and precious Meeting at William Coale's, where the Speaker of their Assembly,[3] with his Wife, and a Justice of Peace, and several other People of Quality were present. Next Day we had a Meeting, six or seven Miles further, at Abraham Birkhead's, where many of the Magistrates and upper sort of People were; and the Speaker of the Parliament or Assembly for that Country was Convinced: A blessed Meeting it was, praised be the Lord. We travelled on next Day; and on the Day following (which was the Twenty eighth of the Eighth Month) had a large and very precious Meeting at Peter Sharp's, on the Clifts, between Thirty and Forty Miles distant from the former. Many of the Magistrates, and upper Rank of People were at this Meeting, and a heavenly Meeting it was. One of the Governour's Council's Wives was

---

[1] At or near Annapolis.

[2] Apparently the western shore of the Severn River is meant. The travellers were already on the western shore of the bay, having crossed at the head.

[3] Thomas Notley was speaker of the lower house of Assembly at the date of this journal.

Convinced; and her Husband very loving to Friends: and one that came from Virginia (Being a Justice of the Peace there) was Convinced; and hath a Meeting since at his House. There was some Papists at this Meeting; and one of them threatned, before he came, that he would Dispute with me: but when he came, he was reached, and could not oppose. Blessed be the Lord, the Truth hath reached into the Hearts of People beyond Words, and it is of a good Savour amongst them. After the Meeting we went about Eighteen Miles to James Preston's, a Friend that liveth on Pottuxon-River; and thither came to us an Indian King, with his Brother, to whom I spake; and I found, they understood the thing I spake of. Now having finished our Service in Mary-land, and intending forthwith to set forward for Virginia, we had a Meeting at Pottuxon on the Fourth Day of the Ninth Month, to take our Leaves of Friends. The Meeting was in the Meeting-Place; and many of the World's People of all sorts were at it; and a powerful Meeting it was.[1] . . .

We passed over Potomack-River also; the Winds being high, the Water very rough, our Sloop open, and the Weather extream Cold; and having a Meeting there-aways also, some People of the World, that came to it, were Convinced: and when we parted thence, some of our Company went amongst them. We steered our Course for Pottuxon-River; and I sate at Helm most part of the Day, and some of the Night. About the First Hour in the Morning we reached James Preston's House in Pottuxon-River; which is accounted about Two hundred Miles from Nancemum[2] in Virginia. We were very weary; yet the next Day (being the First of the Week, and Fifth of the Month) we went to the Meeting not far from thence: and the same week we went to an Indian-King's Cabbin, where several of the Indians were; with whom we had a pretty Opportunity to discourse: and they carried themselves very lovingly. We went also that Week to a General Meeting: from which we went about Eighteen Miles further to John Gearies, where we had a very precious Meet-

---

[1] From November 5, 1672, to January 4, 1673, Fox was occupied in a missionary journey through Virginia to Carolina, in Carolina, and back again through Virginia, crossing the Rappahannock to the northward on January 4.

[2] Nansemond.

ing; praised be the Lord God for ever! But after this the Cold grew so exceeding sharp, such extream Frost and snowy Weather, beyond what was usual in that Country, so that we could hardly endure to be in it. Neither was it easie or safe to stir abroad; yet we got (with some Difficulty) six Miles through the Snow to John Mayor's, where we met with some Friends, that were come from New-England; whom we had left there, when we came away: and glad we were to see each other, after so long and tedious Travels. By these Friends we understood, that William Edmundson, having been at Road-Island and New-England, was gone from thence for Ireland; that Solomon Eccles coming from Jamaica, and landing at Boston in New-England, was taken at a Meeting there, and banished to Barbados; that John Stubbs and another Friend were gone into New-Jersey, and several other Friends to Barbados, Jamaica, and the Leeward-Islands. It was Matter of Joy to us to understand, that the Work of the Lord went on and prospered, and that Friends were unwearied, and diligent in the Service.

On the Twenty Seventh of the Eleventh Month, we had a very precious Meeting in a Tobacco-House: and on the next Day we returned to James Preston's, about Eighteen Miles distant. But when we came there we found, his House was burnt down to the Ground the Night before, through the Carelessness of a Maid-servant: So we lay three Nights on the Ground by the Fire, the Weather being very Cold. We made an Observation, which was somewhat strange, but certainly true; that one Day in the midst of this Cold Weather, the Wind turning into the South, it grew so hot, that we could hardly bear the Heat; and the next Day and Night, the Wind chopping back into the North, we could hardly endure the Cold.

On the Second of the Twelfth Month, we had a glorious Meeting at Pottuxon: and after it went to John Gearie's again, where we waited for a Boat, to carry us to the Monthly Meeting at the Clifts; to which we went, and a living Meeting it was, praised be the Lord: This was on the Sixth of the Twelfth Month. And another Meeting we had on the Ninth, wherein the Glory of the Lord shined over all; blessed and magnified be his Holy Name for ever.

From hence we intended to go to Anamessy;[1] and on the
Twelfth Day of the Twelfth Month we set forward in our
Boat: And travelling by Night, as well as by Day, in the
Night we run our Boat on Ground in a Creek near Manaco-
River. There we were fain to stay, till Morning, that the Tide
came, and lifted her off again: And in the mean time, sitting
in an open Boat, and the Weather being bitter-cold, some
had like to have lost the Use of their Hands, they were so
frozen and benummed with Cold. But in the Morning, when
the Tide had set our Boat a-float again, we got to Land, and
made us a good Fire; at which we warmed our selves well: and
then went to our Boat again, and passed on about ten miles
further to a Friend's House; where next day we had a very
precious Meeting, at which some of the Chiefs of the Place
were. I went after the Meeting to a Friend's House, about
four miles off, at the Head of Anamessy-River; where on the
Day following, the Judge of the Country, and a Justice with
him came to me, and were very loving, and much satisfied with
Friend's Order. The next Day we had a large Meeting at
the Justice's House, but it was in his Barn; for his House
could not hold the Company. There were several of the Great
Folks of that Country; and among the rest there was an
Opposer: but all was preserved quiet and well, and a precious
Meeting it was; and the People were much taken and affected
with the Truth, blessed be the Lord. We went next Day to
see one Capt. Colburn, who was also a Justice of the Peace;
and there we had some Service. Then returning again, we
had a very glorious Meeting at the same Justice's, where we
met before; and there were many People of Account in the
World, Magistrates, Officers, and others at it. It was a large
Meeting, and the Power of the Lord was much felt; so that
the People were generally well satisfied, and taken with the
Truth: and there being several, both Merchants, and Masters
of Ships from New-England, the Truth was spread abroad;
blessed be the Lord!

A Day or two after, departing from this place, we travelled
about sixteen miles through the Woods and Bogs, heading
Anamessy-River, and Amoroca-River; part of which last we

[1] Annamessicks, described in *Archives of Maryland*, III. 452, as four miles
from Manokin, in Somerset County, on the eastern shore of the bay.

went over in a Canooe, and came to Manaoke,[1] to a Friendly
Woman's House: where on the Twenty fourth of the Twelfth
Month, we had a large Meeting in a Barn; and the Lord's living Presence was with us, and among the People: blessed be
his Holy Name for ever-more! Friends had never had a
Meeting in those Parts before. After this Meeting we passed
over the River Wicocomaco,[2] and through many bad and
watry Swamps and Marish Way; and came to James Jones,
a Friend, who was a Justice of the Peace: where we had a
large and very glorious Meeting, praised be the Lord God.
Then passing over the Water in a Boat, we took Horse, and
travelled about Twenty four Miles through Woods and troublesom Swamps, and came to another Justice's House; where
we had a very large Meeting, much People of the World
being at it, and many of Considerable Account amongst
them: and the living Presence of the Lord was amongst us,
praised for ever be his holy Name! This was on the Third
Day of the First Month, 1672/3. And on the Fifth Day
of the same we had another living and heavenly Meeting,
at which divers of the Justices, with their Wives, and many
others of the World's People were; amongst whom we had
very good Service for the Lord, blessed be his Holy Name.
At this Meeting was a Woman that lived at Anamessy, who
had been many Years in Trouble of Mind; and sometimes
would sit moping near two Months together, and hardly
speak or mind any thing. When I heard of her, I was moved
of the Lord to go to her, and tell her, That Salvation was
come to her House. And after I had spoken the Word of
Life to her, and intreated the Lord for her, she mended; and
went up and down with us to Meetings, and is since well:
blessed be the Lord!

Being now clear of these parts, we left Anamessy on the
Seventh Day of the First Month: and passing by Water about
Fifty Miles, came to a Friendly Woman's House at Hunger-
River.[3] We had very rough Weather in our Passage to this
Place, and were in great Danger, for the Boat had like to have
been turned over: and I lost both my Hat and Cap: yet we

---

[1] Manokin, in Somerset County.
[2] This is the Eastern-Shore Wicomico, in Wicomico County.
[3] Honga River.

recovered them again with much ado; and through the good
Providence of God got safe thither, praised be his Name. At
this place we had a Meeting, where we had never any before;
and amongst the People that were at it, there were two Papists, a Man and a Woman: the Man was very tender; and
the Woman confessed to the Truth. This Meeting was not so
large, as it would have been, if many, who intended to have
been at it, could have got to it: but the Weather was so foul,
and the Water by reason of high Winds, so rough, that it was
not safe to pass upon it. I had no Friend now with me, but
Robert Widders; the rest having dispersed themselves into
several parts of the Country in the Service of Truth.

So soon as the Wind would permit, we passed from hence
about Forty Miles by water, rowing most part of the way; and
came to the Head of little Choptanck-River, to Dr. Winsmore's,
who was a Justice of Peace, and lately convinced. Here we
met with some Friends, with whom we staid a while: and then
went on by Land and Water, and had a large Meeting abroad;
for the House we were at, could not receive the People. There
were divers of the Magistrates, and their Wives at this Meeting;
and a good Meeting it was, blessed be the Lord, who is making
his Name known in that Wilderness-Country. We went back
from thence to a Friend's House, whose Name is William Ste-
phen's, where we met with those other Friends, that had been
travelling in other parts; and were much refreshed in the Lord
together, when we imparted to each other the good Success, we
had had in the Lord's Work, and the Prosperity and spreading of
Truth in the places, where we travelled.   John Cartwright and
another Friend had been at Virginia, where were great Desires
in People after the Truth: and being now returned, they staid
but a little with us here; and then set forward for Barbados.
But before we left this place, we had a very glorious Meeting
here, at which were very many of the World's People, and some
of the Chief of them. For there was the Judge of that Country, and three Justices of the Peace, and the High-Sheriff, with
their Wives, and several others: And of Indians there was
he, who was called their Emperor, and one of the Indian Kings,
and their Speaker; who all sate very attentive, and carried
themselves very lovingly: and an establishing, settling Meeting it was. This was on the Twenty third of the First Month.

And on the Twenty fourth we went by Water ten Miles to the Indian Town, where this same Emperor dwelt; whom I had acquainted before with my Coming, and desired him to get their Kings and Councils together. In the Morning the Emperor came himself, and had me to the Town; and they were generally come together, and had their Speaker, and other Officers with them, and the Old Empress sate among them: And to give them their due, they sate very grave and sober, and were all very attentive, beyond many that are called Christians. I had some with me, that could interpret to them; and we had a very good Meeting with them, and of very good Service it was: for it gave them a good Esteem of Truth and Friends; blessed be the Lord!

After this, we had many Meetings in several parts of that Country; one at William Stephens's, which was a general Meeting once a Month: another at Tredhaven-Creek; another at Wye; another at Reconow-Creek; and another at Thomas Taylor's in the Island of Kent. Most of these Meetings were large, there being many of the World's People at them, and divers of them of the most Considerable in the World's Account: And the Lord's Power and living Presence was with us, and plenteously manifested amongst the People, by which their Hearts were tendred, and opened to receive the Truth, which had a good Savour amongst them; blessed be the Lord God over all for ever. Then being clear of that side, we passed over the Bay[1] about Fourteen Miles to a Friend's House, where we met with several Friends; and I sent for Thomas Thurston thither, and had a Meeting with him, to bring the Truth over his bad Actions.

Now having travelled through most parts of that Country, and visited most of the Plantations thereabouts, and had very good Service for the Lord in America, having alarm'd the People of all sorts. where we came, and proclaimed the Day of God's Salvation amongst them; we found, our Spirits began to be clear of those parts of the World, and to draw towards Old England again. Yet we were desirous, and felt Freedom from the Lord to stay, till the General Meeting for that Province of Mary-land was over (which drew nigh;) that we might see Friends generally together, before we de-

---

[1] To the Western Shore.

parted. Wherefore spending our time in the interim, partly
in visiting Friends and Friendly People, and in having Meetings about the Clifts and Pottuxon; and partly in writing
Answers to some Cavilling Objections, which some of Truth's
Adversaries had raised and spread abroad, to hinder People
from receiving the Truth: we were not idle, but laboured in
the Work of the Lord, until that General Provincial Meeting
came on; which began on the Seventeenth Day of the Third
Month, and lasted four Days. On the First of these days the
Men and Women had their Meetings for Business, wherein the
Affairs of the Church of God were taken Care of; and many
things, relating thereunto, were opened unto them to their
Edification and Comfort. The other Three Days were spent
in Publick Meetings for the Worship of God, at which divers of
considerable Account in the Government, and many others
of the World's People were present; who were generally satisfied, and many of them reached: for it was a wonderful,
glorious Meeting, and the mighty Presence of the Lord was
seen and felt over all; blessed and praised be his Holy Name
for ever, who over all giveth Dominion!

REPORTS OF CONFERENCES BETWEEN LORD BALTIMORE AND WILLIAM PENN, AND THEIR AGENTS, 1682, 1683, 1684

INTRODUCTION

On March 4, 1680/1, Charles II., King of England, made a grant to William Penn of the province of Pennsylvania. Its area, in language said to have been settled by Lord Chief Justice North, was described as bounded as follows: "the Delaware on the east, whence it extended westward five degrees of longitude, the 43d degree of latitude on the north, and on the south a circle of twelve miles drawn about New Castle to the beginning of the 40th degree of latitude." This definition of the southern boundary was impossible of gratification under any interpretation that could be put upon it. The question was therefore left open whether the "circle of twelve miles about New Castle" meant a circle having that circumference with Newcastle as its centre; a circle with that diameter, with Newcastle at the centre, or a circle of twelve miles radius drawn about that point. But even with this last, the most favorable construction, the conditions were impossible of fulfilment, for Newcastle lies twenty miles south of the fortieth degree of north latitude.

The boundaries of Maryland, as defined in the charter from Charles I., dated June 20, 1632, included all that part of the peninsula lying between the ocean and the Chesapeake Bay which lay north of a right line running east from Watkins Point on the bay to the ocean, thence northerly to that part of Delaware Bay which lies under the fortieth degree of north latitude where New England is terminated; thence westerly in a right line from Delaware Bay by the degree aforesaid to the true meridian of the first source of the Potomac River, then south to the south bank of the said river, and thence easterly and southerly following the south bank of the river, and then across the Bay by the shortest line to Watkins Point, the place of beginning.[1]

Penn had persuaded himself and assured others that the head of the Chesapeake Bay fell within the area of his grant; but the fortieth degree of north latitude which was named as his south boundary as well as the north boundary of Lord Baltimore's province, lies many miles north of the head of the bay; and when this fact was made plain Penn was eager to secure by some means or other an outlet upon the bay which would not be subject to control by his neighbor on the south. Hence the prolonged and fruitless discussions, the reports of which are here given.

It will be observed that throughout these discussions Lord Baltimore (it was Charles, third Baron, who had succeeded to the title in 1675) made no suggestions whatever. He simply insisted upon the terms of his charter, and that the true location of the fortieth degree of north latitude should be determined by astronomical observations made on the spot with adequate instruments.

In March, 1664, Charles II. had granted to his brother, James, the Duke of York, all the territory lying between the Connecticut River and the eastern shore of the Delaware. This included the region that had been settled by the Dutch and by them called New Netherland. In September of that year the Dutch colonists were reduced to subjection by a force under the command of Colonel Nicholls, and in the following month the Dutch settlements on the west bank of the Delaware, which lay within the territory granted to Lord Baltimore, were likewise reduced to subjection. Penn, apparently feeling doubtful about the success of his efforts to secure an outlet on the Chesapeake, endeavored to make sure of one on the Delaware by obtaining from the Duke of York a grant of land on its west side, north of Cape Henlopen, all

---

[1] Charter of Maryland, p. 102, *supra*.

of which lay within the limits of Lord Baltimore's patent. This grant was made in August, 1682. After the failure of his negotiations with Lord Baltimore, Penn hastened to England to secure a confirmation of his title to this territory upon the Delaware. Against Lord Baltimore's claim to ownership was urged the expression *hactenus inculta* (hitherto uncultivated) which had previously been urged by both Claiborne[1] in respect to Kent Island and the Dutch envoys[2] in 1659. It was also argued that Baltimore's claim was barred by his long acquiescence in the Dutch settlements and his failure to reduce them to obedience by force of arms; and that the Duke of York's title was complete by right of conquest. The Duke in 1685 succeeded to the throne as James II., and by him the application of Penn was referred to the Commissioners of Trade and Plantations. The Commissioners were therefore required to determine the delicate question as to whether a grant made by the King when he was Duke of York was valid or not. They decided in favor of its validity, and directed that to avoid contests in the future the peninsula between the two bays be divided into two equal parts by a line drawn from the latitude of Cape Henlopen northward to the fortieth degree; and declared that the western half belonged to Lord Baltimore, and the eastern to his Majesty, and consequently to his grantee William Penn.[3]

Though running beyond the limits of the narratives here printed, it may be useful briefly to state the outcome of this dispute. After the decision in his favor as to Delaware, Penn procured the issue of a writ of *quo warranto* for the annulment of the charter of Maryland; but proceedings in the case were

---

[1] *Virginia and Maryland*, pp. 190, 201, *supra*.

[2] Journal of the Dutch Embassy, p. 329, *supra*.

[3] In respect to the claim of Claiborne, based on the expression *hactenus inculta*, the Lords Commissioners of Plantations had in 1638, during the reign of Charles I., decided in favor of Lord Baltimore (p. 190 *supra*). That decision and the one mentioned above have only this in common, that each sustained the validity of a grant made by the reigning sovereign.

brought to an abrupt termination by the flight of James II. and the accession of William and Mary to the throne. King William soon assumed direct jurisdiction over both Maryland and Pennsylvania, and appointed governors in the name of the Crown. The authority of the Proprietary of Maryland was not restored until 1716. By reason of the death of the original parties to the contest, and the intervention of royal governors, the boundary dispute slumbered; but eventually it was renewed between the sons of William Penn and Charles, fifth Lord Baltimore. In 1732 the latter entered into an agreement with the Penns for the settlement of the matter in accordance with a map attached to the paper. How he was led to do this it is impossible now to determine, for the map to which he gave his assent was palpably inaccurate and by accepting it he surrendered everything for which his grandfather had vigorously contended. Well-known landmarks were misplaced on this map, and Cape Henlopen, from which one of the lines was to run, was marked at about twenty miles to the south of its true location. The agreement was ingeniously worded that the dividing line should run, not from that cape, but from the point "on the said map *called* Cape Henlopen." It was also agreed that the boundary should be run fifteen miles south of the southernmost point of Philadelphia, while the fortieth degree of latitude, mentioned in both grants as the boundary, lies north of that city. When, upon visiting Maryland during the same year, these errors were pointed out to Lord Baltimore, he repudiated the agreement, and this led to proceedings in chancery for its enforcement. A final decision was not reached until 1750 when the Lord Chancellor held that the agreement of 1732 was binding upon the parties thereto, and issued a decree in accordance with that opinion. By this decision the territory of Maryland was reduced by a strip about twenty miles wide along the entire length of the northern boundary, and in obedience to the decree a line was surveyed, run and marked by monuments to establish the boundary between the two provinces as thus determined. This is the famous Mason and Dixon's line—so called from the names of the English engineers by whom its location was established.

The reports of the two conferences between Lord Baltimore and William Penn were printed in the *Archives of Maryland*, V. 374 *et seq.*, from copies made from the Colonial Papers in the Public Record Office in London; also in the *Pennsylvania Magazine of History*, VI. 414. The report of the conference between William Penn and Colonel Talbot was printed in the *Maryland Historical Magazine*, III. 21, from the original manuscript in the possession of the Maryland Historical Society.

C. C. H.

REPORTS OF CONFERENCES BETWEEN LORD BALTIMORE AND WILLIAM PENN, AND THEIR AGENTS, 1682, 1683, 1684

A narrative of the whole Proceedings betwixt the Lord Balte-more and Captain William Markham Deputy Governor under William Pen Esqre as alsoe betwixt the Lord Balte-more, and the said Pen.

His Majestie having bin graciously pleased to give to Mr William Pen a Tract of Land in America to the northward of Maryland, the said Pen in Aprill (1681) sends one Captain William Markham his kinsman[1] to be his deputy and towards the latter end of August following, Captain Wm Markham came to Maryland with a letter from Mr Pen to the Lord Baltemore and at the same time brought another from His most sacred Majesty bearing date the second day of Aprill in the three and thirtieth year of His Majestie's reign.[2] The Lord Baltemore having perused the king's letter, as also that from Mr Pen, the said Markham was assured by the Lord Baltemore, that the king's commands should be readily and very speedily obeyed, and by that means Mr Pen's desires and request would be likewise complyed with, the said Pen having by his letter requested that the Lord Baltemore would give all the dispatch possible in the business of the bounds.

But by reason of the great heats then in August Captain Markham happened to fall dangerously ill, and because the Lord Baltemore was willing to embrace all opportunities of expressing his great friendshipp, respect and kindness to Mr Pen, he invited Mr Markham to his house where he continued

---

[1] William Markham was deputy for Penn from April, 1681, till Penn's arrival in October, 1682, and at subsequent times deputy-governor or otherwise concerned in the administration of Pennsylvania and Delaware.

[2] April 2, 1681. The letter is printed in *Archives of Maryland*, V. 273.

very dangerously ill for the space of three weeks and better; some time in September the said Markham grew soe well that he resolved to return to Delaware, and before he parted with the Lord Baltemore they both agreed to meete the sixteenth of October next following, in order to take observation for the ascertaineing the fortieth degree of northern latitude; the said Markham haveing promised, and assured the Lord Baltemore, that he would send to New York to borrow of one Col. Lewis Morris there a sextile[1] of six or seaven foote radiis, being the only fit instrument that could be heard of. Captain Markham meeting with a long passage up Chesapeake Bay writes to the Lord Baltemore, that he could not possibly attend the sixteenth as had been agreed on, but desired it might be on the twenty sixth of October. But soone after that, came another letter from Captain Markham, wherein he gave the Lord Baltemore advice, that he was relapsed, and soe ill that he should not be able to attend the business of the bounds till the Spring.

Whilst the said Markham was said to be thus ill, many reports were given out by the friends (vulgarly called Quakers) both of Maryland, as well as those of Pensylvania, that the degree of forty northerly latitude would be as lowe as Pooles Island in the Bay of Cheaspeak; and it seems that Mr Pen had bin so far possesst therewith, that he made bold to write a letter[2] dated the sixteenth of September (1681) and directed the same to James Frisby, Edward Jones, Augustine Herman,[3] George Oulfield, Henry Ward and Henry Johnson, at their Plantations in Pensylvania; for soe was the letter superscribed, the contents of which being, that as he was confident, and ready to beleeve they were within his bounds they should not pay any more taxes, or sessments by any Order or law of Maryland etc. This letter soe alarmed the Inhabitants of Baltemore and Cecell Countys,[4] that they immediately refused paying their levys, which had bin assessed by a Law past but two months afore this happened. Notice hereof being given

---

[1] Sextant.

[2] The original letter is in the possession of the Maryland Historical Society. It is printed in *Calvert Papers* no. 1, p. 323, and in *Archives of Maryland*, V. 285.

[3] See p. 311, *supra*.

[4] Then comprising the whole northeastern part of Maryland.

to the Lord Baltemore and his Councill, orders were immediately issued out to the military Officers of the said Countys to assist the respective Sheriffs in the due execution of theire office, and with great difficulty it was that some of the inhabitants were made to comply with the then Publick leavy; tho' the parties to whom that letter was particularly directed, gave little credit to it, being confident that Mr Pen had been misinformed, as it will sufficiently appeare both he and many others have been, in relation to the fortieth degree of northern latitude.

The trouble and indeed sedition that the said letter had occasioned for some little time, made the Lord Baltemore judge it absolutely necessary to have the bounds speedily fixst; but Captain Markham was said to have a tertian Quartan ague, soe that the Lord Baltemore could not procure the settlement of the bounds, as he then desired; some time after this, reports came down to the Lord Baltemore, that one William Haig a Quaker, and much employed by Mr Pen had taken observation at the head of the Bay, which very much dissatisfied the said Haig and other friends, for upon those observations it was then given out by the Quakers, that if the degree of forty did not afford William Pen a Harbor, he would be forct to buy one of Baltemore, or otherwise that their ships must enter and cleer in Maryland. The said Haig in a short time after this came to the Lord Baltemore's House on Pattuxent river, where, amongst other discourse, the Lord Baltemore askt the said Haig whether he had not taken some observations at Elk river for his private satisfaction, which Haig owned; but with all pretended that the Instrument was soe small, that there could be noe certainty; the Lord Baltemore prest no further but told the said Haig he should be glad that Markham were well, for that he had several reasons to press for a dispatch of the business of the bounds; that the quiet and peace of Maryland very much required it.

The fourteenth of May (1682) the Lord Baltemore writt a letter to Capt: Markham, who, he understood, to be well, to signifie that he appointed the tenth of June to meete him with persons to settle the bounds; to which letter the said Markham gave answer, and with assurance, that he would not faile to meete the Lord Baltemore at Mr Augustin Herman's Plan-

tation on Bohemia river, which was the place the Lord Baltemore appointed to meet him; but some disturbance about that
time happening in Virginia, the Lord Baltemore did not think
it prudent, nor indeed safe for the Province, to be at any distance from Patomeck river, over which the mutineers in Virginia threatened to come to cutt up the tobaccos in Maryland,
as they had don in some Countys of Virginia;[1] The Lord
Baltemore therefore sent away Commissioners who were precisely on the tenth of June at Augustin Herman's Plantation,
but neither finding Capt: William Markham nor any person
else there from him, they immediately writt to him, and sent
their letter by an expresse. But to that no answer was given,
nor to a second they writt, tho' both (as can be proved) came
speedily to the said Markham, who, to be out of the way at
that time, pretended business at New York.

When the Commissioners had expected some days, and
finding noe hopes of seeing Markham, they for the Lord Baltemore's satisfaction made three several observations, in which
they differed not above a minute or two. After this they
being nere New Castle they had a curiosity to see that town,
and being there they were told there was a sloop newly arrived
from New York, that had brought the instrument which
Captain Markham had sent to Colonel Lewis Morris for: with
some difficulty and many entreaties they persuaded the master of the sloope to permitt them the use of it, and with it in
a very cleere day being on the twenty seaventh of June (1682)
they found the latitude of the place of observation which was
in the towne, to be thirty nine degrees forty odd minutes.

After the taking of this observation the Comm[rs] returned,
and then the said Markham sent letters, excuseing his being
absent, and signified that he would be ready when ever the
Lord Baltemore would appoint a second time; upon this
the Lord Baltemore by Letters signified to Captain Markham,
that he would not faile to be up at Augustine Herman's some
time in September following; but a day certaine could not be
fixt, by the Lord Baltemore in regard, as he signified by his
letter, to the said Markham, that two of his Artists were then

[1] The allusion is to the plant-cutting riots in Gloucester, New Kent, and Middlesex Counties, Virginia, in May, 1682. See Hening, *Statutes at Large of Virginia*, II. 562, III. 11.

ill; but on the twelfth of September the Lord Baltemore set saile from Patuxent up the Bay and on the fourteenth the Ld. Baltemore mett at Major Peeter Sawyers a letter from Captain Markham dated the eighth of the same month, wherein he positively promised, and assured the Lord Baltemore that he would attend his coming. This letter put the Lord Baltemore out of all doubts, assureing himself that Markham would not be guilty of such incivilities and indecencies as he had offered the Commissioners.

On the 19th of September the Lord Baltemore being arrived at Elk river he sent a letter to Markham to give him notice of his being there, on the twentieth his Ldp. writt to the said Markham againe. After writeing that letter the Lord Baltemore being certainely advised that Markham was gon up Delaware, and finding little roome, and want of severall conveniences at M[r] Herman's, the Lord Baltemore, with about twelve Gentlemen in Company with him, in all not above twenty persons, went the one and twentieth to New Castle, where staying till the three and twentieth, and heareing noe news of Markham's comeing, tho' it was proved he had received both the L[d] Baltemore's letters, his Ldp the said three and twentieth in the evening procured boats, and that night reacht Upland[1] and tooke his quarters in Captain Markham's lodgeings, who, his Ldp was told, was newly gon up to Burlington in East[2] new Jersey being gon after his receipt of his Lordshipp's first letter of the 19th of September.

Sunday morning being the twenty fourth very early, Markham came into the creeke, at Upland, and was not a little amazed to understand that the Lord Baltemore was there. About tenn of the clock that morning, Captain Markham came to see the Lord Baltemore, but with such a disordered countenance, and odd behaviour, as was easily perceived by all the Company. The L[d] Baltemore not seeming to take any notice of the confusion he saw him in desired of Captain Markham that he might see the new Instrument for observation, which he heard M[r] Pen had sent him, the which he readily yielded to, but for want of some small glasses, which the said Markham said William Haig had taken away, the instrument could not be made use of; Soe then the Lord Baltemore requested he

---

[1] Now Chester, Pennsylvania.   [2] West.

might see the instrument Colonel Lewis Morris had lent, which was likewise brought forth by one richard Noble a quaker, who sett the same up, and it being a very cleer day observacion was taken therewith, by the said Noble, as likewise by those artists the Lord Baltemore had with him and they all agreed that the latitude of Upland was by that sextile of Colonel Morris in 39 degrees forty seven minutes and five seconds;[1] after the taking of this observacion the Lord Baltemore told Captain Markham, that since the degree of north latitude would be about twelve miles more due north from Upland it would be necessary to goe up Delaware river to see where forty did cut the said river; But the said Markham by the advice of Haig (who seemed to govern more than Markham) declined that proposition giving very slight reasons for his refusall, but told the Lord Baltemore that he was ready to goe to the heads of any of the rivers in the Bay to take the fortieth degree of north latitude, and to assure the Lord Baltemore of that, he immediately gave it under his hand; which the Lord Baltemore has ready to produce.

The twenty fifth of September being munday the Lord Baltemore resolved to take his leave at Upland, and in the afternoone the Lord Baltemore, Captain Markham and above forty more, being at the landing in order to take boate, the Ld Baltemore spoake to the said Markham thus: You are sensible, Captain Markham, that by an observacion taken yesterday, that this Plantation is in thirty nine degrees forty seaven minutes and some seconds, and must therefore be sensible that I am here about twelve miles to the southward of the degree of forty, which is my north bounds, as the same is Mr Pen's south bounds. Therefore, afore you and afore all the rest here present I lay claime to this place, and as far further as the degree of forty will reach; to this Captain Markham replied nothing, but immediately conducted the Ld Baltemore to the Boate, assureing the Lord Baltemore that he would not faile the next day being the 26th to be at New Castle with Colonel Lewis Morris' Instrument, which the Lord Baltemore desired, and the said Markham likewise promised faithfully to bring with him to the end the degree of forty might be taken at the head of the Bay.

[1] Actually, 39° 48′ N.

The twenty sixth and twenty seaventh the Lord Baltemore waited at New Castle for Markham, but finding there
was no hopes of seeing him, the Lord Baltemore returned to
Mr Augustin Herman's and thither came a letter from Markham signifying that the persons most concerned for the Government, would noe wise consent that he should meete, as he
had given under his hand, giving this reason that the Quakers
were very much disordered by the Lord Baltemore's laying
claim to a place called Chichester about three or four miles
below Upland. This being all that was don in relacion to
the business of the bounds, notwithstanding His Majestie's
letter of the second of April (1681) procured by the said William Pen, the said letter ordering the Lord Baltemore to appoint with all convenient speed Some person or persons who
might in conjunction with the Agent or Agents of the said
William Pen make a true division and seperacion of the Provinces of Maryland and Pensylvania according to the bounds
and degree of Northern latitude expressed in our letters
Pattents by settling and fixing certaine land marks where they
shall appeare to border upon each other, which are the words
of His Majestie's said letter. This letter of the King's was
little regarded, tho' Mr Pen's letter[1] of the tenth of April (1681)
to the Lord Baltemore gave notable hints for the speedy com-
plying with His Majestie's Commands in that letter of the
second of April, the which the Ld Baltemore was forward
enough to have obey'd, had others had that due regard to His
Majestie's grace and favour therein. But it not serveing the
turne was wholy layd aside by Pen's Agent.

About the twenty fourth of October following Mr Wm Pen
comes into Delaware river, and came to an anchor afore New
Castle, and there demanded and tooke the keyes of that Towne,
and then tooke possession of what else His royal Highness the
Duke of York pretends to; tho' the same hath been justly
claimed by the present Ld Baltemore as also by his Father,
This being don, without taking the least notice of his Highness his Govr at New York, and altho' the said William Pen
sent a letter by his Secretary to the Lord Baltemore bearing
date the second of November (1682) writt at New Castle, yett
Mr Pen made no mention of such his proceedings, nor did he

---

[1] *Calvert Papers* no. 1 (Md. Hist. Soc., *Fund Pub.* no. 28), p. 322.

order his Secretary to take any notice thereof, which seemed a little strange to the Lord Baltemore who had bin told by Mr Pen formerly that His royal Highness the Duke of York had made him offers of his pretentions on Delaware, and that he had refused the Duke in regard (as he signified) he knew it to be the Lord Baltemore's and of this the Lord Baltemore took notice to Mr Pen at their Conference.

On the thirteenth of December last the Lord Baltemore and Mr William Pen had a conference at the house of Colonel Thos Tailler at the ridge in Ann Arrundell County, to which place the said William Pen was so kind as to come; but afore the conference (which Mr Pen desired should have bin private) there was some what spoke by the said Pen, which in short was as followeth. Mr Pen signified, that as the King had given him a considerable Tract of land to the backward of the Lord Baltemore, he was sensible that without the Lord Baltemore's good neighbourhood and kindness to him, a great part of that Countrey soe given him, would prove but a dead lump of earth, for without an Inlett the same would be useless, and therefore he requested the Lord Baltemore to be soe good and kind a neighbour as to afford him but a back door for the improvement of that which otherwise (without such a convenience) would signify nothing to him; Adding this, that what was but the hundredth part of the Lord Baltemore's interest, would be ninety nine parts of the hundred of William Pen's.

As this request of Mr Pen's did not at all seem unreasonable to the Lord Baltemore, soe was it not the Lord Baltemore's intentions to deny the said Pen any neighbourly, and friendly kindness; and all that the Lord Baltemore then replied was that he supposed Mr Pen did not expect a speedy answer to his request; which Mr Pen answered againe he did not; then the Lord Baltemore proposed to Mr Pen, that the Conference he had desired might be afore his friends, and such of the Lord Baltemore's Council as were then there; that it would be best, and safest to have it publick, for that an affaire of that concerne to them both, being publicly debated, would give most satisfaction to the Inhabitants of both Provinces. Mr Pen then demanded how many persons the Lord Baltemore would have present, the Lord Baltemore desired that all the friends he had brought with him might be present if he soe pleased, and that only six Gentleman of the Lord Baltemore's Councill should be the rest. Mr Pen did, at last, declare that what the Lord Baltemore desired was reasonable, faire and honourable; then all persons were called in, and the said Pen began his discourse which he continued for some time, after which he pulls out a letter, and gives it the Ld Baltemore, as the ground and foundacion of theire further discourse.

The Lord Baltemore perceiving it to be a letter from His Majestie, reads the same privately, afterwards, againe, to the whole board; saying he found by that letter, that His Majestie had been misinformed, and to make that out, the Lord Baltemore reads the bounds mentioned in his Patent; after this the Conference held for some howres, the which was taken in short hand by the Clerk of the Assembly in Maryland, and the next morning the Clerk brought it faire writt out; and the same was read, approved and signed by the Gentlemen of the Lord Baltemore's Councill. And had not the said Pen been hastned and hurried away by many Quakers, that are Inhabitants of Maryland, to a meeting that day, Mr Pen had had a Coppy of the said Conference with him; but loath he was to stay soe long, and therefore requested the Lord Baltemore to send him one, which accordingly has bin done. The Lord Baltemore with the Gentlemen of his Council waited on Mr Pen to the place, where the friends meeting was to be that day, and there took his leave and parted with the said Penn, who the next day went to a general meeting at Choptank river in Talbot County, where the Lord Baltemore had ordered Colonel Philæmon Lloyd and his Major with some horsemen to waite on the said Pen in his returne. This is what past between the Lord Baltemore and William Pen who by agreement are to meete some time in March next for the finding out the degree of forty, northerly latitude.

The King's letter which Mr Pen delivered at the Conference to the Lord Baltemore, bearing date the 19th day of August 1682 in the foure and thirtieth yeare of His Majestie's reign[1] makes mention of an admeasurement of two degrees according to the usuall computation of sixty miles to a degree to be the best and certaine method of setting forth and ascertaining

[1] Printed in *Archives of Maryland*, V. 371.

the boundaries between Maryland and Pensilvania; but the Lord Baltemore humbly conceiving that His Majestie had received some misinformation touching the bounds of his Province, did, at the Conferrence, produce his Pattent, and the bounds of the same were read to Mr Pen, and the Gentlemen, then at the Board; After which Mr Pen proposed, as a more equall way for him and the Lord Baltemore to take their commencement from the Capes which (as the said Pen affirmed) lay in thirty seaven degrees, and five minutes,[1] and that having bin received for a long time to be the true latitude of the capes, and by which masters of shipps have governed themselves would be as well for the Lord Baltemore, as the said William Pen, Urgeing that an uncertainty of soe long standing would be better than to runn into new errors, which discourse of Mr Pens seemed to shew a jealousie in him, and not to carry much reason with it, or which many of the Gentlemen, then present, imagined rather proceeded from an unwillingness to have the bounds ascertained the surest, and most certaine way, which, as the Lord Baltemore had often urged might be by a sextant of six, eight or tenn foote, diameter, which being large and fixt in a frame, and the frames standing sure upon firme ground, must by all Artists be held a more certaine way of taking an observacion, then by a small sea quadrant, and that held up by the hand, which is always in motion, and the persons perhaps aboard a ship who tooke the latitude of the capes; where there was the shaking of the hand and error in the Instrument besides the unskillfullness and ignorance of those observators against which Mr Pen spoake soe much; But in a fixt Instrument of the Diameter abovesaid and that set in a frame on firm land a certaine observation may be taken, and that with out the help of an horrison, and this Mr Pen it's beleeved knew well enough to be the surest way; but he having been misinformed as to the degree of forty northerly latitude (which he was assured would fall lower than Saxafras river in the Bay of Chesapeake as by their false mapps appeare, and having assured his friends, and particularly those of his late Society for Trade, that all the head of the said Bay would fall within Pensilvania) is now unwilling to have the truth discovered.

[1] According to the charts of the United States Coast Survey the lighthouse at Cape Charles stands at 37° 07' 22" N. lat.

For whilst Mr Pen and his friends were kept in their said error about the degree of forty then the Lord Baltemore was prest to have an observacion taken, and His Majestie's commands in the first letter of the second of Aprill 1681 complyed with; but that first letter not serveing the turn another was procur'd upon as great a misinformation to His Majesty as could be given. And it will also appeare that upon such blind observations as are usually taken by masters of shipps (who often times are noe more artists than just to saile their shipps to porte by guesse) these great mistakes have risen. For Mr Pen did owne to the Lord Baltemore, that both His Majestie and the Lords of the Councill were assured that New Castle lay seaven, eight or tenn miles to the northward of the fortith degree northerly latitude, whereas Mr Pen, his deputy William Markham and the chiefe of the friends (called Quakers) have since owned that New Castle lyes some miles to the southward of that degree. Now, whereas the said Pen desires to have an admeasurement from the Capes, to the degree of forty, offering that as the most equall way, 'Tis well knowne, that that can never be effected by reason the wayes from the Capes to Watkins Point are not passable, there being not only waters to pass over, but likewise such rotten grounds, as noe person can gett thro; and from Watkins Point (the Lord Baltemore's south bounds) there are severall large rivers to crosse over, besides that a due north line will crosse Chesapeake Bay towards the upper part thereof, and for these reasons (were there noe other) those offers and proposalls of Mr Pen to the Lord Baltemore can never be comply'd with, and soe consequently the degree of forty must be taken as the Lord Baltemore, at the Conferrence, did propose.

[Endorsed]
Delaware, 13th Decr 1682.
Conferrence between my Lord Baltemore and Mr Pen.

*A Conferrence held between the right Honorble the Lord Balte-
more Proprietor of Maryland and William Pen Esqre
Proprietary of Pensilvania at the house of Colonel Thomas
Tailler on the ridge in Ann Arrundell County Wednesday
the 13th of December 1682.[1] Vizt*

William Pen Esqre declares in a very florid manner his reall
and hearty inclinations to maintaine and keepe a neighborly
and friendly correspondence with his Lopp.[2] and the people of
this Province that it was not the ambition of Government or
Dominion that flatter'd him into these parts of the world but
meerely to secure his owne that moved him to come into this
Country which since it was his fortune he well enough liked
and shall study all wayes and meanes imaginable to approve
himselfe a good Neighbor. He then produces a letter from the
King to the Lord Baltemore as a foundation or introduction
to their further discourse.

His Ldp having read the letter answers vizt:

Ld Baltemore. His Majestie's letter I receive with all respect
and with that sense of my duty as becomes me but by the
purport of this letter I conceive His Majesty hath received
some misinformation for the cleering of which I have here not
only a coppy of mine but a Transcript of your Patent by both
which we must be governed I having for my northern Bounds
the fortieth degree of northern latitude which by your Pattent
is your Southern bounds as Watkins point is mine.

His Lopp then reads the Bounds in the Pattent.

W. Pen Esqre. By my Petition to the King I craved five
degrees northward. The Lords told me it was a great deale of
land that my Lord Baltemore had but two to which I replyed
that the difference was vastly great on my Lord Baltemore's
side as for its position being richly accomodated with the Bay
on both sides and severall faire navigable rivers and Creeks

---

[1] This report of the discussion was taken down in shorthand. *Archives of
Maryland*, V. 380.　　　　　　　　　　　　　　　[2] Lordship.

etc. and my reason for soe great a quantity was not out of a covetous humour but only that I might reach the lake of Cannada for the conveniency of an inlett to my Province to which they gave their opinion that I should be answerd to that by having a passage in this Bay but if the Lord Baltemore will stand to and abide by the literall sense of his Pattent, then I think we must lay aside the King's letter untill we shall have first considered the grants and reasons of our Pattents. If the Lord Baltemore will take thirty seaven and half degrees for thirty eight and soe runn on to forty being halfe a degree of difference I think it is considerable and had I covetted to have taken my commencement from Watkins Point as the Lord Baltemore is allowed I had possibly gained more considerably, but confident that he would not endeavor to deprive me of anything that might conduce to my benefitt without any great prejudice to himselfe I was contented to begin where the Lord Baltemore ended, being firmly and stedfastly resolved to approve myself his good neighbor and give him the right hand of fellowship, and it shall be the Lord Baltemore's fault and not mine if there be not as faire and amicable Correspondence between the two Provinces as between any united Provinces whatsoever, but if His Majestie's letter must be waved we must proceed moderately to argue the. grounds and reasons of our Pattents and waite the King's leisure for a further interpretation of his grant to me.

Lord B. It was never my intentions nor indeed in my thoughts to deprive Mr Pen of anything that might conduce to his benefit soe as the same may not tend greatly to my prejudice and what Mr Pen means by a commencement from Watkins Point I understand not but sure I am that had his Pattent given him his commencement anywhere to the southward of the fortieth degree of northern latitude he had deprived me of soe much of my right which yet I beleeve Mr Pen never desired nor coveted. But Mr Pen you seem a little unkind in having proposed any deniall of mine to what you offered and for any kindness you may reasonably expect from me I think it not soe well timed; let but the line be first layd out thereby to ascertaine to each of us his propper and just bounds and then lett it be seen whether I shall deny Mr Pen any neighborly kindness within my power.

Wm Pen. The King it's true did command the laying out the line between us, but if for a more ready way of accommodacion to us both he hath thought fitt to make other proposalls I cannot tell why they may not be taken into consideracion, but I shall concede and wave that letter wholly makeing this further offer. The Capes for several years have bin reputed to lye in the latitude of thirty seaven or between thirty seaven degrees and five minutes or thereabouts and hath bin soe generally taken and approved on by all persons for some considerable space of years and by which calculation all ships and Vessels have proceeded on their Voyages before such time as either interest or prejudice could sway them on the one side or the other. Soe then if the Lord Baltemore please to take his commencement from the Capes which has bin generally and of soe long continuance reputed to lye in thirty seaven degrees and five minutes and from thence measure by line two degrees fifty five minutes will just reach to the fortieth degree.

Lord B. My Pattent gives me the fortieth degree of northern latitude for my northern bounds and there is noe way soe certaine to find that as by an observacion to be taken by a sextant of six or seaven foote radies and such an Instrument you have belonging to Colonel Lewis Morris of New York; besides your commencement by your Pattent is given at the fortieth degree of northern latitude.

Wm Pen. Then I shall only say we will wave and wholy lay aside the King's letter at this time. If the Lord Baltemore will begin at thirty seaven and a halfe insted of thirty eight he will then indeed have more than was designed for him.   I therefore offer as a medium between us the more easily to accommodate this matter, let the Lord Baltemore first begin at the antient and generally reputed and knowne place of thirty seaven degrees and five minutes and thence with a direct line to forty. What falls then within his bounds much good may it doe him. I am contented and doubt not but he is soe worthy and soe much a Gentleman as not to endeavor to deprive me of anything shall appeare to be within my Grant. This I say I offer onely to lett the [Lord] Baltemore know that altho' I am sensible the King's letter is grounded upon strong presumption and sound circumstance yet I am willing to wave that and accommodate the business between us a more equal way as I conceive viz. to commence at the common, generall and soe long reputed know[n] place before either the Lord Baltemore or myselfe could challenge any interest in these parts of the world.

Lord B. It is other discourse that I expected to have heard from you at this time, and well hoped I should have bin soe far favored by you as to have received some small advice from you before you had soe far proceeded upon that part of the Countrey which has bin always reputed and knowne to be justly claimed by me; but to wave that I desire to be informed by you whither you have purchased the Dukes pretentions to Delaware.

Wm Pen. Upon tearmes of the moiety of halfe the revenues thereof to be reserved for himselfe I hold it of his gift; but this leads to other discourse. I would willingly proceed first to the ascertaineing the bounds between us.

Lord B. The certaine bounds betwixt us must be the fortieth degree of northern latitude as I have already shewn you by my grant.

Wm Pen. And to find out that I propose in my judgement the most equall way that can be, which is to begin at the Capes, a place soe generally and soe long knowne and reputed to lye within the latitude of thirty seaven and five minutes, and has not for the space of soe many years bin knowne to vary foure or five minutes by any observacion yet taken and soe from thence to measure two degrees fifty five minutes which will just make the fortieth degree.

Lord B. My southern bounds being Watkins Point was soe determined by Commissioners from His Majesty and others from my father, now had they sett out Watkins Point higher up the Bay my Father must have bin contented therewith and the Northern bounds being the fortieth degree of northern latitude beyond which I am not to runn.

Wm Pen. Possibly the Lord Baltemore's southern bounds might be layd out by Commissioners who may be could or did not see what they did. The uncertainty of an observacion I apprehend and conceive it dangerous to confide in, for by the shakeing of a hand the error in the instrument or the unskillfullness or ignorance of the observator great inconveniences may incurr to the prejudice of either side but I doe offer as the most equall way between us to pitch upon the soe long reputed and generally knowne and received place of thirty seaven degrees odd minutes which for the space of forty, fifty or sixty yeares has bin concluded the latitude of the Capes (speaking now of antiquity and before ever the Lord Baltemore or myselfe were ever concerned in these parts) and from thence to measure by line till we arrive to forty which I conceive farr more safe than to trust to the ignorance of an observator the shakeing of his hand or a bad instrument.

Lord B. A more certaine observation of the fortieth degree may be now taken at the head of the Bay than formerly there was of thirty seaven and halfe where you say the capes lyes and I apprehend it to be more safe and sure for us both to have an observacion taken in the proper place with such an Instrument as I have already spoke of, and surely Mr Pen you will as well confide in your friends as I shall on such as I shall appoint to joyne with them. Now for your owne satisfaction the course you have proposed may be pursued, but that which I shall depend on and be wholy determined by is a due observation to be taken of the fortieth degree being the northern bounds of my Pattent.

W. Pen. I doe not object against the Lord Baltemore's bounds but I say to find that out, which I think a case wherein a man ought to be as cautious as in the choice of a wife well to consider before hand, I propose the most equall way between us both to take our commencem^t from a certaine generall reputed taken and received place of latitude of soe many years standing described by all mapps and by which all masters of shipps and vessels have been governed and soe from thence proceed distinctly to measure to forty, soe to remaine to posterity in order to the waveing any future disputes or differences, which is all the favour I request.

Lord B. Since you owne the case to be so tender, as truely I doe, I think there will therefore be the greater reason to have our business determined the best and surest way, which I have already offered. Tho' for your satisfaction, Mr Pen, I shall not refuse the liberty to any person to doe that which you propose and make report to you, that which I am resolved to trust to and be concluded by is an observation to be taken with an instrument of six or seaven foote diameter, for the sunn will deceive neither of us.

W. Pen. I acknowledge that as a favour from the Lord Baltemore but still I moove the most equal way in my opinion of ascertaining the bounds between us.

Lord B. Mr Pen, you did I remember once propose to me in England that you had offers made you of that part of Delaware from his royale Highness which I lay claime to, but you would not, as you then said, accept thereof because you knew it was mine. The same I heare you have now possesst yourselfe of. I onely desire to know upon what tearmes you claime.

W. Pen. If the Lord Baltemore please I desire we may first conclude our former discourse and then I shall shew myselfe most willing and ready to give you all satisfaction I can in that point.

Lord B. I am willing and have allways been ready to conclude the business of the bounds according as my Pattent directs me.

W. Pen. I conceive that where there is a certaine degree allowed of and generally received for the space of soe many years to commence there and soe proceed by measure to the fortieth degree is the most equall way can be proposed, and am willing to be concluded thereby, and hope the Lord Baltemore may not be opposite to it; and if that which is not the hundredth part of my Lord Baltimore's interest may be ninety nine parts of the hundred of mine, nay possibly *sine quo non*, that upon which the rest wholy depends, the Lord Baltemore I request will not place my eagerness therein to the account of my disrespect but of my interest and honest endeavours to hold a faire and amicable correspondency with him, for that I cannot imagine that fifty or sixty yeares experience and general concurrence in opinion could have any designe of favoure or prejudice either to the Lord Baltemore or myselfe.

Lord B. The latitude of the Capes was taken by a sea Quadrant which by noe artist will be held for exact and certaine as an Instrument of six, eight or tenn foote diameter and with such an instrument I desire to have the degree of forty taken.

W. Pen. I doe not apprehend that a sea quadrant can have any prejudice for the Lord Baltemore more then for William Pen.

Lord B. I say that it was more uncertaine the observation formerly taken at the Capes by a Sea Quadrant then an observation now to be taken of the fortieth degree of Northern latitude with such a fixt land Instrument as I have already made mention of can be.

W. Pen. You say true, the taking of thirty seaven then may be as uncertaine as the taking of forty now, but I say an uncertainety of soe long standing and soe generally received and approved of by all persons when neither the instrument nor observator could be imagined to have any design of interest or prejudice for either of us is safer to depend on then to runn into new errors, and then if it fall within my Lord Baltemore's bounds I hope he will be kind to me and if within mine I shall approve myselfe as kind to the Lord Baltemore as I intended.

Lord B. The way that you propose, should I yield to it, would be but error upon error, therefore let our bounds be ascertained as I have offered. Then possibly I may have an opportunity of shewing my kindnes to Mr Pen and till that be don neither he nor I can approve ourselves as we both desire.

W. Pen. I have I think proposed the most equitable way to that end, but suppose the Capes to lye within the latitude of thirty seaven and this part of the Country in thirty six degrees and thirty minutes, which is halfe a degree difference, what will then follow but to sett the sea and land together by the eares. But waveing disputes of that nature I am contented to take our commencement from the long generally taken and reputed place of thirty seaven degrees and five minutes and thence to run to forty which I apprehend the most faire and equal way and am thereby willing to be concluded.

Lord B. Would it not seeme very strange and preposterous in England for me to proceed upon a bare suggestion or supposition of an observation of thirty seaven taken at the Capes and that by masters of shipps with theire small Quadrants to find out the degree of forty?

W. Pen. Let the Lord Baltemore pitch upon one and I

another to goe and take their observation at the Capes and from thence calculate where Watkins Point lyes, which will not cost above five or six days expense, and from thence proceed to find out the degree of forty, by which, as I have soe often reiterated, I am willing to be concluded. As for the Land in dispute I vallue it not but barely for an Inlett for the conveniency of my Province.

Lord B. It is not to deprive Mr Pen of an Inlett to his Province but my interest which makes me argue this much, for should I consent to take that for my bounds which in truth is not, would be a meanes to destroy the very foundation of my Pattent, which you cannot blame me if I be not soe forward to doe.

W. Pen. If the Lord Baltemore would vouchsafe to discourse with me a word or two in private I should possibly open myselfe more fully and freely in this point and frankly acquaint him what I would request of him, and whether the head of the Bay fall within his or my bounds we should I doubt not make all things commodious between us, for which reason I would crave a little private discourse with the Lord Baltemore.

Lord B. I hope I have not offered anything injurious to Mr Pen, onely am desirous to preserve my own interest, to which end I desire that two able men may be made choice of to find out the degree of forty whereby I am bounded by my Pattent to the Northward. Here is Captaine Connaway a good discreete able man let him be one before he goes out.

W. Pen. Capt: Connaway it's true is a knowing person, but before we goe further I am desirous to purge him of some aspersions have bin cast on him, that he should have advised me. I doe declare that I never had any advice from him in this particular neither indeed did I to my knowledge ever see him before such time as I had my Pattent granted me.

Lord B. What has been said of Capt: Connaway I knowe not, but what ever he hath said or don I doe assure you never tooke any impression upon me; but that some misreports have been made the Mapps and draughts which have bin sett forth sufficiently evince.

W. Pen. Upon the view of the Mapp of Maryland some persons taking the meetes as the same lay displayed found that the Author had either much abused the Lord Baltemore in the wrong calculation or else allowed him more land then indeed was intended for him and accordingly some draughts have bin made.

Lord B. My Pattent gives me, as you and all here present know, the fortieth degree of Northern latitude, and the Sunn with such an Instrument as I have mentioned will soone satisfie us where that is, for thither my Pattent gives me.

W. Pen. Then thus in short I have here produced the King's letter, in answer to which the Lord Baltemore sayeth that he will rather abide by his Pattent which is under the great seale then to the bare contents of a letter.

Lord B. Mr Pen were it your case would you not stick to a Pattent soe plaine as mine is?

W. Pen. I doe not blame the Lord Baltemore. It may be I should doe the same as he does. I have consented to wave that and for the more equal acommodation between us I have proposed that for the ascertaining the bounds between us let us begin and take our commencement from the Capes, so antiently and generally knowne and reputed to lye within thirty seaven degrees and five minutes, and thence proceed till we come to forty, which binds the Lord Baltemore to the North-ward and from whence I must begin. To that the Lord Balte-more doth reply that true he is bounded by the fortieth degree to the Northward and the most exact way to find that out is by an observation taken with a land Instrument. In answer to which I have returned that I conceive that to be an uncertaine way for the reasons I have so often urged, and say lett some persons be jointly commissionated between us to take obser-vation at the Capes and report how much it varies from the antient generally reputed and received opinion and then proceed to find the latitude of Watkins Point and from thence by an exact line measure out to the degree of forty. To that end if the Lord Baltemore please to select foure or five per-sons to be jointly empowered between us soe unanimously to proceed without jarring, which will consequently arise from different parties.

Lord B. That may be don for your private satisfaction by any persons that may make theire report to you.

W. Pen. I doe propose and request that we may accom-modate the business between ourselves.

Lord B. I onely first premise that an observation be duely taken to answer the King's commands.

W. Pen. I question not but if the Lord Baltemore would vouchsafe to discourse the business in private with me we should fairely accommodate all matters.

The afore going is to our certaine knowledge the summe and substance of what materially was argued and spoken by the right hon^{ble} Charles Lord Baltemore and WilliamPen Esqre the day and place aforesaid which hath bin read and approved of by

PHILIP CALVERT
THOMAS TAILLER

A true Copy
examined by me
   C. BALTEMORE.

HENRY COURSEY
HENRY DARNALL
W^M DIGGES
WILL. STEEVENS.

The sume and substance of what was argued and spoken by Charles Lord Baltemore and William Penn Esqr at theire Private Conference at New Castle on Delaware River Tuesday the 29th of May 1683.

Mr Penn having by his letter of the 23rd of Aprill last desired that I would lett him know where in some neere part of my Province he might meete me and that with what speed my affaires would permitt, I wrote him word that I would begin my Voiage up the Bay about the Middle of May, which accordingly I did and being arrived at Saxafras River Wednesday the 23th of the said month I dispatcht from thence Mr John Darnall, one of my Chief Secretaries, with a letter to Mr Penn signifieing my Arrival in that part of my Province; and Tuesday following being the 29th of the Same month I mett Mr Penn about eight miles short of new Castle to which place that day I came in Company with the said Penn.

In the evening the same day I desired to know of Mr Penn what proposall he had to make, signifieing that I was come thither to see what friendly issue might be putt to the buisnes of our bounds; to which he Answered that tho he thought his Majesties Letter of the 19th of August (82) was not to be in-

sisted on by him as to the two degrees mentioned therein he
conceded there was yet an admeasurement to be insisted on,
Still That seeming very strange to me both in regard that M^r
Penn had (at a Conference afore) consented to wave that letter
as also in regard that it was not agreeable to my Pattents, he
tooke some paines (and not without heat) to let me understand what he meant by an other admeasurement, which he
said must Still be insisted on being thus, that as my Northern
bounds was the fortith degree of Northern Latitude he did not
doubt but to have that ascertained by an admeasurement in
this manner, that there should be an observation first taken
at Watkins point and, according to the Latitude that that
place by an observation should be found to lye in, that from
thence there should be an Admeasurement to the degree of
forty, saying that out of every degree he did not doubt but to
gaine six or seaven miles and by that means to gett water at
the head of Chesapeake Bay, and that this was the Mistery
which he was plaine to tell the Lord Baltemore, and did assure
me that he would procure it from his Maj^tie.

To which I answered that if he Could impose his dictates
upon the King and Council it would be in vaine for me to hope
to have Justice don me but I was not (as I told him) of opinion
that he could impose in that kind; and since he discourst of
having an observation taken at Watkins point (my South
Bounds) in order to such an admeasurement as he had last
proposed to himselfe, I did not see any reason why my North
bounds might not also be ascertained by an observation, and
then demanded of him how he Resolved to have the Northern
bounds of his Province (being the 43rd degree of Northern
Latitude) Settled and fixt and answered me, by an observacion, to which I again Replyed that he did not then approve of
an admeasurement for his three degrees, thō he thought it Necessary in my Case and yet I said to him that there was more
reason for admeasurement as to his bounds (there being
Severall degrees mentioned in his grant) then in mine, where I
had nothing given me by any Number of degrees but only
Watkins point for my south bounds, and the degree of forty
for my north-bounds, besides that an admeasurement in my
case might be said not to be rationally practicable as will
easily be made appeare.

This having been argued with some Earnestness Mr Penn at last told me that if I would hearken to accept of a proposal which he had to make me he did not doubt but all matters could Soone receive a friendly issue.   I told him I was desirous of nothing more, then that our differences might be amicably Ended betwixt us; He then proposed this, that if I would lett him have Susquehanna River for an Inlett and Land Enough on Each Side the said River Sufficient of his Occasions and that I would let him know certainly under my hand what price or value I would Sett upon the same, he would then willingly joine with me to bring an observation to find the degree of forty Northerly Latitude and with such instruments as we had then propper for that purpose.   To this I answered that I wondered, should I be willing to dispose of that wch he desired, how he would expect I was able to give him any thing certaine under my hand afore I knew Certainly how far North up Susquehanno River the fortieth degree Northern Lattitude (my North bounds) could reach.

He then desired to know what Latitude Capt James Conaway and some other persons found Palmers Island, which is in Susquehanno River, to lye in by an observation I had caused to be taken the 28th of february last.   For his Satisfaction therein I product to him the observation under their hands and the same read to him, by which he saw that the said Island was 16 miles to the Southward of the degree forty, and then he told me that by that observation he thought New Castle was about twelve miles from the said Degree, and then proposes to me that if I would give him from Under my hand what he must give for as many miles as I should runn up the said River, saying if tenn miles how much should I demand for tenn miles and if sixteen miles how much for 16 miles, and that after I had given him this Certaine under my hand he would then be willing to go with me to the heads of the Rivers and joine with me in the taking observacons as I had all along insisted on; Adding that we should take but a few persons with us and not have the Noise and trouble of any troopes of horse.

As this proposall was New and a very Strange way of proceeding as I thought, I desired some time to consider of what he had offered, but I found he was not willing to give me any longer time then the next day being the 30th of May, so that I tooke that little time to consider of his proposalls, and made him some other offers which he thought not good to yield to, after w[ch] we parted, and this is the sume and Substance, nay (I may almost say) the very words that were Spoken on both sides, But that it is the substance of what was (at that time) argued and Spoken by M[r] Penn and me and I will make oath when required, and I doubt not but M[r] Penn will owne as much when we meet at the Council board.

This 31st May 1683.   C. BALTEMORE.

Report of a conference between Col[l] Talbot[1] and William Penn on various matters connected with his Government of Pen-silvania and Col[l] Talbot's interference therein.

After wee had Sate a minute or two, And the how do you's being over I begann.

Coll. Talbot. S[r] I came to towne accidentally and being told that your honnor was here I thought it the duty of a Gentleman to come and pay my respects to you.

Wm. Penn. I give Coll Talbot many thanks for his kind-nesse.

Talbot. If I had heard at home of your honors being here I had come purposely to waite on you and Indevor to remove the opinion you had of my Incivility in not Leaving a Letter for your honnor when I was at your house in Philadelphia.

Penn. It did seeme strange to me and others that haveing noe way disobliged thee thou shouldst be wanting in soe ordinary a part of common Civility as writeing to me when thou didst not meete my selfe at home.

Talbot. S[r] the tearmes in which my Comission is writt are Sufficient to prove that I had noe more to doe at Phila-delphia, then deliver my Errand to your honnor or your Deputy and then come away, and I should have Exceeded that if I had writt any private Letters to you while I was there, ffor if my

---

[1] George Talbot, who was settled near the head of Chesapeake Bay and was surveyor-general of the province. In 1684, when Charles Lord Baltimore went to England, leaving his infant son Benedict Leonard nominal governor, Talbot was the chief of a commission of deputy governors by whom the government of the province was administered.

Lord Baltemore had thought that to be necessary 'tis like he would have given me orders to that purpose in Case of your honnors absence, But if I had come thither on any buisnesse of my owne I would not have omitted that or any other testimony of my respect to you, for in anything (not opposite to my Lords Interest) you shall find me as willing as any man to serve you.

Penn. Truely I never Expected Lesse from one of thy family, for I know Some of thy relations and found them to be persons of much Integrity and worth But Since thou dost speake of Exceeding thy Comission I think I have something of that kind to object against thee. I am told that in Coll Talbots returne from Philadelphia, he did (at Amersland and other places) use perswasions to certaine Sweades and ffinns to remove into Maryland and live under the Lord Baltemore. Now the question is whether Coll Talbot did this or did it not.

Talbot. S^r I will not disowne my owne act. I certainly did it, for finding severall of them much disatisfied, and declareing theire discontents to me, I thought I should be very remisse if I omitted soe faire an occasion of serveing my Lord Baltemores intrests and tis certaine I did not make it my buisnesse to Lessen theire feares nor doe I see how it may be faulty in any man to tell them the truth that theres better Land and Cheaper rents and greater Incouragements for poore men in Maryland then in Pensilvania.

Penn. But it ended not there for thou didst say that they pay noe taxes in Maryland for getting Children but that they must pay a Crowne per Childe here.

Talbot. Your honor is Sensible that if you are wrongd in that I am not the first author of it for you cannot but know 'twas all over Pensilvania before I went thither.

Penn. It is the Custome in all Countries to keepe account of the Increase and decrease of the people in Registries of births and Burialls and because I doe soe it give occasion for that report, But the Lord is my Witnesse I had noe intent to lay any such tax on the Country for I am soe farr from it that I have Voluntarily given away things of that kind which the Assembly here settled on me. But who were those persons that told thee they were disatisfied with my Government for I think I give none any occasion to be soe.

Talbot. I am not willing to turne Informer nor would my Lorde Baltemore Expect soe meane a Service from me.

Penn. Thou needst not, for I know who the men are and they themselves were the first that told me of it But (as I said already) all this was beyond the Comission thou didst shew at Philadelphia. Hadst thou any Comission to Invite persons out of my Country into Maryland? If thou hadst I hope thou canst produce it, and if thou canst not I am to Looke upon thy actions then as the act of a private person acting of himselfe and not of an officer acting by Commission.

Talbot. I had noe particular Com^ion to that purpose in writeing, but I have a generall written Comission to use my best Endeavors to gett the County of New Ireland[1] planted and Inhabited, and to Invite people thither from all parts, by Vertue of which a Lone I may Justifie what I did and I had Likewise private directions from my Lord to give all reasonable Encouragement to such persons as may be willing to remove out of Pensilvania into Maryland.

Penn. Are those Instructions written?

Talbot. It is not necessary that any of your Councill should have a written warrant under your hand and Seale for every Service they are order'd to doe for you, but 'tis Enough that you bid them doe it.

Penn. Well, well, lay that aside. But the Indian Capt. Mahaloha complaines to me that thou forcedst a paper from him that I gave him wherein I declared that I bought his Land in Delaware and Susquehanno from him and desired that he should not be molested in his hunting in those parts.

Talbot. I had the paper freely from himself without using any thing of force or terror to him.

Penn. Then wilt thou restore it to him againe?

Talbot. That I cannot doe, because there are some passages in it necessary for my Lord to see and I must therefore send it to him.

---

[1] There was no county of this name in Maryland. Talbot, who was an Irishman, had a grant of Susquehannah manor in the northeastern portion of the province. He changed the name to New Connaught, and the surrounding region was known as New Ireland. It was comprised in Cecil County, which was established in 1674. *Calvert Papers* no. 1, *Md. Hist. Soc. Fund Pub.* no. 28, pp. 95, 96.

Penn. But thou didst forbid him and threaten him from hunting in Maryland, which is Complained of as a great grevance by the Inhabitants of this towne, whose Chiefe liveing is by the Indian trade, for thou hast said that thou wilt not suffer them to carry skinns nor furrs out of Maryland hither.

Talbot. There's a Law in Maryland that forbids the Carrying away of Deer skins Elk skins and hides, and there's noe reason that we should give heathens a Liberty which we deny to our Selves; but for theire furrs they may carry them whether they will provided they have my Lord's Licence to hunt in Maryland and not pretend to warrant themselves by any forraigne Licence.

Penn. These Niceties are only Necessary on the Borders of Sweaden and Denmarke where travellers are put to renew theire passports at every Castle they passe by. But if that paper would not doe, The Indians have a native right to hunt, fish, and fowle in all places and are not to be hindered from it by the English.

Talbot. S^r, the Indians (as your honor knowes) are divided into Severall Small Nations. Every Nation has its particular Territory bounded with naturall bounds. Noe one nation was or is to hunt in any part of the others Territory without Licence first obtained. Some of these Territories are Seated by the English by Consent and Composition with the Natives who in all treaties reserved to themselves the rights of hunting, fishing, and fowling in all the lands they sould or gave away, and in these Territories soe obtained by the English the Old Proprietors (and noe other Indians) doe challenge the priviledge of hunting. But the Susquehannoks and theire Country were Conquer'd by the Marylanders at great Expence of blood and money and the Susquehanohs are now noe Nation. That part of theire Country that lyes in Maryland, betweene the 40th degree and the rivers of Patapsco, Elke and Saxafras, was never hunted on in theire time by the Delaware Indians nor any others but the Susquehannohs Indians onely, and now that not onely the Land is my Lord's by his Charter but the Susquehanoh rights of hunting there and barring all others is Invested in my Lord by right of Conquest, The Delaware Indians ought to be Licenced by my Lord's Authority or not permitted to hunt any where west-

ward of Elk river noe more then in the Susquehannoes time,
but to the Eastward of Elk river there's noe man will hinder
them it being theire Antient right to hunt there.

Penn. I have bin the more willing to heare thee discourse
of rights of Conquests because it makes for me in the Case between the Lord Baltemore and mee. But I will justifie that
the Conquest of the Susquehannes was noe just Conquest
nor managed Like a just Conquest, for noe cause of warr was
given by them and they then were betrayed out of theire
Lives by Inviteing them downe among the English and lastly
theire five great men that came out to treat were Inhumanely
knockt in the head against all reason and the Law and Custome of all nations.[1] Oh it is much to be feared that the Cry
of soe much innocent blood will at some time or other bring
downe Gods wrath upon the Children yet unborn in Maryland
though I heartily wish it otherwise.

Talbot. S^r, I have Answerd your honnor in all points that
Concerne my owne Justification and I hope you are Satisfied
that I have don but what I ought to doe and that I did it out of
the duty and obligation I owe my Lord and not out of any
sett purpose to disserve you. But if you be not I hope my
Lord will and then I have my End. But now your honor has
put me upon a discourse that is out of my Element, for I was
not then in America nor have I any Com^ion from my Lord to
talk with your honnor of these things, and doe therefore desire
to be Excused from Answering to any questions relateing to
the Controversy between my Lord and you any further than
Concerns my selfe.

Penn. I had not fallen into it if thy selfe had not begunn
it; but Since we are Enter'd Upon it Let us talk a little more of
it as we have don already calmly, and without passion. How
farr dost thou reckon it to be from this towne to thy hous upon
a Diametricall Line.

Talbot. Some 11 or 12 mile somewhat over or under, S^r.

Penn. Or under—Then if under 12 mile—Coll Talbot (I
suppose) is sensible that he has built his hous within the King's
12 mile Circle of New Castle which I wonder he would doe or

---

[1] The allusion is to the treacherous act of Major Thomas Truman, which
was denounced by the Assembly of Maryland (1676) as a horrid crime against
the laws of God and of nations. *Archives of Maryland.* II. 486. 500.

how he hopes to keepe it knowing how punctuall the King is in reserving the property thereof to himselfe.

Talbot. S^r, I am Likewise sensible that his Majesties reserve layd on th^t Circle was a very late act, and long after the date of the Charter of Maryland and that it was not intended to Cutt any thing from Maryland by it, but to keepe soe much from Pensilvania in Case the 40th degree were found to be to the Southward of New Castle. But that being found to be otherwise I doe not feare that Maryland can loose any part of its Extent upon account of a reserve thats Latter then the date of the Charter.

Penn. The reserve was layd by the King and Duke when they weer in full and Lawfull possession of all Delaware river by Conquest from the Dutch who were seated here long before the Maryland Charter begann.

Talbot. But does it appeare that the Dutch were seated here by any grant or publick Licence from the Crowne of England?

Penn. Why 'tis noe matter whether they did or not. Why dost thou ask?

Talbot. Because there's Lately an order of Councill past in England that the Dutch Settlement in Delaware (although before the Charter of Maryland's date) shall noe more be pleaded against my Lord's right to this place unlesse it be made out that they did it by Licence from the Crowne of England.

Penn. 'Tis impossible any such order should passe, and I not receive as timely notice of it as the Lord Baltemore.

Talbot. I dare assure your honnor that it is soe, and if you have not gott notice of it already your friends in England will not forgett to send you it, or if they neglect it my Lord will not.

Penn. Why 'tis a very unlikely thing that such an order should passe after the reserve made by the King and pattent past to the Duke and after the opinions had of the Learnedst Lawyers in England both in the Civill and Comon Law, that the Lord Baltemore's right was devolved to the Dutch by theire Conquest, and theire right to the Duke by his; for if a Shipp be taken by Piratts and kept 24 houres by them and retaken by a man of warr shee shall be prize to the King and the owner looses his right to her and 'tis the same case here.

Talbot. I [Ay], S^r, if there were noe difference betweene a reall Estate and a Chattell. But the property of a reall Estate is not soe readily made void as that of a Chattell, as is to be seene in hundreds of cases.

Penn. Why there's the mistake of a great many men that take Land in America for a reall Estate, whereas the opinion of all the Judges in England is that it is but a Chattel as it will appeare when the Lord Baltemore and I doe come to tryall.

Talbot. Personall Estates are past from one man to another by Common Bargaines without soe much as a scrowle of paper and never are Intaylable. But we see that land in America is intailable and when it is it passes not from one to another without fine, Recovery, Wife's release of Dower, Conveyance, acknowledgm^t before a judge and Lastly inrowlement, which shews it to differ as much from a Chattel as Land of Inheritance in Middlesex doth.

Penn. It may be soe in Maryland where (perhapps) you have made a Law that Lands shall be tailable but they are not soe in any other part of America.

Talbot. I know of noe law in Maryland more then the old Comon Law of England that makes any mention of Intaileing of Lands or any thing to that purpose or of changeing the Condition of them from a personall to a reall Estate. And that reall Estates if Conquer'd by Enemies and recoverd by the Crown are claimeable by the former Proprietors. The restoreing of the Cavaliers in England to theire reall Estates but not theire Chattells is a Sufficient Instance.

Penn. Theire Case and the Lord Baltimore's Case are very different, for they were Comon Subjects and in the imediate protection of the Crowne and ought by all Law and reason to be restored to the Lands they lost and the case between them and the usurpers might be tryed by the Comon Law. On the contrary the Lord Baltemore is a great Prince, holds onely by two Arrowes, Ought to defend his Territories against forraigners at his owne charge, and if he looses them, and the King recover them, they become the King's property and not his. And if he would be remedied by Law, it must be by the Civill Law and not the Common because the Dutch a forraigne Nation were concerned, and the Civill Law (which is *Lex gentium*) adjudges the right of all conquered Lands to the Conqueror.

And if (by the Civill Law) the Dutch were Lawfully Seized of this place and that (by the same Law) the King (who recoverd it by Armes from them) was Lawfully reinvested in it, what remedy has the Lord Baltemore at the Civill Law, for at the Comon law this case cannot be tryed?

Talbot. S^r, you know that in my Lord's Charter there's a grant of all Royalties in the same manner as the Bishops of Durham Enjoyed at any time heretofore in theire Diocesse. The Bishoprick of Durham lyes neare Scotland and was often in danger of being Conquered by the Kings of Scotland. Now the question is if the Scotts (in those former times when England and Scotland had two Kings) should Conquer and keep Durham for 40 yeares, and then the King should reconq^r it Whither the Bishop might legally clayme and recover his land againe.

Penn. He might but here you must distinguish for Durham is in England and if wonn by the Scotts the losse was upon account of the Crowne and of the people of England and therefore in all equity he ought to be restored. But America is another thing and the losse of a spott of ground here is not of such Concerne to England as the Bishoprick of Durham.

Talbot. That distinction will not alter the Case for I am sure that Maryland is now (by my Lord and his Ancestors) made as profitable to the Crowne of England as ever Durham was. But if it should be soe adjudged that all that the Duke recovered from the Dutch should be his, What right does that give him to the Whore kills, which my Lord tooke and burnt?

Penn. Yea I have heard after what manner that place was taken and Kept.

Talbot. Taken it was Certainely but Capt. Jones that tooke it Neglected to stay and keepe possession untill a plantacon or two were seated on my Lord's account, as I would have stay'd though I had not above one man to keepe me Company. But Jones Neglect of seating then gives noe title to the Duke to enter upon it and Conquer it from my Lord.

Penn. They say that Coll Talbot gives out that he will Suffer noe new Settlements on Christine Creeke but on the Lord Baltemores account. Methinks there is noe need of soe much heate. Young men are more precipitate in Execution then old men in considering. This may be layd aside till the

King and Councill decide the matter. Thou mayst hurt thy selfe by it, for perhapps when the Controversy is Ended thou mayt then prove to be a Pensilvanian for any thing thou knowest yett.

Talbot. S[r], I hardly think I shall, or if I doe, I beleeve your honnor will not like me a jott the worse or employ me the lesse in your businesse for being diligent in the trust my Lord has now reposed in me. But if the Chiefe foundation of your title to the Lower parts of Delaware river, be the possession the Dutch once had here, I doe not see what right that can give you to seate St Jones, St. Georges, the Upper parts of Christine[1] and the forrests backwards where noe settlements were ever made till after the last Conquest from the Dutch. Certainly nothing can be objected against our right beyond all others to seat on those parts which doe lye in Maryland and never were Cultivated by the Dutch.

Penn. If the Lord Baltemore be soe sure of recovering these parts he should not blame me for being a better husband for him then himself is, for I reserve farr greater rents on those Lands then he does on his, the profit of which will be his when he recovers them.

Talbot. No S[r], for I know 'tis his Lo[pps] intent to make the rents here as Easie (when he recovers this Country) as they are in the rest of Maryland and in the meane time the rents of such plantacons goe into others pockets that ought to goe into his, and therefore you need not think it strange that I am unwilling to suffer such new Settlements to goe forwards or shall Endeavor to hinder them when begunn.

Penn. But though the Dutch were not seated in all those places, yet they bought all Delaware river and bay from the Natives and 3 daies journey back into the woods, which would take in a good part of Chesepeake bay besides the whole forrest betwixt it and Delaware bay. Coll Talbot seemed even now to assert the Validity of Indian purchases and Indian Conquests while they made for his purpose; has he any thing to say against them now?

Talbot. I Looke on an Indian Conquest or purchase to be a sufficient title to barr a weaker Indian pretension, but not to

---

[1] St. Jones Creek is in Kent County, St. George's and Christiana in Newcastle County, Delaware.

oppose an English Pattantee that hath his Charter from the Crowne of England, as appeares in the Case of Capt Claybourne that bought Manapousen (now the Isle of Kent) from the Indians before the Maryland Charter and (in that right) seated upon it but was cast out by an order of Councill upon a full hearing in England. And the Like of Capt Brent who in right of his wife the Piscatoway Emperors daughter and only Child pretended a right to the most part of Maryland but could doe noe good on't after a great bustle about it, and your Indian title will Signifie no more or I am much mistaken.

Penn. It seemed strange to me that the Lord Baltemore should promise me (in this towne) another meeting in September and yet when he came up the bay never to send to me to meete him, but tak observacons and runn a Line without giveing me the least notice, and Lastly to send Coll Talbot to me to demand positively the Dukes Land of me, and all this after a solemne promise upon his honor not to doe anything untill our September meeting. I doe not know how the Lord Baltemore will Justifie such proceedings and such breaches of his word when I acquaint the King and Councill with them.

Talbot. S^r, I know that my Lord had intentions of dealing kindly and neighborly with you, had he not received three Letters by Captaine Markham, Mr. Clarke and Mr. Harrison, in which were Expressions which were looked upon to be soe disobligeing as were sufficient to disengage his Lo^pp from any promise of that kind had he past any to your honnor, and as to his takeing private observacons his Lo^pp had a great deale of reason for it, because first Capt. Markham and then your honnor refused to Joine with him in it, for you are sensible that in England if two be at Law, and the defendant refuse to joyne with the plaintiff in Examining Witnesses, the plaintiff may proceed *exparte* and Examine his owne witnesses without the defendants presence, which is the same case here where the 40th degree is the Chiefe and onely Evidence by which this dispute must be Ended. My Lord had reason to Examine *exparte* when none would Joine with him.

Penn. I know the Lord Baltemore took advantage of my agents proceedings in my absence, which was not soe fayre without Inquireing into his Instructions, wherein he might be better satisfied what my Agent could doe and what not.

Talbot. I pray S^r was Capt. Markhams Com^{ion} plenipotentiary or not?

Penn. It was Plenipotentiary with referrence to his Instructions.

Talbot. Then my Lord was onely to take notice of his Comission wch he saw and not of the Instructions wch he saw not.

Penn. Well wee have had Enough of this. But let me desire thee not to molest the Inhabitants of Christine. Thou doest discourage them from improving theire plantations, for it is a present Injury to mee, and a future one to the Lord Baltemore if it prove his fortune to recover these parts.

Talbot. I have given them noe disturbance yet, for I have received noe order from my Lord to turn any out of theire houses that are seated already, but I must not permit new seaters on any account, by my Lords.

Penn. But have a Care of obeying Illegall orders if thou receivest them.

Talbot. S^r, I thank you for your advice, but I am not Lawyer Enough to Judge what orders are legall and what are not; but my Lord knowes better things then to send me Illegall Comands, and therefore I will not dispute the legality of any directions that come from him, and what I doe in obedience thereunto wch may seeme cross to your hono^{rs} Interests I desire once more that they may be understood as don out of affection to his Lo^{pps} Concernes and not any prejudice against your honnor.

Welsh, the Survey Gen^{ll} of Delaware. But Governor, if thou shouldst comand me any thing that were illegal I declare I would not obey it.

Penn. It were not reason to Expect thou shouldest.

Talbot. But I that am not so Versed in law as Mr. Welsh must be guided by my Superiors.

Penn. I see thou wilt pin thy opinions in law as well as Gospel on other mens sleeves.

Talbot. I pray S^r lets change the discourse, or if your honour resolves to Entertaine me alwaies with Controversy you will fright me from Wayting on you here any more, But if yor hono^r will promise to receive my respects as from a private Gentleman and not as from my Lord Prop^{ry} of Marylands officer, I will come constantly to Kisse your hands when I heare you come to towne.

Penn. Coll Talbot shall be kindly welcome wheresoever I am. Then Let us talk of Vineyards etc.

And there the dispute Ended and we talked of other indifferent things.

INDEX

INDEX